RETRACING THE PAST

RETRACING THE PAST

Readings in the History of the American People

Volume One

To 1877

Fourth Edition

Gary B. Nash
University of California, Los Angeles

Ronald Schultz
University of Wyoming

 LONGMAN

An imprint of Addison Wesley Longman, Inc.

New York • Reading, Massachusetts • Menlo Park, California • Harlow, England
Don Mills, Ontario • Sydney • Mexico City • Madrid • Amsterdam

Editor-in-Chief: Priscilla McGeehon
Acquisitions Editor: Jay O'Callaghan
Executive Marketing Manager: Sue Westmoreland
Full Service Production Manager: Valerie Zaborski
Text Design, Project Coordination, and Composition: Elm Street
    Publishing Services, Inc.
Cover Design Manager: Nancy Danahy
Cover Designer: Kay Petronio
Cover Illustration: Kagy, Sheffield. "Past and Present Agriculture and
    Industry of Colleton County" (Mural Study, Waterboro, South
    Carolina Post Office), 1938. National Museum of American Art,
    Smithsonian Institution, Washington, DC/Art Resource, NY.
Senior Print Buyer: Hugh Crawford
Printer and Binder: The Maple-Vail Book Manufacturing Group
Cover Printer: Coral Graphic Services

Library of Congress Cataloging-in-Publication Data
Retracing the past : readings in the history of the American people /
    editors, Gary B. Nash, Ronald Schultz. — 4th ed.
      p. cm.
    Contents: v. 1. to 1877 — v. 2. Since 1865.
ISBN 0-321-04849-0 (v. 1). — ISBN 0-321-04850-4 (v. 2)
1. United States—History. I. Nash, Gary B. II. Schultz,
Ronald, 1946–
E178.6.R45 2000
973—dc21   99-20996
                                            CIP

Please visit our Web site at http://www.awlonline.com

ISBN 0-321-04849-0

 2 3 4 5 6 7 8 9 10-MA-02 01 00 99

CONTENTS

PART THREE
An Expanding People   152

PREFACE

This two-volume reader has been contructed to accompany the fourth edition of *The American People: Creating a Nation and a Society* (New York: Addison Wesley Longman, 1998), but we hope it will also prove a useful supplement to other books in American history. The essays have been selected with three goals in mind: first, to blend political and social history; second, to lead students to a consideration of the roles of women, ethnic groups, and laboring Americans in the weaving of the nation's social fabric; and third, to explore life at the individual and community levels. The book is also intended to introduce students to the individuals and groups that made a critical difference in the shaping of American history or whose experience reflected key changes in society.

A few of the individuals highlighted are famous—Benjamin Franklin, Abraham Lincoln, and Jackie Robinson, for example. A number of others are historically visible but are not quite household names—Squanto, Tecumseh, and John Muir. Some will be totally unknown to students, such as George Robert Twelves Hewes, a Boston shoemaker who witnessed some of the most important events of the American Revolution, and Absalom Jones, who bought his way out of slavery and became a leader of Philadelphia's free African-American community after the Revolution. Often the focus is on groups whose role in history has not been adequately treated—the Chinese in the building of the transcontinental railroad, African-American officeholders during Reconstruction, and the middle class in the 1980s and 1990s.

Some of these essays take us inside American homes, farms, and factories, such as the essays on working women in New York City before the Civil War and the families of Butte, Montana, who welcomed the radio into their lives during the 1920s and 1930s. Such essays, it is hoped, will convey an understanding of the daily lives of ordinary Americans, who collectively helped shape their society. Other essays deal with the vital social and political movements that transformed American society: the debate over the Constitution in the 1780s; reform in the antebellum period; populism and progressivism in the late nineteenth and early twentieth centuries; and the rise of political conservatism in our own time.

Readability has been an important criterion in the selection of these essays. An important indicator of readability, in turn, is how vividly and concretely the authors have brought the past to life. The main objective of this reader is a palpable presentation of the past—one that allows students to sense and feel the forces of historical change and hence to understand them.

Accessibility has been a guiding concern in preparing this edition of *Retracing the Past*. Consequently, we have made several important changes to make the readings more accessible and useful to student readers. First, we have reduced the number of readings to six in each part and have edited each of the readings to make them more straightforward and understandable to students. We have also included glossaries and chapter summaries for each of the readings to help students better understand and focus their attention on the most significant aspects of the essays. In addition, we have begun each part with a brief document taken from the period in order to enliven the past and to make the experiences of the American people more concrete and "real." One of the most important changes in this edition has been the inclusion of a brief introductory essay—Sources and Interpretations—that provides students with a strategy for reading these documents and the essays that follow in a way that is both efficient and effective. This strategy has been used at the University of Wyoming for nearly a decade with excellent results, and we think this strategy will work equally well in any college or high school classroom. In sum, we think these changes in the fourth edition of *Retracing the Past* will make this a more approachable and therefore more useful reader and will make the American past an engaging and rewarding sbject for a new generation of students.

Gary B. Nash
Ronald Schultz

ACKNOWLEDGMENTS

In developing this volume of readings, the editors have been well-advised by the following academic colleagues, who reviewed the previous edition and read preliminary tables of contents:

Matthew Dennise
University of Oregon

Jerrold Hirsch
Truman State University

Monroe Little
Indiana University Purdue University
Indianapolis (or IUPUI)

Susan E. Myers-Shirk
Middle Tennessee State University

Craig H. Roell
Georgia Southern University

John Herbert Roper
Emory & Henry College

Thomas Siefert
Indiana State University

E. Timothy Smith
Barry University

In addition, Ronald Schultz of the University of Wyoming played a major role in preparing the introductory notes and in readying the manuscript for publication.

GBN

INTRODUCTION

Sources and Intrepretations

People often think that history is mostly about facts: Who invented the cotton gin? Where was the nation's first capital? When did women secure the vote? But, while no historian would dispute the importance of facts, historical writers are much more concerned with interpretation, that is, with giving facts historical meaning. In practice, historians normally spend very little time debating the facts of a particular historical process or event; instead they typically differ about what those established facts mean. Take, for example, a letter written by an early nineteenth-century New England farmer outlining his plan to purchase land on the western New York frontier. One historian might recall what she has read about the family-centeredness of New Englanders and find in the letter a father's concern to place each of his sons on freehold land, thus allowing them to re-create his own life as an independent family farmer. On the other hand, the contents of the same letter might lead another historian to remember the economic position of early American farmers and conclude that the father was purchasing land for speculation, hoping to sell the land at a higher price once settlers entered the region. Or a third historian might integrate both of these views and infer from the letter that the farmer's main aim was family continuance but that he was not above a little speculation along the way. In all of these cases, the historians have no dispute with the source (the letter) itself but draw very different and potentially conflicting conclusions from it.

This example points to one of the fundamental features of historical interpretation: the essential ambiguity of sources. Like the farmer's letter, no document or physical artifact is ever perfectly clear to the reader or observer. Instead, it requires the exercise of historical judgment—re-creating the context in which the source was produced and making collateral connections between it and other sources from the same time and place—to give it meaning. It is the historian's job to interrogate a source by asking a series of questions, most importantly, Who produced the source?; What was their purpose in doing so?; For whom was the source intended?; and How was the source received and how was it used? Historians employ this basic arsenal of questions when analyzing a source, and only when the source has been internally scrutinized and these questions answered satisfactorily can the source be used to build an interpretation.

Facts and interpretations are thus closely linked and historians acknowledge this linkage by dividing their materials into two groups: primary sources and secondary interpretations. Primary sources are items produced during the time period being investigated. These items might be written documents—such as letters, diaries, travel accounts, or contemporary books—or they might be statistical compilations—such as census tabulations, business records, or tax lists. They might even be material artifacts—such as houses, home furnishings, or clothing—that have survived from the period in question. It is from the broad array of such primary sources that historians draw the facts they will use in constructing interpretations of past events and processes.

History is a discipline that builds on the work of others, and historians continually measure the primary source data they gather against existing interpretations of their subject. These interpretations (sometimes called secondary sources) most commonly appear as articles in professional journals and as monographs which deal with a specific aspect of the period in question, say an essay about agricultural change in the early republic or a book about the origin of Jim Crow laws in the post–Reconstruction South. Historians use secondary sources to help them place their primary materials in context and to give those materials a wider meaning. In turn, they use primary sources to question the conclusions drawn by other writers. By utilizing primary sources and secondary interpretations in this way, historians advance historical understanding through a process of successive interrogation and refinement. Written history is thus a continuous dialogue between the past and the present, a dialogue that is always ongoing and provisional and one that is never final or complete.

In each part of *Retracing the Past*, you will first encounter "Past Traces," a brief selection of primary documents drawn from the time period of the section. The purpose of these documents is two-fold: first, to give you a sense of the lives and concerns of ordinary people in a particular time period and, second, to involve you in the process of historical evaluation and interpretation. For example, in the opening part of this volume you will find documents from some of the first encounters between Europeans and Native Americans in North America; one from the Indian perspective and one from that of the colonists. Read with care and imagination, the documents tell us much about Native American and European life and culture as well as the nature of their mutual encounters. We learn, for example, that both groups drew upon their own cultural assumptions in interpreting the appearance and actions of the other, the Montagnais villagers by describing the incoming French ships as "floating islands" and the Jesuit missionaries by bristling at what they saw as the native exploitation of women. If we look a little further, we also learn that both groups came from agrarian societies, although both practiced agriculture in different ways. These are just a few of the things that can be learned from the primary documents that follow; there are many others as you will discover. As you read the documents, you will begin to ask your own questions and form your own interpretations. Most importantly, in learning to read the documents for their diverse meanings, you will already be thinking like a historian.

Following the documents, you will find six essays of historical interpretation. In each, a historian has consulted primary and secondary sources and constructed an interpretation which explains what he or she thinks the sources reveal about an individual or group of people in the chronological period in question. Thus in "The Small Circle of Domestic Concerns," Mary Beth Norton uses contemporary women's letters and diaries to reconstruct the lives of eighteenth-century women and finds that household labor lay at the heart of women's roles, no matter what their class or status in life. At the same time, Norton uses these primary sources to challenge historians who have viewed the colonial era as a "golden age" for American women, an age in which gender relations were more equal than they became in later times. This, then, is the procedure of the working historian, a procedure that depends on the mutual interrogation of primary sources and secondary interpretations in the process of reaching historical conclusions.

Reading with Purpose

One of the unusual aspects of written history is that, like literature, it is often read by nonhistorians for no other purpose than simple relaxation and pleasure. Thus, while few people will spend their leisure hours reading a new book on the biochemistry of enzymes, many nonspecialists will read the latest book about the American Civil War. This difference between a work of chemistry and a work of history lays a trap that often snares student readers. The chemistry book will most likely be read pragmatically, that is, it will be read in order to gain specific information about enzymes that can be used later in an experimental or classroom application. The history book, on the other hand, will more likely be read without any expectation of future use or application.

Each of the historical essays that follow can be read as an interesting story in its own right, whether about southern slave resistance, the Populist critique of big business, or the youth culture of the 1960s. As such, each essay invites a casual rather than a pragmatic reading. Yet, most history courses will ask for exactly that: a purposeful, pragmatic, and analytical reading that goes beyond the story line and focuses instead on what the essay and its evidence tell us about a person (or group of people) and their times. In his essay about slave resistance, for example, Peter Wood uses newspapers and contemporary journals to reveal ways in which southern slaves contested the terms of their enslavement and put the lie to slaveholder attempts to dehumanize their bondsmen and women. It is a compelling story in its own right, but in a college classroom or discussion section you would be expected to gain more from Wood's essay than a casual reading would allow. At a minimum, you would be expected to recount the main and subsidiary points of his essay and be able to say something about how the essay adds to our understanding of southern society in the colonial period.

How, then, does one avoid the pitfalls of a casual reading of an essay and grasp its most salient points? One of the most effective ways to accomplish this is to read each essay with a structured set of questions in mind, that is, to read with a purpose. There are five basic questions you should ask yourself as you read the essays in *Retracing the Past*.

First, you should be able to identify the main subject of the essay and place that person or group in the context of their times. Some questions you might wish to ask include: Who are the most important people in the essay? Is the essay about an individual or a group? What are the most important characteristics of this person or group for an understanding of the essay? What is their class? Their race? Their gender? Their occupation? Where did the events discussed in the essay take place? When?

Second, since history deals with human predicaments, you should be able to identify the major problem or problems faced by the subject of the essay. What did the subject hope to accomplish? What was the most important obstacle(s) or impediment(s) standing in the way of the fulfillment of the subject's desires? What was the source of this impediment(s)? Was it individual and personal or structural and impersonal?

Third, because people respond to their predicaments in many different ways, you should be able to locate major actions undertaken by the subject to solve the problem(s). How did the subject go about trying to solve the problem(s)? Does the person or group solve the problem alone? Who provides help? What help was given? Why was it given?

Fourth, since some actions lead to successful conclusions and others do not, make a judgment about the ultimate resolution of the actions taken by the people in the essay. Did they achieve what they set out to accomplish? Or did they realize only some of their goals? If they solved their problem(s), what allowed them to do this? If the problem remained unsolved, why wasn't it solved? What obstacles prevented a solution? What was the person's or group's response to the lack of a solution?

Lastly, since each essay in *Retracing the Past* is a case study of a larger historical process, you should be able to place the subject's problem(s) and resolution(s) into the larger context of the historical period in question. What ideas do you think the author wanted to convey in his or her article? How does the essay relate to other course materials, such as lectures, multimedia presentations, or points made in your textbook and other readings? Do the points made in the essay agree or disagree with other interpretations you've heard or read about in the course? How do they agree or disagree? If they disagree, which interpretation do you accept? Why?

By asking these questions as you read the essays in *Retracing the Past*, you will be engaged in reading pragmatically. This purposeful way of reading will help you to understand and enjoy the essays more fully and, at the same time, will actively engage you in the process of historical interpretation, thus helping you draw your own conclusions and form your own arguments about the historical period in question.

RETRACING THE PAST

PART ONE

A Colonizing People

The expansion of Europe westward across the Atlantic during the sixteenth and seventeenth centuries brought together peoples from Africa, Western Europe, and the Americas to create a new form of multiracial and multiethnic society. The local societies created by this unprecedented mixing of peoples were among the most complex in recorded human history. Reflecting this complexity, the history of colonization in North and South America was largely a story of conflict and accommodation in which people with different cultures and divergent ways of life struggled to create stable patterns of everyday life in a world of constant change.

The early experiences of people in the colonial era were decisively shaped by cultural interactions between the Old World and the New. Neal Salisbury captures one of these early interactions in the poignant story of "Squanto: Last of the Patuxets," in which the kidnapped Native American leader returns to his native Massachusetts to find that his people have been decimated by European disease. His attempt to restore some measure of stability to his society and to elevate his personal position through his actions as a cultural and political broker reminds us that Native Americans were not passive victims of European conquest, but sought to maintain the integrity of their social world in ways that paralleled those of the English settlers.

The realization of a stable social life was no easier for the English than for the Patuxets, as T. H. Breen reveals in his survey of life in the early Chesapeake, "Looking Out for Number One." The single-minded pursuit of individual interest that marked the first generations of Virginia settlers made even the most rudimentary forms of social and political life difficult to achieve. Although faced with mounting conflict with Native Americans and the threat of Spanish invasion, early Virginians refused to put aside their pursuit of profit long enough even to serve in their local militia units.

Individualism posed less of a problem in New England than in Virginia. Settled mostly by established family groups and lacking a lucrative export crop that would attract young, unattached men, as was the case in the tobacco colonies, Massachusetts Bay established social stability from the very beginning. In her study of the original migrants to Massachusetts Bay, Virginia Dejohn Anderson tackles the recurring question of the relative importance of economics and religion in bringing about the settlement of the Bay Colony. She finds that in the early years of the colony, the corporate and religious ethos of Puritanism held sway over the search for individual economic gain.

By 1700 English settlers had achieved a substantial measure of social and political stability. Yet the new century would bring new challenges to colonists living in a changing world. Slavery was one of the most important legacies of the colonial era, creating divisions in American society that would lead to a civil war in 1861 and to distorted social relations for much of our nation's history. In "Patterns of Black Resistance," Peter H. Wood takes us into the private world of South Carolina slaves, showing us the many, often subtle, ways in which African bondspeople resisted the control of their masters and in the process reaffirmed their basic humanity and their own countervailing power. Labor was the heart of slave life, just as it was for colonial women. In tracing "The Small Circle of Domestic Concerns," Mary Beth Norton provides us with an intimate look at the everyday lives of American women, whose experiences ranged from the drudgery faced by frontier wives to the more genteel but no less demanding duties of the plantation mistress.

Beginning in the early eighteenth century, the combined effects of imperial warfare and economic change began to transform America into a recognizably "modern" society. In asking the question "Who Was Benjamin Franklin?," John William Ward invites us to examine an important part of this rising modernity: the ability of some men to manipulate their public image for personal gain. Much like public figures today, Franklin's reputation rested less on his community's intimate knowledge of his character than on his own public image-making and self-advertisement. While much of American society remained traditional in Franklin's time, by mid-century unmistakable signs of change existed as well.

PAST TRACES

The New World encounters of Native American and European peoples during the sixteenth and seventeenth centuries inaugurated a complex period of social, cultural, and psychological adjustment. As both groups of people experienced the unsettling effects of confronting unfamiliar people with very different ways of life, they sought to make sense of what they saw by turning to established and familiar patterns of interpreting the world. In this way, Europeans and Native Americans attempted to explain each other in reference to the world in which they lived.

The following two documents allow us to observe this process first-hand. The first document is an account of a Native American village's first encounter with French explorers in the sixteenth century. In it, Montagnais villagers attempt to explain the strangeness of the explorers' ship and the explorers themselves in terms of their own culture, comparing the French ship to the many islands that dotted the bays surrounding them. In the second, two Jesuit missionaries seek to explain the lives of Native American women in light of European gender roles. In most parts of Atlantic Europe, men, not women, were the primary agriculturists, and it was rare to find a woman performing heavy work in the fields. Thus when Europeans, such as the Jesuit priests, encountered Indian women digging, planting, and harvesting village fields, they could only imagine them to be slaves of their husbands. Only gradually, and often imperfectly, did Europeans come to understand the division of gender roles in Native American society as simply different from their own.

Brief Relation . . .

Pierre Pastedechouan has told us that his grandmother used to take pleasure in relating to him the astonishment of the Natives, when they saw for the first time a French ship arrive upon their shores. They thought it was a moving Island; they did not know what to say of the great sails which made it go; their astonishment was redoubled in seeing a number of men on deck. The women [41] at once began to prepare houses for them, as is their custom when new guests arrive, and four canoes of Savages ventured to board these vessels.

They invited the Frenchmen to come into the houses which had been made ready for them, but neither side understood the other. They were given a barrel of bread or biscuit. Having brought it on shore they examined it; and, finding no taste in it, threw it into the water. In a word, they were as much astonished as was the King of Calecut, in olden times, when he saw the first European ship nearing his shores; for, having sent some one to investigate the character and appearance of the men brought by that great house of wood, the messengers reported to their master that these men were prodigious and horrible; that they were dressed in [42] iron, ate bones, and drank blood. They had seen them covered with their cuirasses, eating biscuits, and drinking wine. Our Savages said the Frenchmen drank blood and ate wood, thus naming the wine and the biscuits.

Now as they were unable to understand to what nation our people belonged, they gave them the name which has since always clung to the French, *ouemichtigouchiou;* that is to say, a man who works in wood, or who is in a canoe or vessel of wood. They saw our ships, which were made of wood, their little canoes being made only of bark.

Jesuit Observations on the "Enslavement" of Native American Women, 1633, 1710

[1633]

To obtain the necessaries of life they [the Indians of Acadia] endure cold and hunger in an extraordinary manner. During eight or ten days, if the necessity is imposed on them, they will follow the chase in fasting, and they hunt with the greatest ardor when the snow is deepest and the cold most severe. And yet these same Savages, the offspring, so to speak, of Boreas [The North Wind] and the ice, when once they have returned with their booty and installed themselves in their tents, become indolent and unwilling to perform any labor whatever, imposing this entirely upon the women. The latter, besides the onerous role of bearing and rearing the children, also transport the game from the place where it has fallen; they are the hewers of wood and drawers of water; they make and repair the household utensils; they prepare food; they skin the game and prepare the hides like fullers; they sew garments; they catch fish and gather shellfish for food; often they even hunt; they make the canoes, that is, skiffs of marvelous rapidity, out of bark; they set up the tents wherever and whenever they stop for the night—in short, the men concern themselves with nothing but the more laborious hunting and the waging of war. For this reason almost every one has several wives, and especially the Sagamores, since they cannot maintain their power and keep up the number of their dependents unless they have not only many children to inspire fear or conciliate favor, but also many slaves to perform patiently the menial tasks of every sort that are necessary. For their wives are regarded and treated as slaves.

[1710]

. . . Now, if you inquire concerning the customs and character of this people [Canadian Indians in general], I will reply that a part of them are nomads, wandering during the winter in the woods, whither the hope of better hunting calls them—in the summer, on the shores of the rivers, where they easily obtain their food by fishing; while others inhabit villages. They construct their huts by fixing poles in the ground; they cover the sides with bark, the roofs with hides, moss and branches. In the middle of the hut is the hearth, from which the smoke escapes through an opening at the peak of the roof. As the smoke passes out with difficulty, it usually fills the whole hut, so that strangers compelled to live in these cabins suffer injury and weakening of the eyes; the savages, a coarse race, and accustomed to these discomforts, ridicule this. The care of household affairs, and whatever work there may be in the family, are placed upon the women. They build and repair the wigwams, carry water and wood, and prepare the food; their duties and position are those of slaves, laborers and beasts of burden. The pursuits of hunting and war belong to the men. Thence arise the isolation and numerical weakness of the race. For the women, although naturally prolific, cannot, on account of their occupation in these labors, either bring forth fully-developed offspring, or properly nourish them after they have been brought forth; therefore they either suffer abortion, or forsake their newborn children, while engaged in carrying water, procuring wood and other tasks, so that scarcely one infant in thirty survives until youth. To this there is added their ignorance of medicine, because of which they seldom recover from illnesses which are at all severe.

1

Squanto: Last of the Patuxets

Neal Salisbury

By the beginning of European colonization in the seventeenth century, Native American tribes had inhabited the eastern seaboard of North America for more than 6000 years. Until recently, historians have paid little attention to the contributions of the Powhatans, Mahicans, Abenaki, and many other tribes to American history. In this essay, Neal Salisbury recasts the familiar story of Squanto in light of this new scholarship and in the process reveals the complex interaction between the original inhabitants and the Europeans who explored and settled along the New England coast.

The central event of Squanto's life was the virtual destruction of his people by European diseases. From the time of Columbus's landing in the New World, Native American peoples, who had lost their immunities to Euro-Asian diseases through centuries of geographic isolation, were devastated by the introduction of smallpox, cholera, and even such relatively minor European diseases as measles and chicken pox. As Salisbury points out, the horrible decimation of the Native American population that followed European contact had profound effects upon those who, like Squanto, survived. With mortality rates as high as 80 percent in a single generation, normal social relations became impossible, the mixed economy of hunting and planting was disrupted, political alliances were shattered, and long-standing cultural systems were destroyed. Survivors were left vulnerable to the designs of European settlers and to the new economic system that they brought with them.

In spite of this devastation and cultural dislocation, the history of early European–Native American contact was more than a tale of death and destruction. It was also the story of the many ways in which early settlers depended on the Native Americans: for the sites of their settlements, for their crops, and for the pelts of indigenous animals with which the colonists paid for their imported goods. As this essay reveals, successful interaction between Native Americans and Europeans depended on *the skills of cultural mediators who worked to bring the disparate cultures together. Without these mediators, New England might have developed very differently.*

....

As every American schoolchild knows, a lone Indian named Squanto rescued the Pilgrims from the wilderness by teaching them how to plant corn and introducing them to friendly natives. In so doing, the textbooks imply, he symbolically brought about the union of the European colonizers and the American land. Though contemporary events and critical historical inquiry are now undermining this myth, Squanto's story retains some significance. For when placed in its historic and cultural context, it reveals the range of truly human, if prosaic, qualities called forth among Native Americans during the early colonization of New England.

As befits a mythic hero, the time and circumstances of Squanto's birth are unknown. His birth date can only be inferred from what the sources say and do not say. The firsthand descriptions of him, written between 1618 and his death in 1622, do not suggest that he was strikingly young or old at that time. All we can safely conclude is that he was probably in his twenties or thirties at the time he was forcibly taken to Europe in 1614.

Though Squanto's early years are obscured by a lack of direct evidence, we know something of the cultural milieu that prepared him for his unexpected and remarkable career. Squanto and his fellow Patuxet spoke an Algonquian dialect that they shared with the other natives around Plymouth Bay and west as far as the near shore of Narragansett Bay. Moreover, its differences from other dialects in what is now southern New England were minimal, so that the Patuxet could communicate with the natives throughout this region. Like other coastal villages below the mouth of the Saco River, Patuxet was positioned to allow its inhabitants to grow crops, exploit marine resources, and have easy access to wild plants and animals. In accordance with the strict sexual division of labor maintained by virtually all eastern North American Indians, Squanto's major activities would have been to hunt game and to engage in certain kinds of fishing. He would also have fashioned a wide variety of tools and other material items and participated in the intensely ritualized world of trade, diplomacy, religious ceremonies, recreation, warfare, and political decision making that constituted a man's public life.

The training of young men in precontact southern New England was designed to prepare them for that world. Of the Pokanoket, closely related to the Patuxet, the Plymouth leader Edward Winslow wrote, "a man is not accounted a man till he do some notable act or show forth such courage and resolution as becometh his place." A New Netherland official noted that young Pokanoket men were left alone in the forest for an entire winter. On returning to his people in the spring, a candidate was expected to imbibe and vomit bitter [poisonous] herbs for several days. At the conclusion of his ordeal, he was brought before the entire band, "and if he has been able to stand it all well, and if he is fat and sleek, a wife is given to him."

As a result of such training, young Algonquians learned not only how to survive but also how to develop the capacities to withstand the severest physical and psychological trials. The result was the Indian personality type that Euroamericans came to characterize as stoic, the supreme manifestation of which was the absolute expressionlessness of prisoners under torture. Though the specific content of such training did little to prepare Squanto for his later experiences in Malaga, London, or Newfoundland, it imparted a sense of psychological independence and prepared him for adapting to the most demanding environments and situations.

Patuxet men such as Squanto also exercised their independence in making political judgments and decisions. As elsewhere in southern New England, the band, consisting of one or more villages, was the primary political unit. Its leader, the sachem, was drawn from one of a select group of lineages elevated in prestige above the rest. The sachems distributed garden plots to families and exercised certain judicial prerogatives. They also represented the band on diplomatic and ceremonial occasions. But a sachem's power was derived directly from the band members. To secure economic and political support he or she needed leadership ability as well as a family name. Band members could oblige a faltering sachem to share the office with a relative or step down altogether. Moreover, major political decisions were reached through a consensus in meetings attended by all adult males. Squanto came from a world, then, where politics was a constant and integral component of a man's life.

Squanto was even better prepared for his unusual career if, as seems probable, he was a *pniese* in his band. In preparation for this position, young men were chosen in childhood and underwent unusually rigorous diets and training. The purpose of this preparation was not simply to fortify them and develop their courage but to enable them to call upon and visualize Hobbamock, a deity capable of inflicting great harm and even death on those he did not favor. Hobbamock appeared in many forms to "the chiefest and most judicious amongst them," in Winslow's words, "though all of them strive to attain to that hellish height of honor." It is clear that those who succeeded in the vision quest had developed the mental self-discipline demanded of all Indians to an extraordinary degree. By calling on Hobbamock, the *pnieses* protected themselves and those near them in battle and frightened their opponents. They constituted an elite group within the band, serving as counselors and bodyguards to the sachems. They were universally respected not only for their access to Hobbamock and for their courage and judgment but for their moral uprightness. Because of his psychological fortitude, his particularly astute grasp of Indian politics and protocol, and his continued sense of duty to his band after its demise, it is quite likely that Squanto was a *pniese*.

The few recorded observations of Patuxet during Squanto's early years show that it was a very different place from the "wilderness" the Plymouth colonists later found there. Both Samuel de Champlain, in 1605 and 1606, and John Smith, in 1614, noted that most of the coast between Massachusetts and Plymouth bays was under cultivation. The colonists were told, probably by Squanto himself, that in Plymouth Bay "in former time hath lived about 2000 Indians." The population of the surrounding area—that is, of the Indians with whom the Patuxet maintained the closest relations—was probably between twenty and twenty-five thousand in 1615. Most of these natives were concentrated in village communities ranging in size from five hundred to fifteen hundred individuals. Squanto was thus accustomed to a more densely settled environment than we might expect and was probably as comfortable in the European cities he later visited as in the tiny colonies.

Though no one could have known it at the time, Squanto was born at a turning point in the history of his people and his region. For a century Europeans had been trading and skirmishing with, and sometimes kidnapping, Indians along the coast. At the time of Squanto's birth, however, these activities had not been extended south of Canada on a regular basis. Infrequent visits from European explorers and traders and the natives' own well-established exchange routes brought some iron tools and glass beads to Patuxet. But these were too scattered to induce any economic or cultural changes of a substantive nature. Unlike the fur-trading Indians to the north, the Patuxet and their neighbors had not become dependent on European trade items for their survival.

The turn of the century marked an intensification of French and British interest in New England's resources. The differing economic goals of the colonizers from the two countries gave rise to differing attitudes and policies toward the natives. The French were concerned primarily with furs. Following Champlain's explorations of the New England coast in 1605 and 1606, French traders using his descriptions and maps began to visit the Indians annually and to cultivate an extensive trade as far south as Cape Cod. Their goals encouraged the maintenance of friendly relations with stable Indian bands and even the development of broad regional ties among the natives.

For the English, however, furs were at best a useful by-product of more pressing interests. Beginning with Bartholomew Gosnold's expedition in 1602, they showed a preference for resources such as fish and sassafras that did not require the cooperation of the natives. Moreover, they thought in long-range terms of making Indian land available to Englishmen for farming, a goal that virtually guaranteed eventual conflict with the natives. Indian allies were cultivated, but only for purposes of assisting the English in establishing themselves, and the methods used were generally more coercive than those of the French. Nearly every English expedition from Gosnold's to that of the *Mayflower* generated hostility with the Indians. By 1610 taking captured Indians to England had become routine. Would-be colonizers such as Sir Ferdinando Gorges hoped to impress their captives with the superiority of English culture, to learn as much as they could about the lay of the land, and to acquire mediators with the local Indians. They also displayed their captives prominently in order to attract financial and public support for their projected colonies.

Squanto and his people were producing substantial fur surpluses by 1614 and had gained at least some acquaintance with the Europeans. From the visits of Champlain, Smith, and the traders, Squanto had learned something of European approaches to trade, diplomacy, and military conflict and had witnessed some of their technological accomplishments. But the regularized trade was less than a decade old. And the ease with which groups of Patuxet men were manipulated by Smith and his officer, Thomas Hunt, in 1614 suggests that they had not developed the wariness toward Europeans, particularly the English, of the more experienced Indians to the north.

Squanto's life reached a sudden and dramatic turning point with Hunt's visit. Smith had returned to England, leaving Hunt in charge of his fishing crew to complete the catch and carry it to Malaga, Spain. Before departing, Hunt stopped at Patuxet. Using his association with Smith, who had left on friendly terms, he lured about twenty natives, including Squanto, aboard. Quickly rounding Cape Cod, he drew off seven more from Nauset and then turned east for Malaga. Hunt's action indelibly marked the English as an enemy of all the Indians in the Patuxet–Cape Cod region. In the words of Sir Ferdinando Gorges, Hunt's action resulted in "a warre now new begunne betweene the inhabitants of those parts and us," and John Smith condemned Hunt for moving the Indians' "hate against our Nation, as well as to cause my proceedings to bee more difficult."

Meanwhile Squanto and his fellow captives [soon] reached Malaga, where Hunt tried to sell them as slaves. A few had already been sold when, according to Gorges, "the Friers of those parts took the rest from them and kept them to be instructed in the Christian faith." What happened to Squanto in the next three years is not clear. Particularly intriguing are questions about the extent and influence of his Catholic instruction and the means by which, in William Bradford's words, "he got away for England." We know only that by 1617 he was residing in the London home of John Slany, treasurer of the Newfoundland Company, where he learned or at least improved his English and his understanding of colonial goals. In the following year he went to Newfoundland itself, presumably at Slany's instigation. Here he met for the second time Thomas Dermer, an officer with Smith in 1614 who now worked for Gorges. Dermer was so impressed with Squanto's tales of Patuxet that he took him back to England to meet Gorges. Though the strategy of employing captive Indians as guides had backfired several times, Gorges was ready to try again. He saw in Squanto the key to countering the recent successes of the French and reestablishing England's reputation among the Indians. For his part Squanto knew, as had earlier captives, how to tell Gorges what he wanted to hear in order to be returned home. In March 1619 he and Dermer were bound for New England.

Moving in the circles he did, Squanto undoubtedly knew something of the epidemic that had ravaged New England, including Patuxet, during his absence. A Gorges expedition under Richard Vines had witnessed what Vines called simply "the plague" at Sagadahoc in 1616 and reported on its effects. Most notable was the immunity of the English; while most of the Indians were dying, Vines and his party "lay in the Cabins with those people, [and] not one of them ever felt their heads to ake." This immunity and the 75 to 90 percent depopulation among the Indians make it clear that a virgin soil epidemic of European origin had been planted in New England's isolated disease environment.

Squanto found his own village completely vacated. Most of its inhabitants had died, but some had fled inland to other villages. He surely noticed, as did others, the undergrowth that had overtaken the formerly cultivated fields and the vast numbers of unburied dead whose "bones and skulls," in one Englishman's words, "made such a spectacle . . . it seemed to me a new found Golgotha."

The ritual worlds and belief systems of the stricken Indians had been badly shaken by the epidemic. The usual practice of gathering with the *pow-wow* (shaman) in a sick person's wigwam could only have served to spread the disease more rapidly. With even the *pow-wows* succumbing, the Indians could only conclude that their deities had aligned against them. And being unable to observe the proper burial rituals, the survivors had to fear the retribution of the dead. The Indians' perception that they had lost touch with the sources of power and that others controlled the access to them would be a critical factor in facilitating Squanto's later political success.

As Dermer's expedition traveled overland from Patuxet in the summer of 1619, Squanto's presence and diplomatic skill enabled the English to break through the antagonisms toward them and to make friendly contacts at Nemasket (near Middleboro) and Pokanoket (near Bristol, Rhode Island). For once an Indian captive had performed as Gorges hoped. But as Dermer returned to his ship and prepared to sail around Cape Cod, Squanto took his leave to search for surviving Patuxets.

In December 1620, word reached Pokanoket that a shipload of English colonists had established a permanent settlement at Patuxet.

Like the other Puritans who later settled New England, the group at Plymouth (for so they renamed Patuxet) was motivated by a combination of religious and economic motives that shaped their attitudes toward the natives. Their experience with persecution in England and exile to the Netherlands had sharpened their desire to practice their exclusionary, intolerant separatism without external inference. Moreover, though seeking distance from English ecclesiastical authorities, the settlers were attempting to reinforce their English identities. They had abandoned their Dutch haven for fear that their children would be assimilated there. Finally, though ostensibly migrating to fish and trade for furs, the colonists sought land to improve themselves materially and, they supposed, spiritually. Though Plymouth lacked the sense of divine mission of the later nonseparatist Puritan colonies, its goals of religious and ethnic exclusivity and an abundance of land had obvious implications for its relations with the natives.

These implications were apparent in Plymouth's early policies and attitudes toward the Indians. In a major promotional pamphlet published in 1622, Robert Cushman restated what had already become a familiar justification for dispossession of native lands:

Their land is spacious and void, and there are few and do but run over the grass, as do also the foxes and wild beasts. They are not industrious, neither have art, science, skill, or faculty to use either the land or the commodities of it, but all spoils or rots, and is marred for want of manuring, gathering, ordering, etc. As the ancient patriarchs therefore removed from straiter places into more roomy . . . so is it lawful now to take a land which none useth, and make use of it.

Cushman's statement was consistent with the emerging European doctrine of *vacuum domicilium,* by which "civil" states were entitled to the uncultivated lands of those in a "natural" state. Though Plymouth's own "civility" was formalized by the hastily contrived *Mayflower* Compact, its financial backers had anticipated its need for more than an abstract principle to press its claim—among its own people as well as among any natives they might encounter. Accordingly, they had hired Miles Standish, a soldier of fortune fresh from the Dutch wars, to organize the colony militarily. It was Standish who would shape Plymouth's Indian policy during its first generation.

Standish began to execute this policy even before the *Mayflower* arrived at Patuxet. Landing first at Cape Cod, the settlers aroused native hostilities by ransacking Indian graves, houses, and grain stores. At Patuxet they also stirred suspicions during the first four months of their stay. But their own situation grew desperate during their first New England winter. They lost half their numbers to starvation and disease, and as inexperienced farmers they were ill-prepared for the approaching planting season. In this condition they could no longer expect to alleviate their shortages through pilferage with impunity. The impasse was broken one day in March 1621 by the appearance of Samoset, a sachem of the Pemaquid River band, which had been trading with the English for more than a decade. Samoset learned the needs and intentions of the colony and returned a few days later with Squanto.

The Pokanoket had been watching the Plymouth group throughout the winter. With Samoset and the newly useful Squanto offering advice and experience, they concluded that the time was ripe to befriend the settlers instead of maintaining a hostile distance. Such an alliance would enable them to break from the hold of the Narragansetts, whose haughty demeanor

stung even more than that of the English. Nevertheless, the decision was not to be taken lightly. Bradford wrote that the Indians did first "curse and execrate them with their conjurations" before approaching the settlers. But this description betrays his fear of witchcraft as it was understood by Europeans, rather than his comprehension of Indian rituals. More likely the Pokanoket were ritually purging themselves of their hostilities toward the English.

Samoset and Squanto arranged the meeting between the Pokanoket and Plymouth colony that resulted in their historic treaty. In it each side agreed to aid the other in the event of attack by a third party, to disarm during their meetings with each other, and to return any tools stolen from the other side. But in addition to these reciprocal agreements, several others were weighted against the natives. Massasoit, the Pokanoket sachem, was to see that his tributaries observed the terms; the Indians were to turn over for punishment any of their people suspected of assaulting any English (but no English had to fear being tried by Indians); and, the treaty concluded, "King James would esteem of him [Massasoit] as his friend and ally." The meaning of the last honor was made explicit by the colony's annalist, Nathaniel Morton, who wrote that by the treaty Massasoit "acknowledged himself content to become the subject of our sovereign lord the King aforesaid, his heirs and successors, and gave unto them all the lands adjacent to them and theirs forever." Morton made clear that among themselves the English did not regard the treaty as one of alliance and friendship between equals but as one of submission by one party to the domination of the other, according to the assumptions of *vacuum domicilium.*

For the Pokanoket, however, the meaning of a political relationship was conveyed in the ritual exchange of speeches and gifts, not in written clauses or unwritten understandings based on concepts such as sovereignty that were alien to one party. From their standpoint, the English were preferable to the Narragansett because they demanded less tribute and homage while offering more gifts and autonomy and better protection.

The treaty also brought a change in status for Squanto. In return for his services, the Pokanoket now freed him to become guide, interpreter, and diplomat for the colony. Thus he finally returned to his home at Patuxet, a move that had, as we shall see, more than sentimental significance. Among his first services was the securing of corn seed and instruction in its planting, including the use of fish fertilizer, which he learned from his own people or from the Newfoundland colonists.

Squanto also enabled Plymouth to strengthen its political position in the surrounding area. He helped secure peace with some bands on Cape Cod and guided an expedition to Massachusetts Bay. His kidnapping by anti-English Indians at Nemasket and subsequent rescue by a heavily armed Plymouth force speaks compellingly of his importance to the colony. Moreover, this incident led to a new treaty, engineered in part by Squanto, with all the Indian groups of Massachusetts Bay to the tip of Cape Cod, including even Epenow and his band. By establishing a tributary system with the surrounding Indian bands, the colony was filling the political vacuum left by the epidemic and creating a dependable network of corn suppliers and buffers against overland attack. But it also incurred the resentment of the Narragansett by depriving them of tributaries just when Dutch traders were expanding their activities in the bay. The Narragansett challenged Plymouth's action in January 1622 by sending a snakeskin filled with arrows. On Squanto's advice Plymouth's leaders returned the skin filled with powder and shot. The Narragansett sachem, Canonicus, refused to accept this counterchallenge, in effect acknowledging the colony's presence and political importance.

However effective in appearance, Plymouth's system of Indian diplomacy was fraught with tensions that nearly destroyed it. A Pokanoket *pniese,* Hobbamock (named for his patron deity), became a second advisor to Plymouth in the summer of 1621. Whether the English

thought that Hobbamock would merely assist Squanto or would serve to check him is unclear. In any event, Squanto was no longer the only link between the colony and the Indians; indeed, as a Pokanoket, Hobbamock had certain advantages over him. As one whose very life depended on the colony's need for him, Squanto had to act decisively to check this threat to his position. His most potent weapon was the mutual distrust and fear lingering between English and Indians; his most pressing need was for a power base so that he could extricate himself from his position of colonial dependency. Accordingly, he began maneuvering on his own.

Squanto had been acting independently for several months before being discovered by the English in March 1622. As reconstructed by Edward Winslow:

> his course was to persuade [the Indians] he could lead us to peace or war at his pleasure, and would oft threaten the Indians, sending them word in a private manner we were intended shortly to kill them, that thereby he might get gifts to himself, to work their peace; . . . so that whereas divers were wont to rely on Massasoit for protection, and resort to his abode, now they began to leave him and seek after Tisquantum [Squanto].

In short, he sought to establish himself as an independent native political leader. At the same time he endeavored to weaken the Pokanoket's influence on Plymouth by provoking armed conflict between the two allies. He circulated a rumor that Massasoit was conspiring with the Narragansett and Massachusett to wipe out the colony. The English quickly verified the continued loyalty of the Pokanoket but, though angry at Squanto, were afraid to dispense with him. Instead they protected him from Massasoit's revenge, which brought tensions into the Pokanoket–Plymouth relationship that were only finally assuaged when Squanto died later in the year.

In seeking to establish his independence of Plymouth, Squanto was struggling for more than his survival. As Winslow put it, he sought "honor, which he loved as his life and preferred before his peace." What did honor mean to

Squanto? For one thing, of course, it meant revenge against the Pokanoket, not only for threatening his position at Plymouth but for his earlier captivity. But it meant more than that. Squanto appears to have made substantial inroads among Indians loyal to Massasoit in a short period of time. Winslow indicated, unknowingly and in passing, the probable key to this success. The news of Massosoit's alleged treachery against Plymouth was brought, he said, by "an Indian of Tisquantum's family." Contrary to the Plymouth sources (all of which were concerned with establishing the colony's unblemished title to the land around Plymouth Bay), there were certainly a few dozen Patuxet survivors of the epidemic at Pokanoket, Nemasket, and elsewhere. Though Squanto undoubtedly sought the loyalty and tribute of others, it was to these relatives and friends that he would primarily have appealed. The honor he sought was a reconstituted Patuxet band under his own leadership, located near its traditional home.

Squanto's hopes were shattered when his plot collapsed. With Massasoit seeking his life, he had, in Bradford's words, "to stick close to the English, and never durst go from them till he dies." This isolation from other Indians and dependence on the colonists helps explain the latter's willingness to protect him. In July, Squanto again engineered an important breakthrough for Plymouth by accompanying an expedition to Monomoy, where suspicion of all Europeans persisted. The Indians here had attacked Champlain's party in 1606 and Dermer's in 1619. Standish's men had taken some of their corn during their stop at Cape Cod in November 1620. Now, as Winslow phrased it, "by Tisquantum's means better persuaded, they left their jealousy, and traded with them." The colony's take was eight hogsheads of corn and beans. But as the expedition prepared to depart, Squanto "fell sick of an Indian fever, bleeding much at the nose (which the Indians take for a symptom of death) and within a few days died there."

By the time of Squanto's death, Plymouth colony had gained the foothold it had sought for two and a half years. The expedition to Monomoy marked the establishment of firm relations with the last local band to withhold loyalty. Moreover, the trade in corn was no longer an economic necessity, remaining important primarily as a means of affirming tributary relationships. These accomplishments would have been infinitely more difficult, if not impossible, without Squanto's aid. But it is questionable whether his contributions after the summer of 1622 would have been as critical. Thereafter, the colony's principal dealings were with the hostile Massachusett and Narragansett Indians beyond Patuxet's immediate environs. Moreover, the world in which Squanto had flourished was vanishing. A rationalized wampum trade had begun to transform Indian-European relations in southern New England. And the end of the decade would bring a mighty upsurge in English colonization that would surround and dwarf Plymouth. Within the restrictions imposed by his dependence on Plymouth's protection, Squanto would have adapted to these changes. But his knowledge and skills would no longer have been unique nor his services indispensable.

It is difficult to imagine what direction the life of this politically and historically isolated man, who valued "honor" above all else, might have taken in the coming decades. It is in this light that we should read his well-known deathbed conversion wherein he requested Bradford "to pray for him that he might go to the Englishmen's God in Heaven; and bequeathed sundry of his things to sundry of his English friends as remembrances of his love." He was acknowledging that after eight years of acting with honor in alien settings, he had been cornered. Dying so ignominiously, the last Patuxet would have found it ironic that later generations of Americans celebrated him as a hero.

KEY TERMS

Pilgrims: Along with the Puritans, the most important dissenting group in England; believed that separation from the Church of England was the only path to reform.

Samuel de Champlain (1567?–1635): French explorer who explored present-day Canada and in 1608 established the settlement of Quebec.

John Smith (1580?–1631): One of the early leaders of the Virginia Colony; explored New England as well as the Chesapeake.

Mayflower: The ship which brought the Pilgrims to their Plymouth settlement.

Virgin soil epidemic: The catastrophic spread of communicable disease among a population without active immunities, leading to high mortality.

Golgotha: A graveyard or charnel house.

Mayflower Compact: The agreement reached by the original Pilgrims regulating the government of the Plymouth settlement.

DISCUSSION TOPICS

After reading this essay, you should be able to discuss:

1. The impact of European diseases on Native American peoples.

2. The meaning of Squanto's position as a *pniese*.

3. The implications of the European doctrine of *vacuum domicilium*.

4. Squanto's motives in Anglo-Indian relations.

2

Looking Out for Number One:
Conflicting Cultural Values in Early
Seventeenth-Century Virginia

T. H. Breen

Emigration to the New World in the seventeenth century was an arduous undertaking. The journey required two to six months at sea, with passengers huddled in cramped quarters with little provision for privacy. During the long voyage one could expect minimal—and at times rotten—provisions. Seasickness, fevers, contagious diseases, and boredom afflicted most sojourners. Death itself often awaited the very young, the old, and the infirm. For those who set sail for the Chesapeake, the voyage was only the first part of the ordeal. Once ashore, virtually every immigrant contracted yellow fever, malaria, or some other parasitic disease from the mosquitoes that thrived in the lowly-ing tidewater swamps. Contemporary records suggest that up to half of all English immigrants died of disease within a few years of reaching Virginia or Maryland.

Yet despite the rigors and dangers of such a crossing, thousands of English men and women left their homeland for the Chesapeake in the first half of the seventeenth century. In this essay, T. H. Breen explores the character of those who made this fateful choice. What drew these people to the Chesapeake, most of them as indentured servants? And what about these people inspired them to risk disease and death to come to a region with so little in the way of typical English social and family life?

The answer, Breen suggests, is a simple one. Wave after wave of immigrants came to the Chesapeake to make money from the tobacco crop that was the sole reason for colonization of the region. The well-off and poor alike arrived in Virginia with the hope of obtaining the land and labor that would enable them to rise in the expanding economic world of the seventeenth century. The stakes and risks were both high, Breen concludes, and those who attempted to follow the Chesapeake's quick way to wealth were "adventurers"—atypically individualistic, competitive, and materialistic English people with few concerns other than their own advancement.

....

Despite their common English background, the thousands of European men and women who migrated to Barbados, Virginia, and New England during the seventeenth century created strikingly different societies in the New World.

This essay examines the creation of a distinct culture in Virginia roughly between 1617 and 1630. Although early Virginians shared certain general ideas, attitudes, and norms with other English migrants, their operative values were quite different from those that shaped social and institutional behavior in places such as Massachusetts Bay. Virginia's physical environment, its extensive network of navigable rivers, its rich soil, its ability to produce large quantities of marketable tobacco, powerfully reinforced values which the first settlers carried to America. The interplay between a particular variant of Jacobean culture and a specific New World setting determined the character of Virginia's institutions, habits of personal interaction, and patterns of group behavior that persisted long after the early adventurers had died or returned to the mother country.

An ethnographic reconstruction of Virginia between 1617 and 1630 begins with an analysis of the values that the settlers carried with them to the New World. Here the distinction that social anthropologists make between "dominant" and "variant" values becomes relevant. The men and women who sailed for the Chesapeake Bay in the early seventeenth century were certainly part of a general English culture. They shared a set of views, customs, and expectations with other Jacobeans, with New Englanders and Barbadians, with those persons who remained in the mother country. Historians of colonial America have closely analyzed this

common cultural background, and there is no need to repeat their findings in detail.

From these accounts we learn that the crucial formative values transferred to Virginia were religious and political. Their constitutional heritage provided the colonials with civil and legal imperatives; their religion with a world view that structured their daily lives.

Early Virginians undoubtedly subscribed to these general constitutional and religious values and, whenever feasible, attempted to translate them into action. Anyone who has read the colony's history knows the first settlers saw God's hand behind human affairs, marched to church to the beat of a drum, and formed a representative legislative body called the House of Burgesses. But this sort of analysis does not carry us very far in understanding why Virginia society was unlike those formed by English migrants in other parts of the New World, or why despite the presence of common dominant values various groups of settlers created distinctive patterns of social and institutional behavior.

Such problems are reduced when we realize that the early settlers in Virginia were an unusual group of Jacobeans. In no way did they represent a random sample of seventeenth-century English society or a cross section of English values. While little is known about the specific origins or backgrounds of most settlers, we do have a fairly clear idea of what sort of inducements persuaded men and women to move to Virginia. The colony's promotional literature emphasized economic opportunity, usually quick and easy riches. In his "True Relation of the State of Virginia" written in 1616, for example, John Rolfe pitied England's hardworking farmers who barely managed to make ends meet. "What happiness might they enjoy in

Virginia," Rolfe mused, "where they may have ground for nothing, more than they can manure, reap more fruits and profits with half the labour." And in 1622 Peter Arundle, overlooking the colony's recent military setbacks at the hands of the Indians, assured English friends that "any laborious honest man may in a short time become rich in this Country." It was a compelling dream, one which certain Englishmen were all too willing to accept as truth. Indeed, so many persons apparently risked life and possessions in the illusive search for the main chance that John Harvey, a future Royal Governor of Virginia, begged men of integrity on both sides of the Atlantic to control "the rumors of plenty to be found at all tyme[s] in Virginia."

The lure of great wealth easily obtained held an especially strong appeal for a specific type of seventeenth-century Englishman, individuals who belonged to a distinct subculture within Jacobean society. By all accounts, early Virginia drew a disproportionately large number of street toughs, roughnecks fresh from the wars in Ireland, old soldiers looking for new glory, naive adventurers, mean-spirited sea captains, marginal persons attempting to recoup their losses. If contemporaries are to be believed, Virginia found itself burdened with "many unruly gallants packed thether by their friends to escape ill destinies." Even Sir Thomas Dale, himself a recent veteran of English military expeditions in Holland, was shocked by the colony's settlers, "so prophane, so riotous, so full of Mutenie and treasonable Intendments" that they provided little "testimonie beside their names that they are Christians."

Even if Dale exaggerated, there is no reason to question that the colonists were highly individualistic, motivated by the hope of material gain, and in many cases, not only familiar with violence but also quite prepared to employ it to obtain their own ends in the New World. By and large, they appear to have been extremely competitive and suspicious of other men's motives. Mutiny and anarchy sometimes seemed more attractive than obeying someone else's orders.

Few of the colonists showed substantial interest in creating a permanent settlement. For the adventurer, Virginia was not a new home, not a place to carry out a divine mission, but simply an area to be exploited for private gain. It was this "variant" strain of values—a sense of living only for the present or near future, a belief that the environment could and should be forced to yield quick financial returns, an assumption that everyone was looking out for number one and hence that cooperative ventures of all sorts were bound to fail—that help to account for the distinctive patterns of social and institutional behavior found in early Virginia.

The transfer of these variant values, of course, only partially explains Virginia's cultural development. The attitudes, beliefs, and ideas that the founders brought with them to the New World interacted with specific environmental conditions. The settlers' value system would certainly have withered in a physical setting that offered no natural resources capable of giving plausibility to the adventurers' original expectations. If by some chance the Virginians had landed in a cold, rocky, inhospitable country devoid of valuable marketable goods, then they would probably have given up the entire venture and like a defeated army, straggled home. That is exactly what happened in 1607 to the unfortunate men who settled in Sagadohoc, Maine, a tiny outpost that failed to produce instant wealth. Virginia almost went the way of Sagadohoc. The first decade of its history was filled with apathy and disappointment, and at several points, the entire enterprise seemed doomed. The privatistic values that the colonists had carried to Jamestown, a tough, exploitive competitive individualism were dysfunctional—even counter-productive—in an environment which offered up neither spices nor gold, neither passages to China nor a subject population easily subdued and exploited. In fact, before 1617 this value system generated only political faction and petty personal violence, things that a people struggling for survival could ill afford.

The successful cultivation of tobacco altered the course of Virginia's cultural development.

Clearly, in an economic sense, the crop saved the colony. What is less obvious but no less true, is that the discovery of a lucrative export preserved the founders' individualistic values. Suddenly, after ten years of error and failure, the adventurers' transported values were no longer at odds with their physical environment. The settlers belatedly stumbled across the payoff; the forests once so foreboding, so unpromising, could now be exploited with a reasonable expectation of quick return. By 1617 the process was well-advanced, and as one planter reported, "the streets, and all other spare places planted with Tobacco . . . The Colonie dispersed all about, planting *Tobacco.*"

The interplay between the settlers' value system and their environment involved more than economic considerations. Once a market for tobacco had been assured, people spread out along the James and York Rivers. Whenever possible, they formed what the directors of the Virginia Company called private hundreds, small plantations frequently five or more miles apart which groups of adventurers developed for their own profit. By 1619 forty-four separate patents for private plantations had been issued, and by the early 1620's a dispersed settlement pattern, long to be a characteristic of Virginia society, was well established. The dispersion of the colony's population was a cultural phenomenon. It came about not simply because the Virginia soil was unusually well suited for growing tobacco or because its deep rivers provided easy access to the interior, but because men holding privatistic values regarded the land as an exploitable resource, and within their structure of priorities, the pursuit of private gain outranked the creation of corporate communities.

The scattering of men and women along the colony's waterways, their self-imposed isolation, obviously reduced the kind of ongoing face-to-face contacts that one associates with the villages of seventeenth-century New England. A migrant to Virginia tended to be highly competitive and to assume that other men would do unto him as he would do unto them—certainly

an unpleasant prospect. Dispersion heightened this sense of suspicion. Because communication between private plantations was difficult, Virginians possessed no adequate means to distinguish the truth about their neighbors from malicious rumor, and lacking towns and well-developed voluntary organizations, without shared rituals, ceremonies, even market days, they drew increasingly distrustful of whatever lay beyond the perimeter of their own few acres.

The kind of human relationships that developed in colonial Virginia graphically reveal the effect of highly individualistic values upon social behavior. In this settlement only two meaningful social categories existed: a person was either free or dependent, either an exploiter or a resource. There was no middle ground. Those men who held positions of political and economic power treated indentured servants and slaves not as human beings, but as instruments to produce short-run profits. As a consequence of this outlook, life on the private plantations was a degrading experience for thousands of men and women who arrived in Virginia as bonded laborers. Whatever their expectations about the colony may have been before they migrated, the servants' reality consisted of poor food, meager clothing, hard work, and, more often than not, early death. The leading planters showed little interest in reforming these conditions. The servants were objects, things to be gambled away in games of chance, beaten or abused, and then replaced when they wore out.

But dependence has another side. In Virginia dominance went hand in hand with fear, for no matter how tractable, how beaten down, the servants may have appeared, both masters and laborers recognized the potential for violence inherent in such relationships. In the early 1620's several worried planters complained that Captain John Martin, a long-standing troublemaker for the Virginia Company, "hath made his owne Territory there a receptacle of Vagabonds and bankerupts & other disorderly persons." Whether the rumors of Martin's activities were accurate is not the point. In such a society a gathering of "Vagabonds" represented a grave threat, a base from which the exploited could harass their former masters. The anxiety resurfaced in 1624 when the Virginia Company lost its charter and no one in the colony knew for certain who held legitimate authority. In shrill rhetoric that over the course of a century would become a regular feature of Virginia statute books, the colony's Assembly immediately ordered that "no person within this Colonie upon the rumor of supposed change and alterations [may] presume to be disobedient to the presente Government, nor servants to theire privatt officers masters or overseers, at their utmost perills."

The distrust that permeated Virginia society poisoned political institutions. Few colonists seem to have believed that local rulers would on their own initiative work for the public good. Instead, they assumed that persons in authority would use their office for personal gain. One settler called Governor George Yeardley, a man who grew rich directing public affairs, "the right worthy statesman for his own profit." William Capps, described simply as an old planter, referred to the governor as an "old smoker" and claimed that this official had "stood for a cypher whilst the Indians stood ripping open our guts." Cynicism about the motives of the colony's leaders meant that few citizens willingly sacrificed for the good of the state. In fact, Virginia planters seem to have regarded government orders as a threat to their independence, almost as a personal affront. William Strachey, secretary of the colony, condemned what he labeled the general "want of government." He reported, "every man over-valuing his owne worth, would be a Commander: every man underprising anothers value, denied to be commanded." Other colonists expressed agreement with Strachey's views. During the famous first meeting of the House of Burgesses in 1619, the representatives of the various plantations twice commented upon the weakness of Virginia's governing institutions. Toward the end of the session, they declared that whatever laws they passed in the future should go into immediate effect without

special authorization from London, "for otherwise this people . . . would in a shorte time grow so insolent, as they would shake off all government, and there would be no living among them."

The colonists' achievements in education and religion were meager. From time to time, Virginians commented upon the importance of churches and schools in their society, but little was done to transform rhetoric into reality. Church buildings were in a perpetual state of decay; ministers were poorly supported by their parishioners. An ambitious plan for a college came to nothing, and schools for younger children seem to have been nonexistent. The large distances between plantations and the pressure to keep every able-bodied person working in the fields, no doubt discouraged the development of local schools and parish churches, but the colony's dispersed settlement plan does not in itself explain the absence of these institutions. A colonywide boarding school could have been constructed in Jamestown, a Harvard of Virginia, but the colony's planters were incapable of the sustained, cooperative effort that such a project would have required. They responded to general societal needs as individuals, not as groups. Later in the seventeenth century some successful planters sent their sons at great expense to universities in England and Scotland, but not until the end of the century did the colonists found a local college.

An examination of Virginia's military policies between 1617 and 1630 provides the clearest link between social values and institutional behavior. During this important transitional period, military affairs were far better recorded than were other social activities, and the historian can trace with a fair degree of confidence how particular military decisions reflected the colonists' value system. And second, in any society military efforts reveal a people's social priorities, their willingness to sacrifice for the common good, and their attitudes toward the allocation of community resources. Certainly, in early Virginia, maintaining a strong defense should have been a major consideration. Common sense alone seemed to dictate that a group of settlers confronted with a powerful Indian confederation and foreign marauders would, in military matters at least, cooperate for their own safety. But in point of fact, our common sense was not the rule of the seventeenth-century Virginian. The obsession with private profits was a more compelling force than was the desire to create a dependable system of self-defense. This destructive individualism disgusted John Pory, at one time the colony's secretary of state. In 1620 he reported that Governor Yeardley asked the men of Jamestown "to contribute some labor to a bridge, and to certaine platformes to mounte greate ordinance upon, being both for the use and defense of the same Citty, and so of themselves; yet they repyned as much as if all their goods had bene taken from them."

Virginians paid dearly for their failure to work together. On March 22, 1622, the Indians of the region launched a coordinated attack on the scattered, poorly defended white settlements, and before the colonists could react, 347 of them had been killed. The details of this disaster are well known. The Massacre and the events of the months that followed provide rare insight into the workings of the Virginia culture. The shock of this defeat called into question previous institutional policies—not just military ones—and some colonists even saw the setback as an opportunity to reform society, to develop a new set of values.

Virginia's vulnerability revealed to some men the need to transform the privatistic culture into a more tightly knit, cooperative venture. Local rulers bravely announced that "this Massacre will prove much to the speedie advancement of the Colony and much to the benefitt of all those that shall nowe come thither." No longer would the planters live so far apart. Shortsighted dreams of tobacco fortunes would be laid aside, and the people would join together in the construction of genuine towns. And most important, the settlers would no longer evade their military responsibilities. As the members of the Virginia Council wrote only a month after the Massacre, "our

first and princypall care should have beene for our safetie . . . yet its very necessarie for us yett at last, to laye a better and surer foundation for the tyme to come." But despite the death and destruction and despite the bold declarations about a new start, the colonists proceeded to repeat the very activities that contemporary commentators agreed had originally caused the people's immense suffering.

Even though the Indians remained a grave threat to security throughout the 1620's, the settlers continued to grumble about the burden of military service. Each person seemed to assess the tragedy only in personal terms—how, in other words, had the Indian Massacre affected his ability to turn a profit. By the end of the summer of 1622, there were unmistakable signs that many people no longer regarded the defeat of the Indians as a community responsibility. Few men talked of the common good; fewer still seemed prepared to sacrifice their lives or immediate earning power in order to preserve the colony from a second disaster.

In Virginia long before the massive enslavement of black Africans, human relationships were regarded as a matter of pounds and pence, and each day one man chased the Indians through the wilderness or helped build a fortification, another man grew richer growing tobacco. When William Capps in 1623 attempted to organize a raiding party of forty men to go against the Indians, he was greeted with excuses and procrastination. Almost in disbelief, he informed an English correspondent of the planters' train of thought, "take away one of my men, there's 2000 Plantes gone, thates 500 waight of Tobacco, yea and what shall this man doe, runne after the Indians. . . . I have perhaps 10, perhaps 15, perhaps 20, men and am able to secure my owne Plantacion; how will they doe that are fewer? let them first be Crusht alittle and then perhaps they will themselves make up the Nomber for theire own safeties." Perhaps Frethorne's anxiety grew out of the knowledge that no one beyond Martin's Hundred really cared what the Indians might do to him and his comrades.

Virginia's extreme individualism was not an ephemeral phenomenon, something associated only with the colony's founding or a peculiar boom-town atmosphere. Long after the 1620's, values originally brought to the New World by adventurers and opportunists influenced patterns of social and institutional behavior, and instead of providing Virginia with new direction or a new sense of mission, newcomers were assimilated into an established cultural system. Customs became statute law, habitual acts tradition.

The long-term effects of these values upon society are too great to be considered here. It should be noted, however, that seventeenth-century Virginians never succeeded in forming a coherent society. Despite their apparent homogeneity, they lacked cohesive group identity; they generated no positive symbols, no historical myths strong enough to overcome individual differences. As one might expect, such a social system proved extremely fragile, and throughout the seventeenth century Virginians experienced social unrest, even open rebellion.

Nor should the grand life style of the great eighteenth-century planters, the Byrds, the Carters, the Wormeleys, mislead one into thinking that their value system differed significantly from that of Virginia's early settlers. The apparent political tranquillity of late colonial Virginia grew not out of a sense of community or new value-orientations, but out of more effective forms of human exploitation. The mass of tobacco field laborers were now black slaves, men and women who by legal definition could never become fully part of the privatistic culture. In Byrd's Virginia, voluntaristic associations remained weak; education lagged, churches stagnated, and towns never developed. The isolation of plantation life continued, and the extended visits and the elaborate balls of the period may well have served to obscure the competition that underlay planter relationships. As one anthropologist reminds us, "in a society in which everyone outside the nuclear family is immediately suspect, in which one is at every moment believed to be vulnerable to the underhanded attacks of others, reliability and trust can never be taken for granted." In the course of a century of cultural development, Virginians transformed an extreme form of individualism, a value system suited for soldiers and adventurers, into a set of regional virtues, a love of independence, an insistence upon personal liberty, a cult of manhood, and an uncompromising loyalty to family.

KEY TERMS

Jacobean: The era of the reign of King James I of England, 1603–1625.

John Rolfe (1585–1622): An early leader of the Virginia colony; eventually became the husband of Pocahontas.

Jamestown: Capital and principal settlement of the Virginia settlement.

Martin's Hundred: The plantation owned by John Martin, "hundred" referring to the original land grants of a hundred acres to free immigrants.

Sagadahoc, Maine: Site of a failed Plymouth Company colony, 1607–1609.

Ethnographic: From ethnography—the study of the customs, habits, and way of life of human societies.

DISCUSSION TOPICS

After reading this essay, you should be able to discuss:

1. The values of English migrants to the Chesapeake.

2. The ways in which the Chesapeake environment reinforced English individualism.

3. The various ways in which individualistic values were expressed in early Virginia.

4. The reasons that educational and religious institutions were slow to develop in Virginia.

5. The ways in which Virginia's military policies demonstrated the individualism of Chesapeake society.

3

Migrants and Motives: Religion and the Settlement of New England, 1630–1640

Virginia Dejohn Anderson

English men and women emigrated from their native land for many reasons. Some, such as the Chesapeake settlers, came to the New World seeking to better their lot in life. Others sought to add a measure of adventure to their lives. For many English dissenters, however, the New World offered the unique prospect of recreating what they saw as God's true church free from the interfering hand of the established Church of England. One of the most important of these dissenting groups was the English Puritans. The Puritans had been staunch critics of the established Church of England since the late sixteenth century, believing that the English church was insufficiently reformed in both structure and doctrine. Drawing on the ideas of the French Protestant reformer John Calvin, the Puritans criticized not only the doctrines of the established English church but its elaborate ceremonies and its close connections with the monarchy as well. For Puritans, who believed that God had predestined some souls to salvation and others to damnation, only the "saved" ought to form and control the congregations of God's "true" church. The Church of England, which admitted every English man and woman to membership and was controlled by an established church hierarchy, was for the Puritans as distant from their vision of the true church as was the church in Rome.

By the 1620s, the spread of Puritanism to a growing number of English communities became a threat to the established church as well as to Charles I's ambition to make England into an absolutist state. Under the policy of William Laud, Archbishop of

From "Migrants and Motives: Religion and the Settlement of New England, 1630–1640." *New England Quarterly,* 58, pp. 339–383. Reprinted by Permission.

Canterbury and titular head of the national church, Puritan ministers and their congregations were harshly persecuted both as heretics and as enemies of the state. In the minds of many Puritans, their only hope lay in migration to the wilderness of New England, where they hoped to create the kind of pure and religiously cohesive communities that English conditions prevented them from achieving at home. It was against this backdrop that over 16,000 Puritan men, women, and children uprooted themselves from their local communities between 1630 and 1641 and set sail for the unpredictable wilderness of New England.

Given the risks and uncertainties of moving to the New World, some historians have doubted that religion alone can explain the source of the Puritan migration. More prosaic motives—escaping the effects of economic decline in England or the hope of economic gain—they claim, were at least as important as religious commitment in explaining the Puritan exodus. In this study of the Puritan "Great Migration," Virginia Dejohn Anderson answers these historians with a close study of the original migrants to Massachusetts Bay. The early Massachusetts Puritans, she finds, were little different from typical English men and women. New England Puritans, Anderson concludes, were not religious ascetics who dismissed economic well-being in their pursuit of religious perfection. Rather they were pragmatic realists who kept a firm eye on God's ordinances while providing amply for themselves in the New World.

....

No man, perhaps, would seem to have been an unlikelier candidate for transatlantic migration than John Bent. He had never shown any particular interest in moving; indeed, in 1638, at the age of forty-one, Bent still lived in Weyhill, Hampshire, where both he and his father before him had been born. Having prospered in the village of his birth, John Bent held enough land to distinguish himself as one of Weyhill's wealthiest inhabitants. One might reasonably expect that Bent's substantial economic stake, combined with his growing familial responsibilities—which by 1638 included a wife and five children—would have provided him with ample incentive to stay put. By embarking on a transatlantic voyage—moving for the first time in his life and over a vast distance—Bent would exchange an economically secure present for a highly uncertain future and venture his family's lives and fortunes no less than his own. Yet in the spring of 1638, Bent returned his Weyhill land to the lord of the manor, gathered

his family and possessions, and traveled twenty-five miles to the port of Southampton. There, he and his family boarded the *Confidence*, bound for Massachusetts Bay.

In doing so, the Bent family joined thousands of other men, women, and children who left for New England between 1630 and 1642. We know more about John Bent than about the vast majority of these other emigrants because certain information has fortuitously survived. Bent's name appears on one of the few extant ship passenger lists of the Great Migration, and genealogists and local historians have compiled enough additional data to sketch in the outlines of his life in Old and New England. Yet despite this rare abundance of information, John Bent's reasons for moving to Massachusetts remain obscure. In fact, the surviving biographical details render the question of motivation all the more tantalizing because they provide no identifiable economic reason for leaving but rather depict a man firmly rooted in his English homeland.

Most accounts of early New England include a general discussion of the emigrants' motivations, but none has dealt with the issue systematically. If we are ever to comprehend the nature and significance of the Great Migration, however, we must understand why men like John Bent left their homes. The Great Migration to New England, unlike the simultaneous outpouring of Englishmen to other New World colonies, was a voluntary exodus of families and included relatively few indentured servants. The movement, which began around 1630, effectively ceased a dozen years later with the outbreak of the English Civil War, further distinguishing it from the more extended period of emigration to other colonies.

These two factors—the emigrants' voluntary departure and the movement's short duration—suggest that the Great Migration resulted from a common, reasoned response to a highly specific set of circumstances. Such circumstances must have been compelling indeed to dislodge a man like John Bent from a comfortable niche in his community. And while Bent and his fellows could not have known it, their reasons for embarking for New England would not only change their own lives but also powerfully shape the society they would create in their new home.

The New England settlers more closely resembled the nonmigrating English population than they did other English colonists in the New World. The implications of this fact for the development of colonial societies can scarcely be overstated. While the composition of the emigrant populations in the Chesapeake and the Caribbean hindered the successful transfer of familiar patterns of social relationships, the character of the New England colonial population ensured it. The prospect of colonizing distant lands stirred the imaginations of young people all over England, but most of these young adults made their way to the tobacco and sugar plantations of the South. Nearly half of a sample of Virginia residents in 1625 were between the ages of twenty and twenty-nine, and groups of emigrants to the Chesapeake in the seventeenth century consistently included a majority of people in their twenties. In contrast, only a quarter of the New England settlers belonged to this age group.

The age structure of New England's emigrant population virtual mirrored that of the country they had left. Both infancy and old age were represented: the *Rose* of Great Yarmouth carried one-year-old Thomas Baker as well as Katherine Rabey, a widow of sixty-eight. The proportion of people over the age of sixty was, not surprisingly, somewhat higher in the general English population than among the emigrants. Although Thomas Welde reported in 1632 that he traveled with "very aged" passengers, "twelve persons being all able to make well nigh one thousand years," a transatlantic voyage of three months' duration was an ordeal not easily undertaken, and the hardships involved in settling the wilderness surely daunted prospective emigrants of advanced years. On the whole, however, New England attracted people of all ages and thus preserved a normal pattern of intergenerational contact.

Similarly, the sex ratio of the New England emigrant group resembled that of England's population. If women were as scarce in the Chesapeake as good English beer, they were comparatively abundant in the northern colonies. In the second decade of Virginia's settlement, there were four or five men for each woman; by the end of the century, there were still about three men for every two women. Among the emigrants studied here, however, nearly half were women and girls. Such a high proportion of females in the population assured the young men of New England greater success than their southern counterparts in finding spouses.

These demographic characteristics derive directly from the fact that the migration to New England was primarily a transplantation of families. Fully 87.8 percent (597 out of 680) of the emigrants traveled with relatives of one sort or another. Nearly three-quarters (498 out of 680) came in nuclear family units, with or without children. Occasionally, single spouses migrated with their children, either to meet a partner already in the New World or to wait for his or her arrival on a later ship. Grandparents comprised a relatively inconspicuous part of the migration, but a few hardy elders did make the trip. In 1637, Margaret Neave sailed to Massachusetts with her granddaughter Rachel Dixson, who was probably an orphan. In the following year, Alice Stephens joined her sons William and John and their families for the voyage to New England. More frequently, emigrant family structure extended horizontally, within a generation, rather than vertically, across three generations. Several groups of brothers made the trip together, and when the three Goodenow brothers decided to leave the West Country, they convinced their unmarried sister Ursula to come with them as well.

Thus, for the majority of these New England settlers, transatlantic migration did not lead to permanent separation from close relatives. Some unscrupulous men and women apparently migrated in order to flee unhappy marriages, but most nuclear family units arrived intact. When close kin were left behind, they usually joined their families within a year or so. Samuel Lincoln, for instance, who traveled aboard the *Rose* in 1637, soon joined his brother Thomas, who had settled in Hingham in 1633. Another brother, Stephen, arrived in the following year with both his family and his mother. Edward Johnson, who had first crossed the ocean with the Winthrop fleet in 1630, returned to England in 1637 to fetch his wife and seven children. For Thomas Starr, who left Sandwich in 1637, migration meant a reunion with his older brother Comfort, a passenger on the *Hercules* two years earlier. Although some disruption of kin ties was unavoidable, it was by no means the rule.

Further exploration of demographic patterns reveals other subtle but significant differences between the migrating population and that of England. These differences illustrate the important fact that migration was a selective process; not all people were equally suited to or interested in the rigors of New World settlement. Since the movement to New England was a voluntary, self-selective affair, most of this winnowing-out process occurred before the hearths of English homes, as individuals and families discussed whether or not to leave.

Although family groups predominated within the emigrant population, many individuals came to New England on their own. The vast majority of these solitary travelers were male—men outnumbered women by a factor of ten to one—and together they constituted 38 percent of the emigrant households. This figure stands in sharp contrast to England's population, where only about 5 percent of all households were composed of one individual. About one in six emigrants aged twenty-one to thirty sailed independently, perhaps drawn to New England by hopes of employment or freeholdership. These men were hardly freewheeling adventurers; instead, they provided the new settlements with skilled labor. The unaccompanied travelers included shoemakers, a carpenter, butcher, tanner, hempdresser, weaver, cutler, physician, fuller, tailor, mercer, and skinner. Some were already married at the time of the voyage, and those who were single seldom remained so for more than a couple of years after their arrival. Through marriage, the men became members of family networks within their communities. Within a few years of his arrival in 1635, for instance, Henry Ewell, a young shoemaker from Sandwich in Kent, joined the church in Scituate and married the daughter of a prominent local family. William Paddy, a London skinner, managed to obtain land, find a wife, and get elected to Plymouth's first general court of deputies within four years of his voyage.

New England clearly attracted a special group of families. The average age of emigrant husbands was 37.4 years; for their wives the average was 33.8. The westward-bound ships carried couples who were mature, who had probably been married for nearly a decade, and who had established themselves firmly within their communities. The typical migrating family was complete—composed of husband, wife, and three or four children—but was not yet completed. They were families in process, with parents who were at most halfway through their reproductive cycle and who would continue to produce children in New England. They would be responsible for the rapid population growth that New England experienced in its first decades of settlement. Moreover, the numerous children who emigrated with their parents contributed their efforts to a primitive economy sorely lacking in labor.

The task of transforming wilderness into farmland, however, demanded more labor than parents and their children alone could supply, and more than half of the emigrating families responded to this challenge by bringing servants with them to the New World. Perhaps some had read William Wood's advice in *New England's Prospect* and learned that "men of good estates may do well there, always provided that they go well accommodated with servants." In any case, servants formed an integral part, just over 17 percent, of the colonizing population and in fact were at first somewhat more commonplace in New England than in England. Most were males (80 of 114) and labored alongside their masters, clearing land, planting corn, and building houses and barns. Their presence substantially increased the ratio of producers to consumers in the newly settled towns.

Household heads, however, knew that servants might easily become a drain on family resources in the critical early months of settlement. Their passages had to be paid and food and shelter provided at a time when those commodities were at a premium. Hence, when arranging for a suitable labor supply, masters heeded the advice of writers like William Wood, who emphasized that emigrants should not take too many servants and should choose men and women of good character. "It is not the multiplicity of many bad servants (which presently eats a man out of house and harbor, as lamentable experience hath made manifest)," he warned, "but the industry of the faithful and diligent laborer that enricheth the careful master; so that he that hath many dronish servants shall soon be poor and he that hath an industrious family shall as soon be rich." Most families attempted to strike a balance between their need for labor and available resources by transporting only a few servants. Nearly half of the families brought just one and another quarter of them brought only two.

The diversity of the emigrants' English backgrounds—and their urban origins in particular—influenced the distribution of their occupations. Virtually the same number of men were engaged in farming and in artisanal trades not involved with cloth manufacture; slightly fewer earned their livings in the textile industry. Most of the cloth workers emigrated from cities well known for their textile manufacture; half of the fourteen weavers left Norwich, while five of the sixteen tailors had lived in Salisbury. The geographical distribution of the other artisans was more even, yet many also had congregated in urban areas. Ten of the eleven shoemakers came from Norwich, Great Yarmouth, Sandwich, and Marlborough, while the only two joiners had lived in Canterbury and Norwich. Nearly all of the men with highly specialized skills lived in large towns; the locksmith William Ludkin in Norwich, the cutler Edmund Hawes in London, the surgeon John Greene (who appears to have been a physician, not a barber-surgeon) in Salisbury. Artisans, both in the cloth trades and in other pursuits, formed a greater proportion of the emigrant population than tradesmen did in the English population as a whole. In 1696, Gregory King estimated that "freeholders" and "farmers" outnumbered "artizans and handicrafts" by a factor of more than seven to one; among the emigrants to New England, however, artisans predominated by a ratio of nearly two to one.

The occupational spectrum of future New Englanders placed them at the more prosperous end of English society. As farmers and artisans, prospective emigrants belonged to that part of the population that—according to Gregory King—"increased the wealth of the kingdom." Yet in striking contrast to Virginia, where, at least initially, the population included "about six times as large a proportion of gentlemen as England had," New England attracted very few members of the upper class. Sir Henry Vane and Sir Richard Saltonstall were unique among the leaders of the migration, and for the most part even they submitted to government by such gentle but untitled figures as John Winthrop and Thomas Dudley. On the whole, emigrants were neither very high nor very low in social and economic status. Husbandmen predominated among the farmers who came to Massachusetts; thirty of them emigrated compared to just five yeomen. By the seventeenth century, the legal distinctions between the status of yeoman and that of husbandman had largely eroded and evidence indicates that the labels generally denoted relative position on the economic and social ladder. Both groups primarily made their livings from the land, but yeomen were generally better off. New England, however, was peopled by less affluent—but not necessarily poor—husbandmen.

Emigrant clothworkers practiced trades that also placed them on the middle rungs of the economic ladder. Textile manufacturing in the early seventeenth century employed the skills of dozens of different craftsmen, from the shearmen, carders, and combers who prepared wool for spinning to the wealthy clothiers who sold the finished product. But the emigrant clothworkers did not represent the entire spectrum of skills; most were weavers and tailors who made a modest living at their trade. While it is true that, during his impeachment trial, the former bishop of Norwich was accused of harrying some of the city's most important and prosperous tradesmen—including the weavers Nicholas Busby, Francis Lawes, and Michael Metcalf—out of the land, these emigrants' economic status was probably exaggerated. Most urban weavers from Norfolk in this period had goods worth no more than £100, and one out of five did not even own his own loom. Among the non-clothworking artisans, shoemakers and carpenters predominated, and they too worked in trades that would bring comfort, if not riches.

All in all, the New England-bound ships transported a population characterized by a greater degree of social homogeneity than existed in the mother country. Despite Winthrop's reminder to his fellow passengers on the *Arbella* that "some must be rich some poor, some highe and eminent in power and dignitie; others meane and in subieccion," New Englanders would discover that the process of migration effectively reduced the distance between the top and the bottom of their social hierarchy.

In a letter to England written in 1632, Richard Saltonstall commented on the social origins of New England's inhabitants. "It is strange," he wrote, "the meaner sort of people should be so backward [in migrating], having assurance that they may live plentifully by their neighbors." At the same time, he expressed the hope that more "gentlemen of ability would transplant themselves," for they too might prosper both spiritually and materially in the new land. For young Richard, the twenty-one-year-old son of Sir Richard Saltonstall, New England promised much but as yet lacked the proper balance of social groups within its population that would ensure its success. The migration of the "meaner sort" would help lower the cost of labor, while richer emigrants would "supply the want we labor under of men fitted by their estates to bear common burdens." Such wealthy men would invest in the colony's future even as they enhanced their own spiritual welfare by becoming "worthy instruments of propagating the Gospel" to New England's natives.

Saltonstall wrote early in the migration decade, but the succeeding years did little to redress the social imbalance he perceived in Massachusetts. Two years later, William Wood could still write that "none of such great estate went over yet." Throughout the decade of the 1630s, New England continued to attract colonists who were overwhelmingly ordinary. Demographically they presented a mirror image of the society they had left behind, and socially and economically they fairly represented England's relatively prosperous middle class. The question is inescapable: why did so many average English men and women pass beyond the seas to Massachusetts' shores?

Whether or not they have assigned it primary importance, most historians of the period have noted that economic distress in England in the early seventeenth century must have been causally related to the Great Migration. These were years of agricultural and industrial depression, and farmers and weavers were conspicuous passengers on the transatlantic voyages. A closer examination of the connections between economic crisis and the movement to New England, however, indicates that the links were not as close as they have been assumed to be.

Agriculture—especially in the early modern period—was a notoriously risky business. Success depended heavily upon variables beyond human control. A dry summer or an unusually wet season rendered futile the labor of even the most diligent husbandman, and English farmers in the early seventeenth century had to endure more than their share of adversity. While the decade of the 1620s began propitiously, with excellent harvests in 1619 and 1620, the farmers' luck did not hold. The next three years brought one disastrous harvest after another; improvement in 1624 was followed by dearth in 1625. The beginning of the 1630s, especially in the eastern counties, was marked by further distress; in 1630, the mayor of Norwich complained that "scarcity and dearth of corn and other victuals have so increased the number and misery of the poor in this city" that civic taxes had to be boosted to unprecedented heights and the city's stock of grain dwindled dangerously. In 1637, a severe drought spawned further hardship.

Although this period of agricultural depression undoubtedly touched the lives of many English families, it did not necessarily compel them to emigrate. The worst sustained period of scarcity occurred in the early 1620s, a decade or so before the Great Migration began; if agrarian distress was a "push" factor, it produced a curiously delayed reaction. Furthermore, annual fluctuations were endemic in early modern agriculture. Englishmen knew from experience that times would eventually improve, even if that day were unpleasantly distant; moreover, they had no reason to suppose that farmers in New England would somehow lead charmed lives, exempt from similar variations in the weather. In addition, dearth was not an unmitigated disaster for families engaged in husbandry: as supplies of grain and other products shrank, prices rose. In 1630, a year with one of the worst harvests in the first half of the seventeenth century, the price of grain was twice what it had been in the more plentiful years of 1619 and 1620. Thus for farmers involved in market agriculture, a bad year, with half the yield of a good one, could still bring the same income. As the Norwich mayor's lament amply demonstrates, the people really hurt in times of scarcity were city-dwellers dependent on the countryside for their food. That urban dwellers left for New England to assure themselves of a steady food supply, however, is highly unlikely. Emigrants would surely have anticipated the primitive state of the region's agriculture; reports of scarcity at Plymouth and the early Massachusetts Bay settlements had quickly filtered back to England. Moreover, emigrating urban artisans certainly understood that, in the New World, responsibility for feeding their families would lie in their own hands—hands more accustomed to the loom or the last than the plow.

The slump in England's textile industry has also been accounted an incentive for emigration. The industry was indeed mired in a severe depression in the early seventeenth century; it is true as well that a quarter of the adult male emigrants were employed in a trade related to cloth manufacture. The weavers Nicholas Busby, Francis Lawes, and Michael Metcalf of Norwich all completed their apprenticeships at a time when the textile trade "like the moon [was] on the want," and the future of Norfolk's preeminent industry was growing dimmer each year. Throughout the sixteenth century, the county's traditional worsted manufacture had steadily lost ground in its European markets to a developing continental industry. In southern England and the West Country, broadcloth producers suffered reverses as well. In 1631, the clothiers of Basingstoke, Hampshire—a town about fifteen miles southwest of the home of the emigrant weaver Thomas Smith of Romsey—informed the county's justices that the "poor do daily increase, for there are in the said town 60 householders, whose families do amount to 300 persons and upwards being weavers, spinners, and clothworkers, the most of them being heretofore rated towards the relief of the poor, do now many of them depend upon the alms of the parish" and begged for some kind of relief.

The decline in sales of the white, undressed fabric that had been the mainstay of English clothiers proved to be irreversible. At the same time, however, certain sectors in the textile industry recovered by switching over to the production of "new draperies." These fabrics, lighter in weight and brighter in color than the traditional English product, were made from a coarser—and therefore cheaper—type of wool. They were introduced in England largely by immigrant Dutch and Walloon artisans, who were frequently encouraged by local authorities to take up residence in England. East Anglia and Kent became centers of the revitalized industry; the cities of Norwich, Canterbury, and Sandwich counted scores of these north European "strangers" among their inhabitants. With the end of hostilities between England and Spain in 1604, trade expanded, and the new fabrics found ready markets in the Mediterranean and the Levant. By the mid-seventeenth century, the production of Norwich stuffs—new versions of worsted wool—had "probably raised the prosperity of the industry to an unprecedented level" and brought renewed prosperity to a number of beleaguered artisans as well.

We cannot know whether worsted weavers like Nicholas Busby, William Nickerson, or Francis Lawes adapted to prevailing trends in their trade, but they seem not to have been in serious economic straits at the time they decided to go to Massachusetts. The identification of Busby, Lawes, and Michael Metcalf among Norwich's most important tradesmen at Bishop Wren's impeachment trial, even if those claims were somewhat exaggerated, attested to their standing in the community. Busby's service as a *jurat* responsible for checking the quality of worsted wool produced in the city certainly indicated that he had achieved considerable status in his profession. Economic advancement attended professional prominence: before their departure for the New World, Busby and his wife owned a houselot in a prospering parish in the northern part of the city. In the countryside as well, some cloth workers managed to make a good living in hard times. Thomas Payne, a weaver from the village of Wrentham in Suffolk, emigrated to Salem in 1637 but died soon thereafter. His will, written in April 1638, not only listed property recently acquired in Salem, but also mentioned his share in the ship *Mary Anne*, on which he had sailed to Massachusetts. At the time of the departure from Suffolk, then, Payne could not only afford his family's transportation costs but also had funds to invest in the New England enterprise.

Even if evidence did suggest that emigrant weavers were compelled by economic adversity to leave their homeland, Massachusetts would not have been a wise choice of destination if they hoped to continue in their trade. Flight to the Netherlands, a place with a well-developed textile industry, would have been a more rational choice for artisans worried about the fate of their trade in England and anxious to persist in its practice. Massachusetts lacked both the wool supply and the intricate network of auxiliary tradesmen—such as combers, carders, calenderers, fullers, dyers, etc.—upon which England's weavers depended. Several of the emigrants packed up their looms along with their other belongings, but there is little evidence that they were able to earn their livings in Massachusetts solely by weaving.

Arguments linking the Great Migration to economic hardship in England all share an important weakness. Although historians have discovered that many *places* from which emigrants came suffered from agricultural or industrial depression, they have had little success in connecting those unfavorable economic circumstances to the fortunes of individual emigrants. On the contrary, it appears that the families that went to New England had largely avoided the serious setbacks that afflicted many of their countrymen during those years.

An alternative interpretation of the colonists' economic motivation has recently been proposed by Peter Clark, who discovered similarities between the New England settlers and "betterment migrants" traveling within the county of Kent during the decades preceding the English Civil War. Betterment migrants, like the New England colonists, were persons of solid means who, Clark argues, sought further to improve their economic positions. Most betterment migrants traveled only a short distance, usually to a nearby town; the New Englanders differed from them primarily through the immense length of their transatlantic journeys. On the whole, betterment migrants were not especially mobile; in their search for opportunity, they generally moved just once in their lives. New England emigrants like John Bent, while they lived in England, also tended to be geographically stable. In addition, betterment migrants shared with the Massachusetts settlers a tendency to rely on kin connections in their choice of destinations.

Clark's model of betterment migration fits the New England movement in certain particulars, but it makes little sense within the larger context of the transatlantic transplantation. If migration to New England was not a sensible economic decision for farmers or weavers hurt by hard times in England, it was even less sensible for people doing well. Most emigrants exchanged an economically viable present for a very uncertain future. As we have seen, nearly one in ten was over forty years old at the time of the migration and had little reason to expect to live long enough to enjoy whatever prosperity the New World might bring. The emigrant groups studied here all left England five or more years after the Great Migration had begun and a decade and a half after the landing at Plymouth; they surely heard from earlier arrivals that New England was no land of milk and honey. If any had a chance to read Edward Winslow's *Good Newes from New England,* published in 1624, he or she would have learned that the "vain expectation of present profit" was the "overthrow and bane" of plantations. People might prosper through "good labor and diligence," but in the absence of a cash crop, great wealth was not to be expected. The message of William Wood's *New England's Prospect,* published a decade later, was similar. Some colonists were lured westward by descriptions of plenty, Wood acknowledged, but they soon fell to criticizing the new society, "saying a man cannot live without labor." These disgruntled settlers "more discredit and disparage themselves in giving the world occasion to take notice of their dronish disposition that would live off the sweat of another man's brows. Surely they were much deceived, or else ill informed, that ventured thither in hope to live in plenty and idleness, both at a time." Letters as well as published reports informed would be settlers that New England was not a particularly fertile field for profit. In 1631, one young colonist wrote to his father in Suffolk, England, that "the cuntrey is not so as we ded expecte it." Far from bringing riches, New England could not even provide essentials; the disillusioned settler begged his father to send provisions, for "we do not know how longe we may subeseiste" without supplies from home.

If prospective emigrants were not hearing that New England offered ample opportunities for economic betterment, they *were* informed that life in Massachusetts could bring betterment of another sort. When Governor Thomas Dudley provided the countess of Lincoln with an account of his first nine months in New England, he announced that "if any come hether to plant for worldly ends that canne live well at home hee comits an errour of which he will soon repent him. But if for spirituall [ends] and that noe particular obstacle hinder his removeall, he may finde here what may well content him." Dudley worried that some might be drawn to

Massachusetts by exaggerations of the land's bounty and wanted to make clear who would benefit most from emigration. "If any godly men out of religious ends will come over to helpe vs in the good worke wee are about," the governor wrote, "I think they cannot dispose of themselves nor of their estates more to God's glory and the furtherance of their owne reckoninge." New England promised its settlers *spiritual* advantages only; men merely in search of wealth could go elsewhere. Emmanuel Downing, in a letter to Sir John Coke, clarified the important difference between New England and other colonial ventures. "This plantation and that of Virginia went not forth upon the same reasons nor for the same end. Those of Virginia," he explained, "went forth for profit. . . . These went upon two other designs, some to satisfy their own curiosity in point of conscience, others . . . to transport the Gospel to those heathen that never heard thereof."

Both published tracts and private correspondence advertised New England's religious mission. In *The Planter's Plea*, Rev. John White proclaimed that "the most eminent and desirable end of planting Colonies, is the propagation of Religion." Prospective emigrants learned from the Rev. Francis Higginson's *New-England's Plantation*, published in 1630, that "that which is our greatest comfort . . . is, that we haue here the true Religion and holy Ordinances of Almightie God taught amongst us: Thankes be to God, we haue here plentie of Preaching, and diligent Catechizing, with strickt and carefull exercise, and good and commendable orders to bring our People into a Christian conuersation with whom we haue to doe withall." Indeed, New England's Puritan predilections were so well known that colonial leaders feared retribution from the Anglican establishment in England. *The Planter's Plea* specifically sought to dispel rumors that Massachusetts was overrun with Separatists, and, during the early 1630s, Edward Howes maintained a steady correspondence with John Winthrop, Jr. concerning similar allegations of New England radicalism. In 1631, Howes reported that "heare is a mut-

teringe of a too palpable seperation of your people from our church gouernment." The following year, he again informed Winthrop of claims that "you neuer vse the Lords prayer, that your ministers marrie none, that fellowes which keepe hogges all the weeke preach on the Saboth, that euery towne in your plantation is of a seuerall religion; that you count all men in England, yea all out of your church, and in the state of damnacion." Howes knew such rumors were false but feared that many other Englishmen believed them. The spread of such lies endangered not only the colony's reputation but perhaps its very survival as well.

Prospective emigrants, then, could hardly have been unaware of the peculiar religious character of New England society. Accounts of the region's commitment to Puritanism were too numerous to be overlooked; those who made the voyage had to know what they were getting into. Adherence to Puritan principles, therefore, became the common thread that stitched individual emigrants together into a larger movement. As John White declared, "Necessitie may presse some; Noveltie draw on others; hopes of gaine in time to come may prevaile with a third sort: but that the most and most sincere and godly part have the advancement of the *Gospel* for their maine scope I am co[n]fident."

White's confidence was by no means misplaced. The roster of passengers to New England contains the names of scores of otherwise ordinary English men and women whose lives were distinguished by their steadfast commitment to nonconformity, even in the face of official harassment. The *Hercules* left Sandwich in 1635 with William Witherell and Comfort Starr aboard; both men had been in trouble with local ecclesiastical authorities. Anthony Thacher, a nonconformist who had been living in Holland for two decades, returned to Southampton that same year to embark for New England on the *James*. Two years later, the *Rose* carried Michael Metcalf away from the clutches of Norwich diocesan officials. Metcalf had appeared before ecclesiastical courts in 1633 and again in 1636 for refusing to bow at the name of Jesus or to adhere to the "stinking tenets of Arminius" adopted by the established Church. Before his departure, Metcalf composed a letter "to all the true professors of Christs gospel within the city of Norwich" that chronicled his troubled encounters with church officials and explained his exclusively religious reasons for emigration. Thomas and Mary Oliver, Metcalf's fellow parishioners at St. Edmund's in Norwich, had also been cited before the archepiscopal court in 1633 and set sail for Massachusetts the same year as Metcalf. Other emigrants leaving in 1637 were John Pers and John Baker, two Norwich residents evidently also in trouble with church officials; Joan Ames, the widow of the revered Puritan divine William Ames, who had only recently returned from a lengthy stay in Rotterdam; and Margaret Neave and Adam Goodens, whose names appeared on Separatist lists in Great Yarmouth. Peter Noyes, who emigrated in 1638, came from a family long involved in nonconformist activities in England's southwest.

Although New England was not populated solely by unsuccessful defendants in ecclesiastical court proceedings, the nonconformist beliefs of other emigrants should not be underestimated merely because they avoided direct conflict with bishops and deacons. John Winthrop's religious motivation has never been in doubt even though he was never convicted of a Puritan offense. Winthrop's "General Observations for the Plantation of New England," like Metcalf's letter to the citizens of Norwich, emphasized the corrupt state of England's ecclesiastical affairs and concluded that emigration "wilbe a service to the church of great consequens" redounding to the spiritual benefit of emigrants and Indians alike. Those few men who recorded their own reasons for removal likewise stressed the role of religion. Roger Clap, who sailed in 1630, recalled in his memoirs that "I never so much as heard of *New-England* until I heard of many godly Persons that were going there" and firmly believed that "God put it into my Heart to incline to Live abroad" in Massachusetts. John Dane, who seems to have spent most of his youth fighting off his evil incli-

nations, "bent myself to cum to nu ingland, thinking that I should be more fre here then thare from temptations." Arriving in Roxbury in the mid-1630s, Dane soon discovered that relocation would not end his struggle with sinfulness; the devil sought him out as readily in the New World as in the Old.

To declare that most emigrants were prompted by radical religious sentiment to sail to the New World, however, does not mean that these settlers resembled Hawthorne's memorable "stern and blackbrowed Puritans" in single-minded pursuit of salvation. The decision to cross the seas indelibly marked the lives of those who made it. Even the most pious wrestled with the implications of removal from family, friends, and familiar surroundings. Parents often objected to the departure of their children; a son following the dictates of his conscience might risk the estrangement of a disappointed father. Although religious motivation is the only factor with sufficient power to explain the departure of so many otherwise ordinary families, the New England Puritans should not be seen as utopians caught up in a movement whose purpose totally transcended the concerns of daily life.

Solitary ascetics can afford to reject the things of this world in order to contemplate the glories of the next; family men cannot. Even as prospective settlers discussed the spiritual benefits that might accompany a move to New England, they worried about what they would eat, where they would sleep, and how they would make a living. In the spring of 1631, Emmanuel Downing wrote with considerable relief to John Winthrop that the governor's encouraging letters "haue much refreshed my hart and the myndes of manie others" for "yt was the Iudgement of most men here, that your Colonye would be dissolved partly by death through want of Food, howsing and rayment, and the rest to retorne or to flee for refuge to other plantacions." Other leaders and publicists of the migration continued both to recognize and to sympathize with the concerns of families struggling with the decision of whether or not to move, and they sought to reassure prospective settlers that a decision in favor of emigration would not doom their families to cold and starvation in the wilderness. At the same time, the way in which these writers composed their comforting messages to would-be emigrants underscored the settlers' understanding of the larger meaning of their mission.

Although several of the tracts and letters publicizing the migration contained favorable descriptions of the new land, they were never intended to be advertisements designed to capture the interest of profit seekers. When John White, Thomas Dudley, and others wrote about the blessings of New England's climate, topography, and flora and fauna, they simply hoped to assure godly English men and women that a move to the New World would not engender poverty as well as piety. In *The Planter's Plea,* John White succinctly answered objections that New England lacked "meanes if wealth." "An unanswerable argument," White replied, "to such as make the advancement of their estates, the scope of their undertaking." But, he added, New England's modest resources were in "no way a discouragement to such as aime at the propagation of the Gospell, which can never bee advanced but by the preservation of Piety in those that carry it to strangers." For, White concluded, "nothing sorts better with Piety than Compete[n]cy." He referred his readers to Proverbs 30:8—"Remove far from me vanity and lies: give me neither poverty nor riches; feed me with food convenient for me." Thomas Dudley in effect explicated the meaning of "competency" in a New England context when he listed such goods as "may well content" a righteous colonist. In Massachusetts, Dudley noted, settlers could expect to have "materialls to build, fewell to burn, ground to plant, seas and rivers to fish in, a pure ayer to breath in, good water to drinke till wine or beare canne be made, which togeather with the cowes, hoggs, and goates brought hether allready may suffffice for food." Such were the amenities that emigrants not only could but should aspire to enjoy.

John White repeatedly assured his readers that "all Gods directions"—including the divine imperative to settle New England—"have a double scope, mans good and Gods honour." "That this commandement of God is directed unto mans good *temporall and spirituall,*" he went on, "is as cleere as the light." The Lord, in other words, would take care of His own. To providentialists steeped in the conviction that God intervened directly in human lives, that divine pleasure or disapproval could be perceived in the progress of daily events, White's statement made eminent sense. If emigrant families embarked on their voyages with the purpose of abandoning England's corruption in order to worship God according to biblical precepts in their new homes, and if they adhered to this purpose, they might expect as a sign of divine favor to achieve a competency, if not riches. Thus John Winthrop could assert that "such thinges as we stand in neede of are vsually supplied by Gods blessing vpon the wisdome and industry of man." The governor's firm belief in the connection between divine favor and human well-being explains why in his "Particular Considerations" concerning his own removal out of England, he admitted that "my meanes heere [in England] are so shortned (now my 3 eldest sonnes are come to age) as I shall not be able to continue in this place and imployment where I now am." If he went to Massachusetts, Winthrop anticipated an improvement in his fortunes, noting that "I [can] live with 7. or 8: servants in that place and condition where for many years I have spent 3: or 400 *li.* per an[num]." Winthrop, despite these musings on his worldly estate, did not emigrate in order to better his economic condition. Rather, he removed in order to undertake the "publike service" that God had "bestowed" on him and hoped that God might reward him if his efforts were successful. In similar fashion, thousands of other emigrants could justify their decisions to move to New England. They believed that, by emigrating, they followed the will of God and that their obedience would not escape divine notice. In return for their submission to His will, the emigrants sincerely hoped that God might allow them—through their own labor—to enjoy a competency of this world's goods.

KEY TERMS

Nonconformity: Refusing to conform to the doctrines and practices of the Church of England; also dissent; the people known as dissenters.

Covenant: Literally, a contract with God struck by the first settlers of New England villages, who agreed to live in harmony with one another while following God's ordinances.

DISCUSSION TOPICS

After reading this essay, you should be able to discuss:

1. The social composition of the Great Migration to New England.

2. The similarities and differences between Massachusetts Bay immigrants and ordinary seventeenth-century English men and women.

3. The role of servants in early Massachusetts Bay.

4. The balance between economic and religious motivations for migrating to New England.

4

Patterns of Black Resistance

Peter H. Wood

As English colonists gained a foothold on the mainland of North America and began the process of establishing permanent communities, the need for labor became increasingly acute. The small farmers of New England and the Middle Atlantic colonies needed labor to clear land, harvest crops, and maintain livestock. In the South, large plantations required flocks of fieldhands to tend labor-intensive crops such as tobacco and rice. And in the growing seaport cities, labor was needed to handle a growing volume of goods, to build houses for a burgeoning population, and to augment the production of local artisans. During the colonial period, much of this labor was supplied by indentured servants, who exchanged four to seven years of their labor for passage to America.

But by the end of the seventeenth century, colonists began to turn to a new source of labor: African slaves. Slavery was not new to the Americas: Spain and Portugal had been conducting a profitable slave trade since the sixteenth century. English mainland colonists could also draw upon the experiences of their West Indian counterparts, whose sugar plantations depended on a constant supply of slaves for their operation. By the early eighteenth century, southern plantation owners as well as northern artisans and merchants had turned to large-scale importations of slaves in order to maintain their tobacco and rice plantations, their shops, and their homes.

While the importance of early American slavery has long been recognized, historians have only recently turned their attention to the lives of the slaves themselves. One of the most important outcomes of this research is our growing understanding of the African-American response to enslavement. In this essay, Peter H. Wood explores one aspect of this response, the subtle and varied ways in which slaves resisted their bondage. Slave resistance was continuous, he suggests, and took place along a

From *Black Majority* by Peter H. Wood (New York: Alfred A. Knopf, 1974), pp. 285–307. Copyright © 1974 by Peter H. Wood. Reprinted by permission of Alfred A. Knopf, Inc.

continuum that ranged from collective violence at one extreme to individual acts of defiance and dissimulation on the other. While America witnessed no successful large-scale
rebellions, African-American slaves nonetheless engaged in a continuous struggle with
their owners and overseers throughout the colonial and antebellum periods.

....

It is by no means paradoxical that increasingly
overt white controls met with increasingly
forceful black resistance. The stakes for Negroes
were simply rising higher and the choices
becoming more hopelessly difficult. As the individual and collective tensions felt by black
slaves mounted, they continued to confront the
immediate daily questions of whether to accept
or deny, submit or resist, remain or flee. Given
their diversity of background and experience, it
is not surprising that slaves responded to these
pressures in a wide variety of ways. To separate
their reactions into docility on the one hand and
rebellion on the other, as has occasionally been
done, is to underestimate the complex nature of
the contradictions each Negro felt in the face of
new provocations and new penalties. It is more
realistic to think in terms of a spectrum of
response, ranging from complete submission to
total resistance, along which any given individual could be located at a given time.

At one end of the spectrum of individual
resistance were the extreme incidents of physical
violence. There are examples of slaves who, out
of desperation, fury, or premeditation, lashed
out against a white despite the consequences.
Jemmy, a slave of Capt. Elias Ball, was sentenced to death in 1724 "for striking and
wounding one Andrew Songster." The master
salvaged the slave's life and his own investment
by promising to deport Jemmy forever within
two months. For others who vented individual
aggression there was no such reprieve. In
August 1733 the *Gazette* reported tersely: "a
Negro Man belonging to Thomas Fleming of
Charlestown, took an Opportunity, and kill'd
the Overseer with an Axe. He was hang'd for
the same yesterday." An issue during 1742
noted: "Thursday last a Negro Fellow belonging
to Mr. Cheesman, was brought to Town, tried,

condemn'd and hang'd, for attempting to
murder a white lad."

Such explosions of rage were almost always
suicidal, and the mass of the Negro population
cultivated strict internal constraints as a means
of preservation against external white controls.
(The fact that whites accepted so thoroughly the
image of a carefree and heedless black personality is in part a testimony to the degree to which
black slaves learned the necessity of holding
other emotional responses in outward check.)
This essential lesson of control, passed on from
one generation to the next, was learned by early
immigrants through a painful process of trial
and error. Those newcomers whose resistance
was most overt were perceived to be the least
likely to survive, so there ensued a process of
conscious or unconscious experimentation
(called "seasoning" or "breaking" by the whites)
in which Africans calculated the forms and
degrees of resistance which were most possible.

Under constant testing, patterns of slave
resistance evolved rapidly, and many of the
most effective means were found to fall at the
low (or invisible) end of the spectrum. For
example, for those who spoke English, in whatever dialect, verbal insolence became a consistent means of resistance. Cleverly handled, it
allowed slaves a way to assert themselves and
downgrade their masters without committing a
crime. All parties were aware of the subversive
potential of words (along with styles of dress
and bearing), as the thrust of the traditional
term "uppity" implies, and it may be that both
the black use of this approach and the white
perception of it increased as tensions grew. In
1737 the Assembly debated whether the patrols
should have the right "to kill any resisting or
saucy Slave," and in 1741 the Clerk of the
Market proposed that "if any Slave should in

Time of Market behave him or herself in any insolent abusive Manner, he or she should be sent to the Work-house, and there suffer corporal Punishment."

At the same time traits of slowness, carelessness, and literal-mindedness were artfully cultivated, helping to disguise countless acts of willful subterfuge as inadvertent mistakes. To the benefit of the slave and the frustration of the historian, such subversion was always difficult to assess, yet considerable thought has now been given to these subtle forms of opposition. Three other patterns of resistance—poisoning, arson, and conspiracy—were less subtle and more damaging, and each tactic aroused white fears which sometimes far exceeded the actual threat. All three are recognized as having been methods of protest familiar in other slave colonies as well, and each is sufficiently apparent in the South Carolina sources to justify separate consideration.

African awareness of plants and their powers [was widespread], and it was plain to white colonists from an early date that certain blacks were particularly knowledgeable in this regard. In 1733 the *Gazette* published the details of a medicine for yaws, dropsy, and other distempers "for the Discovery whereof, a Negroe Man in Virginia was freed by the Government, and had a Pension of Thirty Pounds Sterling settled on him during his Life." Some of the Negroes listed by the name "Doctor" in colonial inventories had no doubt earned their titles. One South Carolina slave received his freedom and £100 per year for life from the Assembly for revealing his antidote to poison; "Caesar's Cure" was printed in the *Gazette* and appeared occasionally in local almanacs for more than thirty years.

In West Africa, the obeah-men and others with the herbal knowledge to combat poisoning could inflict poison as well, and use for this negative capability was not diminished by enslavement. In Jamaica, poisoning was a commonplace means of black resistance in the eighteenth century, and incidents were familiar on the mainland as well. At least twenty slaves were

executed for poisoning in Virginia between 1772 and 1810. In South Carolina, the Rev. Richard Ludlam mentioned "secret poisonings" as early as the 1720s. The administering of poison by a slave was made a felony (alongside arson) in the colony's sweeping Negro Act of 1740. No doubt in times of general unrest many poisoning incidents involved only exaggerated fear and paranoia on the part of whites, but what made the circle so vicious was the fact that the art of poisoning was undeniably used by certain Africans as one of the most logical and lethal methods of resistance.

The year 1751 was striking in this regard. The Rev. William Cotes of Dorchester expressed discouragement about the slaves in St. George's Parish, a "horrid practice of poisoning their Masters, or those set over them, having lately prevailed among them. For this practice, 5 or 6 in our Parish have been condemned to die, altho [sic] 40 or 50 more were privy to it." In the same year the assemblymen attempted to concoct a legal antidote of their own. They passed an addition to the existing Negro Act, noting that "the detestable crime of poisoning hath of late been frequently committed by many slaves in this Province, and notwithstanding the execution of several criminals for that offence, yet it has not been sufficient to deter others from being guilty of the same." The legislation declared that any Negroes convicted of procuring, conveying, or administering poison, and any other privy to such acts, would suffer death. A £4 reward was offered to any Negro informing on others who had poison in their possession, and a strict clause was included against false informers.

Three additional clauses in the measure of 1751 suggest the seriousness with which white legislators viewed the poisoning threat. They attempted belatedly to root out longstanding Negro knowledge about, access to, and administration of medicinal drugs. It was enacted "That in case any slave shall teach or instruct another slave in the knowledge of any poisonous root, plant, herb, or other poison whatever, he or she, so offending, shall, upon conviction thereof, suffer death as a felon." The student was to receive a lesser punishment. "And to prevent, as much as may be, all slaves from attaining the knowledge of any mineral or vegetable poison," the act went on, "it shall not be lawful for any physician, apothecary or druggist, at any time hereafter, to employ any slave or slaves in the shops or places where they keep their medicines or drugs." Finally, the act provided that "no negroes or other slaves (commonly called doctors,) shall hereafter be suffered or permitted to administer any medicine, or pretended medicine, to any other slave; but at the instance or by the direction of some white person," and any Negro disobeying this clause was subject to "corporal punishment, not exceeding fifty stripes." No other law in the settlement's history imposed such a severe whipping upon a Negro.

A letter written years later by Alexander Garden, the famous Charlestown physician, sheds further light on the subject of poisonings. The outspoken Garden was forthright in criticizing his own profession, observing to his former teacher in Edinburgh that among South Carolina's whites, "some have been actually poisoned by their slaves and hundreds [have] died by the unskilfulness of the practitioners in mismanaging acute disorders." He claimed that when local doctors confronted cases

> proving both too obstinate and complicated for them, they immediately call them poisonous cases and so they screen their own ignorance, for the Friends never blame the doctors neglect or ignorance when they think that the case is poison, as they readily think that lies out of the powers of medicine. And thus the word *Poison* . . . has been as good a screen to ignorance here as ever that of *Malignancy* was in Britain.

But apparently neither strict legislation nor scientific observation could be effective in suppressing such resistance, for in 1761 the *Gazette* reported that "The negroes have again begun the hellish practice of poisoning." Eight years later several more instances were detected, and although the apparent "instigator of these

horrid crimes," a mulatto former slave named Dick, made good his escape, two other Negroes were publicly burned at the stake. According to the account in a special issue of the *Gazette*, Dolly, belonging to Mr. James Sands and a slave man named Liverpool were both burned alive on the workhouse green, "the former for poisoning an infant of Mr. Sands's which died some time since, and attempting to put her master out of the world the same way; and the latter (a Negro Doctor) for furnishing the means." The woman was reported to have "made a free confession, acknowledged the justice of her punishment, and died a penitant," but the man denied his guilt until the end.

The act of arson, highly destructive and difficult to detect, provided another peculiarly suitable means of subversion. Early in the century, with considerable forced labor being used to produce naval stores, the governor urged the Assembly "to make it ffelony without benefitt of Clergy, willfully to Sett ffire to any uncovered Tarrkiln or Pitch and Tarr in Barrells, as in like cases, ffiring Houses and Barnes." In later decades arsonists also fired stores of rice, and the Negro Act of 1740 was explicit in declaring death for "any slave, free negro, mulattoe, Indian or mustizoe, [who] shall wilfully and maliciously burn or destroy any stack of rice, corn, or other grain."

Indeed, as rice production intensified, the number of barns which burned between the months of October and January (when the majority of slaves were being pressed to clean and barrel the annual crop) increased suspiciously. A telling to the *Gazette* in October 1732 reads:

> Sir,
> I Have taken Notice for Several Years past, that there has not one winter elapsed, without one or more Barns being burnt, and two winters since, there was no less than five. Whether it is owing to Accident, Carelessness, or Severity, I will not pretend to determine; but am afraid, chiefly to the two latter. I desire therefore, as a Friend to the Planters, that you'll insert the following Account from Pon Pon, which, I hope, will forewarn the

Planters of their Danger, and make them for the future, more careful and human.

About 3 Weeks since, Mr. James Gray work'd his Negroes late in his Barn at Night and the next Morning before Day, hurried them out again, and when they came to it, found it burnt down to the Ground, and all that was in it.

Several years later, just after Christmas, "the Barn of Mr. John Fairchild at Wassamsaw, with all his Crop was burnt down to the Ground," and in November 1742, "a Barn, belonging to Mr. Hume, at Goose-Creek, was burnt in the Night, and near 70 Barrels of Rice consumed."

Undoubtedly Negroes were occasionally made the scapegoats for fires which occurred by chance. The Rev. Le Jau relates vividly how a woman being burned alive on the charge of setting fire to her master's house in 1709 "protested her innocence . . . to the last." But as with accusations of poisoning, numerous Negroes charged with burning their masters' homes had actually resorted to such sabotage. Moreover, arson could occur in conjunction with other offenses, serving to cover evidence or divert attention. Runaways sometimes resorted to setting fires, and arson was occasionally linked to crimes of violence as well. The following news item from South Carolina appeared in Ireland's *Belfast News Letter*, May 10, 1763:

Charlestown, March 16. A most shocking murder was committed a few weeks ago, near Orangeburg by a Negro fellow belonging to one John Meyer, who happened to come to Charlestown; the cruel wretch murdered Mrs. Meyer, her daughter, about 16 years of age, and her sucking infant; he then dressed himself in his Master's best cloaths and set fire to the house, which was burnt to the ground; three other children of Mr. Meyers made their escape and alarmed the neighbors, some of whom did not live above half a mile distant. The murderer was taken up next day and by a Jury of Magistrates and Freeholders condemned to be burnt alive at a stake which was accordingly executed. The unfortunate husband and father, we are told, is almost, if not entirely distracted by his misfortunes; it is said both he and his wife used

the barbarous destroyer of their family and substance with remarkable tenderness and lenity.

It was fires within the town limits which aroused the greatest concern among white colonists, for not only were numerous lives and buildings endangered, but the prospect of subsequent disorder and vandalism by the city's enslaved residents was obvious. A fire engine was purchased by public subscription in the 1730s. But it proved of little use in 1740, when the Carolina colony, having experienced several epidemics and a series of slave conspiracies in rapid succession, added a severe fire to its "Continued Series of misfortunes." On the afternoon of Tuesday, November 18, flames broke out near the center of Charlestown, and whipped by a northwest wind, burned out of control for six hours, consuming some three hundred houses, destroying crucial new fortifications, and causing property losses estimated at £250,000 sterling.

Even though 2 P.M. seemed an unlikely hour for slave arson, there were strong suspicions about the origin of the holocaust. Not long before, in the strained atmosphere following the Stono Uprising, a slave had been accused of setting fire to the home of Mr. Snow and had been burned to death for the crime. Officials suspected the Spanish of instigating arson by Negroes as one form of resistance, for an act passed the previous April charged the Spaniards in St. Augustine with, "encouraging thither the desertion of our Slaves and . . . exciting them to rise here in Rebellion and to commit Massacres and Assassinations and the burning of Houses in divers parts of this Province of which practices there have of late been many proof[s]."

Word of the November fire reaching northern ports was accompanied by rumors of arson and insurrection. In January a Boston paper had to print a revised account of the fire, saying the story "that the Negroes rose upon the Whites at the same Time, and that therefore it was supposed to be done by them, turns out to be a Mistake, it happening by some Accident." The story finally reaching London was that the flames were "said to have begun among some Shavings in a Saddler's Shop."

Whatever the actual cause of the fire, the white minority feared Negro violence in the aftermath of the blaze. "It is inexpressible to relate to you the dismal Scheme [scene?] . . . ," Robert Pringle wrote to his brother in London, "the best part of this Town being laid in Ashes." He blamed his "Incorrect Confus'd Scrawl" on the fact that he had hardly slept in the three days since the fire. He cited as an explanation "the great Risque we Run from an Insurrection of our Negroes which we were very apprehensive of but all as yet Quiet by the strict Guards & watch we are oblig'd to keep Constantly night & Day." In a letter the next week he mentioned that much property had been stolen and concealed apparently by freemen and slaves alike. But large-scale disorder was prevented, and Negro labor was soon at work "pulling down the Ruin of Charles Town" and clearing away rubble for the arduous task of rebuilding.

Regardless of its true origins, the November fire could only have confirmed to slaves the effectiveness of arson. Moreover, there was word the following spring of Negro incendiaries at work in the northern colonies, supposedly with Spanish connections. On July 30, 1741, the *Gazette* contained a front-page story about a rash of barn-burnings in Hackensack, New Jersey. The next page was given over to details of an arson plot in New York City, for which nine Negroes had already been burned at the stake. The conspiracy, stated the report from New York,

> was calculated, not only to ruin and destroy this city, but the whole Province, and it appears that to effect this their Design was first to burn the Fort, and if Opportunity favoured to seize and carry away the Arms in store there, then to burn the whole Town, and kill and murder all the Male Inhabitants thereof (the Females they intended to reserve for their own use) and this to be effected by seizing their Master's Arms and a general Rising, it appears also as we are informed, that these Designs were not only carried on in this City, but had also spread into the country. . . . And so

far had they gone that the particular Places to be burnt were laid out, their Captains and Other Officers appointed, and their places of general Rendezvous fixed, and the Number of Negroes concern'd is almost incredible, and their barbarous Designs still more so. . . .

It may not be coincidence that within five days after these lurid reports appeared in Charlestown several slaves attempted to kindle another fire in the city. After dark a mulatto slave woman named Kate and a man named Boatswain entered Mrs. Snowden's house in Unity Alley, climbed to the roof, and placed a small bundle of straw on the shingles so that it rested under the gables of the adjoining house, belonging to Moses Mitchell and fronting on Union Street. They lit the tinder with a brand's end, and the fire they started might have been capable "of burning down the remaining Part of the Town," had not Mrs. Mitchell, walking in her yard, spotted the blaze so promptly that it could be dowsed with several pails of drinking water.

An old Negro woman who heard one of the arsonists stumble descending the stairs testified against Kate, and within forty-eight hours she had been tried, convicted, and sentenced to die. At the eleventh hour, upon promise of pardon, Kate named Boatswain as a co-conspirator, and he in turn was sentenced to burn alive. According to the *Gazette's* account, "On his Tryal after much Preverication and accusing many Negroes, who upon a strict Examination were found to be innocent, he confessed that none but he and *Kate* were concerned." Since Boatswain "looked upon every white Man he should meet as his declared Enemy," his prosecutors concluded that the incident stemmed from "his own sottish wicked Heart," and that there was probably no larger plot. The same people may have been somewhat less sanguine several months later, when two slaves were found guilty of attempting to set fire to the city's powder magazine.

Arson, real and suspected, remained a recurring feature in eighteenth-century South Carolina. In 1754, for example, a slave named

Sacharisa was sentenced to burn at the stake for setting fire to her owner's house in Charlestown. Two years later a suspicious fire started on a town wharf in the middle of the night. In 1797 two slaves were deported and several others were hanged for conspiring to burn down the city. In some ways the protracted Charleston Fire Scare of 1825 and 1826, which came four years after the Denmark Vesey Plot, was reminiscent of the concern for arson which followed in the wake of the Stono Uprising of 1739.

While poisoning and arson rarely involved more than one or two compatriots, organized forms of resistance, which involved greater numbers (and therefore higher risks), were not unknown in the royal colony. In fact uprisings appear to have been attempted or planned repeatedly by slaves. For obvious reasons, published sources are irregular on these matters—the *South Carolina Gazette* refrained from mentioning the Stono incident, which occurred within twenty miles of Charlestown—but a number of conspiracies were recorded. In these instances it is sometimes difficult to categorize the objectives of the insurgents, since often a will to overpower the Europeans and a desire to escape from the colony were intertwined in the same plot. The province's first major conspiracy, uncovered in 1720, provides a case in point. "I am now to acquaint you," wrote a Carolina correspondent to the colony's London agent in June, "that very lately we have had a very wicked and barbarous plott of the designe of the negroes rising with a designe to destroy all the white people in the country and then to take the town in full body." He continued that through God's will "it was discovered and many of them taken prisoners and some burnt some hang'd and some banish'd." At least some participants in the scheme "thought to gett to Augustine" if they could convince a member of the Creek tribe to guide them, "but the Savanna garrison tooke the negroes up half starved and the Creeke Indians would not join them or be their pylott." A party of whites and Indians had been dispatched to "Savanna Towne," where fourteen captives were being held, and it was planned that these rebels would "be executed as soon as they came down."

Despite harsh reprisals, however, secret gatherings of slaves, sometimes exceeding one hundred people, were again reported within several years. In February 1733 the Assembly urged the slave patrols to special watchfulness and ordered a dozen slaves brought in for questioning, but there is no sign that any offense was uncovered. Late in 1736 a white citizen appears to have sought a reward for uncovering a Negro plot. Early in the following year the provost marshal took up three Negroes "suspected to be concerned in some Conspiracy against the Peace of this Government," and although the Assembly cleared and released the most prominent suspect, it did not deny the existence of a plot.

By September 1738 the government had completed "An Act for the further Security and better Defence of this Province" and given instructions that the two paragraphs relating to slaves were to be reprinted in the *Gazette*. The paper complied several days later by publishing the section which ordered that within a month every slaveowner in the colony was to turn in to the militia captain of his local precinct "a true and faithful List, in Writing, of all the Slaves of such Persons, or which are under their Care or Management, from the Age of 16 Years to the Age of Sixty Years." Each list was required to specify "the Names, Ages and Country of all such Slaves respectively, according to the best of the Knowledge and Belief of the Persons returning the same."

The statute imposed a heavy fine of £100 upon any master who neglected or refused to comply, so that the required local lists (if collected and sent to the governor annually as authorized) must have constituted a thorough census of the colony's adult slaves. The unlikely reappearance of even a portion of these lists would be a remarkable boon to historians, in light of the unique request for the original country of all slaves. This detail appears to bear witness to the fact that masters were generally interested and informed as to the origins of the Negroes they owned. It may also reflect the belief, commonly accepted in the Carolinas as elsewhere, that new slaves from Africa posed the greatest threat to the security of the white settlers. John Brickell explained at this time, "The Negroes that most commonly rebel, are those brought from Guinea, and who have been inured to War and Hardship all their lives; few born here, or in the other Provinces have been guilty of these vile Practices." When country-born slaves did contemplate rebellion, Brickell claimed, it was because they were urged to it by newcomers "whose Designs they have sometimes discovered to the Christians" in order to be "rewarded with their Freedom for their good Services."

The thought that newcomers from Africa were the slaves most likely to rebel does not appear to have been idle speculation, for the late 1730s, a time of conspicuous unrest, was also a time of massive importation. In fact, at no earlier or later date did recently arrived Africans (whom we might arbitrarily define as all those slave immigrants who had been in the colony less than a decade) comprise such a large proportion of South Carolina's Negro population. By 1740 the black inhabitants of the colony numbered roughly 39,000. During the preceding decade more than 20,000 slaves had been imported from Africa. Since there is little evidence that mortality was disproportionately high among newcomers, this means that by the end of the 1730s fully half of the colony's Negroes had lived in the New World less than ten years. This proportion had been growing steadily. In 1720 fewer than 5 per cent of black adults had been there less than a decade (and many of these had spent time in the West Indies); by 1730 roughly 40 per cent were such recent arrivals. Heavy importation and low natural increase sent the figure over 50 per cent by 1740, but it dropped sharply during the nearly total embargo of the next decade, and after that point the established black population was large enough so that the percentage of newcomers never rose so high again.

Each of the lowland parishes must have reflected this shift in the same way. In St. Paul's for example, where the Stono Uprising origi-nated, there were only 1,634 slaves in 1720, the large majority of whom had been born in the province or brought there long before. By contrast, in 1742 the parish's new Anglican minister listed 3,829 "heathens and infidels" in his cure, well over 3,000 of whom must have been slaves. Of these, perhaps as many as 1,500 had been purchased in Charlestown since 1730. A predominant number of the Africans reaching the colony between 1735 and 1739 have been shown to have come from Angola, so it is likely that at the time of the Stono Uprising there were close to 1,000 residents of St. Paul's Parish who had lived in the Congo-Angola region of Africa less than ten years before. While this figure is only an estimate, it lends support to the assertion in one contemporary source that most of the conspirators in the 1739 incident were Angolans. The suggestion seems not only plausible, but even probable.

European settlers contemplating the prospects of rebellion, however, seem to have been more concerned with the contacts the slaves might establish in the future than with experience that came from their past. White colonists were already beginning to subscribe to the belief that most Negro unrest was necessarily traceable to outside agitators. Like most shibboleths of the slave culture, this idea contained a kernel of truth, and it is one of the difficult tasks in considering the records of the 1730s and 1740s to separate the unreasonable fears of white Carolinians from their very justifiable concerns.

Of the various sources of outside agitation none seemed so continually threatening after 1720 as St. Augustine, for the abduction and provocation of slaves by the Spanish were issues of constant concern. While London and Madrid were reaching a peace settlement in 1713, Charlestown and St. Augustine had renewed their agreement concerning the mutual return of runaways, but Spanish depredations continued long after the conclusion of the Yamasee War.

In June 1728 Acting Gov. Arthur Middleton sent a formal complaint to authorities in London that not only were the Spanish "receivieing and harbouring all our Runaway Negroes," but also, "They have found out a New way of sending our own slaves against us, to Rob and Plunder us;— They are continually fitting out Partys of Indians from St. Augustine to Murder our White People, Rob our Plantations and carry off our slaves," Middleton stated, "soe that We are not only at a vast expence in Guarding our Southern Frontiers, but the Inhabitants are continually Allarmed, and have noe leizure to looke after theire Crops." The irate leader added that "the Indians they send against us are sent out in small Partys . . . and sometimes joined wth Negroes, and all the Mischeife they doe, is on a sudden and by surprize."

These petty incursions soon subsided. Nevertheless, rumors reached South Carolina in 1737 from the West Indies of a full-scale Spanish invasion intended, in the words of Lt. Gov. Thomas Broughton, to "unsettle the colony of Georgia, and to excite an Insurrection of the Negroes of this Province." He reported to the Lords of Trade that the militia had been alerted, "and as our Negroes are very numerous An Act of the General Assembly is passed, to establish Patrols throughout the Country to keep the Negroes in order."

The threatened assault never materialized, but in the meantime a new element was added to the situation. Late in 1733 the Spanish king issued a royal *cédula* granting liberty to Negro fugitives reaching St. Augustine from the English colonies. The edict was not immediately put into effect, and incoming slaves continued to be sold, but in March 1738 a group of these former runaways appealed successfully to the new governor for their freedom and obtained it. Seignior Don Manuel de Montiano established them on land two and a half miles north of St. Augustine at a site called the Pueblo de Gracia Real de Santa Terese de Mose, which soon became known as "Moosa." With the approval of the Council of the Indies, the governor undertook to provision this settlement of several dozen families until its first harvest and arranged for a Catholic priest to offer them

instruction. He may also have urged other slaves to join them, for the captain of an English coasting schooner returning to Beaufort the following month testified that "he heard a Proclamation made at St. Augustine, that all Negroes, who did, or should hereafter, run away from the English, should be made free." As a result, according to the captain, "several Negroes who ran away thither, and were sold there, were thereupon made free, and the Purchasers lost their Money."

In November 1738 nineteen slaves belonging to Capt. Caleb Davis "and 50 other Slaves belonging to other Persons inhabiting about Port Royal ran away to the Castle of St. Augustine." Those who made it joined the Negro settlement at Moosa. It was apparently at this time that the Catholic king's edict of 1733 was published (in the words of a South Carolina report)

by Beat of Drum round the Town of St. Augustine (where many Negroes belonging to English Vessels that carried thither Supplies of Provisions &c. had the Opportunity of hearing it) promising Liberty and Protection to all Slaves that should desert thither from any of the English Colonies but more especially from this. And lest that should not prove sufficient of itself, secret Measures were taken to make it known to our Slaves in general. In consequence of which Numbers of Slaves did from Time to Time by Land and Water desert to St. Augustine, and the better to facilitate their Escape carried off their Master's Horses, Boats &c. some of them first committing Murder; and were accordingly received and declared free.

When Capt. Davis went to St. Augustine to recover his slaves he was pointedly rebuffed, a sign for Carolina's legislature that this difficulty might grow worse in the coming year. Any premonitions which colonial officials might have felt were to prove justifiable, for the year 1739 was a tumultuous and decisive one in the evolution of South Carolina. Only the merest twist of circumstances prevented it from being remembered as a fateful turning point in the social history of the early South.

KEY TERMS

Stono Uprising: British America's only "successful" slave revolt, taking place along the Stono River, South Carolina, in 1739; the slaves were all eventually killed or captured.

Denmark Vesey Plot: A failed slaved uprising in South Carolina in 1822.

St. Augustine, Florida: Spanish fortress and city which offered freedom to any slave fleeing their English master or mistress.

Yamasee War: War between British and native peoples of coastal South Carolina and Georgia. Allied with the Spanish, the Yamassees had raided English plantations and welcomed escaping slaves; they were defeated by British forces in 1715.

Cédula: A formal Spanish imperial decree or law.

DISCUSSION TOPICS

After reading this essay, you should be able to discuss:

1. The spectrum of slave responses to enslavement.

2. The role of power in shaping the forms that resistance took.

3. The slave use of arson to regulate labor.

4. The role played by the Spanish colonies in shaping patterns of resistance.

5

The Small Circle of Domestic Concerns
Mary Beth Norton

Throughout the colonial period, American women lived their lives in a world dominated by men. Subject to the will of their fathers from birth until marriage, once married they became wards of their husbands with no legal rights of their own. Yet despite their subordinate status, women formed a vital and indispensable part of the family economy, as Mary Beth Norton reveals in this essay. Whether their fathers and husbands farmed, traded, or crafted manufactured goods, women spent their days near the household, cooking, cleaning, rearing children, making cloth and clothing, tending vegetables, and maintaining the pigs, chickens, and cows that supplemented the family diet.

But while domestic concerns dominated the lives of all early American women, the character of their lives varied considerably, depending upon their race and class as well as the region in which they lived. Thus Norton shows that while everyday life on the frontier was dominated by an unremitting round of daily and weekly chores with little chance for recreation and sociability, the markets and density of urban life permitted middling-class women a much greater measure of leisure and conviviality. Equally, while northern wives might have overseen the work of apprentices or household servants as part of their family duties, the wives of southern planters were veritable managers of households that extended far beyond the Great House to encompass the welfare of all those who lived on the estate. Domesticity, this essay demonstrates, took many different forms in seventeenth- and eighteenth-century America.

The household, the basic unit of eighteenth-century American society, had a universally understood hierarchical structure. At the top was the man, the lord of the fireside; next came the mistress, his wife and helpmate; following her, the children, who were expected to assist the parent of their own sex; and, finally, any servants or slaves, with the former taking precedence over the latter. Each family was represented in the outside world by its male head, who cast its single vote in elections and fulfilled its obligations to the community through service in the militia or public office. Within the home, the man controlled the finances, oversaw the upbringing of the children, and exercised a nominal supervision over household affairs. Married men understandably referred to all their dependents collectively as "my family," thereby expressing the proprietary attitude they so obviously felt.

The mistress of the household, as befitted her inferior position, consistently employed the less proprietary phrase "our family." Yet she, and not her husband, directed the household's day-to-day activities. Her role was domestic and private, in contrast to his public, supervisory functions. As the Marylander Samuel Purviance told his teenaged daughter Betsy in 1787, "the great Province of a Woman" was "Economy and Frugality in the management of [a] Family." Even if the household were wealthy, he stressed, "the meanest Affairs, are all and ought to be Objects of a womans cares." Purviance and his contemporaries would have concurred with the position taken in an article in Caleb Bingham's *The American Preceptor*, a textbook widely used in the early republic: "[N]eedle work, the care of domestic affairs, and a serious and retired life, is the proper function of women, and for this they were designed by Providence."

Of course, such statements applied only to whites, for no eighteenth-century white American would have contended that enslaved black women should work solely at domestic tasks. But the labor of female slaves too was affected by their sexual identity, for they were often assigned jobs that differed from those of male slaves, even though such tasks were not exclusively domestic. Appropriately, then, an analysis of black and white women's experiences in eighteenth-century America must begin with an examination of their household responsibilities.

I

"I have a great and longing desire to be very notable," wrote a Virginia bride in 1801, declaring her allegiance to the ideal of early American white womanhood. In this context, the adjective "notable" connoted a woman's ability to manage her household affairs skillfully and smoothly. Thus the prominent clergyman Ezra Stiles asked that his daughter be educated in such a way as to "lay a founda[tion] of a notable Woman," and a Rhode Islander wrote of a young relative that she "Sets out to be a Notable house Wife." When the Virginian Fanny Tucker Coalter exuberantly told her husband, John, "I'm the picture of bustling notability," he could have had no doubt about her meaning.

The characteristics of the notable wife were best described by Governor William Livingston of New Jersey in his essay entitled "Our Grand-Mothers," which was printed posthumously in two American magazines in the early 1790s. Decrying his female contemporaries' apparent abandonment of traditional values, Livingston presented a romanticized picture of the colonial women of the past. Such wives "placed their renown" in promoting the welfare of their families, Livingston asserted. "They were strangers to dissipation; . . . their own habitation was their delight." They not only practiced economy, thereby saving their husbands' earnings, but they also "augmented their treasure, by their industry." Most important, "they maintained good order and harmony in their empire" and "enjoyed happiness in their chimney corners," passing on these same qualities to the daughters they carefully raised to be like themselves. Their homes, in short, were "the source of their pleasure; and the foundation of their glory."

Although other accounts of the attributes of notable housewives were couched in less sentimental form, their message was the same. Ministers preaching funeral sermons for women often took as their text Proverbs 31, with its description of the virtuous woman who "looketh well to the Ways of her Household and eateth not the Bread of Idleness." So too drafters of obituaries and memorial statements emphasized the sterling housewifely talents of the women they eulogized. Such a model of female perfection did not allow a woman an independent existence: ideally, she would maintain no identity separate from that of her male-defined family and her household responsibilities. A man like James Kent, the distinguished New York lawyer, could smugly describe himself as "the independent . . . *Lord of my own fireside*," while women, as William Livingston had declared, were expected to tend the hearth and find "happiness in their chimney corners."

These contrasting images of autonomy and subordination were translated into reality in mideighteenth-century American household organization. Although the mistress directed the daily life of the household, her position within the home was secondary to that of her husband. She was expected to follow his orders, and he assumed control over the family finances. In 1750, the anonymous author of *Reflections on Courtship and Marriage*, a pamphlet long erroneously attributed to Benjamin Franklin, told men that it "would be but just and prudent to inform and consult a wife" before making "very important" decisions about monetary matters, but evidence drawn from a variety of sources indicates that few colonial husbands followed this advice. Instead, they appear to have kept the reins of financial management firmly in their own hands, rarely if ever informing their wives about even the basic details of monetary transactions.

The most comprehensive evidence of this phenomenon comes from an analysis of the claims for lost property submitted by 468 white loyalist refugee women after the Revolution.

The evidence of women's ignorance of financial affairs takes a variety of forms in the claims records. Rural wives often were unable to place a precise value on tools, lands, or harvested grain, even if they knew a farm's total acreage or the size of the harvest. Urban women frequently did not know their husbands' exact income or the cost of the houses in which they lived. The typical wealthy female was not aware of her husband's net worth because she did not know the amount of his outstanding debts or what was owed to him, and poor women occasionally failed to list any value at all for their meager possessions. Women of all descriptions, moreover, shared an ignorance of legal language and an unfamiliarity with the details of transactions concerning property with which they were not personally acquainted. The sole exceptions to their rule were a few widows who had already served several years as executrices of the family estates; some wives of innkeepers, grocers, or other shopkeepers who had assisted their husbands in business; and a small number of single women who had supported themselves through their own efforts.

Loyalist husbands, then, did not normally discuss economic decisions with their wives. The women lacked exactly that information which their husbands alone could have supplied, for they were able to describe only those parts of the property with which they came into regular contact. That the practice in these loyalist homes was not atypical is shown when one looks at patriot families as well.

American wives and widows alike repeatedly noted their lack of information about their husbands' business dealings. "I don't know anything of his affairs," a Virginian resident in London wrote in 1757; "whether his income will admit of our living in the manner we do, I am a stranger to." Elizabeth Sandwith Drinker, a Philadelphia Quaker, commented years later, "I am not acquainted with the extent of my husband's great variety of engagements," quoting an apposite poem that began, "I stay much at home, and my business I mind." To such married women, their spouses' financial affairs were not of immediate import. But widows, by contrast, had to cope with the consequences of their ignorance. On his deathbed, a New England cleric surprised his wife with the news that she would have "many debts to pay that [she] knew nothing about," and her subsequent experience was replicated many times over—by the Marylander whose husband left no records to guide her administration of his estate, by the Virginian who had to tell her husband's employer that he had evidently neglected to maintain proper rent rolls, by the New Yorker who admitted to her son-in-law that she had known "very little" of her spouse's affairs before his death.

It might seem extraordinary that colonial men failed to recognize the potential benefits—to their children and their estates, if not to themselves—of keeping their wives informed about family finances. Yet the responsibility was not theirs alone. Married women rarely appear to have sought economic information from their husbands, whether in anticipation of eventual widowhood or simply out of a desire to understand the family's financial circumstances. On the contrary, women's statements reveal a complete acceptance of the division of their world into two separate, sexually defined spheres.

"Nature & Custom seems to have destined us for the more endearing & private & the Man for the more active & busy Walks of Life," remarked Elizabeth Willing Powel, a leader of Philadelphia society, in 1784. A similar sense of the character of the difference between male and female realms shone through the 1768 observation of a fellow Philadelphian of Mrs. Powel, the teenager Peggy Emlen, who described the men she saw hurrying about the city streets: they "all seem people of a great deal of business and importance, as for me I am not much of either." Men shared this same notion of the dichotomy between male public activity and female private passivity. In 1745, an essayist warned women that they were best "confined within the narrow Limits of Domestick Offices," for "when they stray beyond them, they move excentrically, and consequently without grace." A New Englander twelve years later worried that women might want "to obtain the

other's Sphere of Action, & become Men," but he reassured himself that "they will again return to the wonted Paths of true Politeness, & shine most in the proper Sphere of domestick Life."

If women were accordingly out of place in the world beyond the household, so men were not entirely at home in the female realm of domestic affairs. The family property may have been "his" in wives' terminology, but at the same time the household furnishings were "hers" in the minds of their spouses. Wartime letters from American husbands confirm the separation of male and female spheres, more because of what they do not contain than as a result of what they do. When couples were separated by the Revolutionary War, men for the most part neglected to instruct their wives about the ordinary details of domestic life. Since they initially sent explicit directions about financial affairs, their failure to concern themselves with household management would seem to indicate that they had been accustomed to leave that realm entirely to their wives. Only if they had not previously issued orders on domestic subjects would they have failed to include such directives in their correspondence.

The evidence, then, suggests that female whites shared a universal domestic experience that differentiated their world from that of men. Their lives were to a large extent defined by their familial responsibilities, but the precise character of those obligations varied according to the nature of the household in which they resided. Although demographic historians have concentrated upon determining the size of colonial households, from the standpoint of an American woman, size—within a normal range—mattered less than composition. It meant a great deal to a housewife whether she had daughters who could assist her, whether her household contained a helpful servant or demanding elderly relative, or whether she had to contend with a resident mother-in-law for control of her own domestic affairs.

But ultimately of greater significance were differences in the wealth and location of colonial households. The chief factors that defined a white woman's domestic role arose from the family's economic status, which determined whether there would be servants or slaves, and from the household's location in a rural or urban setting. With a similarity of household roles as a basis, one can divide eighteenth-century women into four groups: poor and middling white farm women, north and south; white urban women of all social ranks; wealthy southerners who lived on plantations; and the female blacks held in bondage by those same wealthy southerners.

II

A majority of white women in eighteenth-century America resided in poor or middling farm households, and so it is reasonable to begin a discussion of female domestic work patterns with an assessment of their experience. Their heavy responsibilities are revealed most vividly in accounts left by two city families who moved to rural areas, for farm women were so accustomed to their burdensome obligations that they rarely remarked upon them.

Christopher Marshall and his wife abandoned Philadelphia when the British occupied the city in the fall of 1777, shifting their large family to Lancaster, Pennsylvania. There Marshall marveled at his wife's accomplishments, at how "from early in the morning till late at night, she is constantly employed in the affairs of the family." She not only did the cooking, baking, washing, and ironing, all of which had been handled by servants in their Philadelphia home, but she also milked cows, made cider and cheese, and dried apples. The members of the Palmer family of Germantown, Massachusetts, had a comparable experience when they moved in 1790 to Framingham, about twenty miles west of Boston. Mary Palmer, who was then fifteen and the oldest daughter in the home, later recalled that her father had had difficulty in adjusting to the change in his womenfolk's roles. "It took years to wean him from the idea that we must be ladies," she wrote, "although he knew that we

must give up all such pretensions." Mary herself thrived in the new environment. "Kind neighbors" taught her mother how to make butter and cheese, and the girls "assisted in the laborious part, keeping churn, pans, cheese-hoops and strainers nice and sweet." After she married Royall Tyler and set up housekeeping in Brattleboro, Vermont, Mary continued to practice the skills of rural housewifery she had gained as a teenager. Between managing her dairy in the summer and supervising spinning and weaving in the winter, not to mention raising five children, she observed, "I never realized what it was to have time hang heavy."

Mary Palmer's recollections disclose the seasonal nature of much of farm women's labor. Such annual rhythms and the underlying, invariable weekly routine are revealed in the work records kept by farm wives like Sarah Snell Bryant, of Cummington, Massachusetts, and Mary Cooper, of Oyster Bay, Long Island. Each week Mrs. Bryant devoted one day to washing, another to ironing, and a third at least partly to baking. On the other days she sewed, spun, and wove. In the spring she planted her garden; in the early summer she hived her bees; in the fall she made cider and dried apples; and in mid-December came hog-killing time. Mary Cooper recorded the same seasonal round of work, adding to it spring housecleaning, a midsummer cherry harvest, and a long stretch of soap-making, boiling "souse," rendering fat, and making candles that followed the hog butchering in December. In late 1769, after two weeks of such work, she described herself as "full of freting discontent dirty and miserabel both yesterday and today."

Unlike the laconic Mrs. Bryant, who simply noted the work she had completed each day, Mrs. Cooper frequently commented on the fatiguing nature of her life. "It has been a tiresome day it is now Bed time and I have not had won minutts rest," she wrote in November 1768. One Sunday some months later she remarked, "I hoped for some rest but I am forst to get dinner and slave hard all day long." On those rare occasions when everyone else in the household was away, Mary Cooper under-standably breathed a sigh of relief. "I have the Blessing to be quite alone without any Body greate or Small," she noted in late October 1768, and five years later another such day brought thanks for "some quiate moments which I have not had in weeks."

Perhaps one of the reasons why Mrs. Cooper seemed so overworked was her obsession with cleanliness. Since travelers in rural America commented frequently upon the dirt they encountered in farmhouses and isolated taverns, it seems clear either that cleanliness was not highly valued or that farm wives, fully occupied with other tasks, simply had no time to worry about sweeping floors, airing bedding, or putting things away. Mary Cooper's experience suggests that the latter explanation was more likely. Often describing herself as "dirty and dis-trest," she faithfully recorded her constant battle against filth. "We are cleaning the house and I am tired almost to death," she wrote in December 1768; the following spring, after seven straight days of cleaning, she complained, "O it has been a week of greate toile and no Comfort or piece to Body or mind." Another time she noted with satisfaction, "I have got some clean cloths on thro mercy some little done to clean the house," and again, "Up very late But I have got my Cloths Ironed." Obviously, if a farm woman was not willing to invest almost superhuman effort in the enter-prise, keeping her household clean was an impossible task.

Mary Cooper's diary is unique in that it con-veys explicitly what is only implicit in other farm wives' journals: a sense of drudgery and bore-dom. Sarah Snell Bryant would record that she had engaged in the same tasks for days on end, but she never noted her reaction to the repeti-tion. This sameness was the quality that differen-tiated farm women's work from that performed by their husbands. No less physically demanding or difficult, men's tasks varied considerably from day to day and month to month. At most— during planting or harvest time, for example— men would spend two or three weeks at one job.

But then they would move on to another. For a farmer, in other words, the basic cycle was yearly; for his wife, it was daily and weekly, with addi-tional obligations superimposed seasonally. Moreover, men were able to break their work routine by making frequent trips to town or the local mill on business, or by going hunting or fishing, whereas their wives, especially if they had small children, were tied to the home.

Rural youngsters of both sexes were expected to assist their parents. "Their children are all brought up in industry, and have their time fully employed in performing the necessary duties of the house and farm," remarked a foreign visitor to a western Pennsylvania homestead in 1796. His inclusion of both sons and daughters was entirely accurate, for although historians have tended to emphasize the value of boys' labor to their fathers, extensive evidence suggests that girls were just as important as aides to their mothers. The fifteen-year-old Elizabeth Fuller, of Princeton, Massachusetts, for example, recorded occasionally baking pies, making can-dles, scouring floors, mincing meat for sausages, making cheese, and doing laundry, in addition to her primary assignments, spinning and weav-ing. Nabby and Betsy Foote, sisters who lived in Colchester, Connecticut, likewise noted helping their mother with housework, again in conjunc-tion with their major chores of sewing, spin-ning, and weaving. When the parents of Ruth Henshaw, of Leicester, Massachusetts, called her home in mid-July 1789 after she had been visit-ing a relative for four days, saying, she recounted, that they "could not Subsist with out me any longer," they were only expressing what is evident in all these diaries: the labor of daugh-ters, like that of wives, was crucial to the suc-cess of a farm household.

Brissot de Warville, an astute foreign trav-eler, recognized both the value of women's work and the clearly defined gender role distinctions visible in rural life in his observations upon a fellow Frenchman's Pennsylvania farm in 1788. It is a "great disadvantage," Brissot remarked, that "he does not have any poultry or pigeons and makes no cheese; nor does he have any spinning done or collect goose feathers." The reason: he was a bachelor, and "these domestic farm industries . . . can be carried on well only by women." Brissot's friend had two women indentured servants, so he did not lack female labor as such; what was missing was a wife or daughters to supervise the servants. Significantly, neither he nor Brissot seems to have considered the possibility that he could himself keep poultry or learn enough about cheesemaking to direct the servants. That was clearly "woman's work," and if there was no woman present, such work was not done, no matter how pressing the need or how great the resulting loss of potential income.

Yet in some frontier areas the gender role divisions so apparent in more settled regions did blur, although they did not break down entirely. Farmers' wives and daughters occasionally worked in the fields, especially at harvest time. Travelers from the East were unaccustomed to the sight of white female fieldworkers and wrote about it at length. In 1778, for example, a doctor from Dorchester, Massachusetts, told his wife in some amazement that he had seen Pennsylvania German women "at work abroad on the Farm mowing, Hoeing, Loading Dung into a Cart." A New Hampshire farmer, by contrast, matter-of-factly recorded in his diary his use of female relatives and neighbors for field work. In that same colony in the early 1760s the pendulum swung the other way, and men helped with women's work. In the winters, recalled one woman many years later, "the boys did as much Knitting as the Girls, and the men and boys also did the milking to spare the women."

Backcountry women had to cope with a far more rough-and-ready existence than did their counterparts to the east and south. The log cabins in which many of them lived were crudely built and largely open to the elements. Even the few amenities that brightened the lives of their poor contemporaries in areas of denser settlement were denied them; the Reverend Charles Woodmason, an Anglican missionary in western South Carolina, commented in 1768 that "in many Places they have nought but a

Gourd to drink out off Not a Plate Knife or Spoon, a Glass, Cup, or any thing—It is well if they can get some Body Linen, and some have not even that." Later in the century, one woman on the Ohio frontier, lacking a churn, was reduced to making butter by stirring cream with her hand in an ordinary pail. Under such circumstances, simple subsistence would require most of a woman's energies.

How, then, did frontier women react to these primitive conditions? At least one group of pioneer men termed their wives "the greatest of Heroines," suggesting that they bore such hardships without complaint, but other evidence indicates that some women, especially those raised in genteel households, did not adapt readily to their new lives. Many, like a Pennsylvanian, must have vetoed their husbands' plans to move west because of an unwillingness to exchange a civilized life for a residence in "what she deems a Wilderness." Others must have resembled the Shenandoah Valley woman, a mother of eight, who descended into invalidism shortly after her husband moved her and their children to what their son described as a "valuable Farm but with a small indifferent house . . . & almost intirely in woods." Perhaps, like a female traveler in the west, the Virginian "felt oppress'd with so much wood towering above . . . in every direction and such a continuance of it." This was not a unique reaction: a Scottish immigrant, faced with his wife's similar response to the first sight of their new home, comforted her by promising, "[W]e would get all these trees cut down . . . [so] that we would see from house to house."

At least in this case the husband knew of his wife's discontent and reacted to it. In other instances, the lack of communication between spouses resulting from their divergent roles appears to have been heightened on the frontier, as wives deliberately concealed their unhappiness from their husbands, revealing their true feelings only to female relatives. Mary Hooper Spence, who described herself as having been beset by "misfortunes" ever since the day of her marriage, lived with her husband on the "dreary

& cold" island of St. Johns (now Prince Edward Island) in the 1770s. In letters to her mother in Boston she repeatedly told of her loneliness and depression, of how she found a primitive, isolated existence "hard to bear." By contrast, her husband characterized their life as "happy" and reported to a relative that they were "comfortably" settled. Likewise, Mrs. Joseph Gilman, said by her husband to be pleased with living in the new settlement of Marietta, Ohio, in 1789, later recounted that on many occasions while milking their cows she would think of her New England home, "sob and cry as loud as a child, and then wipe her tears and appear before her husband as cheerful as if she had nothing to give her pain."

To point out the apparent dissatisfaction of many frontier women with their lives in the wilderness is not to say that they and others did not cope successfully with the trials they encountered. To cite just one example: Mrs. Hutchens, a Mississippi woman whose husband was kidnapped and whose slaves were stolen, pulled her family together in the face of adversity almost by sheer force of will alone. Her son subsequently recalled that she had told her children they could survive if they were willing to work. Accordingly, she and her three sons cultivated the fields while her daughters did the housework, spun cotton, and wove the fabric for their clothing. By the time her husband returned seven years later, she had prospered sufficiently to be able to replace all the slaves taken by the robbers.

The fact that Mrs. Hutchens put her daughters to work spinning and weaving is significant, for no household task was more time-consuming or more symbolic of the female role than spinning. It was, furthermore, a task quintessentially performed by young, single women; hence, the use of the word "spinster" to mean an unmarried female and the phrase "the distaff side" to refer to women in general. Farm wives, and especially their daughters, spent a large proportion of their time, particularly in the winter months, bending over a flax wheel or loom, or walking beside a great wheel,

spinning wool. No examination of the domestic sphere can be complete without detailed attention to this aspect of household work.

Before 1765 and the subsequent rise in home manufacturing caused by colonial boycotts of British goods, spinning and weaving as ordinary chores were largely confined to rural areas of the northern and middle colonies and the backcountry South. Planters and even middling farmers who lived along the southeastern coast and city residents throughout America could usually purchase English cloth more cheaply than they could manufacture it at home, and so they bought fabric rather than asking their wives, daughters, or female slaves to spend the requisite amount of time to produce it. But rural women outside the plantation South spent much of their lives spinning. They began as girls, helping their mothers; they continued after their marriages, until their own daughters were old enough to remove most of the burden from their shoulders; and they often returned to it in old age or widowhood, as a means of supporting themselves or making use of their time. Not all farm women learned weaving, a skill open to men as well, but spinning was a nearly universal occupation among them.

Rural girls understood at an early age that spinning was "a very proper accomplishment for a farmers daughter," as the New Jersey Quaker Susanna Dillwyn put it in 1790. Susanna's niece Hannah Cox began trying to spin on an "old wheel which was in the house" when she was only seven, so her mother bought her a little new wheel, upon which Hannah soon learned to spin "very prettily." Similarly, the tutor on Robert Carter's Virginia plantation observed that his small pupils would tie "a String to a Chair & then run buzzing back to imitate the Girls spinning." Such playful fascination with the process of cloth production later turned for many girls into monotonous daily labor at wheels or looms during the months between December and May. The normal output of an experienced spinner who carded the wool herself was four skeins a day, or six if an assistant carded for her. Teenaged girls like

Elizabeth Fuller, who were less practiced than their mothers, produced on the average two or three skeins a day. After a long stint of spinning tow (short coarse linen fibers) in January and February 1792, Elizabeth exploded in her diary, "I should think I might have spun up all the Swingling Tow in America by this time." Later that same year, she switched to weaving, at last completing her annual allotment on June 1. In three months she had woven 176 yards of cloth, she recorded, happily inscribing in her journal, "Welcome sweet Liberty, once more to me. How have I longed to meet again with thee."

But clothwork, which could be a lonely and confining occupation, as Elizabeth Fuller learned, could also be an occasion for socializing. Rural girls sometimes attended "spinning frolics" or quilting bees, many of which lasted for several days and ended with dancing. Even more frequently farm women "changed work," trading skills with others experienced in different tasks. Mary Palmer recalled that after her family moved to Framingham her mother would change work with other women in the area, "knitting and sewing for them while they would weave cotton and flax into cloth" for her, since as a city dweller she had never learned that skill. In a similar way Ruth Henshaw and her mother repaid Lydia Hawkins, who warped their loom for them, by helping her quilt or making her a pair of stays. Ruth regularly exchanged chores with girls of her own age as well; in December 1789, for example, she noted, "Sally here Spining Changeing works with Me," while ten days later she was at Sally's house, carding for her.

From such trading of labor farm women could easily move on to work for pay. By 1775 Betsy and Nabby Foote had taken that step. Nabby, like Lydia Hawkins of Leicester, specialized in warping webs and making loom harnesses; her sister Betsy worked in all phases of cloth production, carding wool, hatcheling flax, and spinning, as well as doing sewing and mending for neighbors. In the rural North and South alike white women spun, wove, and sold butter, cheese, and soap to their neighbors, participating on a small scale in the market econ-

omy long before the establishment of textile factories in New England and the consequent introduction of widespread wage labor for young northern women.

Given the significance of spinning in women's lives, it is not surprising that American men and women made that occupation the major symbol of femininity. William Livingston had declared that "country girls . . . ought to be at their spinning-wheels," and when Benjamin Franklin sought a wedding present for his sister Jane, he decided on a spinning wheel instead of a tea table, concluding that "the character of a good housewife was far preferable to that of being only a pretty gentlewoman."

Compelling evidence of the link between spinning and the female role in the eighteenth-century American mind comes from the observations of two visitors to Indian villages. Confronted by societies in which women did not spin but instead cultivated crops while their husbands hunted and fished, both the whites perceived Indian sex roles as improper and sought to correct them by introducing the feminine task of spinning. Benjamin Hawkins, United States agent for the Creek tribe, admired the industrious Creek women and encouraged them to learn to spin and weave. This step, he believed, would lead to a realignment of sex roles along proper lines, because the women would be freed from dependence upon their hunter husbands for clothing, and they would also no longer have time to work on the crops. The men in turn would therefore be "obliged to handle the ax & the plough, and assist the women in the laborious task of the fields." A similar scheme was promoted by the Quaker woman Anne Emlen Mifflin, who traveled in the Seneca country as a missionary in 1803. Men should work in agriculture, she told her Indian audience, so that women would be able to learn spinning and dairy management, which were "branches suited to our sex," as opposed to "drudging alone in the labors of the field."

As Mifflin's comment shows, women, too, found spinning a necessary component of femininity, a fact best illustrated by reference to

Elizabeth Graeme Fergusson's poem "The Contemplative Spinner." In 1792, Mrs. Fergusson, one of the leaders of intellectual life in republican Philadelphia, composed a poem in which she compared her spinning wheel to a wheel of fortune, leading her to a series of observations on life, death, and religion. But the wheel did more: it also reminded her of other women, linking her inextricably to "a train of Female Hands/Chearful uniting in Industrious Bands." And so, she wrote:

> In such Reflections I oft passed the Night,
> When by my Papas solitary Light
> My Wheel I turned, and thought how others toild
> To earn a morsel for a famishd Child.

To Elizabeth Graeme Fergusson, spinning symbolized her tie to the female sisterhood, just as to Benjamin Hawkins and other eighteenth-century men that occupation above all somehow appertained to femininity. It is consequently ironic that the one factor that differentiated the lives of urban women most sharply from those of their rural counterparts was the fact that they did not have to engage in cloth production. Women who had access to stores saw no point in spending hour after tedious hour at the wheel or loom. Not, at least, until doing so came to have political significance in the late 1760s, as Americans increasingly tried to end their dependence on British manufactured goods.

III

Although urban women did not have to spin and weave, the absence of that time-consuming occupation did not turn their lives into leisured ones. Too often historians have been misled by the lack of lengthy work entries in urban women's diaries, concluding therefrom that city "ladies" contributed little or nothing to the family welfare. Admittedly, white urban women of even moderate means worked shorter hours and at less physically demanding tasks than did their rural counterparts, but this did not mean that their households ran themselves. Women still had the responsibility for food preparation,

which often included cultivating a garden and raising poultry. The wives of artisans and shop-keepers also occasionally assisted their husbands in business. Furthermore, their homes were held to higher standards of cleanliness—by themselves and by their female friends—than were the homes of farm women like Mary Cooper. Even if they could afford to hire servants, they frequently complained that supervising their assistants took almost as much time and effort as doing the work themselves.

Middling and well-to-do urban women who described their daily routines in letters or diaries disclosed a uniform pattern of mornings devoted to household work, a late dinner at about two o'clock, and an afternoon of visiting friends, riding, or perhaps reading quietly at home. Although some women arose as late as eight o'clock (which one female Bostonian termed "a lazy hour"), others, including Abigail Adams, recorded that they habitually rose at five. A Pennsylvanian summed up the common practice in a poem:

> Like a notable house wife *i rise with the sun*
> Then bustle about till the business is done,
> Consult with the Cook, and *attend to the spiting*
> [*sic*]
> Then quietly seat myself down to my *knitting*—
> Should a neighbour step in we *talk of the weather*
> Retail all the *news* and the *scandle* together, . . .
> The *tea things removed* our party disperses,
> And of course puts an end to my *very fine verses*.

The chores that city women performed in the mornings resembled those of farm wives. Their diaries noted hours devoted to washing and ironing, cooking and baking, sewing and knitting. Like that of their rural counterparts, their labor was affected by the seasons, although less consistently so: in the autumn they preserved fruit and stored vegetables, and early in the winter they salted beef and pork and made sausage. Yet there were differences. Most notably, urban dwellers made daily trips to large markets, where they bought most of their meat, vegetables, cheese, and butter. Rebecca Stoddert, a Marylander who had moved to Philadelphia, marveled that her neighbors quickly killed chickens they had purchased without "think[ing] of fattening them up," a practice she deplored as wasteful and shortsighted.

Although urban women were not burdened with the major stock-tending and clothmaking chores that devolved upon farm wives, some of the time thus saved was devoted to cleaning their homes. Many of the travelers in rural areas most horrified by dirty farmhouses and taverns were themselves urban women, who had adopted standards of cleanliness for their homes, clothes, and beds that were utterly alien to farm wives. Certainly no rural woman except Mary Cooper would have written a journal entry resembling that of a Philadelphian in 1781: "As we were whitewashing & cleaning house this day I seemed anxious, I fear over anxious to have every thing clean, & in order." Another Philadelphia resident, the Quaker Sally Logan Fisher, seems to have painted, white-washed, or wallpapered her house each spring, even though she remarked in April 1785 that it was "troublesome work indeed, the pleasure afterwards of being nice, hardly pays for the trouble." Other wives in smaller towns similarly recorded their commitment to keeping their homes neat and clean.

Cleaning, though, was perhaps the only occupation at which city dwellers of moderate means expended more energy than women living in agricultural regions. One of the benefits of residing in a city or a good-sized town was the availability of a pool of female workers who could be hired at relatively low rates. If a woman decided that she could not afford even a minimal payment, she could take a girl into her home as a sort of apprentice in housewifery, compensating her solely with room, board, and clothes. . . .

The mistresses of such [middling and wealthy] homes felt caught in a dilemma. On the one hand, servants were impertinent, lazy, untrustworthy, careless, and slovenly (to list just a few of their complaints), but on the other hand it was impossible to run a household without some help. The women who offered themselves for hire were usually either single girls or elderly widows; only in rare cases can one identify white females who spent their entire lives as servants. Instead, girls worked as maids, cooks, or laundresses for a few years before marriage, often for a series of employers. From the diaries and letters of mistresses of urban households one gains the impression of a floating population of "young Giddy Headed Girls" who did largely as they pleased, knowing that with the endemic American shortage of labor they could always find another position. Few seem to have stayed in the same household for more than a few months, or a year at most, before moving on to another post. For example, in just the five years from 1794 to 1799, Deborah Norris Logan, Sally Logan Fisher's sister-in-law, employed at least ten different female servants in fairly rapid succession. Among them were two widows, some immigrants from Ireland and Germany, a pair of sisters, and several girls.

Deborah Logan had no daughters to assist her in the home, but even if she had, she, like other urban mothers, would not have expected them to contribute as much work to the household as did their rural counterparts. City daughters from well-to-do homes were the only eighteenth-century American women who can accurately be described as leisured. The causes of their relative lack of employment have already been indicated: first, the work of an urban household was less demanding than that of a farm, so that mothers and perhaps one or two servants could do all that was necessary; and, second, city girls did not have to produce the cloth supply for the family. Accordingly, they could live at a relaxed pace, sleeping late, learning music and dancing, spending hours with male and female friends, and reading the latest novels.

This is not to say, as some historians have argued, that these young women were entirely idle and decorative, for they did extensive amounts of sewing for their families. Girls began to sew at an early age—Hannah, Sally Logan Fisher's daughter, was only eight when she made her first shirt—and they thereafter devoted many hours each day to their needles. Most of their tasks were mundane: mending and altering clothes; making shirts for their fathers and brothers; and stitching apparently innumerable aprons, caps, and shifts for themselves, their mothers, and their aunts. Such "common sewing" won a girl "no great Credit," the New Englander Pamela Dwight Sedgwick admitted in 1789, but at the same time, she pointed out to her daughter, "[I]t will be thought unpardonable negligence . . . not to doe it very nicely." Sometimes girls would work samplers or make lace, but even the wealthiest among them occasionally felt apologetic for spending a considerable amount of their time on decorative stitchery. Betsy DeLancey, a daughter of the prominent New York family, defended such evidently frivolous employment to her sister Anne in 1768 by referring to Proverbs: "I must be industrious and make myself fine with my own Hands, and who can blame me for spending some of my time in that manner when it is part of the virtuous Womans Character in the Bible."

In poor households, daughters' sewing skills could contribute significantly to family income, as may be demonstrated by reference to the Banckers of New York City. Christopher Bancker was an alcoholic, and his wife Polly tried to support the family by working as a seamstress. Yet she alone could not "du the whole," as she wrote in 1791, and so her two oldest daughters, Peggy and Betsy, also sought employment as seamstresses. Even with the girls' help the family experienced severe economic difficulties, yet the combined income of wife and daughters, coupled with charity proffered by reluctant relatives, kept the Banckers out of the poor house. Peggy and Betsy—and, by implication, other urban girls as well—thus proved to be economic assets to their families in a way that sons were not. The best that could be done with the two oldest Bancker boys was to send them out of the household to learn trades, so that they would no longer be a drag on family resources. Not until they had served apprenticeships of several years, with the

expenses being borne by relatives, could they make positive contributions to the support of their parents and siblings. But their sisters had been "apprenticed" to their mother, and so they had developed salable skills at an early age. The other side of the coin was the fact that the Bancker boys' advanced training eventually paid off in higher wages, whereas the girls had little hope of ever improving their position, except through a good marriage.

Because sewing was readily portable, and because they lived so close to each other, well-to-do urban girls frequently gathered to work in sizable groups. While one of their number read, usually from a popular novel, the others would pass the afternoon or evening in sewing. Like farm girls, they created an opportunity for socializing out of the necessity for work, but as a result of their proximity they were able to meet more often, more regularly, and in greater numbers. One sewing group called itself the "Progressive Society" and confined its reading to edifying tracts. "Our design is to ameliorate, by every probable method, the morals, opinions, manners and language of each other," one of the members wrote, explaining why they excluded cardplaying, gossip, and men from their meetings.

In addition to sewing, city girls, like their rural counterparts, were taught what one of them termed "the mysteries of housewifery" by conscientious mothers. Sally Logan Fisher began to instruct her daughter Hannah in "Family affairs" when she was just ten, so that she would become "a good Housewife & an active Mistress of a Family." Daughters did some cooking, baking, and cleaning, helped to care for younger siblings, and on occasion took charge of the household. Sometimes they acquired this responsibility only when their mothers became ill, but in other cases adults deliberately adopted it as a training device. Abigail Adams, who believed it "an indispensable requisite, that every American wife, should herself know, how to order, and regulate her family," commented approvingly in 1788 that her son-in-law William Stephens Smith's four sisters were "well educated for wives as well as daughters" because "their Mamma had used them to the care of her Family by Turns. Each take it a week at a Time."

The words chosen by Mrs. Adams and Mrs. Fisher revealed a key difference in the domestic roles of urban and rural girls. Farm daughters learned to perform household tasks because their family's current well-being required their active involvement in daily work, whereas city girls acquired domestic skills primarily so that they could eventually become good wives and mothers. The distinction was crucial. Urban daughters participated sporadically in household tasks as a preparation for their own futures, but farm girls worked regularly at such chores as a direct contribution to their family's immediate welfare. The difference points up the overall contrast between the lives of urban and rural white women. In both city and farm, women made vital contributions to the success and survival of the household, but in rural areas those contributions were both more direct and more time-consuming.

IV

Wealthy southern women were directly responsible for even fewer household tasks than northerners with comparable means. But northerners who moved south soon realized the falsity of an initial impression that "a mrs of a family in Carolina had nothing to doe but be waited on as their was so many negros." Anna Bowen, a young Rhode Island woman who first went to South Carolina to visit a married sister and subsequently married a planter herself, told another sister in 1790 about the problems of running a large household. Required to "think incessantly of a thousand articles of daily supply," she sometimes did not know "which way to turn," Bowen admitted, but, she added confidently, "I shall learn in time."

The daily schedules of mistresses of large plantations resembled those of wealthy urban women in the North, with the exception of the fact that social visits were confined to one or two afternoons a week because of the distance between plantations. The mornings were devoted to household affairs, although white southerners spent their time supervising the work of slaves instead of doing such chores themselves. The day began, sometimes before breakfast, with what one southern man termed "Grand Rounds from the Kitchen to the Larder, then to the Poultry Yard & so on by the Garret & Store Room home to the Parlour." After she had ascertained that the daily tasks were proceeding as planned, the mistress of the household could spend some time reading or playing music before joining her husband for dinner in early to mid-afternoon. Afterward, she would normally turn to needlework until evening, and then again to reading and writing.

The supervision of what were the largest households on the north American continent involved plantation mistresses in varied activities, almost always in the role of director rather than performer. What were small-scale operations on northern farms—running a dairy, raising poultry, tending a garden—were magnified many times on southern plantations, but they remained within the female sphere. Chores that northern women could do in a day, such as laundry, took nearly one week of every two on at least one South Carolina plantation. Food management, easily accomplished in small northern urban families with access to markets, occupied a significant amount of time and required much forethought on large plantations, where each year's harvest had to feed perhaps one hundred or more people for months. White women, it is true, did not usually make the decisions about how many hogs to kill or how many barrels of corn to set aside for food and seed, but they did manage the distribution of food once it had been stored, not to mention the supervision of its initial preservation. Furthermore, they coordinated the manufacture of the slaves' clothing, spending many hours cutting out garments or superintending that work, in addition to making, altering, and mending their families' clothes.

Such women invariably aroused the admiration of observers, who regularly commended their "industry and ingenuity," their "very able and active manner," or their character as "worthy economists" and "good managers." Surviving correspondence indicates that the praise could be completely deserved. A prime example is provided by the Marylander Hannah Buchanan, who in August 1809 returned alone to Woburn plantation while her husband remained in Baltimore on business. She reported to him in anger that the white couple they had left in charge did not have "the smallest idea of the proper economy of a Farm." Among the abuses she discovered were a misassignment of slave women to nonessential tasks, a lack of planning for the slaves' winter clothing, and extremely poor handling of food supplies, including such errors as allowing the slaves to have wheat flour, consuming all the pork, and having no vegetables at all. "This is miserable management," she declared, and set herself to correct the situation. A month later the work on winter clothes was coming along "Wonderfully," and she was filled with ideas on how to prepare and distribute the food more efficiently. Although she expressed a desire to rejoin her husband in the city, she proposed, "[L]et me direct next year and you will spend less believe me and the people will live much better."

Appropriately, then, the primary task of girls from wealthy southern families was to gain expertise in running large estates. Like their northern counterparts, they did some cooking and baking and a fair amount of sewing, but their household roles differed from those of both farm and city girls. Whereas one New England father told his daughter, "[L]earn to work as fast as you can to make Shirts etc & assist your Mother," Thomas Jefferson advised his younger daughter, Maria, who was usually called Polly, that she should know how to "manage the kitchen, the dairy, the garden, and other appendages of the hous[e]hold." Teenaged girls like Eleanor Parke (Nelly) Custis accordingly served as "deputy Housekeeper" to the mistress of the family, who in her case was her grandmother Martha Washington. If this training was successful, parents could look with

pleasure upon the accomplishments of such excellent managers as Martha Jefferson Randolph, who assured her father in 1791 that at Monticello under her direction "there is as little wasted as possible," or Harriott Pinckney Horry, whose fond mother, Eliza Lucas Pinckney, had herself managed three South Carolina plantations in the 1740s while she was still a teenager. "I am glad your little wife looks well to the ways of [her] hou[se]," Mrs. Pinckney told her new son-in-law within a month of his marriage, especially remarking upon her daughter's ability to run a "perfectly neat" dairy.

In the end, being a good plantation mistress involved very different skills from those of the usual notable housewife of northern communities. Most importantly, the well-to-do southern white woman had to know how to command and direct the activities of others, often a great many others, not just the one or two servants common to northern households. It was less essential for a wealthy female southerner to know how to accomplish tasks herself than it was for her to know how to order blacks to perform them, and to ensure that her orders were carried out. Thus when the Virginian Elizabeth Foote Washington, who feared that she would not survive until her baby daughter reached maturity, decided to leave her a book of household advice, she devoted most of its pages to hints on the management of slaves. A mistress should behave with "steadiness," she advised; she should show the servants that she would not be "impos'd upon." The most important goal was to maintain "peace & quietness" in the household, and to this end a mistress should be careful not to complain about the slaves to her husband or her friends. Such a practice would make the servants grateful and perhaps encourage their industry, she wrote.

As it happened, both the daughters born to Mrs. Washington died in infancy, and so her detailed delineation of the way to handle house servants was not passed on as she had hoped. But other white southern girls early assumed the habit of command. A telling incident involved

Anne, the daughter of James Iredell, the North Carolina attorney and eventual associate justice of the Supreme Court. At the early age of four, she showed how well she had learned her lessons by "strutting about in the yard after Susanna (whom she had ordered to do something) with her work in her hand & an Air of as much importance as if she had been Mistress of the family."

The story of Anne Iredell's behavior inevitably forces one to confront a difficult question: how did Susanna, a mature black woman, react to being ordered about by a white child? Or, to broaden the issue, what sort of lives were led by the black women who, with their husbands and children, constituted the vast majority of the population on southern plantations? Many female slaves resided on small farms and presumably worked in both field and house, but the discussion here will concentrate upon larger plantations, for it was in such households that most black women lived, since the relatively small proportion of white families who possessed slaves tended to own large numbers of them.

Significantly, the size of these plantations allowed the specialization of domestic labor. White northern farm wives had to be, in effect, jills-of-all-trades, whereas planters often assigned slave women more or less permanently to particular tasks. A wide variety of jobs were open to black women, jobs that demanded as much skill as those performed by such male artisans as blacksmiths and carpenters. The slave list prepared by Thomas Middleton for his Goose Creek, South Carolina, plantation in 1784 included a dairymaid, a nurse, two laundresses, two seamstresses, and three general house servants. On other plantations women were also employed as cooks, spinners and weavers (after the mid-1760s), midwives, and tenders of poultry and livestock.

Female blacks frequently worked at the same job for a number of years, but they were not necessarily restricted to it for a lifetime, although practices varied from plantation to plantation. Thomas Jefferson used children of both sexes under ten as infant nurses; from the ages of ten to sixteen he assigned girls to spinning and boys to nailmaking; and then either put them into the fields or had them learn a skilled occupation. Even as adults their jobs might be changed: when Jefferson went to France as ambassador in 1784, his "fine house wench" Dinah, then twenty-three, began to work in the fields, continuing at that assignment at least until 1792. The descriptions of slaves bought or sold on other plantations likewise showed women accustomed to different occupations. Colonel Fitzgerald's Nell, aged thirty-four, was "a stout able field wench & an exceeding good Washer and Ironer"; her daughter Sophy, eighteen, was a "Stout Wench & used to both field & [hou]se Work."

All field work was not the same, of course, and women who labored "in the crop" performed a variety of functions. Evidence of work assignments from both the Jefferson and Washington plantations shows that there were some field jobs reserved for men, most notably cradling wheat and cutting and hauling timber for fences, but that women sometimes built fences. Women plowed, hoed and grubbed the land, spread manure, sowed, harrowed, and at harvest time threshed wheat or husked corn. At Landon Carter's Sabine Hall plantation in Virginia two women, Grace and Maryan, each headed a small gang of female field workers.

On outlying quarters, most women were agricultural laborers, with the occasional exception of a cook or a children's nurse. But female slaves raised at the home plantation could sometimes attain a high level of skill at conventionally "feminine" occupations. White masters and mistresses frequently praised the accomplishments of their cooks, seamstresses, and housekeepers. In a typical passage, Alice DeLancey Izard, a wealthy South Carolinian returning home after a long absence, commended her dairymaid Chloe because she found "the Dairy in excellent order, & plentifully supplied with Milk, & Butter," further observing that Chloe "has made little Chloe very useful in her line."

Mrs. Izard thereby called attention to the transmission of skills among generations of female blacks. Thomas Jefferson's censuses of his plantations demonstrate that women who were house servants tended to have daughters who also worked in the house, and the inventory of a Pinckney family plantation in 1812 similarly included a mother-daughter midwife team. Indeed, midwifery, which was most likely an occupation passed on from woman to woman rather than one taught deliberately by a master, was one of the most essential skills on any plantation. Slave midwives were often called upon to deliver white children as well as black, and masters recognized the special demands of their profession. In 1766, the midwife at Landon Carter's Fork Quarter, who was also the poultry tender, left her post to deliver a baby, an act resulting in the death of four turkeys. Even the petulant Carter realized that her midwifery duties came first, and so he did not punish her.

In this case, a conflict arose between the midwife's divergent duties within her master's household. More commonly, slave women must have had to contend with contradictory demands placed upon them by their plantation tasks and the needs of their own husbands and children. Only a few aspects of the domestic lives led by black women within their own families can be traced in the records of white planters, for masters and mistresses did not, on the whole, concern themselves with the ways in which female slaves organized their homes. Yet occasional comments by slaveowners suggest that black women carefully made the most of what little they had and were even able to exercise some entrepreneurial initiative on occasion. Slave families occasionally maintained their own garden plots and supplemented their meager food and clothing allowances through theft or guile. Further, black women established themselves as the "general Chicken Merchants" in the plantation South. Whites often bought fowls from their female slaves instead of raising chickens themselves, as a means, Thomas Jefferson once explained, of "drawing a line between what is theirs & mine."

That some black women had a very strong sense indeed of what was "theirs" was demonstrated on Nomini Hall plantation in the summer of 1781. Robert Carter had authorized two white overseers to begin making salt, and in order to accomplish that task they commandeered an iron pot from its two female owners. Joan and Patty, the aggrieved slaves, awaited their chance and then removed the pot from the saltworks. After the whites repossessed it, the women dispatched Patty's husband, Jesse, to complain to Carter about the treatment they had received. Carter sided with the women, agreeing that their pot had been taken in an "arbitrary" manner, and he ordered it returned to them.

One could argue that Joan and Patty were emboldened to act as they did because they anticipated that Carter, a well-meaning master who eventually emancipated his slaves, would sympathize with their position. But bondwomen less favorably circumstanced also repeatedly displayed a desire to control as much of their lives as was possible under the conditions of servitude. Robert Carter's relative Landon was quick to anger, impatient with his servants and children. He frequently had recalcitrant slaves whipped, a tactic to which Robert rarely resorted, yet the women at Sabine Hall were no less insubordinate than those at Nomini. If Robert Carter's "Young & Stout" Jenny deliberately had fits "upon her being reprimanded," Landon Carter's Sarah pretended to be pregnant for a full eleven months so that she could avoid work, and Criss sent her children to milk his cows in the middle of the night in retaliation for a whipping. Similarly ingenious was James Mercer's Sall, who in August 1777 convinced her master that she had consumption and persuaded him to send her to the mountain quarter where her parents lived. That summer he ordered that she should be well fed and allowed to ride six or seven miles on horseback each day until she recovered her health, but by the following year, Mercer had concluded she was faking and directed that "she must turn out at all events unless attended with a fever."

The same willful spirit asserted itself when masters and mistresses attempted to move female slaves from their accustomed homes to other locations. A North Carolina woman who was visiting Boston wanted to have her servant Dorinda sent north to join her, but learned from a relative that Dorinda "would by no means go to Boston or North Carolina, from Cape Fear." Some years later a Pennsylvanian who had sent a slave woman to Cuba to be sold learned that she had managed to convince the white woman accompanying her that she should be returned to her Philadelphia home, because she was "Very Unhappy and always Crying." And "Miss Charlotte," an East Florida black, demonstrated her autonomy by her reaction to a dispute over who owned her. One of the two whites involved reported that she lived with neither of them, but instead "goes about from house to house," saying "now she's a free woman."

Charlotte, Sall, Dorinda, and the others gained at least a little freedom of movement for themselves, but they were still enslaved in the end. All their victories were minor ones, for they could have only limited impact upon the conditions of their bondage. White women were subject to white men, but black women had to subordinate themselves to all whites, men, women, and children alike. The whites demanded always that their needs come first, before those of black women's own families. Female slaves' work lives were thus complicated by conflicting obligations that inflicted burdens upon them far beyond those borne by most whites.

V

White Americans did not expect their slaves to gain satisfaction from their work, for all that masters and mistresses required of their bond servants was proper behavior and a full day's labor. But white women, as already indicated, were supposed to find "happiness in their chimney corners," to return to William Livingston's striking phrase. Men certainly believed that women should enjoy their domestic role. As a Georgian told his married sister in 1796, "I am sure that those cares which duty requires to your husband, and your child—must fill up every moment of time—and leave you nothing but those sensations of pleasure—which invariably flow—from a consciousness of having left no duty unperformed." Women too anticipated happiness from achieving the goal of notable housewifery. "Domestick oeconomy . . . is the female dignity, & praise," declared Abigail Adams's younger sister, Elizabeth Smith, in the late 1760s, and a Virginian observed to a friend nearly forty years later that she had "always been taught, that within the sphere of domestic life, Woman's chief glory & happiness ought to consist."

The expectation, then, was clear: domesticity was not only a white American woman's inevitable destiny, but it was also supposed to be the source of her sense of pride and satisfaction. Regardless of the exact shape of her household role—whether she was a rural or an urban wife, or the mistress of a southern plantation—she should find fulfillment in it, and she should take pleasure in performing the duties required of her as mistress of the home.

Unsurprisingly, women rarely found the ideal as attractive in reality as it was in theory. But the reasons for their dissatisfaction with the restrictions of notable housewifery, which required them to be consistently self-effacing and constantly employed at domestic tasks, are both illuminating and unanticipated.

First, it must be noted that Mary Cooper was alone among her contemporaries in emphasizing the difficult, fatiguing nature of housework as the primary source of her complaints. Only she wrote of "the continnel cross of my famaly," only she filled her diary with accounts of weariness and endless drudgery. Women's unhappiness with their domestic lives, in other words, stemmed not from the fact that the work was tiring and demanding. Their husbands' labor was also difficult, and in eighteenth-century America there were few models of a leisured existence for either men or women to emulate. Rather, women's expressed dissatisfaction with their household role derived from its basic nature, and from the way it contrasted with their husbands' work.

As has been seen, farmers' lives were much more varied than those of their wives, not only because they rarely repeated the same chore day after day in immediate succession, but also because they had more breaks from the laboring routine. The same was true of southern planters and of urban husbands, regardless of their occupation. The diaries of planters, professional men, and artisans alike demonstrate that their weeks were punctuated by travel, their days enlivened not only by visits with friends—which their wives also enjoyed—but also by a variety of business activities that took them on numerous errands. It was an unusual week, for example, when Thomas Hazard, a Rhode Island blacksmith, worked in his shop every day without any sort of respite from his labors, or when Ebenezer Parkman, a New England clergyman, did not call on parishioners, confer with neighbors about politics, or meet with other ministers.

Against the backdrop of their husbands' diverse experiences, the invariable daily and weekly routines of housewifery seemed dull and uninteresting to eighteenth-century women, especially those who lived in urban areas, where the housework was less varied and their spouses' opportunities for socializing simultaneously greater. "The same cares and the same wants are constantly returning in domestic Life to take up my Time and attention," Pamela Dwight Sedgwick told her husband, Theodore, the Massachusetts Federalist, in words that reappeared in other women's assessments of their lives. "A continual sameness reigns throughout the Year," wrote Christian Barnes, the wife of a Marlborough, Massachusetts, merchant, and Mary Orne Tucker, a Haverhill lawyer's wife, noted in her diary that she did not record her domestic tasks in detail because "each succeeding day with very little variety would present a compleat history of the last."

New England city dwellers were not the only women who made such observations about the unchanging character of their experiences. The transplanted Rhode Islander Anna Bowen

Mitchell reported from her new South Carolina home in 1793, "[T]he detail of one day . . . would be the detail of the last six months of my life," while hastening to add that her days were not "insipid," but rather filled with "heart-soothing tranquility." A Virginia planter's wife was more blunt about her situation in 1785, describing herself and her friends as "almost in a State of vegitation" because of their necessary attention to the "innumerable wants" of their large households.

She thus touched upon yet another source of housewives' discontent with their lot: the fact that their all-encompassing domestic responsibilities left them little time to themselves. In 1755, a New England woman remarked longingly to a correspondent, "[T]he little scraps of time that can be rescued from Business or Company, are the greatest cordials to my tired Spirits that I meet with." Thirty years later Pamela Sedgwick echoed her sentiments, telling her unmarried friend Betsy Mayhew, "[W]e that have connected ourselves in the famely way, find the small circle of domestic concerns engross almost all our attention." Sally Logan Fisher too commented, "[I] find so much to do in the Family that I have not all the time for retirement and improvement of my own mind in the best things that I wish," revealingly referring to her domestic duties as "these hindering things." Again, such complaints were not confined to northerners. A young Virginia wife observed in 1769 that "Domestic Business . . . even deprives thought of its Native freedom" by restricting the mind "to one particular subject without suffering it to entertain itself with the contemplation of any thing New or improving." A wry female poet made the same point in verse: "Ah yes! 'tis true, upon my Life! / No *Muse* was ever yet a *Wife*," she wrote, explaining that "Muses . . . in *poultry yards* were never seen," nor were they required "from Books and Poetry to Turn / To mark *the Labours of the Churn*."

The point of all these remarks was the same, despite their divergent geographical and chronological origins. White American women recognized not only that their domestic obligations were never-ending, but also that their necessary concentration upon those obligations deprived them of the opportunity to contemplate "any thing New and improving." So Elizabeth Smith Shaw told her oldest sister, Mary Cranch, in 1781, several years after her marriage to the clergyman John Shaw, "[I]f Ideas present themselves to my Mind, it is too much like the good seed sown among Thorns, they are soon erased, & swallowed up by the Cares of the World, the wants, & noise of my Family, & Children." Abigail Adams in particular regretted her beloved younger sister's preoccupation with domestic concerns during her second marriage, to another clergyman, who boarded a number of students. In February 1800 she told Elizabeth (then Mrs. Stephen Peabody) that her "brilliant" talents were "encumbered" and "obstructed" by her household chores, lamenting "that the fire of imagination should be checked, that the effusions of genious should be stifled, through want of leisure to display them." Abigail's characterization of the impact of domestic responsibilities on her sister's life bore little resemblance to William Livingston's glorification of those same activities: "The mind which is necessarily imprisoned in its own little tenement: and fully occupied by keeping it in repair: has no time to rove abroad for improvement," she observed. "The Book of knowledge is closely clasped against those who must fullfil there [sic] daily task of manual labour."

Even with their expressed dissatisfaction at the endless, unchanging nature of housework, one might theorize that late eighteenth-century American women could nevertheless have found their domestic lives meaningful if they and their husbands had highly valued their contributions to the family well-being. But such was not the case. Women revealed their assessments of the importance of their work in the adjectives they used to describe it: "my Narrow sphere," my "humble duties," "my little Domestick affairs."

Always the words belittled their domestic role, thereby indicating its low status in contemporary eyes. Modern historians can accurately point to the essential economic function of women within a colonial household, but the facts evident from hindsight bear little relationship to eighteenth-century subjective attitudes. In spite of the paeans to notable womanhood, the role of the household mistress in the family's welfare was understood only on the most basic level. Such minimal recognition did not translate itself into an awareness that women contributed to the wider society. Instead, just as a woman's activities were supposed to be confined to the domestic sphere, so, too, was any judgment of her importance. Americans realized that a successful household needed a competent mistress, but they failed to endow that mistress with an independent social standing or to grant to her domestic work the value it deserved. Notable housewifery was conceived to be an end in itself, rather than as a means to a greater or more meaningful goal. As such, it was an inadequate prop for feminine self-esteem.

Accordingly, it comes as no surprise to learn that women generally wrote of their household work without joy or satisfaction. They spoke only of "the discharge of the necessary duties of life," of "perform[ing] the duties that are annex'd to my Station." Even the South Carolinian Martha Laurens Ramsay, described by her husband, David, as a model wife, regarded her "self denying duties" as "a part of the curse denounced upon Eve," as a penalty to be endured, instead of as a fulfilling experience. The usage was universal and the message unmistakable: their tasks, with rare exceptions, were "duties," not pleasures. The only Americans who wrote consistently of the joys of housewifery and notable womanhood were men like William Livingston. In contrast, Christian Barnes found the household a prison that offered no intellectual stimulation, describing it as a place where women were "Chain'd down to domestic Dutys" that "Stagnate[d] the Blood and Stupefie[d] the Senses."

Yet still women did not question the overall dimensions of the ideal domestic role. Sometimes, to be sure, they inquired about its details, as when Esther Edwards Burr, Jonathan Edwards's daughter, and her close friend Sarah

Prince carried on a learned discussion about the precise meaning of the parts of Proverbs 31 that outlined the virtuous woman's daily routine. But ultimately they saw no alternative to domesticity. Many were simply resigned to the inevitable, for they had few options. Certainly some expressed the philosophy that "the height of happiness is Contentment" with one's lot, that although their life had "no great veriety . . . custom has made it agreeable . . . and to desire more would be ungreatfull." More probable, though, is the fact that the household duties women found unsatisfying were intertwined in their own minds with responsibilities from which they gained a great deal of pleasure. Their role as mistress of the household, in the end, constituted but a third of their troika of domestic duties. They were wives and mothers as well as housekeepers, and these components of domesticity gave them the emotional and psychological rewards they did not receive from running their households efficiently.

KEY TERMS

Loyalist: An adherent of the British cause during the American Revolution.

Body linen: Undergarments.

Middling: People of middle rank, neither rich nor poor.

Troika: A group of three, from the Russian troika, a carriage drawn by a team of three horses abreast.

DISCUSSION TOPICS

After reading this essay, you should be able to discuss:

1. The contributions made by women to the functioning of early American society.

2. Women's roles in early America.

3. The ways in which English society defined the household as the domain of women.

4. The ways in which race, class, and geography shaped women's lives in early America.

6

Who Was Benjamin Franklin?
John William Ward

Much like his contemporary George Washington, Benjamin Franklin has become one of the staples of American mythology. As John William Ward makes clear, however, Franklin was in reality no mythological being but a very complex and even contradictory man. The essence of Franklin, according to Ward, was his existence as a symbol of upward mobility. Beginning life as an apprentice printer, Franklin achieved business success before he was thirty, earned an international reputation in science through his experiments in electricity, became influential in politics at the state and national levels, and served as one of the new nation's most successful diplomats in the Revolutionary era. The key to Franklin's rise, Ward contends, was his ability to separate appearance and reality: to appear to conform to community norms in public life while following his own desires in private affairs.

In fashioning his own public image, both by managing his behavior and by constructing an emulous persona in his *Autobiography*, Franklin emerges as one of the first truly "modern" men in American life. In a society where the worth of a man or woman was measured by his or her personal and family reputations and by connections with others above and below them in the world, Franklin pioneered a new way to measure a person's character. Divorcing himself from the personal world of family and personal connections and relying instead on commonly held moral principles and an ethic of individualism, Franklin forged a reputation that rested on his personal attributes rather than his family position. As America's population grew at an explosive rate during the eighteenth and early nineteenth centuries, increasing numbers of Americans took advantage of the anonymity large-scale population growth provided and, like Franklin, created their own self-images and public representations.

From "Who Was Benjamin Franklin?" Reprinted by permission from Mrs. John William Ward.

Benjamin Franklin bulks large in our national consciousness, sharing room with Washington and Jefferson and Lincoln. Yet it is hard to say precisely what it means to name Franklin one of our cultural heroes. He was, as one book about him has it, "many-sided." The sheer variety of his character has made it possible to praise him and damn him with equal vigor.

Part of the difficulty in comprehending Franklin's meaning is due to the opposites he seems to have contained with complete serenity within his own personality. He was an eminently reasonable man who maintained a deep skepticism about the power of reason. He was a model of industriousness who, preaching the gospel of hard work, kept his shop only until it kept him and retired at forty-two. He was a cautious and prudent man who was a revolutionist. And, to name only one more seeming contradiction, he was one who had a keen eye for his own advantage and personal advancement who spent nearly all his adult life in the service of others. Small wonder that there have been various interpretations of so various a character.

Yet there still remains the obstinate fact that Franklin could mean so many things to so many men, that he was so many-sided, that he did contain opposites, that he was, in other words, so many different characters. One suspects that here is the single most important thing about Franklin. Rather than spend our energies trying to find some consistency in this protean, many-sided figure, trying to resolve who Franklin truly was, we might perhaps better accept his variety itself as our major problem and try to understand that. To insist on the importance of the question, "Who was Benjamin Franklin?" may finally be more conclusive than to agree upon an answer.

The place to begin to ask the question is with the *Memoirs*, with the *Autobiography*, as we have come to call them, and the place to begin there is with the history of the text. Fascinating in and of itself, the history of the text gives us an initial lead into the question of the elusiveness of Franklin's personality.

The *Autobiography* was written in four parts. The first part, addressed by Franklin to his son, William, was begun during some few weeks in July and August, 1771, while Franklin was visiting with his friend, Jonathan Shipley, the Bishop of St. Asaph, in Hampshire, England. Franklin was then sixty-five years old. As he wrote the first part he also carefully made a list of topics he would subsequently treat. Somehow the manuscript and list fell into the hands of one Abel James who eleven years later wrote Franklin, returning to him the list of topics but not the first part of the manuscript, urging him to take up his story once again. This was in 1782, or possibly early in January, 1783. Franklin was in France as one of the peace commissioners. He wrote the second part in France in 1784, after the achievement of peace, indicating the beginning and the ending of this short second part in the manuscript itself.

In 1785, Franklin returned to America, promising to work on the manuscript during the voyage. Instead he wrote three of his utilitarian essays: on navigation, on how to avoid smoky streetlamp chimneys, and on his famous stove. He did not return to his life's story until 1788. Then, after retiring from the presidency of the state of Pennsylvania in the spring, Franklin, quite sick, made his will and put his house in order before turning again to his own history. This was in August, 1788. Franklin was eighty-three years old, in pain, and preparing for death. The third part is the longest part of the autobiography, less interesting than the first two, and for many years was thought to conclude the manuscript.

In 1789, Franklin had his grandson, Benjamin Franklin Bache, make two fair copies of Parts I, II, and III in order to send them to friends abroad, Benjamin Vaughan in England and M. le Veillard in France. Then, sometime before his death in April, 1790, Franklin added the last and fourth part, some seven and one-half manuscript pages, which was not included, naturally, in the fair copies sent abroad. For the rest, Mr. Max Farrand, our authority on the history of the text:

After [Franklin's] death, the publication of the autobiography was eagerly awaited, as its existence was widely known, but for nearly thirty years the reading public had to content itself with French translations of the first and second parts, which were again translated from the French into other languages, and even retranslated into English. When the authorized English publication finally appeared in 1818, it was not taken from the original manuscript but from a copy, as was the preceding French version of the first part. The copy, furthermore, did not include the fourth and last part, which also reached the public in a French translation in 1828.

. . . The complete autobiography was not printed in English from the original manuscript until 1868, nearly eighty years after Franklin's death.

The story is, as I have said, interesting in and of itself. The tangled history of one of our most important texts has its own fascination, but it also provides us the first clue to our question. Surely, it must strike any reader of the *Autobiography* as curious that a character who speaks so openly should at the same time seem so difficult to define. But the history of the text points the way to an answer. All we need to do is ask why Franklin wrote his memoirs.

When the Quaker Abel James wrote Franklin, returning his list of topics and asking "kind, humane, and benevolent Ben Franklin" to continue his life's story, "a work which would be useful and entertaining not only to a few but to millions," Franklin sent the letter on to his friend, Benjamin Vaughan, asking for advice. Vaughan concurred. He too urged Franklin to publish the history of his life because he could think of no "more efficacious advertisement" of America than Franklin's history. "All that has happened to you," he reminded Franklin, "is also connected with the detail of the manners and situation of a rising people." Franklin included James's and Vaughan's letters in his manuscript to explain why he resumed his story. What had gone before had been written for his family; "what follows," he said in his "Memo," "was written . . . in compliance with the advice contained in these letters, and accordingly

intended for the public. The affairs of the Revolution occasioned the interruption."

The point is obvious enough. When Franklin resumed his story, he did so in full self-consciousness that he was offering himself to the world as a representative type, the American. Intended for the public now, his story was to be an example for young Americans, as Abel James would have it, and an advertisement to the world, as Benjamin Vaughan would have it. We had just concluded a successful revolution; the eyes of all the world were upon us. Just as America had succeeded in creating itself a nation, Franklin set out to show how the American went about creating his own character. As Benjamin Vaughan said, Franklin's life would "give a noble rule and example of self-education" because of Franklin's "discovery that the thing is in many a man's private power." So what follows is no longer the simple annals of Franklin's life for the benefit of his son. Benjamin Franklin plays his proper role. He becomes "The American."

How well he filled the part that his public urged him to play, we can see by observing what he immediately proceeds to provide. In the pages that follow James's and Vaughan's letters, Franklin quickly treats four matters: the establishment of a lending library, that is, the means for satisfying the need for self-education; the importance of frugality and industriousness in one's calling; the social utility of religion; and, of course, the thirteen rules for ordering one's life. Here, in a neat package, were all the materials that went into the making of the self-made man. This is how one goes about making a success of one's self. If the sentiments of our Declaration were to provide prompt notes for European revolutions, then Franklin, as the American Democrat, acted them out. Family, class, religious orthodoxy, higher education: all these were secondary to character and common sense. The thing was in many a man's private power.

If we look back now at the first part, the opening section addressed by Franklin to his son, William, we can see a difference and a similarity. The difference is, of course, in the easy and personal tone, the more familiar manner, appropriate to a communication with one's son. It is in these early pages that Franklin talks more openly about his many *errata*, his "frequent intrigues with low women," and displays that rather cool and calculating attitude toward his wife. Rather plain dealing, one might think, at least one who did not know that William was a bastard son.

But the similarity between the two parts is more important. The message is the same, although addressed to a son, rather than to the world: how to go about making a success. "From the poverty and obscurity in which I was born and in which I passed my earliest years," writes the father to the son, "I have raised myself to a state of affluence and some degree of celebrity in the world." A son, especially, must have found that "some" hard to take. But the career is not simply anecdotal: "my posterity will perhaps be desirous of learning the means, which I employed, and which, thanks to Providence, so well succeeded with me. They may also deem them fit to be imitated." The story is exemplary, although how the example was to affect a son who was, in 1771, about forty years old and already Royal Governor of New Jersey is another matter.

The story has remained exemplary because it is the success story to beat all success stories: the runaway apprentice printer who rose to dine with kings; the penniless boy, walking down Market Street with two large rolls under his arms, who was to sit in Independence Hall and help create a new nation. But notice that the story does not deal with the success itself. That is presumed, of course, but the *Autobiography* never gets to the later and more important years because the *Autobiography* is not about success. It is about the formation of the character that makes success possible. The subject of the *Autobiography* is the making of a character. Having lifted himself by his own bootstraps, Franklin described it that way: "I have raised myself." We were not to find the pat phrase until the early nineteenth century when the age of the common man made the style more

common: "the self-made man." The character was for life, of course, and not for fiction where we usually expect to encounter the made-up, but that should not prevent us from looking a little more closely at the act of creation. We can look in two ways: first, by standing outside the *Autobiography* and assessing it by what we know from elsewhere; second, by reading the *Autobiography* itself more closely.

A good place to begin is with those years in France around the end of the [American] Revolution. It is so delicious an episode in plain Ben's life. More importantly—as Franklin said, one can always find a principle to justify one's inclinations—it is in these very years at Passy that Franklin, in response to James's and Vaughan's letters, wrote those self-conscious pages of the second part of the *Autobiography*. Just as he wrote the lines, he played them. As Carl Van Doren has written, "the French were looking for a hero who should combine the reason and wit of Voltaire with the primitive virtues celebrated by Rousseau. . . . [Franklin] denied them nothing." This is the period of the simple Quaker dress, the fur cap and the spectacles. France went wild in its adulation and Franklin knew why. "Think how this must appear," he wrote a friend, "among the powdered heads of Paris."

But he was also moving with equal ease in that world, the world of the powdered heads of Paris, one of the most cosmopolitan, most preciously civilized societies in history. Although he was no Quaker, Franklin was willing to allow the French to think so. They called him "*le bon Quackeur*." The irony was unintentional, a matter of translation. But at the same time that he was filling the role of the simple backwoods democrat, the innocent abroad, he was also playing cavalier in the brilliant salon of Madame Helvétius, the widow of the French philosopher. Madame Helvétius is supposed to have been so beautiful that Fontenelle, the great popularizer of Newton, who lived to be one hundred years old, was said to have paid her the most famous compliment of the age: "Ah, madame, if I were only eighty again!" Madame Helvétius was sixty when Franklin knew her and the classic anecdote of their acquaintance is that Madame Helvétius is said to have reproached him for not coming to see her, for putting off his long anticipated visit. Franklin replied, "Madame, I am waiting until the nights are longer." There was also Madame Brillon, not a widow, who once wrote to Franklin, "People have the audacity to criticize my pleasant habit of sitting on your knee, and yours of always asking me for what I always refuse."

Some, discovering this side of Franklin, have written him off simply as a rather lively old lecher. Abigail Adams, good New England lady that she was, was thoroughly shocked. She set Madame Helvétius down as a "very bad woman." But Franklin, despite his public style, was not so provincial. He appealed to Madame Brillon that he had spent so many days with her that surely she could spend one night with him. She mockingly called him a sophist. He then appealed to her charity and argued that it was in the design of Providence that she grant him his wish. If somehow a son of the Puritans, Franklin had grown far beyond the reach of their sermonizing. Thomas Hooker had thought, "It's a grievous thing to the loose person, he cannot have his pleasures but he must have his guilt and gall with them." But Franklin wrote Madame Brillon, "Reflect how many of our duties [Providence] has ordained naturally to be pleasures; and that it has had the goodness besides, to give the name of sin to several of them so that we might enjoy them the more."

All this is delightful enough, and for more one need only turn to Carl Van Doren's biography from which I have taken these anecdotes, but what it points to is as important as it is entertaining. It points to Franklin's great capacity to respond to the situation in which he found himself and to play the expected role, to prepare a face to meet the faces that he met. He could, in turn, be the homespun, rustic philosopher or the mocking cavalier, the witty sophist. He knew what was expected of him.

The discovery should not surprise any reader of the *Autobiography*. Throughout it, Franklin insists always on the distinction between appearance and reality, between what he is and what he seems to be.

> In order to secure my credit and character as a tradesman, I took care not only to be in *reality* industrious and frugal, but to avoid all *appearances* of the contrary. I dressed plain and was seen at no places of idle diversion. I never went out a fishing or shooting; a book, indeed, sometimes debauched me from my work, but that was seldom, snug, and gave no scandal; and to show that I was not above my business, I sometimes brought home the paper I purchased at the stores, thro' the streets on a wheelbarrow. Thus being esteemed an industrious, thriving young man, and paying duly for what I bought, the merchants who imported stationery solicited my custom; others proposed supplying me with books, and I went on swimmingly.

Now, with this famous passage, one must be careful. However industrious and frugal Franklin may in fact have been, he knew that for the business of social success virtue counts for nothing without its public dress. In Franklin's world there has to be someone in the woods to hear the tree fall. Private virtue might bring one to stand before the King of kings, but if one wants to sit down and sup with the kings of this world, then one must help them see one's merit. There are always in this world, as Franklin pointed out, "a number of rich merchants, nobility, states, and princes who have need of honest instruments for the management of their affairs, and such being so rare [I] have endeavoured to convince young persons, that no qualities are so likely to make a poor man's fortune as those of probity and integrity."

Yet if one wants to secure one's credit in the world by means of one's character, then the character must be of a piece. There can be no false gesture; the part must be played well. When Franklin drew up his list of virtues they contained, he tells us, only twelve. But a Quaker friend "kindly" informed him that he was generally thought proud and overbearing and rather insolent; he proved it by examples. So Franklin added humility to his list; but, having risen in the world and content with the degree of celebrity he had achieved, he could not bring himself to be humble. "I cannot boast of much success in acquiring the *reality* of this virtue, but I had a good deal with regard to the *appearance* of it."

He repeats, at this point, what he had already written in the first part of his story. He forswears all "positive assertion." He drops from his vocabulary such words as "certainly" and "undoubtedly" and adopts a tentative manner. He remembers how he learned to speak softly, to put forward his opinions, not dogmatically, but by saying, "'I imagine' a thing to be so or so, or 'It so appears to me at present.'" As he had put it to his son earlier, he discovered the Socratic method, "was charmed with it, adopted it, dropped my abrupt contradiction and positive argumentation, and put on the humble enquirer." For good reason, "this habit . . . has been of great advantage to me."

What saves all this in the *Autobiography* from being merely repellent is Franklin's self-awareness, his good humor in telling us about the part he is playing, the public clothes he is putting on to hide what his public will not openly buy. "In reality," he writes, drawing again the distinction from appearance, "there is perhaps no one of our natural passions so hard to subdue as *pride*; disguise it, struggle with it, beat it down, stifle it, mortify it as much as one pleases, it is still alive and will every now and then peep out and show itself. You will see it perhaps often in this history. For even if I could conceive that I had completely overcome it, I should probably be proud of my humility." Here, despite the difference in tone, Franklin speaks like that other and contrasting son of the Puritans, Jonathan Edwards, on the nature of true virtue. Man, if he could achieve virtue, would inevitably be proud of the achievement and so, at the moment of success, fall back into sin.

The difference is, of course, in the tone. The insight is the same but Franklin's skeptical and untroubled self-acceptance is far removed from Edwards' troubled and searching self-doubt. Franklin enjoys the game. Mocking himself, he quietly lures us, in his Yankee deadpan manner, with the very bait he has just described. After having told us that he early learned to "put on the humble enquirer" and to affect a self-depreciating pose, he quotes in his support the line from Alexander Pope, "To speak, though sure, with seeming diffidence." Pope, Franklin immediately goes on to say, "might have joined with this line that which he has coupled with another, I think less properly, 'For want of modesty is want of sense.'"

> If you ask why *less properly,* I must repeat the lines,
>
> *Immodest words admit of* no defense,
> For *want of modesty is want of sense.*
>
> Now is not the "want of sense" (where a man is so unfortunate as to want it) some apology for his "want of modesty"? and would not the lines stand more justly thus?
>
> *Immodest words admit* but *this defense*
> That want of modesty is want of sense.
>
> This, however, I should submit to better judgements.

Having been so bold as to correct a couplet of the literary giant of the age, Franklin quietly retreats and defers to the judgment of those better able to say than he. Having just described the humble part he has decided to play, he immediately acts it out. If we get the point, we chuckle with him; if we miss the point, that only proves its worth.

But one of the functions of laughter is to dispel uneasiness and in Franklin's case the joke is not enough. Our uneasiness comes back when we stop to remember that he is, as his friends asked him to, writing his story as an efficacious advertisement. We must always ask whether Franklin's disarming candor in recounting how things went on so swimmingly may not be yet another role, still another part he is playing. Actually, even with Yale's sumptuous edition of Franklin's papers, we know little about Franklin's personal life in the early years, except through his own account. The little we do know suggests that his way to wealth and success was not the smooth and open path he would have us believe. This leads us, then, if we cannot answer finally the question who Franklin was, to a different question. What does it mean to say that a character so changeable, so elusive, somehow represents American culture? What is there in Franklin's style that makes him, as we say, characteristic?

At the outset in colonial America there was always the assumption that one would be called to one's appropriate station in life and labor in it for one's own good and the good of society. Magistrates would be magistrates and printers would be printers. But in the world in which Franklin moved, the magistrates, like Governor Keith of Pennsylvania who sends Franklin off on a wild-goose chase to England, prove to be frauds while the plain, leather-aproned set went quietly about the work of making society possible at all, creating the institutions—the militia, the fire companies, the libraries, the hospitals, the public utilities—that made society habitable. The notion that underlay an orderly, hierarchical society failed to make sense of such a world. It proved impossible to keep people in their place.

One need only consider in retrospect how swiftly Franklin moved upward through the various levels of society to see the openness, the fluidity of his world. Simply because he is a young man with some books, Governor Burnet of New York asks to see him. While in New Jersey on a job printing money he meets and makes friends with all the leaders of that provincial society. In England, at the coffeehouses, he chats with Mandeville and meets the great Dr. Henry Pemberton who was seeing the third edition of Newton's *Principia* through the press. As Franklin said, diligent in his calling, he raised himself by some degree.

The Protestant doctrine of calling, of industriousness in the world, contained dynamite for the orderly, hierarchical, social structure it was originally meant to support. The unintended consequence showed itself within two generations. Those who were abstemious, frugal and

hardworking made a success in the world. They rose. And society, rather than the static and closed order in which, in Winthrop's words, "some must be rich some poor, some high and eminent in power and dignities; others meane and in subieccion," turned out to be dynamic, fluid and open.

If there is much of our national character implicit in Franklin's career, it is because, early in our history, he represents a response to the rapid social change that has remained about the only constant in American society. He was the self-made man, the jack-of-all-trades. He taught thirteen rules to sure success and purveyed do-it-yourself kits for those who, like himself, constituted a "rising" people. Franklin stands most clearly as an exemplary American because his life's story is a witness to the uncertainties about social status that have characterized our society, a society caught up in the constant process of change. The question, "Who was Benjamin Franklin?" is a critical question to ask of Franklin because it is the question to which Franklin himself is constantly seeking an answer. In a society in which there are no outward, easily discernible marks of social status, the question always is, as we put it in the title of reference works that are supposed to provide the answer, "Who's Who?"

Content with his success, blandly sure it must be in the design of Providence that printers hobnob with kings. Franklin simply passes by the problem of the relation between reality and appearance. In this world, appearance is sufficient. Humanely skeptical that the essence can ever be caught, Franklin decided to leave the question to be answered in the next world, if there proved to be one. For this world, a "tolerable character" was enough and he "valued it properly." The result was a common sense of utilitarianism which sometimes verges toward sheer crassness. But it worked. For this world, what others think of you is what is important.

We admire, I think, the lusty good sense of the man who triumphs in the world that he accepts, yet at the same time we are uneasy with the man who wears so many masks that we are never sure who is there behind them. Yet it is this, this very difficulty of deciding whether we admire Franklin or suspect him, that makes his character an archetype for our national experience. There are great advantages to be had in belonging to a culture without clearly defined classes, without an establishment, but there is, along with the advantages, a certain strain, a necessary uneasiness. In an open and pluralistic society we have difficulty "placing" people, as we say. Think how often in our kind of society when we meet someone for the first time how our second or third question is apt to be, "What do you do?" Never, "Who are you?" The social role is enough, but in our more reflective moments we realize not so, and in our most reflective moments we realize it will never do for our own selves. We may be able to, but we do not want to go through life as a doctor, lawyer, or Indian chief. We want to be ourselves, as we say. And at the beginning of our national experience, Benjamin Franklin not only puts the question that still troubles us in our kind of society, "Who's Who?" He also raises the question that lies at the heart of the trouble: "Who am I?"

KEY TERMS

Peace commissioners: U.S. representatives at negotiations for the Treaty of Paris in 1783, which ended the Revolutionary War.

Carl van Doren: Franklin's most famous modern biographer.

Thomas Hooker (1586?–1647): English cleric and founder of the Hartford, Connecticut colony.

Jonathan Edwards (1703–1758): American theologian most famous for encouraging the Great Awakening and for attempting to reconcile traditional Puritanism and Enlightenment thought.

Alexander Pope (1688–1744): English poet especially well-known among contemporaries for his statement of new social attitudes in his *Essay on Man*.

Bernard Mandeville (1670?–1733): Dutch-born British physician, philosopher, and satirist whose *Fable of the Bees* (1714) depicts all activity as being motivated by self-interest.

John Winthrop (1588–1649): Founder and first governor of the Massachusetts Bay Colony.

DISCUSSION TOPICS

After reading this essay, you should be able to discuss:

1. The means Franklin used to fashion his public persona.

2. The ways in which Franklin's formula for success both built on and challenged accepted social and cultural norms.

3. Why it is so difficult to know who Franklin really was.

4. The changes in eighteenth-century society that permitted Franklin to fashion his own public identity.

PART TWO

A Revolutionary People

The history of the American Revolution is no longer thought of simply as a story of patriotic ardor overcoming British corruption in the crucible of war. As historians have investigated the meaning of the Revolution to nonelite men and women, to Native Americans, and to African Americans (both bound and free), they have discovered a world of complexity and dispute in which people's allegiance to the patriot cause depended as much on their place in society as on abstract political or constitutional principles.

The Revolutionary War itself was a complex affair. As the essays by Alfred F. Young and James Kirby Martin reveal, ordinary artisans, farmers, laborers, and mariners had their own reasons for supporting the American cause. Like many other artisans, George Robert Twelves Hewes was attracted to the patriot cause because he found in it a way to reject the deference he had been forced to give his "superiors" during the colonial era, and because it allowed him to claim an independent political voice for the first time in his life. The men who joined Washington's Continental Army, on the other hand, composed a "Most Undisciplined, Profligate Crew" of poor men from eastern North America's farms and cities. These men from the lower ranks of society risked their lives less from patriotism, Martin claims, than from the promise of the wartime pay and land bounties that might permit them to join the ranks of independent landowners after the Revolution.

The Treaty of Paris, signed in 1783, ended the Revolutionary War and established the United States as an independent nation. At the same time, it posed many new questions to the American people. Robert E. Shalhope's essay discusses two of the most momentous of these questions: What sort of policy would the national government establish? And what sort of society would its policies promote? In the contrasting visions of Federalists and Anti-Federalists, Shalhope argues, lay the future model for American social and political development.

The questions raised by the debate over the Constitution hardly touched the lives of American women. As Wayne Bodle shows in his essay, Jane Bartram's long and often daunting struggle for control of the property she acquired during her marriage to a Philadelphia Tory attests to the continued dependency which was women's legal legacy of the Revolution. Not until well into the nineteenth century would married women gain any degree of legal recognition for the vital economic contribution they made to their marriages.

The Revolution had a profound impact on those outside the political realm as well. The wartime rhetoric that counterposed American liberty to British slavery brought many Americans to reconsider the institution of slavery in the new nation. Especially in the northern states, where slavery was less important economically, but in the Virginia assembly as well, state legislatures debated the question of abolition, and by the end of the eighteenth century the northern states had sent slavery on the road to extinction. In "Absalom Jones," Gary B. Nash discusses the difficult birth of the nation's most important free black community in Philadelphia. Focusing on Jones, an ex-slave who purchased his own freedom and went on to found the first independent African-American church in America, Nash points to the vital importance of religion in the struggle to form free black communities.

Religion played an equally important role in Native American resistance to white expansion into the trans-Appalachian West. No sooner had the Revolutionary War ended than land-hungry settlers surged over the Appalachians, claiming land in Kentucky, Tennessee, and the Northwest Territory by right of conquest. Faced with internal political divisions, wavering British support, and general white hostility, Native American leaders searched for new ways to deal with the imminent threat to their ancestral homelands. Some, like the Cherokee, chose the path of assimilation, hoping that by adopting white ways, they would be accepted into mainstream American society. Others, like the Shawnee leaders Tecumseh and Tenskwatawa—discussed in R. David Edmunds's essay—chose the path of pan-Indian alliance and armed resistance, arguing that whites would never permit Indian assimilation into the white republic.

PAST TRACES

The American Revolution disrupted the lives of most Americans, whether they were patriots, royalists, or neutral. Nowhere was this more true than for those living in areas where the British and American armies confronted each other. As the contending armies maneuvered for position prior to battle, no one was spared the depredations of war. In this document, an elder New Jersey farmer recounts the sufferings and losses experienced by local farmers during the Battle of Princeton in December 1776. The British Regulars, he recounts, showed little concern for non-combatants in the region and followed a policy of destruction, expropriation, and intimidation among the rural populace. In reading his account, there is little wonder why British military operations often served to cement local allegiance to the patriot cause.

A Brief Narrative of the Ravages committed by the Regular and Hessian Soldiers at Trenton & Princeton

I have Often Read and heard of the horror of the war but was never near it Until I was in the Eighty fifth Year of my age and I was born the 25th of September 1691 Old Stile. The regular army left Brunswick on the 7th of December 1776. The Remainder of the our men left Princetown and Marcht to Trenton (for the most of them had gone on before) and Were followed by Gen[l] How with his army in the afternoon of the same day Within a Short time after Passing Stony Brook, our men delaying their Pursuit by Pulling up Stoney Brook Bridge. But they finding the ford past Over one of their light horsemen was shot on his horse from over the brook, and the man who shot him being on rising Ground beyond him, escaped . . . [half line].

The next Morning, having crossed the Delaware in the night, when the Regulars came to the River our men saw them and fired at the Regulars Which we heard at Princetown the Same morning, Which Prevented their crossing the River (and it is said) Killed and Wounded Several of their men.

Most of the Inhabitants of Prince Town a Day or two before [the battle] left their Dwelling Houses and went where they Could go with their Family to Escape From the Regular Army and left a Great Part of their goods behind them in their Houses for want of Carriages to take them away, Great part of Which fell into the regulars hands, and They not only Burnt up all the fire wood that the Inhabitants had Provided for Winter, but Stript Shops, out Houses and Some Dwelling houses of the boards that Covered them, and all the loose boards and Timber That the Joiners and

78

Carpenters had in Store to work up, they Burnt with all their Fences and Garden Inclosures with in the Town & After sent their Carriages and Drew away the Farmers Fences adjoining within a mile, and laid all in Common. They also cut down Apple trees and other fruit bearing trees and burnt them, And either by Accident or Wilfully burnt a Large House lately finisht belonging to Jonathan Seargant Esq in Prince town.

And at new New Market about two short miles from thence they burnt the best Gristmill in these Parts, with a Quantity of Wheat and flower in it, and with it a Fulling mill with a large Quaintity of Cloth in it. The fuller told those Soldiers that set it on fire that he might be Accountable to the owners of the Cloth and Intreated them to let him take it out, Which they refused to do and burnt all together. They also Burnt the grist mill and a Framed dwelling House that had Six rooms in it and which Belonged to Major William Scudder and his fulling mill they burnd. These are said to be Burnt by the Regular army who took from the Neighbouring Farmhouse not only the wood but also Straw, Part of it the soldiers slept on and used in various ways to defend them from the cold and the rest they took and burnt and the wheat lost These are some of the ruins made by fire in and near Princetown contrary to that Justice which is due to all men. It is said that at a house a little out of the Western end of the Town where were a number of Regulars, for Gen[l] Sterling's Brigade belonged to the British, part of them one very cold night before the battle stripped both Wheat fields and upland Meadows setting fire not only to firewood and Carriages but to all sorts of timber and specially fences, So that if

they were Refenced this spring to guard their foder and feed, that that they will cost them (?). . . .[half line]. . . . . and much more than this in labor and time . . . . . [one line]. . . . .

I am informed that they went to tanners and robbed them both of their Tanned, as well as their untanned Leather taken from their Vats. What use the latter may be to them I Know not, Unless it be to make leather Scarce in the Country and impoverish the owners. I am Also Inform'd That they have taken great Quantitys of Unbroken Flax Whether Rotted or not, To use in making Fortifycations and that from several they have taken all they had.

On the same day the 8th of December there followed the Regular Army a Parcel of Hessians and took away four Horses from the People to the westard of the town, One of them was said to be valued at a 100 pound, and commited Several other Outrages the same day In pulling of mens hats from their heads, Though the Regular Officers had given them Protections as they went before, In these Words or near it, Viz. Let no Man Presume to Injure A; B. In his Person or Property. Yet these men had no Regard to it But Directly to the Contrary Injured the Protected Men both in their Persons and Propertys, by Insulting their Persons and by Robing them of their Propertys. Two of these men came to David Oldens (where I then was) Mounted on Poor horses, and in an Insolent manner Demanded his Horses: But as it hapened he had sent them away, before the Regular Army came with all his Household goods and provisions Except what was absolutely Necessary for present use, and many of his Neighbours In and about Princetown had done the like and by that means Saved a good part of their Property. This Method was the very best (if not all) the Safe Protections that could be obtained so much better it is for any Man to be Protected by himself or his friends then to trust his Enemys, Yet this Method did not allways avail as I design to to show hereafter.

There went four of these Hessians to a Gentleman's House (who is called a Quaker) And after they had treated him and his Family in an Insolent Manner a Stout fellow among them laid hold of his Hat on his head and puled it of And he (though but a Smal man and between Fifty and Sixty Years of age) laid hold of their Champion and Struck up his heels and threw him on the Ground and clapt his foot on his Sword and Prevented his drawing it, And took his Hat again from him Upon that the three Other Paltroons Drew their Swords, and he was obligded to Yield up a very good Hat Though he had a Protection several days before, which was of so little Effect that Afterwards the Regulars Robed him of a fine mare, and broke the door of his Stable to get her out, They also Robed his four Store Hogs being all he had before his face, And (as it is said) Three of their Generals were Present Cornwallice, Grant, & Leshly looking on to see how the Regular Soldiers ran After the Hogs about the Pen to Catch them. This is one Instance among many to show the Power of their Protections And Wether they are given to Protect, Or to Allure People to depend on them that they may be Plundered the Easier I shal leave to Others to Determin.

The Regulars and Hessians together Robed and Plundered two wealthy Farmers (that were brothers) of the Greatest part of their moveable Estates About four or five miles from Princetown, and not only took away their Cretures but robed their Houses and ript open their Beds and turned out the feathers and took away the Ticken and left the owners but very little to cover them, or even to live on.

They had yet some other ways to Plunder and Distress the People besides these two that I have Already Mentioned of fire and sword. They go out late in the night and Steal and Kill Sheep and cattle Even Milch Cows and skin them, leave their skins and hides and take away the meat. Another method is this their Officers Bargains with the Inhabitants for forage and other Necessarys and upon the Delivery gives the owners Receipts of the sorts and Quantitys with the Prices, but pays no money thus many Farmers are served. Others are ser'vd in a different manner the Regular Officers with their Soldiers Are by Orders boarded out at the Farmers Houses, and they take their Horses with them and take the Farmers Indian corn, Oats, and the very best of his fodder to feed them on.

At a Gentleman Farmers house the next to that where I now live There was with Officers and all one hundred and Seventy of those Genteel Unwelcome Guests. His best Rooms and beds in his House were taken up by the Officers who was fed upon the best Diet that the House afforded. In the mean time The Soldiers took and wasted what they Pleasd of his stalk tops and Oats in the sheif in Makeing sheds to keep them from the Cold when they Stood on Gaurd, besides what their Horses Devoured, And at their Departure he Desired the Officers to give him Receipts for what they had and damage done Which they Refused and only paid him twenty shillings for fifty Pounds Damage as he Computed it.

Another officer went to another Farmers House And Imperiously Demanded two of the first Rooms in his house each with a good bed in it for him to lodge in and another to Receive in which he accordly took and the owner with his family was Oblidged to live in his Kitchen, While their horses were Eating and Destroying the very best of his Provender and hay for Which the owner never was paid a farthing.

To give a Particular Account of Every Robery and outrage comited by the Hessians and Regulars In and within five miles of Princetown (which is the Extent of these Observations of villanys done) would fill a Vollum therefore I have only Mentioned a few particulars out of a Multitude.

7

George Robert Twelves Hewes:
A Boston Shoemaker and
the American Revolution

Alfred F. Young

By the mid-eighteenth century, questions of political and social authority occupied the minds of Americans of all ranks. While the prosperous governing elites debated the nature of British parliamentary authority in the colonies, those of more humble station challenged existing social arrangements. In rural communities in which land scarcity meant that fathers could no longer offer the promise of propertied independence to their children, sons and daughters began to question the patriarchal control of their fathers and conceived children to force marriage on their own terms. In towns and cities, middling- and laboring-class people joined in questioning the customary authority that the rural gentry and urban merchants exercised. In the mobilization against Britain, these people of lower status demanded a voice in their own affairs that threatened the system of patronage and deference that had dominated social relations for generations.

In Boston, as Alfred F. Young shows, popular questioning of elite control grew in force as the Revolution approached. By following the career of George Robert Twelves Hewes, a humble shoemaker whose experiences were typical of ordinary artisans in America's pre-Revolutionary cities, Young reveals the breakdown of the system of deference that dominated much of the political and social history of colonial America. As the imperial bonds that bound British America to the mother country began to loosen following the Seven Years' War, social relations within the colonies began to change as well. Whereas in 1763 someone such as Hewes felt intimidated and socially inferior when dealing with wealthy and politically influential men such as John Hancock, fifteen years later men of Hewes's rank routinely declared themselves equal to all men, regard-

From "George Robert Twelves Hewes," *William and Mary Quarterly*, 38:4, pp. 561–623. Copyright © 1981 by Alfred F. Young. Reprinted by permission.

less of wealth or social position. The rise of this popular egalitarianism was a prominent feature of the Revolutionary era, as ordinary farmers and artisans placed their lives and livelihoods at risk for the patriot cause. By the end of the eighteenth century, these wartime sacrifices brought ordinary men such as Hewes to make unprecedented demands for social equality and popular political participation in the affairs of the new republic.

Seeing the American Revolution through the eyes of a poor shoemaker rather than from the perspective of founding fathers such as Washington, Jefferson, and John Adams has a twofold advantage. First, it enables us to see the role of ordinary people as history makers; second, it shows that a social upheaval such as the American Revolution can involve many agendas—not always shared by the various participants.

....

Late in 1762 or early in 1763, George Robert Twelves Hewes, a Boston shoemaker in the last year or so of his apprenticeship, repaired a shoe for John Hancock and delivered it to him at his uncle Thomas Hancock's store in Dock Square. Hancock was pleased and invited the young man to "come and see him on New Year's day, and bid him a happy New Year," according to the custom of the day, a ritual of noblesse oblige on the part of the gentry. We know of the episode through Benjamin Bussey Thatcher, who interviewed Hewes and wrote it up for his *Memoir* of Hewes in 1835. On New Year's Day, as Thatcher tells the story, after some urging by his master,

George washed his face, and put his best jacket on, and proceeded straightaway to the Hancock House (as it is still called). His heart was in his mouth, but assuming a cheerful courage, he knocked at the front door, and took his hat off. The servant came:

"Is 'Squire Hancock at home, Sir?" enquired Hewes, making a bow.

He was introduced directly to the *kitchen,* and requested to seat himself, while report should be made above stairs. The man came down directly, with a new varnish of civility suddenly spread over his face. He ushered him into the 'Squire's sitting-room, and left him to make his obeisance. Hancock remembered him, and addressed him kindly. George was anxious to get through, and he commenced a desperate speech—"as pretty a one," he says, "as he any way knew how,"—intended to announce the

purpose of his visit, and to accomplish it, in the same breath.

"Very well, my lad," said the 'Squire—"now take a chair, my lad."

He sat down, scared all the while (as he now confesses) "almost to death," while Hancock put his hand into his breeches-pocket and pulled out a crown-piece, which he placed softly in his hand, thanking him at the same time for his punctual attendance, and his compliments. He then invited his young friend to drink his health—called for wine—poured it out for him—and ticked glasses with him,—a feat in which Hewes, though he had never seen it performed before, having acquitted himself with a creditable dexterity, hastened to make his bow again, and secure his retreat, though not till the 'Squire had extorted a sort of half promise from him to come the next New-Year's—which, for a rarity, he never discharged.

The episode is a demonstration of what the eighteenth century called deference.

Another episode catches the point at which Hewes had arrived a decade and a half later. In 1778 or 1779, after one stint in the war on board a privateer and another in the militia, he was ready to ship out again, from Boston. As Thatcher tells the story: "Here he enlisted, or engaged to enlist, on board the Hancock, a twenty-gun ship, but not liking the manners of the Lieutenant very well, who ordered him one day in the streets to take his hat off to him—which he refused to do for any man,—he went aboard the 'Defence,' Captain Smedley, of Fairfield Connecticut." This, with a vengeance, is the casting off of deference.

What had happened in the intervening years? What had turned the young shoemaker tongue-tied in the face of his betters into the defiant person who would not take his hat off for any man? And why should stories like this have stayed in his memory sixty and seventy years later?

George Robert Twelves Hewes was born in Boston in 1742 and died in Richfield Springs, New York, in 1840. He participated in several of the principal political events of the American Revolution in Boston, among them the Massacre and the Tea Party, and during the war he served as a privateersman and militiaman. A shoemaker all his life, and intermittently or concurrently a fisherman, sailor, and farmer, he remained a poor man. He never made it, not before the war in Boston, not at sea, not after the war in Wrentham and Attleborough, Massachusetts, not in Otsego County, New York. He was a nobody who briefly became a somebody in the Revolution and, for a moment near the end of his life, a hero.

Hewes was one of the "humble classes" that made the success of the Revolution possible. How typical he was we can only suggest at this point in our limited knowledge of the "humble classes." Probably he was as representative a member of the "lower trades" of the cities and as much a rank-and-file participant in the political events and the war as historians have found. The two biographies, which come close to being oral histories (and give us clues to track down Hewes in other ways), provide an unusually rich cumulative record, over a very long period of time, of his thoughts, attitudes, and values. Consequently, we can answer, with varying degrees of satisfaction, a number of questions about one man of the "humble classes." About the "lower trades": why did a boy enter a craft with such bleak prospects as shoemaking? what was the life of an apprentice? what did it mean to be a shoemaker and a poor man in Boston? About the Revolution: what moved such a rank-and-file person to action? what action did he take? may we speak of his "ideology"? does the evidence of his loss of deference permit us to

speak of change in his consciousness? About the war: how did a poor man, an older man, a man with a family exercise his patriotism? what choices did he make? About the results of the Revolution: how did the war affect him? to what extent did he achieve his life goals? why did he go west? what did it mean to be an aged veteran of the revolution? What, in sum, after more than half a century had passed, was the meaning of the Revolution to someone still in the "humble classes"?

Where one ended up in life depended very much on where one started out. George was born under the sign of the Bulls Head and Horns on Water Street near the docks in the South End. His father—also named George— was a tallow chandler and erstwhile tanner. Hewes drew the connections between his class origins and his life chances as he began his narrative for Hawkes:

> My father, said he, was born in Wrentham in the state of Massachusetts, about twenty-eight miles from Boston. My grandfather having made no provision for his support, and being unable to give him an education, apprenticed him at Boston to learn a mechanical trade. . . .
>
> In my childhood, my advantages for education were very limited, much more so than children enjoy at the present time in my native state. My whole education which my opportunities permitted me to acquire, consisted only of a moderate knowledge of reading and writing; my father's circumstances being confined to such humble means as he was enabled to acquire by his mechanical employment, I was kept running of errands, and exposed of course to all the mischiefs to which children are liable in populous cities.

Hewes's family on his father's side was "no better off than what is called in New England *moderate*, and probably not as good." The American progenitor of the line seems to have come from Wales and was in Salisbury, near Newburyport, in 1677, doing what we do not know. Solomon Hewes, George Robert's grandfather, was born in Portsmouth, New Hampshire, in 1674, became a joiner, and moved with collateral members of his family to

Wrentham, originally part of Dedham, near Rhode Island. There he became a landholder; most of his brothers were farmers; two became doctors, one of whom prospered in nearby Providence. His son—our George's father—was born in 1701. On the side of his mother, Abigail Seaver, Hewes's family was a shade different. They had lived for four generations in Roxbury, a small farming town immediately south of Boston across the neck. Abigail's ancestors seem to have been farmers, but one was a minister. Her father, Shubael, was a country cordwainer who owned a house, barn, and two acres. She was born in 1711 and married in 1728.

George Robert Twelves Hewes, born August 25, 1742, was the sixth of nine children, the fourth of seven sons. Five of the nine survived childhood—his three older brothers, Samuel, Shubael, and Solomon, and a younger brother, Daniel. He was named George after his father, Robert after a paternal uncle, and the unlikely Twelves, he thought, for his mother's great uncle, "whose Christian name was Twelve, for whom she appeared to have great admiration. Why he was called by that singular name I never knew." More likely, his mother was honoring her own mother, also Abigail, whose maiden name was Twelves.

The family heritage to George, it might be argued, was more genetic than economic. He inherited a chance to live long: the men in the Seaver line were all long-lived. And he inherited his size. He was unusually short—five feet, one inch. "I have never acquired the ordinary weight or size of other men," Hewes told Hawkes, who wrote that "his whole person is of a slight and slender texture." In old age he was known as "the little old man." Anatomy is not destiny, but Hewes's short size and long name helped shape his personality. It was a big name for a small boy to carry. He was the butt of endless teasing jibes—George Robert what?—that Thatcher turned into anecdotes the humor of which may have masked the pain Hewes may have felt.

"Moderate" as it was, Hewes had a sense of family. Wrentham, town of his grandfather and uncles, was a place he would be sent as a boy, a place of refuge in the war, and after the war his home. He would receive an inheritance three times in his life, each one a reminder of the importance or potential importance of relatives. And he was quite aware of any relative of status, like Dr. Joseph Warren, a distant kinsman on his mother's side.

His father's life in Boston had been an endless, futile struggle to succeed as a tanner. Capital was the problem. In 1729 he bought a one-third ownership in a tannery for £600 in bills of credit. Two years later, he sold half of his third to his brother Robert, who became a working partner. The two brothers turned to a rich merchant, Nathaniel Cunningham, who put up £3500 in return for half the profits. The investment was huge: pits, a yard, workshops, hides, bark, two horses, four slaves, journeymen. For a time the tannery flourished. Then there was the disastrous falling out with Cunningham: furious fights, a raid on the yards, debtor's jail twice for George, suits and countersuits that dragged on in the courts for years. The Hewes brothers saw themselves as "very laborious" artisans who "managed their trade with good skill," only to be ruined by a wealthy, arrogant merchant. To Cunningham, they were incompetent and defaulters. Several years before George Robert was born, his father had fallen back to "butchering, tallow chandlering, hog killing, soap, boiling &c."

The family was not impoverished. George had a memory as a little boy of boarding a ship with his mother to buy a small slave girl "at the rate of two dollars a pound." And there was enough money to pay the fees for his early schooling. But beginning in 1748, when he was six, there was a series of family tragedies. In 1748 an infant brother, Joseph, died, followed later in the year by his sister Abigail, age thirteen, and brother Ebenezer, age two. In 1749 his father died suddenly of a stroke, leaving the family nothing, it would seem, his estate tangled in debt and litigation. George's mother would have joined the more than one thousand widows in Boston, most of whom were on poor relief. Sometime before 1755 she died. In 1756 Grandfather Seaver died, leaving less than £15 to be divided among George and his four surviving brothers. Thus in 1756, at the age of fourteen, when boys were customarily put out to apprenticeship, George was an orphan, the ward of his uncle Robert, as was his brother Daniel, age twelve, each with a legacy of £2 17s. 4d. Uncle Robert, though warmly recollected by Hewes, could not do much to help him: a gluemaker, he was struggling to set up his own manufactory. Nor could George's three older brothers, whom he also remembered fondly. In 1756 they were all in the "lower" trades. Samuel age twenty-six, and Solomon, twenty-two, were fishermen; Shubael, twenty-four, was a butcher.

The reason why George was put to shoemaking becomes clearer: no one in the family had the indenture fee to enable him to enter one of the more lucrative "higher" trades. Josiah Franklin, also a tallow chandler, could not make his son Benjamin a cutler because he lacked the fee. But in shoemaking the prospects were so poor that some masters would pay to get an apprentice. In addition, George was too small to enter trades that demanded brawn; he could hardly have become a ropewalk worker, a housewright, or a shipwright. Ebenezer McIntosh, the Boston shoemaker who led the annual Pope's Day festivities and the Stamp Act demonstrations, was a small man. The trade was a sort of dumping ground for poor boys who could not handle heavy work. Boston Overseers of the Poor acted on this assumption in 1770; so did recruiting officers for the American navy forty years later. The same was true in Europe. Getting into a good trade required "connections"; the family connections were in the leather trades, through Uncle Robert, the gluemaker, or brother Shubael, the butcher. Finally, there was a family tradition. Grandfather Shubael had been a cordwainer, and on his death in 1756 there might even have been a prospect of acquiring his tools and lasts. In any case, the capital that would be needed to set up shop of one's own was relatively small.

And so the boy became a shoemaker—because he had very little choice.

Josiah Franklin had known how important it was to place a boy in a trade that was to his liking. Otherwise there was the threat that Benjamin made explicit: he would run away to sea. Hawkes saw the same thrust in Hewes's life: shoemaking "was never an occupation of his choice," he "being inclined to more active pursuits." George was the wrong boy to put in a sedentary trade that was not to his liking. He was what the Bostonians called "saucy"; he was always in Dutch. The memories of his childhood and youth that Thatcher elicited were almost all of defying authority—his mother, his teachers at dame school, his schoolmaster, his aunt, his shoemaker master, a farmer, a doctor.

Hewes spoke of his mother only as a figure who inflicted punishment for disobedience. The earliest incident he remembered could have happened only to a poor family living near the waterfront. When George was about six, Abigail Hewes sent him off to the nearby shipyards with a basket to gather chips for the fire. At the water's edge George put the basket aside, straddled some floating planks to watch the fish, fell in, and sank to the bottom. He was saved only when some ship carpenters saw the basket without the boy, "found him motionless on the bottom, hooked him out with a boat hook, and rolled him on a tar barrel until signs of life were discovered." His mother nursed him back to health. Then she flogged him.

The lesson did not take, nor did others in school with Miss Tinkum, wife of the town crier. He ran away. She put him in a dark closet. He dug his way out. The next day she put him in again. This time he discovered a jar of quince marmalade and devoured it. A new dame school with "mother McLeod" followed. Then school with "our famous Master Holyoke," which Hewes remembered as "little more than a series of escapes made or attempted from the reign of the birch."

Abigail Hewes must have been desperate to control George. She sent him back after one truancy with a note requesting Holyoke to give him a good whipping. Uncle Robert took pity and sent a substitute note. Abigail threatened, "If you run away again I shall go to school with you myself." When George was about ten, she took the final step: she sent him to Wrentham to live with one of his paternal uncles. Here, George recalled, "he spent several years of his boyhood . . . in the monotonous routine of his Uncle's farm." The only incident he recounted was of defying his aunt. His five-year-old cousin hit him in the face with a stick "without any provocation." George cursed the boy out, for which his aunt whipped him, and when she refused to do the same with her son, George undertook to "chastise" him himself. "I caught my cousin at the barn" and applied the rod. The aunt locked him up but his uncle let him go, responsive to his plea for "equal justice."

Thus when George entered his apprenticeship, if he was not quite the young whig his biographers made him out to be, he was not a youth who would suffer arbitrary authority easily. His master, Downing, had an irascible side and was willing to use a cowhide. Hewes lived in Downing's attic with a fellow apprentice, John Gilbert. All the incidents Hewes recalled from this period had two motifs: petty defiance and a quest for food. There was an escapade on a Saturday night when the two apprentices made off for Gilbert's house and bought a loaf of bread, a pound of butter, and some coffee. They returned after curfew to encounter an enraged Downing, whom they foiled by setting pans and tubs for him to trip over when he came to the door. There was an excursion to Roxbury on Training Day, the traditional apprentices' holiday in Boston, with fellow apprentices and his younger brother. Caught stealing apples, they were taken before the farmer, who was also justice of the peace and who laughed uproariously at Hewes's name and let him go. There was an incident with a doctor who inoculated Hewes and a fellow worker for smallpox and warned them to abstain from food. Sick, fearful of death, Hewes and his friend consumed a dish of venison in melted butter and a mug of flip—and lived to tell the tale.

These memories of youthful defiance and youthful hunger lingered on for seventy years: a loaf of bread and a pound of butter, a parcel of apples, a dish of venison. This shoemaker's apprentice could hardly have been well fed or treated with affection.

The proof is that Hewes tried to end his apprenticeship by the only way he saw possible: escape to the military. "After finding that my depressed condition would probably render it impracticable for me to acquire that education requisite for civil employments," he told Hawkes, "I had resolved to engage in the military service of my country, should an opportunity present." Late in the 1750s, possibly in 1760, as the fourth and last of England's great colonial wars with France ground on and his majesty's army recruiters beat their drums through Boston's streets, Hewes and Gilbert tried to enlist. Gilbert was accepted, but Hewes was not. Recruiting captains were under orders to "enlist no Roman-Catholic, nor any under five feet two inches high without their shoes." "I could not pass muster," Hewes told Hawkes, "because I was not tall enough." As Thatcher embroiders Hawkes's story, Hewes then "went to the shoe shop of several of his acquaintances and heightened his heels by several taps[;] then stuffing his stocking with paper and rags," he returned. The examining captain saw through the trick and rejected him again. Frustrated, humiliated, vowing he would never return to Downing, he took an even more desperate step: he went down to the wharf and tried to enlist on a British ship of war. "His brothers, however, soon heard of it and interfered," and, in Thatcher's words, "he was compelled to abandon that plan." Bostonians like Solomon and Samuel Hewes, who made their living on the waterfront, did not need long memories to remember the city's massive resistance to the impressment sweeps of 1747 and to know that the British navy would be, not escape, but another prison.

About this time, shoemaker Downing failed after fire swept his shop (possibly the great fire of 1760). This would have freed Hewes of his indenture, but he was not qualified to be a shoe-maker until he had completed apprenticeship. As Hewes told it, he therefore apprenticed himself "for the remainder of his minority," that is, until he turned twenty-one, to Harry Rhoades, who paid him $40. In 1835 he could tell Thatcher how much time he then had left to serve, down to the month and day. Of the rest of his "time" he had no bad memories.

Apprenticeship had a lighter side. Hewes's anecdotes give tantalizing glimpses into an embryonic apprentice culture in Boston to which other sources attest—glimpses of pranks played on masters, of revelry after curfew, of Training Day, when the militia displayed its maneuvers and there was drink, food, and "frolicking" on the Common. One may specu-late that George also took part in the annual Pope's Day festival, November 5, when appren-tices, servants, artisans in the lower trades, and young people of all classes took over the town, parading effigies of Pope, Devil, and Pretender, exacting tribute from the better sort, and engag-ing in a battle royal between North End and South End Pope's Day "companies."

Hewes's stories of his youth hint at his win-ning a place for himself as the small schoolboy who got the better of his elders, the apprentice who defied his master, perhaps even a leader among his peers. There are also hints of the adult personality. Hewes was punished often, but if childhood punishment inured some to pain, it made Hewes reluctant to inflict pain on others. He developed a generous streak that led him to reach out to others in trouble. When Downing, a broken man, was on the verge of leaving for Nova Scotia to start anew, Hewes went down to his ship and gave him half of the $40 fee Rhoades had paid him. Downing broke into tears. The story smacks of the Good Samaritan, of the Methodist of the 1830s counting his good deeds; and yet the memory was so vivid, wrote Thatcher, that "his features light up even now with a gleam of rejoicing pride." Hewes spoke later of the "tender sympathies of my nature." He did not want to be, but he was, a fit candidate for the "gentle craft" he was about to enter.

In Boston from 1763, when he entered his majority, until 1775, when he went off to war, Hewes never made a go of it as a shoemaker. He remembered these years more fondly than he had lived them. As Hawkes took down his story, shifting from the third to the first person:

Hewes said he cheerfully submitted to the course of life to which his destinies directed.

He built him a shop and pursued the private avocation of his trade for a considerable length of time, until on the application of his brother he was induced to go with him on two fishing voy-ages to the banks of New Foundland, which occu-pied his time for two years.

After the conclusion of the French war . . . he continued at Boston, except the two years absence with his brother.

During that period, said Hewes, when I was at the age of twenty-six, I married the daughter of Benjamin Sumner, of Boston. At the time of our intermarriage, the age of my wife was seventeen. We lived together very happily seventy years. She died at the age of eighty-seven.

At the time when British troops were first sta-tioned at Boston, we had several children, the exact number I do not recollect. By our industry and mutual efforts we were improving our condition.

He had his own shop—this much is clear, but the rest is surmise. There were at that time in Boston about sixty to seventy shoemakers, most of whom seem to have catered to the local market. If Hewes was typical, he would have made shoes to order, "bespoke" work; this would have made him a cordwainer. And he would have repaired shoes: this would have made him a cob-bler. Who were his customers? No business records survive. A shoemaker probably drew his customers from his immediate neighborhood. Located as he was near the waterfront and rope-walks, Hewes might well have had customers of the "meaner" sort. In a ward inhabited by the "middling" sort he may also have drawn on them. When the British troops occupied Boston, he did some work for them. Nothing suggests that he catered to the "carriage trade."

Was his business "improving" or "growing better"? Probably it was never very good and grew worse. From his own words we know that he took off two years on fishing voyages with his brothers. He did not mention that during this period he lived for a short time in Roxbury. His prospects were thus not good enough to keep him in Boston. His marriage is another clue to his low fortune. Sally (or Sarah) Sumner's father was a sexton so poor that his wife and daughters had to take in washing. The couple was married by the Reverend Samuel Stillman of the First Baptist Church, which suggests that this was the church that Benjamin Sumner served. Though Stillman was respected, First Baptist was not "one of the principal churches in town," as Thatcher guessed, but one of the poorest and smallest, with a congregation heavy with laboring people, sailors, and blacks. Marriage, one of the few potential sources of capital for an aspiring tradesman, as Benjamin Franklin made clear in his autobiography, did not lift Hewes up.

Hewes stayed poor. The Boston tax records of 1771, the only ones that have survived for these years, show him living as a lodger in the house of Christopher Ranks, a watchmaker, in the old North End. He was not taxed for any property. In 1773 he and his family, which now included three children, were apparently living with his uncle Robert in the South End; at some time during these years before the war they also lived with a brother. After almost a decade on his own, Hewes could not afford his own place. In January 1774 he inadvertently summed up his condition and reputation in the course of a violent street encounter. Damned as "a rascal" and "a vagabond" who had no right to "speak to a gentlemen in the street," Hewes retorted that he was neither "and though a poor man, in a good credit in town" as his well-to-do antagonist.

Between 1768 and 1775, the shoemaker became a citizen—an active participant in the events that led to the Revolution, an angry, assertive man who won recognition as a patriot. What explains the transformation? We have enough evidence to take stock of Hewes's role in three major events of the decade: the Massacre (1770), the Tea Party (1773), and the tarring and feathering of John Malcolm (1774).

On the night of the Massacre, March 5, Hewes was in the thick of the action. What he tells us about what brought him to King Street, what brought others there, and what he did during and after this tumultuous event gives us the perspective of a man in the street. The presence of British troops in Boston beginning in the summer of 1768—four thousand soldiers in a town of fewer than sixteen thousand inhabitants—touched Hewes personally. Anecdotes about soldiers flowed from him. He had seen them march off the transports at the Long Wharf; he had seen them every day occupying civilian buildings on Griffin's Wharf near his shop. He knew how irritating it was to be challenged by British sentries after curfew (his solution was to offer a swig of rum from the bottle he carried).

More important, he was personally cheated by a soldier. Sergeant Mark Burk ordered shoes allegedly for Captain Thomas Preston, picked them up, but never paid for them. Hewes complained to Preston, who made good and suggested he bring a complaint. A military hearing ensued, at which Hewes testified. The soldier, to Hewes's horror, was sentenced to three hundred fifty lashes. He "remarked to the court that if he had thought the fellow was to be punished so severely for such an offense, bad as he was, he would have said nothing about it." And he saw others victimized by soldiers. He witnessed an incident in which a soldier sneaked up behind a woman, felled her with his fist, and "stripped her of her bonnet, cardinal muff and tippet." He followed the man to his barracks, identified him (Hewes remembered him as Private Kilroy, who would appear later at the Massacre), and got him to give up the stolen goods, but decided this time not to press charges. Hewes was also keenly aware of grievances felt by the laboring men and youths who formed the bulk of the crowd—and the principal victims—at the Massacre. From extant accounts, three causes can be pieced together.

First in time, and vividly recalled by Hewes, was the murder of eleven-year-old Christopher Seider on February 23, ten days before the

Massacre. Seider was one of a large crowd of schoolboys and apprentices picketing the shop of Theophilus Lilly, a merchant violating the anti-import resolutions. Ebenezer Richardson, a paid customs informer, shot into the throng and killed Seider. Richardson would have been tarred and feathered, or worse, had not whig leaders intervened to hustle him off to jail. At Seider's funeral, only a week before the Massacre, five hundred boys marched two by two behind the coffin, followed by two thousand or more adults, "the largest [funeral] perhaps ever known in America," Thomas Hutchinson thought.

Second, Hewes emphasized the bitter fight two days before the Massacre between soldiers and workers at Gray's ropewalk down the block from Hewes's shop. Off-duty soldiers were allowed to moonlight, taking work from civilians. On Friday, March 3, when one of them asked for work at Gray's, a battle ensued between a few score soldiers and ropewalk workers joined by others in the maritime trades. The soldiers were beaten and sought revenge. Consequently, in Thatcher's words, "quite a number of soldiers, in a word, were determined to have a row on the night of the 5th."

Third, the precipitating events on the night of the Massacre, by Hewes's account, were an attempt by a barber's apprentice to collect an overdue bill from a British officer, the sentry's abuse of the boy, and the subsequent harassment of the sentry by a small band of boys that led to the calling of the guard commanded by Captain Preston. Thatcher found this hard to swallow—"a dun from a greasy barber's boy is rather an extraordinary explanation of the origin, or one of the occasions, of the massacre of the 5th of March"—but at the trial the lawyers did not. They battled over defining "boys" and over the age, size, and degree of aggressiveness of the numerous apprentices on the scene.

Hewes viewed the civilians as essentially defensive. On the evening of the Massacre he appeared early on the scene in King Street, attracted by the clamor over the apprentice. "I

was soon on the ground among them," he said, as if it were only natural that he should have turned out in defense of fellow townsmen against what was assumed to be the danger of aggressive action by soldiers. He was not part of a conspiracy; neither was he there out of curiosity. He was unarmed, carrying neither club nor stave as some others did. He saw snow, ice, and "missiles" thrown at the soldiers. When the main guard rushed out in support of the sentry, Private Kilroy dealt Hewes a blow on his shoulder with his gun. Preston ordered the townspeople to disperse. Hewes believed they had a legal basis to refuse: "they were in the king's highway, and had as good a right to be there" as Preston.

The five men killed were all workingmen. Hewes claimed to know four: Samuel Gray, a ropewalk worker; Samuel Maverick, age seventeen, an apprentice to an ivory turner; Patrick Carr, an apprentice to a leather breeches worker; and James Caldwell, second mate on a ship—all but Christopher Attucks. Caldwell, "who was shot in the back was standing by the side of Hewes, and the latter caught him in his arms as he fell," helped carry him to Dr. Thomas Young in Prison Lane, then ran to Caldwell's ship captain on Cold Lane.

More than horror was burned into Hewes's memory. He remembered the political confrontation that followed the slaughter, when thousands of angry townspeople faced hundreds of British troops massed with ready rifles. "The people," Hewes recounted, "then immediately choose a committee to report to the governor the result of Captain Preston's conduct, and to demand of him satisfaction." Actually the "people" did not choose a committee "immediately." In the dark hours after the Massacre a self-appointed group of patriot leaders met with officials and forced Hutchinson to commit Preston and the soldiers to jail. Hewes was remembering the town meeting the next day, so huge that it had to adjourn from Fanueil Hall, the traditional meeting place that held only twelve hundred, to Old South Church, which had room for five to six thousand. This meeting approved a committee to wait on officials and then adjourned, but met again the same day, received and voted down an offer to remove one regiment, then accepted another to remove two. This was one of the meetings at which property bars were let down.

What Hewes did not recount, but what he had promptly put down in a deposition the next day, was how militant he was after the Massacre. At 1:00 A.M., like many other enraged Bostonians, he went home to arm himself. On his way back to the Town House with a cane he had a defiant exchange with Sergeant Chambers of the 29th Regiment and eight or nine soldiers, "all with very large clubs or cutlasses." A soldier, Dobson, "ask'd him how he far'd; he told him very badly to see his townsmen shot in such a manner, and asked him if he did not think it was a dreadful thing." Dobson swore "it was a fine thing" and "you shall see more of it." Chambers "seized and forced" the cane from Hewes, "saying I had no right to carry it. I told him I had as good a right to carry a cane as they had to carry clubs."

The Massacre had stirred Hewes to political action. He was one of ninety-nine Bostonians who gave depositions for the prosecution that were published by the town in a pamphlet. Undoubtedly, he marched in the great funeral procession for the victims that brought the city to a standstill. He attended the tempestuous trial of Ebenezer Richardson, Seider's slayer, which was linked politically with the Massacre. ("He remembers to this moment even the precise words of the Judge's sentence," wrote Thatcher.) He seems to have attended the trial of the soldiers or Preston or both.

It was in this context that he remembered something for which there is no corroborating evidence, namely, testifying at Preston's trial on a crucial point. He told Hawkes:

When Preston, their captain, was tried, I was called as one of the witnesses, on the part of the government, and testified, that I believed it was the same man, Captain Preston, that ordered his soldiers to make ready, who also ordered them to fire. Mr. John Adams, former president of the

United States, was advocate for the prisoners, and denied the fact, that Captain Preston gave orders to his men to fire; and on his cross examination of me asked whether my position was such, that I could see the captain's lips in motion when the order to fire was given; to which I answered, that I could not.

Perhaps so: Hewes's account is particular and precise, and there are many lacunae in the record of the trial (we have no verbatim transcript) that modern editors have assiduously assembled. Perhaps not: Hewes may have "remembered" his brother Shubael on the stand at the trial of the soldiers (although Shubael was a defense witness) or his uncle Robert testifying at Richardson's trial. Or he may have given pretrial testimony but was not called to the stand.

In one sense, it does not matter. What he was remembering was that he had become involved. He turned out because of a sense of kinship with "his townsmen" in danger; he stood his ground in defense of his "rights"; he was among the "people" who delegated a committee to act on their behalf; he took part in the legal process by giving a deposition, by attending the trials, and as he remembered it, by testifying. In sum, he had become a citizen, a political man.

Four years later, at the Tea Party on the night of December 16, 1773, the citizen "volunteered" and became the kind of leader for whom most historians have never found a place. The Tea Party, unlike the Massacre, was organized by the radical whig leaders of Boston. They mapped the strategy, organized the public meetings, appointed the companies to guard the tea ships at Griffin's Wharf (among them Daniel Hewes, George's brother), and planned the official boarding parties. As in 1770, they converted the town meetings into meetings of "the whole body of the people," one of which Hutchinson found "consisted principally of the Lower ranks of the People & even Journeymen. Tradesmen were brought in to increase the number & the Rabble were not excluded yet there were divers Gentlemen of Good Fortunes among them."

The boarding parties showed this same combination of "ranks." Hawkes wrote:

On my inquiring of Hewes if he knew who first proposed the project of destroying the tea, to prevent its being landed, he replied that he did not; neither did he know who or what number were to volunteer their services for that purpose. But from the significant allusion of some persons in whom I had confidence, together with the knowledge I had of the spirit of those times, I had no doubt but that a sufficient number of associates would accompany me in that enterprise.

The recollection of Joshua Wyeth, a journeyman blacksmith, verified Hewes's story in explicit detail: "It was proposed that young men, not much known in town and not liable to be easily recognized should lead in the business." Wyeth believed that "most of the persons selected for the occasion were apprentices and journeyman, as was the case with myself, living with tory masters." Wyeth "had but a few hours warning of what was intended to be done." Those in the officially designated parties, about thirty men better known, appeared in well-prepared Indian disguises. As nobodies, the volunteers—anywhere from fifty to one hundred men—could get away with hastily improvised disguises. Hewes said he got himself up as an Indian and daubed his "face and hands with coal dust in the shop of blacksmith." In the streets "I fell in with many who were dressed, equipped and painted as I was, and who fell in with me and marched in order to the place of our destination."

At Griffin's Wharf the volunteers were orderly, self-disciplined, and ready to accept leadership.

When we arrived at the wharf, there were three of our number who assumed an authority to direct our operations, to which we readily submitted. They divided us into three parties, for the purpose of boarding the three ships which contained the tea at the same time. The name of him who commanded the division to which I was assigned was Leonard Pitt [Lendell Pitts]. The names of the other commanders I never knew. We were immediately ordered by the respective commanders to board all the ships at the same time, which we promptly obeyed.

But for Hewes there was something new: he was singled out of the rank and file and made an officer in the field.

The commander of the division to which I belonged, as soon as we were on board the ship, appointed me boatswain, and ordered me to go to the captain and demand of him the keys to the hatches and a dozen candles. I made the demand accordingly, and the captain promptly replied, and delivered the articles; but requested me at the same time to do no damage to the ship or rigging. We then were ordered by our commander to open the hatches, and take out all the chests of tea and throw them overboard, and we immediately proceeded to execute his orders; first cutting and splitting the chests with our tomahawks, so as thoroughly to expose them to the effects of the water. In about three hours from the time we went on board, we had thus broken and thrown overboard every tea chest to be found in the ship; while those in the other ships were disposing of the tea in the same way, at the same time. We were surrounded by British armed ships, but no attempt was made to resist us. We then quietly retired to our several places of residence, without having any conversation with each other, or taking any measure to discover who were our associates.

As the Tea Party ended, Hewes was stirred to further action on his own initiative, just as he had been in the hours after the Massacre. While the crews were throwing the tea overboard, a few other men tried to smuggle off some of the tea scattered on the decks. "One Captain O'Connor whom I well knew," said Hewes, "came on board for that purpose, and when he supposed he was not noticed, filled his pockets, and also the lining of his coat. But I had detected him, and gave information to the captain of what he was doing. We were ordered to take him into custody, and just as he was stepping from the vessel, I seized him by the skirt of his coat, and in attempting to pull him back, I tore it off." They scuffled. O'Connor recognized him and "threatened to 'complain to the Governor.' 'You had better make your will first,' quoth Hewes, doubling his fist expressively," and O'Connor escaped, running the gauntlet of the crowd on the wharf. "The next day we nailed the skirt of his coat, which I had pulled off, to the whipping post in Charlestown, the place of his residence, with a label upon it," to shame O'Connor by "popular indignation."

A month later, at the third event for which we have full evidence, Hewes won public recognition for an act of courage that almost cost his life and precipitated the most publicized tarring and feathering of the Revolution. The incident that set it off would have been trivial at any other time. On Tuesday, January 25, 1774, at about two in the afternoon, the shoemaker was making his way back to his shop after his dinner. According to the very full account in the *Massachusetts Gazette,*

> Mr. George-Robert-Twelves-Hewes was coming along Fore-Street, near Captain Ridgway's, and found the redoubted John Malcolm, standing over a small boy, who was pushing a little sled before him, cursing, damning, threatening and shaking a very large cane with a very heavy ferril on it over his head. The boy at that time was perfectly quiet, notwithstanding which Malcolm continued his threats of striking him, which Mr. Hewes conceiving if he struck him with that weapon he must have killed him out-right, came up to him, and said to him, Mr. Malcolm I hope you are not going to strike this boy with that stick.

Malcolm had already acquired an odious reputation with patriots of the lower sort. A Bostonian, he had been a sea captain, an army officer, and recently an employee of the customs service. He was so strong a supporter of royal authority that he had traveled to North Carolina to fight the Regulators and boasted of having a horse shot out from under him. He had a fiery temper. As a customs informer he was known to have turned in a vessel to punish sailors for petty smuggling, a custom of the sea. In November 1773, near Portsmouth, New Hampshire, a crowd of thirty sailors had "genteely tarr'd and feather'd" him, as the *Boston Gazette* put it: they did the job over his clothes. Back in Boston he made "frequent complaints" to Hutchinson of "being hooted at in the streets" for this by "tradesmen"; and the lieutenant governor cautioned him, "being a passionate man," not to reply in kind.

The exchange between Malcolm and Hewes resonated with class as well as political differences:

> Malcolm returned, you are an impertinent rascal, it is none of your business. Mr. Hewes then asked him, what had the child done to him. Malcolm damned him and asked him if he was going to take his part? Mr. Hewes answered no further than this, that he thought it was a shame for him to strike the child with such a club that, if he intended to strike him. Malcolm on that damned Mr. Hewes, called him a vagabond, and said he would let him know he should not speak to a gentleman in the street. Mr. Hewes returned to that, he was neither a rascal nor vagabond, and though a poor man was in as good credit in town as he was. Malcolm called him a liar, and said he was not, nor ever would be. Mr. Hewes retorted, be that as it will, I never was tarred nor feathered any how. On this Malcolm struck him, and wounded him deeply on the forehead, so that Mr. Hewes for some time lost his senses. Capt. Godfrey, then present, interposed, and after some altercation, Malcolm went home.

Hewes was rushed to Joseph Warren, the patriot doctor, his distant relative. Malcolm's cane had almost penetrated his skull. Thatcher found "the indentation as plainly perceptible as it was sixty years ago." So did Hawkes. Warren dressed the wound, and Hewes was able to make his way to a magistrate to swear out a warrant for Malcolm's arrest "which he carried to a constable named Justice Hale." Malcolm, meanwhile, had retreated to his house, where he responded in white heat to taunts about the half-way tarring and feathering in Portsmouth with "damn you let me see the man that dare do it better."

In the evening a crowd took Malcolm from his house and dragged him on a sled into King Street "amidst the huzzas of thousands." At this point "several gentlemen endeavored to divert the populace from their intention." The ensuing dialogue laid bare the clash of conceptions of justice between the sailors and laboring people heading the action and Sons of Liberty leaders. The "gentlemen" argued that Malcolm was "open to the laws of the land which would undoubtedly award a reasonable satisfaction to the parties he had abused," that is, the child and Hewes. The answer was political. Malcolm "had been an old impudent and mischievous [sic] offender—he had joined in the murders at North Carolina—he had seized vessels on account of sailors having a bottle or two of gin on board—he had in other words behaved in the most capricious, insulting and daringly abusive manner." He could not be trusted to justice. "When they were told the law would have its course with him, they asked what course had the law taken with Preston or his soldiers, with Capt. Wilson or Richardson? And for their parts they had seen so much partiality to the soldiers and customhouse officers by the present Judges, that while things remained as they were, they would, on all such occasions, take satisfaction their own way, and let them take it off."

The references were to Captain Preston who had been tried and found innocent of the Massacre, the soldiers who had been let off with token punishment, Captain John Wilson, who had been indicted for inciting slaves to murder their masters but never tried, and Ebenezer Richardson, who had been tried and found guilty of killing Seider, sentenced, and then pardoned by the crown.

The crowd won and proceeded to a ritualized tarring and feathering, the purpose of which was to punish Malcolm, force a recantation, and ostracize him.

> With these and such like arguments, together with a gentle crouding of persons not of their way of thinking out of the ring they proceeded to elevate Mr. Malcolm from his sled into a cart, and stripping him to buff and breeches, gave him a modern jacket [a coat of tar and feathers] and hied him away to liberty-tree, where they proposed to him to renounce his present commission, and swear that he would never hold another inconsistent with the liberties of his country; but this he obstinately refusing, they then carried him to the gallows, passed a rope round his neck, and threw the other end over the beam as if they intended to hang him: But this manoeuvre he set at defiance. They then

basted him for some time with a rope's end, and threatened to cut his ears off, and on this he complied, and then they brought him home.

Hewes had precipitated an electrifying event. It was part of the upsurge of spontaneous action in the wake of the Tea Party that prompted the whig leaders to promote a "Committee for Tarring and Feathering" as an instrument of crowd control. The "Committee" made its appearance in broadsides signed by "Captain Joyce, Jun.," a sobriquet meant to invoke the bold cornet who had captured King Charles in 1647. The event was reported in the English newspapers, popularized in three or four satirical prints, and dramatized still further when Malcolm went to England, where he campaigned for a pension and ran for Parliament (without success) against John Wilkes, the leading champion of America. The event confirmed the British ministry in its punitive effort to bring rebellious Boston to heel.

The denouement of the affair was an incident several weeks later. "Malcolm recovered from his wounds and went about as usual. 'How do you do, Mr. Malcolm?' said Hewes, very civilly, the next time he met him. 'Your humble servant, Mr. George Robert Twelves Hewes,' quoth he,—touching his hat genteely as he passed by. 'Thank ye,' thought Hewes, 'and I am glad you have learned *better manners at last.*'" Hewes's mood was one of triumph. Malcolm had been taught a lesson. The issue was respect for Hewes, a patriot, a poor man, an honest citizen, a decent man standing up for a child against an unspeakably arrogant "gentleman" who was an enemy of his country.

Hewes's role in these three events fits few of the categories that historians have applied to the participation of ordinary men in the Revolution. He was not a member of any organized committee, caucus, or club. He did not attend the expensive public dinners of the Sons of Liberty. He was capable of acting on his own volition without being summoned by any leaders (as in the Massacre). He could volunteer and assume leadership (as in the Tea Party). He was at home on the streets in crowds but he could also reject a crowd (as in the tarring and feathering of Malcolm). He was at home in the other places where ordinary Bostonians turned out to express their convictions: at funeral processions, at meetings of the "whole body of people," in courtrooms at public trials. He recoiled from violence to persons if not to property. The man who could remember the whippings of his own boyhood did not want to be the source of pain to others, whether Sergeant Burk, who tried to cheat him over a pair of shoes, or John Malcolm, who almost killed him. It is in keeping with his character that he should have come to the aid of a little boy facing a beating.

Hewes was moved to act by personal experiences that he shared with large numbers of other plebeian Bostonians. He seems to have been politicized, not by the Stamp Act, but by the coming of the troops after 1768, and then by things that happened to him, that he saw, or that happened to people he knew. Once aroused, he took action with others of his own rank and condition—the laboring classes who formed the bulk of the actors at the Massacre, the Tea Party, and the Malcolm affair—and with other members of his family: his uncle Robert, "known for a staunch Liberty Boy," and his brother Daniel, a guard at the tea ship. Shubael, alone among his brothers, became a tory. These shared experiences were interpreted and focused more likely by the spoken than the written word and as much by his peers at taverns and crowd actions as by leaders in huge public meetings.

But what ideas did Hewes articulate? He spoke of what he did but very little of what he thought. In the brief statement he offered Hawkes about why he went off to war in 1776, he expressed a commitment to general principles as they had been brought home to him by his experiences. "I was continually reflecting upon the unwarrantable sufferings inflicted on the citizens of Boston by the usurpation and tyranny of Great Britain, and my mind was excited with an unextinguishable desire to aid in chastising them." When Hawkes expressed a doubt "as to the correctness of his conduct in absenting himself from his family," Hewes "emphatically reiterated" the same phrases, adding to a "desire to aid in chastising them" the phrase "and securing our independence." This was clearly not an afterthought; it probably reflected the way many others moved toward the goal of Independence, not as a matter of original intent, but as a step made necessary when all other resorts failed. Ideology thus did not set George Hewes apart from Samuel Adams or John Hancock. The difference lies in what the Revolution did to him as a person. His experiences transformed him, giving him a sense of citizenship and personal worth. Adams and Hancock began with both; Hewes had to arrive there, and in arriving he cast off the constraints of deference.

KEY TERMS

John Hancock (1737–1793): Wealthy Boston merchant and Revolutionary leader, President of the Continental Congress (1775–1777) and first signer of the Declaration of Independence.

Dr. Joseph Warren (1741–1775): Physician and political leader in Revolutionary Boston, killed in the Battle of Bunker Hill (June 17, 1775).

Training Day: A day set aside in Massachusetts for compulsory military training.

Anti-Importation resolutions: A voluntary agreement of American merchants in the Continental Association not to trade with Britain.

Tea Party: Popular protest on December 16, 1773, directed against the British tea tax retained after the repeal of the Townshend Acts. Protesters disguised as Native Americans boarded three tea ships and threw the tea into Boston harbor.

DISCUSSION TOPICS

After reading this essay, you should be able to discuss:

1. The concept of deference.

2. The ways in which Hewes's attitudes changed during the Revolutionary era.

3. The experiences that brought about these changes in attitude.

4. The expectations that Hewes had about the position of men like himself in the aftermath of the Revolution.

8

A "Most Undisciplined, Profligate
Crew": Protest and Defiance in
the Continental Ranks, 1776–1783

James Kirby Martin

During the first year of the Revolutionary War, the patriot cause enjoyed wide-spread enthusiasm and support. Expecting a short war with relatively little loss of life and damage to property, American men of all ranks joined local militia units in 1775–1776 to defend their homes and families from British "corruption" and from the red-coated army that had been sent to put down the colonial "rebellion." But as it became clear that this would be a long and costly struggle, men of middling and upper rank began to purchase substitutes or pay nominal fines for nonservice and withdrew to private life. After 1777, the bulk of military service fell to the lower ranks of American society—to poor farmers, laborers, indentured servants, slaves, and free men of color.

In this essay, James Kirby Martin recounts the struggles of these "dispensable" men as they battled not only the British army and epidemic disease but also a lack of support from the Continental Congress and the populace. Martin suggests that these men—poorly equipped and ill-fed, their pay always months in arrears—persevered less from patriotic commitment than from the Congress's promises of freedom to bondsmen and free western land to those who enlisted for the duration of the war. More than any other consideration, the prospects of escaping from the bottom of eighteenth-century society and of achieving freedom and a modest foothold on the social ladder kept Washington's army in the field during the long years of the war.

"A 'Most Undisciplined, Profligate Crew': Protest and Defiance in the Continental Ranks, 1776–1783" from *Arms and Independence: The Military Character of the American Revolution*, eds. Ronald Hoffman and Peter J. Albert (Charlottesville: Virginia, 1984), pp. 119–140. Reprinted by permission of the University Press of Virginia.

Martin's account attempts to sort out the motivations and political consciousness of ordinary people. In the heroic version of the American Revolution, men were motivated by "the Spirit of '76"—a love of liberty and a hatred of arbitrary authority. In this more sober account, ordinary people looked to their own interests and chances for advancement. In reading this essay, keep in mind the possibility that both considerations played a role in popular allegiance to the revolutionary cause.

A sequence of events inconceivable to Americans raised on patriotic myths about the Revolution occurred in New Jersey during the spring of 1779. For months the officers of the Jersey brigade had been complaining loudly about everything from lack of decent food and clothing to pay arrearages and late payments in rapidly depreciating currency. They had petitioned their assembly earlier, but nothing had happened. They petitioned again in mid-April 1779, acting on the belief that the legislature should "be informed that our pay is now only *minimal*, not *real*, that four months' pay of a private will not procure his wretched wife and children a single bushel of wheat." Using "the most plain and unambiguous terms," they stressed that "unless a speedy and ample remedy be provided, the total dissolution of your troops is inevitable." The Jersey assembly responded to this plea in its usual fashion—it forwarded the petition to the Continental Congress without comment. After all, the officers, although from New Jersey, were a part of the Continental military establishment.

The assembly's behavior only further angered the officers, and some of them decided to demonstrate their resolve. On May 6 the brigade received orders to join John Sullivan's expedition against the Six Nations. That same day, officers in the First Regiment sent forth yet another petition. They again admonished the assembly about pay and supply issues. While they stated that they would prepare the regiment for the upcoming campaign, they themselves would resign as a group unless the legislators addressed their demands. Complaints had now turned into something more than gentlemanly protest. Protest was on the verge of becoming nothing less than open defiance of

civil authority, and the Jersey officers were deadly serious. They had resorted to their threatened resignations to insure that the assembly would give serious attention to their demands—for a change.

When George Washington learned about the situation, he was appalled. "Nothing, which has happened in the course of the war, . . . has given me so much pain," the commander in chief stated anxiously. It upset him that the officers seemingly had lost sight of the "principles" that governed the cause. What would happen, he asked rhetorically, "if their example should be followed and become general?" The result would be the "ruin" and "disgrace" of the rebel cause, all because these officers had *"reasoned wrong about the means of obtaining a good end."*

So developed a little known but highly revealing confrontation. Washington told Congress that he would have acted very aggressively toward the recalcitrant officers, except that "the causes of discontent are too great and too general and the ties that bind the officers to the service too feeble" to force the issue. What he did promise was that he would not countenance any aid that came "in [such] a manner extorted." On the other hand, the officers had been asking the assembly for relief since January 1778, but to no avail. They, too, were not about to be moved.

The New Jersey legislature was the political institution with the ability to break the deadlock. Some of the legislators preferred disbanding the brigade. The majority argued that other officers and common soldiers might follow the First Regiment's lead and warned that the war effort could hardly succeed without a Continental military establishment. The moment was now ripe for compromise. The assemblymen agreed to provide the officers with whatever immediate relief could be mustered in return for the latter calling back their petitions. That way civil authorities would not be succumbing to intimidation by representatives of the military establishment, and the principle of subordination of military to civil authority would remain inviolate. The assembly thus provided an immediate payment of £200 to each officer and $40 to each soldier. Accepting the compromise settlement as better than nothing, the brigade moved out of its Jersey encampment on May 11 and marched toward Sullivan's bivouac at Easton, Pennsylvania. Seemingly, all now had returned to normal.

The confrontation between the New Jersey officers and the state assembly serves to illuminate some key points about protest and defiance in the Continental ranks during the years 1776–83. Most important here, it underscores the mounting anger felt by Washington's regulars as a result of their perceived (and no doubt very real) lack of material and psychological support from the society that had spawned the Continental army. It is common knowledge that Washington's regulars suffered from serious supply and pay shortages throughout the war. Increasingly, historians are coming to realize that officers and common soldiers alike received very little moral support from the general populace. As yet, however, scholars have not taken a systematic look at one product of this paradigm of neglect, specifically, protest and defiance. The purpose of this essay is to present preliminary findings that will facilitate that task.

Given that there was a noticeable relationship between lack of material and psychological support from the civilian sector and mounting protest and defiance in the ranks, it is also important to make clear that patterns of protest were very complex. A second purpose of this essay is to outline those basic patterns and to indicate why protest and defiance did not result in serious internal upheaval between army and society in the midst of the War for American Independence. To begin this assessment, we must bring Washington's Continentals to the center of the historical arena.

During the past twenty years, historians have learned that there were at least two Continental armies. The army of 1775–76 might be characterized as a republican constabulary, consisting of citizens who had respectable amounts of property and who were defending hearth and home. They came out for what they believed would be a rather short contest in which their assumed virtue and moral commitment would easily carry the day over seasoned British regulars not necessarily wedded to anything of greater concern than filling their own pocketbooks as mercenaries.

The first army had a militialike appearance. Even though phrases of commitment were high sounding, there was not much discipline or rigorous training. These early soldiers had responded to appeals from leaders who warned about "our wives and children, with everything that is dear to us, [being] subjected to the merciless rage of uncontrolled despotism." They were convinced that they were "engaged . . . in the cause of virtue, of liberty, of *God*." Unfortunately, the crushing blows endured in the massive British offensive of 1776 against New York undercut such high-sounding phrases about self-sacrifice. The message at the end of 1775 had been "Persevere, ye guardians of liberty." They did not.

The second Continental establishment took form out of the remains of the first. Even before Washington executed his magnificent turnabout at Trenton and Princeton, he had called for a "respectable army," one built on long-term enlistments, thorough training, and high standards of discipline. The army's command, as well as many delegates in Congress, now wanted soldiers who could stand up against the enemy with more than notions of exalted virtue and moral superiority to upgird them. They called for able-bodied men who could and would endure for the long-term fight in a contest that all leaders now knew could not be sustained by feelings of moral superiority and righteousness alone.

To assist in overcoming manpower shortages, Congress and the states enhanced financial promises made to potential enlistees. Besides guarantees about decent food and clothing, recruiters handed out bounty moneys and promises of free land at war's end (normally only for long-term service). Despite these financial incentives, there was no great rush to the Continental banner. For the remainder of the war, the army's command, Congress, and the states struggled to maintain minimal numbers of Continental soldiers in the ranks.

In fact, all began to search diligently for new recruits. Instead of relying on propertied freeholders and tradesmen of the ideal citizen-soldier type, they broadened the definition of what constituted an "able-bodied and effective" recruit. For example, New Jersey in early 1777 started granting exemptions to all those who hired substitutes for long-term Continental service—and to masters who would enroll indentured servants and slaves. The following year Maryland permitted the virtual impressment of vagrants for nine months of regular service. Massachusetts set another kind of precedent in 1777 by declaring blacks (both slave and free) eligible for the state draft. Shortly thereafter, Rhode Islanders set about the business of raising two black battalions. Ultimately, Maryland and Virginia permitted slaves to substitute for whites. The lower South, however, refused to do so, even in the face of a successful British invasion later in the war.

The vast majority of Continentals who fought with Washington after 1776 were representative of the very poorest and most repressed persons in Revolutionary society. A number of recent studies have verified that a large proportion of the Continentals in the second establishment represented ne'er-do-wells, drifters, unemployed laborers, captured British soldiers and Hessians, indentured servants, and slaves. Some of these new regulars were in such desperate economic straits that states had to pass laws prohibiting creditors from pulling them from the ranks and having them thrown in jail for petty debts. (Obviously, this was not a problem with the unfree.)

The most important point to be derived from this dramatic shift in the social composition of the Continental army is that few of these new common soldiers had enjoyed anything close to economic prosperity or full political (or legal) liberty before the war. As a group, they had something to gain from service. If they could survive the rigors of camp life, the killing diseases that so often ravaged the armies of their times, and the carnage of skirmishes and full-scale battles, they could look forward to a better life for themselves at the end of the war. Not only were they to have decent food and clothing and regular pay until the British had been irrevocably beaten, they had also been promised free land (and personal freedom in the cases of indentured servants, black slaves, and criminals). Recruiters thus conveyed a message of personal upward mobility through service. In exchange for personal sacrifice in the short run, there was the prospect of something far better in the long run, paralleling and epitomizing the collective rebel quest for a freer political life in the New World.

To debate whether these new Continentals were motivated to enlist because of crass materialism or benevolent patriotism is to sidetrack the issue. A combination of factors was no doubt at work in the mind of each recruit or conscript. Far more important, especially if we are to comprehend the ramifications of protest and defiance among soldiers and officers, we must understand that respectably established citizens after 1775 and 1776 preferred to let others perform the dirty work of regular, long-term service on their behalf, essentially on a contractual basis. Their legislators gave bounties and *promised* many other incentives. Increasingly, as the war lengthened, the civilian population and its leaders did a less effective job in keeping their part of the agreement. One significant outcome of this obvious civilian ingratitude, if not utter disregard for contractual promises, was protest and defiance coming from Washington's beleaguered soldiers and officers.

That relations between Washington's post-1776 army and Revolutionary society deteriorated dramatically hardly comes as a surprise to those historians who have investigated surviving records. Widespread anger among the rank and file became most demonstrable in 1779 and 1780, at the very nadir of the war effort. Pvt. Joseph Plumb Martin captured the feelings of his comrades when he reflected back on support for the army in 1780. He wrote: "We therefore still kept upon our parade in groups, venting our spleen at our country and government, then at our officers, and then at ourselves for our imbecility in staying there and starving in detail for an ungrateful people who did not care what became of us, so they could enjoy themselves while we were keeping a cruel enemy from them." Gen. John Paterson, who spoke out in March 1780, summarized feelings among many officers when he said, "It really gives me great pain to think of our public affairs; where is the public spirit of the year 1775? Where are those flaming *patriots* who were ready to sacrifice their lives, their fortunes, their all, for the public?" Such thoughts were not dissimilar from those of "A Jersey Soldier" who poured his sentiments into an editorial during May 1779 in support of those regimental officers who were trying to exact some form of financial justice from their state legislature. The army, he pointed out, had put up with "a load . . . grown almost intolerable." "It must be truly mortifying to the virtuous soldier to observe many, at this day, displaying their cash, and sauntering in idleness and luxury," he went on, including "the gentry . . . [who] are among the foremost to despise our poverty and laugh at our distress." He certainly approved the actions of his comrades because he resented "the cruel and ungrateful disposition of the people in general, in withholding from the army even the praise and glory justly due to their merit and services," just as he resented society's failure to live up to its contract with the soldiers. These statements, which are only a representative sampling, indicate that the army had come to believe that Revolutionary civilians had taken advantage of them—and had broken their part of the contract for military services.

There were real dangers hidden behind these words. With each passing month beginning in 1777, Washington's regulars, especially that small cadre that was signing on for the long-term fight, became more professional in military demeanor. Among other things, including their enhanced potential effectiveness in combat, this meant that soldiers felt the enveloping (and reassuring) bonds of "unit cohesion." The immediate thoughts of individual soldiers, whether recruited, dragooned, or pressed into service, became attached to their respective primary units in the army, such as the particular companies or regiments in which they served. The phenomenon was nothing more than a developing comradeship in arms. Any threat or insult thus became an assault on the group, especially if that threat or insult were directed at all members of the group. The bonding effect of unit cohesion suggests that collective protest and defiance would become more of a danger to a generally unsupportive society with each passing month, unless civilians who had made grand promises started to meet their contractual obligations more effectively.

Indeed, the most readily observable pattern in Continental army protest and defiance was that it took on more and more of a collective (and menacing) character through time. At the outset, especially beginning in 1776, most protest had an individual character. Frequently it was the raw recruit, quite often anxious for martial glory but quickly disillusioned with the realities of military service once in camp, who struck back against undesirable circumstances. Protest could come through such diverse expressions as swearing, excessive drinking, assaulting officers, deserting, or bounty jumping. One source of such behavior was the dehumanizing, even brutal nature of camp life. Another had to do with broken promises about pay, food, and clothing. A third was a dawning sense that too many civilians held the soldiery in disregard, if not utter contempt.

It must be remembered that middle- and upper-class civilians considered Washington's new regulars to be representative of the "vulgar herd" in a society that still clung to deferential values. The assumption was that the most fit in terms of wealth and community social standing were to lead while the least fit were to follow, even when that meant becoming little more than human cannon fodder. Perhaps James Warren of Massachusetts summarized the social perceptions of "respectable" citizens as well as any of the "better sort" when he described Washington's troops in 1776 as "the most undisciplined, profligate Crew that were ever collected" to fight a war.

While civilians often ridiculed the new regulars as riffraff, troublemakers, or mere hirelings (while conveniently ignoring the precept that military service was an assumed obligation of all citizens in a liberty-loving commonwealth), individual soldiers did not hold back in protesting their circumstances. In many cases, they had already acknowledged the personal reality of downtrodden status before entering the ranks. Acceptance of these circumstances and the conditions of camp life did not mean, however, that these new soldiers would be passive. Thus it may be an error to dismiss heavy swearing around civilians or repeated drunkenness in camp as nothing more than manifestations of "time-honored military vices," to borrow the words of one recent student of the war period.

At least in some instances, individual soldiers could have been making statements about their sense of personal entrapment. Furthermore, protest through such methods as drunkenness (this was a drinking society but not one that condoned inebriety) was a defensive weapon. One of Washington's generals, for instance, bitterly complained in 1777 that too many soldiers consistently made it "a practice of getting drunk . . . once a Day and thereby render themselves unfit for duty." To render themselves unfit for duty was to give what they had received—broken promises. Defiance that came in the form of "barrel fever" for some soldiers thus translated into statements about how society looked upon and treated them.

Only over time did individual acts of protest take on a more collective character. That transition may be better comprehended by considering the phenomenon of desertion. While it is true that a great many soldiers did not think of desertion as a specific form of protest, they fled the ranks with greater frequency when food and clothing were in very short supply or nonexistent, as at Valley Forge. However, primary unit cohesion worked to militate against unusually high desertion levels. Sustained involvement with a company or regiment reduced the likelihood of desertion. Hence as soldiers came to know, trust, and depend upon one another, and as they gained confidence in comrades and felt personally vital to the long-term welfare of their primary group, they were much less likely to lodge a statement of individual protest through such individualized forms as desertion.

So it appears to have been with Washington's new regulars. Thad W. Tate discovered that, in the regiments of New York, Maryland, and North Carolina, about 50 percent of all desertions occurred within six months of enlistments. Mark Edward Lender, in studying New Jersey's Continentals, also found that the rate of desertion dropped off dramatically for those soldiers who lasted through just a few months of service. The first few days and weeks in the ranks were those in which these poor and desperate new regulars asked themselves whether vague promises of a better lot in life for everyone, including themselves, in a postwar republican polity was worth the sacrifice now being demanded. Many enlistees and conscripts concluded that it was not, and they fled. Since they had little proof that they could trust the civilian population and its leaders, they chose to express their defiance through desertion. Unit cohesion, in turn, helped sustain those who read the equation differently, and it eased the pain of enduring a long war in return for the remote prospect of greater personal freedom, opportunity, and prosperity.

Then there were those individuals who neither deserted nor became hard-core regulars. By and large, this group defied civil and military authority through the practice of bounty jumping. The procedure, which Washington once referred to as "a kind of business" among some soldiers, was straightforward. It involved enlisting, getting a bounty, and deserting, then repeating the same process with another recruiting agent in another location. Some of the most resourceful bounty jumpers got away with this maneuver seven, eight, or even nine times, if not more. Most jumpers appear to have been very poor young men without family roots. The most careful of them went through the war unscathed. Bounties thus provided a form of economic aggrandizement (and survival) in a society that generally treated its struggling classes with studied neglect. To accept a bounty payment, perhaps even to serve for a short period, and then to run off, was a strongly worded statement of personal defiance.

Bounty jumping was invariably the act of protesting individuals; looting and plundering (like desertion) combined individual with collective protest. Certainly there were numerous occasions when hungry soldiers looted by themselves. Just as often, groups of starving men "borrowed" goods from civilians. Even before the second establishment took form, looting had become a serious problem. Indeed, it probably abetted unit cohesion. One sergeant, for example, described how he and his comrades, searching desperately for food, "liberated" some geese belonging to a local farmer in 1776 and devoured them "Hearty in the Cause of Liberty of taking what Came to their Hand." Next "a sheep and two fat turkeys" approached this band of hungry soldiers, but "not being able to give the countersign," they were taken prisoner, "tried by fire and executed" for sustenance "by the whole Division of the freebooters."

When army looting of civilian property continued its unabated course in 1777, General Washington threatened severe penalties. He emphasized that the army's "business" was "to give protection, and support, to the poor, distressed Inhabitants; not to multiply and increase their calamities." These pleas had little impact. Incident after incident kept the commander in chief and his staff buried in a landslide of civilian complaints. Threats of courts martial, actual trials, and severe punishments did not deter angry, starving, protesting soldiers. In 1780 and 1781 Washington was still issuing pleas and threats, but to little avail. Not even occasional hangings contained an increasingly defiant and cohesive soldiery that wondered who the truly poor and distressed inhabitants were—themselves or civilians ostensibly prospering because of the army's travail. To strike back at hoarding, unsupportive citizens, as they had come to perceive the populace whom they were defending, seemed only logical, especially when emboldened by the camaraderie of closely knit fellow soldiers.

Above all else, two patterns stand out with respect to common soldier protest. First, as the war effort lengthened, defiance became more of a collective phenomenon. Second, such protest had a controlled quality. While there was unremitting resentment toward civilians who were invariably perceived as insensitive and unsupportive, protest rarely metamorphosed into wanton violence and mindless destruction. Soldiers may have looted and pillaged, they may have grabbed up bounties, and they may have deserted. But they rarely maimed, raped, or murdered civilians. Pvt. Joseph Plumb Martin attempted to explain why. Even though "the monster Hunger, . . . attended us," he wrote, and the new regulars "had borne as long as human nature could endure, and to bear longer we considered folly," he insisted that his comrades had become, in the end, "truly patriotic." They were persons who "loved their country, and they had already suffered everything short of death in its cause." The question by 1779 and 1780 was whether these hardened, cohesive veterans would be willing to endure even more privation.

In reflecting positively on the loyalty of his comrades, Martin was commenting on a near mutiny of the Connecticut Line in 1780. Indeed, the specter of collective defiance in the form of line mutinies had come close to reality with the near insubordination of the New Jersey officers in 1779. They had not demonstrated in the field, but they had made it clear that conditions in the army were all but intolerable—and that civil society, when desperate to maintain a regular force in arms, could be persuaded to concede on basic demands. Washington had used the phrase "extorted"; he had also pointed out that, "notwithstanding the expedient adopted for saving appearances," this confrontation "cannot fail to operate as a bad precedent." The commander in chief was certainly right about the setting of precedents.

Among long-term veterans, anger was beginning to overwhelm discipline. There had been small-scale mutinies before, such as the rising of newly recruited Continentals at Halifax, North Carolina, in February 1776. In 1779 Rhode Island and Connecticut regiments threatened mutinies, but nothing came of these incidents. Then in 1780 another near uprising of the Connecticut Line occurred. Invariably, the issues had the same familiar ring: lack of adequate civilian support as demonstrated by rotten food, inadequate clothing, and worthless pay (when pay was available). On occasion, too, the heavy hand of company- and field-grade officers played its part. The near mutiny of the Connecticut Line in 1780 had been avoided by a fortuitous shipment of cattle and by promises from trusted officers of better treatment. In the end, the Connecticut Line calmed itself down, according to Martin, because the soldiery was "unwilling to desert the cause of our country, when in distress." Nevertheless, he explained that "we knew her cause involved our own, but what signified our perishing in the act of saving her, when that very act would inevitably destroy us, and she must finally perish with us."

By the end of 1780, there were some veterans who would have disputed Martin's reasoning. They had all but given up, let come what might for the glorious cause. On January 1, 1781, the Pennsylvania Line proved that point. Suffering through yet another harsh winter near Morristown, New Jersey, the Pennsylvanians mutinied. Some one thousand determined comrades in arms (about 15 percent of the manpower available to Washington) ostensibly wanted nothing more to do with fighting the war. On a prearranged signal, the Pennsylvanians paraded under arms, seized their artillery, and marched south toward Princeton, their ultimate target being Philadelphia. These veterans had had their fill of broken promises, of the unfulfilled contract. They maintained that they had signed on for three years, not for the duration. If they were to stay in the ranks, then they wanted the same benefits (additional bounty payments, more free land, and some pay in specie) that newer enlistees had obtained.

Formal military discipline collapsed as the officers trying to contain the mutineers were brushed aside. The soldiers killed one and wounded two other officers, yet their popular commander, Anthony Wayne, trailed along, attempting to appeal to their sense of patriotism. Speaking through a committee of sergeants, the soldiers assured Wayne and the other officers that they were still loyal to the cause, and they proved it by handing over two spies that Sir Henry Clinton had sent out from New York to monitor the situation. Moreover, the mutineers, despite their anger and bitterness, behaved themselves along their route and did not unnecessarily intimidate civilians who got in their way.

Later checking demonstrated that many of the mutineers were duration enlistees, yet that was a moot point. When the soldiers reached Trenton, representatives of Congress and the Pennsylvania government negotiated with them and agreed to discharge any veteran claiming three years in rank. Also, they offered back pay and new clothing along with immunity from prosecution for having defied their officers in leaving their posts. Once formally discharged, the bulk of the mutineers reenlisted for a new bounty. By late January 1781 the Pennsylvania Line was once more a functioning part of the Continental army.

These mutineers won because Washington was in desperate need of manpower and because they had resorted to collective defiance, not because their society wanted to address what had been grievances based on the contract for service. Unlike their officers, who had just won a major victory in driving for half-pay pensions, they were not in a position to lobby before Congress. Hence they employed one of the most threatening weapons in their arsenal, collective protest against civil authority, but only after less extreme measures had failed to satisfy their claims for financial justice. They were certainly not planning to overthrow any government or to foment an internal social revolution against better-placed members of their society. They had staked their hopes on a better life in the postwar period and had already risked their lives many times for the proposed republican polity. All told, the extreme nature of this mutiny demonstrated, paradoxically, both that Washington's long-term Continentals were the most loyal and dedicated republican citizens in the new nation, and that they were dangerously close to repudiating a dream that far too often had been a personal nightmare because of the realities of societal support and of service in the Continental army.

KEY TERMS

Six Nations: The six nations of the Iroquois Confederacy, composed of the Mohawk, Oneida, Onondaga, Cayuga, and Seneca in 1570 and joined by the Tuscarora in 1722.

Pennsylvania Line: The Pennsylvania contingent of Washington's Continental Army.

Continental: A soldier in the Continental Army.

Sir Henry Clinton (1738–1795): British general in the American Revolution who was commander in chief of British forces in North America from 1778 to 1781.

DISCUSSION TOPICS

After reading this essay, you should be able to discuss:

1. The reasons why ordinary people enlisted in the Continental Army.

2. The reasons they remained in the army despite the lack of pay and public support.

3. The major experiences of ordinary soldiers in the Continental Line.

4. The different forms that protest took during the Revolution.

9

The Constitution and the Competing Political Cultures of Late-Eighteenth-Century America

Robert E. Shalhope

The men who met in 1787 to consider how best to reform the national government were of a variety of minds. Northerners and southerners, from cities and the countryside, these men represented the diverging interests that marked early America. Yet whatever their differences, these men shared a common concern: As leaders of the world's newest republic, how could they prevent the inevitable slide into decline and despotism that marked the history of all previous republics? To these men, schooled in the classical doctrine that republics required a virtuous people who could put self-interest aside, the competing interests of class, region, and party were sure signs of decay and impending doom. How, then, could they act to prevent these social divisions from developing in America?

As Robert E. Shalhope demonstrates, political thought at the close of the eighteenth century offered two answers. Localists—mostly small farmers and rural artisans with few connections to the commercial world—saw the answer in a continuation of America as a decentralized republic of small property holders. With every American a small holder of property, there would be no large accumulations of wealth to challenge the virtuous government of the republic, and every citizen would have a stake—and thus an interest—in society.

A different and more modern view was offered by Alexander Hamilton, who thought the entire Republican conception of government, upon which so much of contemporary thought rested, misconceived. A cosmopolitan Federalist, Hamilton envisioned America as a great commercial and industrial empire on the model of Great Britain. For him, the

From *The Roots of Democracy: American Thought and Culture, 1760–1800* by Robert E. Shalhope (Boston: Twayne Publishers, 1990), pp. 94–111. Reprinted by permission.

creation of classes and competing interests was both inevitable and ultimately desirable. Much like modern-day conservatives, Hamilton saw capitalists as the creators of national wealth and sought to link the state with these men of wealth, augmenting their power and influence in society and ensuring American economic development. In this way, Hamilton hoped to move America away from the agrarian republic of Franklin and Jefferson and make it into a modern industrial state.

As Shalhope shows, it was ultimately these two notions of national development that competed in the mind of James Madison, principal architect of the Constitution, and came to structure American politics for a half-century following the Constitutional Convention of 1787.

....

In each state legislature two relatively well-defined opposing political blocs emerged to contest the issues. These groups did not form systematic organizations, nor did they extend into the electorate through institutional forms or organized electioneering. Rather they provided political expression within the legislatures to socioeconomic and cultural tensions that had been building for several decades. While no party labels or appellations appeared during the period, the terms *localist* and *cosmopolitan* best capture the essential nature of these opposing legislative blocs.

The opposing perspectives of cosmopolitans and localists resulted from their contrasting experiences. Cosmopolitans resided along the Atlantic coast or major navigable streams in long-established counties and townships, as well as the urban and more heavily populated districts. Cosmopolitanism thrived in those areas that had been most thoroughly Anglicized. The cosmopolitan delegate pursued an occupation—merchant, trader, laywer, commercial farmer—that compelled him to deal with a broader world and permitted him to share in the cultural and social activities of his community. He enjoyed wealth, or at least comfortable circumstances. He very likely owned slaves or employed servants, had assets well beyond his debts, had served as a Continental officer during the war or in an important civil capacity, and had the benefit of formal education. His view of the world, particularly when compared to his localist colleagues, was extensive.

Localists represented isolated, independent, and relatively egalitarian communities scattered through the inland regions of the nation located far from or inaccessible to established trade routes. The localist delegate was very likely a farmer and might also, like most of his constituents, be in debt. If he had seen military service, it was as a militia officer, and so the experience was brief and likely did not take him far from home. Few localist delegates had held previous civil office, and if they had, it entailed only local responsibilities. They had little if any formal education and, given their restricted experiences, had difficulty perceiving a world much larger than their own neighborhoods or counties. Their goal was to represent the needs of their own people—their fellow debtors, small property holders, and newly emergent market farmers.

These divergent cultural backgrounds were reflected in the voting patterns that emerged in the state legislatures. Localists worked constantly to reduce governmental expenses. They did not fill newly created governmental offices or hold redeemable state certificates or notes. By and large localists took care of their own needs. They built roads, paid their ministers' salaries, supported what schools they had, and took care of their poor. In essence they wanted to be left alone. Consequently they resented having to pay taxes on land and other necessaries when that tax revenue seemed to benefit others. Localist delegates pressed for many forms of debtor relief. They consistently supported inflationary policies that eased the conditions of debtors, provided relief for taxpayers, and supplied publicly supported money or credit at low interest to promote economic expansion and prevent foreclosures. Above all, they demanded a plentiful supply of money that would be considered legal tender in the payment of debts and taxes.

Localist representatives took negative stands on a number of other issues. They opposed the creation of banks and legislation to aid businessmen in urban areas. They resisted the unimpeded return of loyalists, who, once they had regained their property, would support the cosmopolitan cause. They were cynical about state-supported colleges and systems of public education, hesitant to support congressional demands for enlarged powers, and violently opposed to the idea of strengthening the central government. These people, trusting no one but their own kind, supported a simple egalitarian form of democracy that left them in control of their own affairs and free from hostile and corrupt outside forces.

In contrast, cosmopolitans believed most governmental activity fostered the greater good of society. This was particularly true if they themselves exercised political power. They supported payment of the debt in full, not merely because they held most of the state certificates and would thus benefit directly but also because they believed that government must, in order to maintain a good reputation, create solvent economic substructures with an outstanding basis of credit among the world at large. As the personal beneficiaries of good government, they supported higher salaries for public officials.

Cosmopolitans also supported a solid judicial system, improved transportation, subsidies to promote economic expansion, a stable monetary system, and the maintenance of good order. Never hesitating to pay their portion to receive such benefits, they demanded that all residents of the state share in these expenses by paying their taxes promptly, and preferably in specie. All private debts as well should also be paid promptly and in full. To these men, paper money and debtor relief schemes appeared ill conceived and dangerously irresponsible. Cosmopolitans supported the authority and majesty of government. They consistently voted

in favor of granting requests from the Confederation government for greater powers and looked favorably upon the creation of a stronger national government. Being broad-minded, urbane individuals, they quickly forgave loyalists, favored state-supported colleges, and endorsed the cultural and economic development of towns. Therefore the sort of democracy the localists advocated seemed like no government at all. It meant the domination of rational, educated, and propertied men by those of little property and even less insight into what responsible government was all about. Localism, to the cosmopolitan, meant narrow, selfish interests being pressed by ambitious provincials with little regard for order, decorum, station, and morals. It stood, in short, for the destruction of the sort of government that gentlemen had known—and controlled—for ages.

Beneath the tension within the legislatures coursed a deep cultural antagonism that repeatedly surfaced in newspaper essays, pamphlets, and public orations. In the minds of cosmopolitans, American society faced a crisis resulting from a combination of licentiousness and excessive democracy. Legislatures should be composed of men of property, independence of mind, firmness, education, and a wide knowledge of history, politics, and the laws of their society. Unfortunately, according to a Boston newspaper, such "men of sense and property" were being rapidly displaced in the legislative halls of the states by "blustering ignorant men." A Massachusetts gentlemen claimed that government was increasingly falling into the hands of those who, though perhaps honest, "yet from the contractedness of their Education, and whose views never extended further than a small farm or a bond of 50 or 100£ cannot, from long habit, be persuaded to view Matters on a large or national scale." Such men, "being unacquainted with the nature of Commerce view the Merchants as real positive Evils hence as well from Obstinacy as Ignorance, Trade, by which only a Nation can grow rich, is neglected." Cosmopolitans worried over the future, "when almost every office is in the hands of those who are not distinguished by property, family, education, manners or talents."

For their part localists remained suspicious of gentlemen who constantly assumed it to be their privilege to draw power into their hands at the expense of the common people. An incident in South Carolina in 1784, involving an alleged insult to John Rutledge by a tavern keeper, William Thompson, became a *cause célèbre* and led to a clear articulation of localist resentments—resentments that had festered for years. When the state legislature threatened to banish Thompson for his indiscretion against one of its own, the tavern keeper and ex-captain in the Revolutionary service struck back. His public address of April 1784, a classic articulation of the resentment building against social superiority, spoke out on behalf of the people, or "those more especially, who go at this day, under the opprobrious appellation of, the *Lower Orders of Men*." Thompson not only attacked those aristocratic "Nabobs" attempting to humiliate him but upended the predominant eighteenth-century belief that only a natural aristocracy was peculiarly qualified to rule. He argued that the "persons and conduct" of Rutledge and other "Nabobs" of South Carolina "in *private* life, may be unexceptionable, and even amiable, but their pride, influence, ambition, connections, wealth and political principles, ought, in *public* life, ever to exclude them from *public confidence*." All that republican leadership required was "being *good, able, useful*, and *friends to social quality*," because in a republican government "consequence is from the *public opinion*, and not from *private fancy*." Then, in tones heavy with irony, Thompson related how he, a tavern keeper, "a *wretch* of no higher rank in the Commonwealth than that of Common-Citizen," was debased by "those *self-exalted* characters, who affect to compose the *grand hierarchy* of the State, . . . for having dared to dispute with a *John Rutledge*, or any of the NABOB *tribe*." No doubt, Thompson exclaimed, Rutledge had "conceived me his inferior." However, the tavern keeper, like so many others in similar circumstances, could no longer

"comprehend the *inferiority*." The animosity between those considering men like Thompson as their inferiors and those like Thompson who would no longer accept such treatment underlay the social ferment that boiled just beneath the surface of the legislatures and throughout American society in the 1780s.

DEMOCRATIC EXCESSES

Within this environment many cosmopolitan gentlemen became convinced that their society faced a social crisis. For men well versed in eighteenth-century political theory, it was not difficult to diagnose the illness plaguing their society. If British rule twenty years previously had degenerated into a perversion of power, the excesses of the people now had become a perversion of liberty. By this the gentry did not necessarily mean mob violence, although Shays' Rebellion in the winter of 1786–87 shocked them; rather they meant the quite legal democratic actions of the state legislatures. The delegates, elected in as fair a manner and based upon as equal a representational scheme as the world had ever seen, openly perpetrated the excesses that so disturbed the gentry. In those assemblies paper money schemes, the confiscation of property, and the whole panoply of debtor-relief legislation that undercut creditors and violated property rights achieved legitimacy.

James Madison's experience in the Virginia legislature from 1784 through 1787 epitomized the unease cosmopolitans throughout the nation endured. Madison quickly discovered that not all of his fellow legislators were gentlemen. In his opinion most cared little for public honor or honesty and seemed intent upon serving only narrow, local interests. Calm reason and order gave way to clamorousness and chaos. Lawmakers during Madison's tenure appeared to him to scramble to secure the demands of their constituents with little regard for consistency or the systematic creation of a body of laws to promote the overall interests of the state. Government, in the hands of "Individuals of extended views, and of national pride," could enlighten, but that standard would never be served by "the multitude," who could rarely conceive of issues except in terms of their own pocketbooks and their own neighborhoods.

Such a perception was by no means unique to Madison. Gentlemen everywhere grew increasingly disillusioned with the "characters too full of Local attachments and Views to permit sufficient attention to the general interest" who disgraced the state legislatures by ceaselessly advancing particular causes and pandering "to the vulgar and sordid notions of the populace." For Madison and his gentlemanly colleagues, the legislative branch of state governments, long considered the expression of the people's will as well as the best protector of their liberties, now seemed to have become a democratic despot. A tremendously important shift occurred in their thoughts; the fear and suspicion of political power long associated with the executive now became fixed upon the individual state assemblies.

Again James Madison offered the most cogent insights into the matter: "Wherever the real power in a Government lies, there is the danger of oppression. In our Governments the real power lies in the majority of the Community, and the invasion of private rights is chiefly to be apprehended, not from acts of Government contrary to the sense of its constituents, but from acts in which the Government is the mere instrument of the major number of the constituents." The people were just as capable of becoming despotic as any king or prince. Consequently the classical perception, in which the people's liberties faced a constant threat from the power of their rulers, made little sense. In America, rather than the many fearing the few, "It is much more to be dreaded that the few will be unnecessarily sacrificed to the many." This fear of the power of the majority, when combined with the gentry's growing apprehension regarding the character of the American people, created the most profound despair for men like Madison and his colleagues. In Madison's mind Americans must discover "a republican remedy for the diseases most incident to republican government."

Others agreed with Madison and set about reforming the state constitutions that had been written in 1776–77, adopting the Massachusetts Constitution of 1780 as their model. With a legislature balanced between a House that embodied the people and a Senate apportioned according to property valuation, a strong executive, and a judiciary appointed by the governor, this constitution represented a check on the unrestrained power of the people. A bill of rights spelled out the principle of the separation of powers in great detail. Some genteel reformers wanted to go beyond the Massachusetts Constitution as a model. They hoped to change the very character of the lower houses, first by decreasing the number of delegates so as to make the assembly more stable and energetic, and second by reducing their powers.

These efforts did not go unnoticed. Localists, who had welcomed changes in their state governments wrought by the Revolution, became apprehensive. For them the Revolution, by granting greater powers to much-enlarged legislatures, had been a success. From their perspective, the Revolution was just beginning to achieve its goals: a more equitable republican society where each individual and locale could gain autonomy and control.

By 1786–1787, the reformation of the central government became the primary concern of those worried about America's ability to sustain republican governments and a prosperous republican society. As a result, when the Constitutional Convention gathered in Philadelphia in 1787, it represented the culmination of reform efforts to curb the democratic excesses of the state legislatures and to provide an institutional framework that could safely accommodate the dynamic changes taking place within American society.

THE CONSTITUTION

The convention that met in Philadelphia throughout the summer of 1787, attended almost entirely by men of a cosmopolitan frame of mind, effected a political revolution as great as the one that gained independence from Great Britain. The delegates scrapped the Articles of Confederation and created a truly national government, a single continental republic that penetrated the state governments to the people themselves. At its head stood a powerful executive with broad appointive powers within the executive and judicial branches, who also served as commander in chief of armed forces and exercised virtual control over the nation's diplomatic affairs. Chosen by electors elected by the people rather than by the legislature, the president gained further independence during his four-year term of office, and he was eligible for perpetual reelection. The Constitution also created a separate, potentially powerful national judiciary branch, whose justices would hold office during good behavior and so gained immunity from the vagaries of popular election. The legislative branch consisted of a House of Representatives elected by the people and apportioned according to population and a Senate selected by the individual states composed of two senators from each state, each with one vote. Both houses of Congress enjoyed extensive legislative prerogatives, and Congress gained wide powers under the Constitution that had been denied it by the Articles. Most important, it now had the power to tax and to regulate commerce. In addition the new document specifically denied certain prerogatives to the states; they could no longer print paper money, impair the obligation of contracts, be involved in foreign affairs, or lay imposts or duties on imports and exports. The Constitution, unlike the Articles, created a true national state with extensive coercive powers.

The new government reflected the central cosmopolitan tenets of its authors. According to Alexander Hamilton, it suited "the commercial character of America"; John Jay felt that it mirrored the true "manners and circumstances" of the nation, which were "not strictly democratical." The new arrangement must control the democratic excesses of the states by insulating the federal government from the populist forces that had sprung up with the Revolution. In addition, it should restore political influence to selfless gentlemen of broad vision and education. Madison believed that the best way to ensure this was to create "such a process of elections as will most certainly extract from the mass of Society the purest and noblest characters which it contains; such as will at once feel most strongly the proper motives to pursue the end of their appointment, and be most capable to devise the proper means of attaining it." This desire to attract the best men to the government and then to allow them to exercise independent judgment resulted in the complexity of separate constituencies, staggered terms of office, and elaborate mechanisms of election created by the new form of government. Only such a filtration of talent and modification of the undiluted expression of the people could safeguard the hierarchical world of America's gentlemen.

At the same time the creation of an active, energetic government promised to unleash the commercial potential of the nation that had been inhibited by state control over commerce. With a national framework within which to work, the entrepreneurial interests of the gentry could develop the tremendous economic potential of the young republic. The new government, empowered to deal aggressively with foreign powers and to control the nation's commercial activities, could now actively promote national prosperity. Geographical expansion, commercial development, and the consolidation and mobilization of mercantile capital seemed a real possibility at last.

JAMES MADISON AND THE CONSTITUTION

These two impulses—to control democratic excesses and to create a more beneficial commercial environment—lay at the heart of the cosmopolitan's view of the good society; yet they also constituted the source of his greatest tension and frustration. Backward looking in his political beliefs—desperate in his desire to hang on to the neoclassical political and social world of the eighteenth century—and yet modern in his economic outlook, the cosmopolitan became a victim of his own success. The capitalistic practices of his economic world fostered an individualistic ethos that eroded his neoclassical world of hierarchy and deference from which he derived his sense of identity and security.

James Madison's intellectual search for a way to preserve republican government and society from its own worst excesses led him to a careful reconsideration of what American society had become by the mid-1780s. Struggling to comprehend the changes that were transforming the new republic, he caught glimpses of the weaknesses in the conflicting sources of authority—hierarchy and localism—that struggled for dominance. Out of his effort to think through the work accomplished at Philadelphia, he arrived at the conclusion that the Constitution provided a framework for government and society resting on entirely different principles of authority than any previous governmental system. He presented this new understanding of political science, as well as his still inchoate perceptions of America's changing culture, in his contributions to the *Federalist* essays, published with those of Hamilton and Jay to support the ratification of the Constitution.

In these essays Madison spoke to the tension emerging in American society between the individual and the community. He attempted to find a system to oblige self-interested, self-governing men to respect the rights of others and to promote the interests of the larger community. He thus explored a middle ground between the potential tyranny of unrestrained majorities and the potential oppression of a hierarchy of centralized power. "The practicable sphere of a republic," he reasoned, must be large enough to "break and control the violence of faction," but it should never be so large as to sever the democratic bond between governors and the governed. While republican government should restrain the undiluted will of the people, that will must never be denied. In Madison's view governments existed solely to protect and enlarge the freedom of the people as well as

their equality of opportunity. The best guarantee of such a purpose was to be certain that governmental power and authority rested on the consent of the governed. This constituted the most vital republican principle to which all just government must adhere. Therefore Madison's primary intent became to discover the proper mechanism that would provide such insurance while at the same time maintaining order and integrity in government.

Madison believed this mechanism existed in the federal structure created by the Constitution. That system would be able to refine and purify the will of the majority by causing it to pass through the successive filters of state and national governments while simultaneously guaranteeing that government at either level, however purified, always rested upon the will of the people. State authorities would attend to issues requiring a particular understanding of the parochial needs of local situations, while federal representatives would handle national issues requiring broader vision and scope. Because each level of government had been carefully balanced, no separate branch of either the state or federal government would be able to operate in opposition to the interest of the whole people. In addition, the state and national governments acted as checks upon one another. Given the creation of these safeguards, future generations of Americans would be able to enjoy as much self-government as human nature would allow.

Within this system Madison could constantly seek the middle ground. If the heedless pursuit of local interests threatened to overwhelm national authority or erode republican principles, Madison could throw his support to the central government and emphasize majority rule. Such was the case in 1787. If, however, a group of power-hungry leaders were to capture the central government at some future time and thereby threaten to destroy republican government through an oppressive oligarchy, he could emphasize anticentralist, libertarian principles and organize the countervailing powers of the state governments. For Madison, such a shifting of forces to achieve a proper equilibrium was necessary in order to ensure a lasting American republic.

In *Federalist* No. 10, Madison offered his clearest statement of the diseases that most commonly threatened a republic and their proper remedies. Sensing the emergence of a diverse individualism within the new republic, Madison knew that to gain legitimacy within this society government must rest upon the sacredness of the individual and each citizen's right to the fullest and freest expression of that individuality. He knew also that "as long as the reason of man continues fallible, and he is at liberty to exercise it, different opinions will be formed." Such "diversity in the faculties of men" must always be given free reign. Indeed, for Madison, "the protection of these faculties is the first object of government." In making such a commitment, however, Madison realized full well that a diverse society composed of self-interested individuals must inexorably result in the creation of fiercely competitive antagonistic factions. Such factions naturally resulted from the liberties cherished in a republican society. To remove their causes was to destroy the very essence of a republican society. Thus, since the causes of faction could not be eliminated, "relief is only to be sought in the means of controlling, its *effects*." This meant creating a governmental structure that simultaneously protected the peoples' liberties from the emergence of a single oppressive power and vitiated the power of factions themselves.

In Madison's mind, the Constitution accomplished this by dispersing power between state and central authorities and by dividing and balancing it among the executive, legislative, and judicial branches of the national government. While nearly every element of government at both the state and federal levels was elected by the people, these elections took place at different times and within such a variety of diverse electoral districts as to make it extremely difficult for one self-interested faction to gain simultaneous control of all branches of government throughout the nation. If a faction did control several state legislatures and gained a majority in the federal House, the Senate, the president, and the judiciary still stood as checks upon its excesses.

The surest means to control the effects of faction, however, lay in extending the geographic extent of government. The larger the republican government is, contrary to Montesquieu's dictums, the more secure the republican society is. Thus, "The influence of factious leaders may kindle a flame within their particular states, but will be unable to spread a general conflagration through the other states: a religious sect may degenerate into a political faction in a part of the confederacy; but the variety of sects dispersed over the entire face of it, must secure the national councils against any danger from that source: a rage for paper money, for an abolition of debts, for an equal division of property, or for any other improper or wicked project, will be less apt to pervade the whole body of the union than a particular member of it."

Madison's view of American society rested on the realization that a self-interested and diverse population had emerged within the young republic. No longer could an outmoded hierarchy or a localism based upon majoritarian sentiments offer entirely legitimate bases of authority. The one smacked entirely too much of aristocracy, and the other promised only chaos. For Madison, then, the Constitution fostered a diverse individualistic society, but at the same time it produced a checked and balanced government of real authority and power. The Constitution had indeed designed a government to protect a republican society from itself.

THE FEDERALISTS

Like Madison, the great bulk of Federalists—the name assumed by the cosmopolitan supporters of the Constitution—believed that the new government could preserve American republicanism from the democratic excesses they saw all around them. Republicanism to these gentlemen meant mobility, equality of opportunity, and careers open to men of talent. Such a perception of equality, however, was not incompatible with their commitment to hierarchy. In their minds all societies consisted of gradations of social orders held together by the deference owed to individuals in higher stations by those in lower ones. In a republic any person of ability should be free to move upward, but Federalists naturally assumed that individuals who rose in a republican society would first acquire the requisites of social superiority—property, education, social connections, broad experiences—before they took on the responsibilities of political authority. For this reason respectable people stood aghast as they witnessed men "whose fathers they would have disdained to have sit with the dogs of their flocks, raised to immense wealth, or at least to carry the appearance of a haughty, supercilious and luxurious spendthrift." Worse, state legislatures, the traditional Whig bastions of liberty, filled up with "men without reading, experience, or principle." Authority rested in "the Hands of those whose ability or situation in Life does not entitle them to it."

In spite of, or perhaps because of, the changes taking place in their society, Federalists clung desperately to classical traditions of disinterested public leadership. For them the Constitution promised a last hope to preserve the republican ideal of a government in the hands of the "worthy" rather than the "licentious."

Many Federalists accepted Madison's argument in *Federalist* No. 10. The "better sort" might be overpowered by localists in the many small electoral districts required by state legislatures, but in enlarged congressional districts men of broad contacts and experience would surely gain election and thus control of the national government, which, with its enhanced powers, now had the opportunity to shape American society. Thus, the Constitution offered a filtration of talent that seemed to promise the reassertion of genteel authority.

To accept the logic of *Federalist* No. 10, however, enmeshed the Federalists in several paradoxes. First, by recognizing that American society had become fragmented into a multiplicity of conflicting interests—interests that could become overbearing local majorities in

particular state legislatures—they accepted a conception of society that undermined the traditional social justification for a natural aristocracy and an elitist style of politics. The notion of the organic unity of society had always undergirded the existence of a disinterested natural aristocracy. Now Federalists seemed to believe that such a society no longer existed.

Also, by depending upon the new governmental structure to solve the social and political problems arising from the Revolution, Federalists acquiesced to the very democratic politics that they blamed for the ills of their society. Indeed democratic elections became the basis for the perpetuation of the natural elite's continued domination of politics. So long as constituencies could be made large enough to stifle the opportunities for social upstarts to gain office, the popular vote would elect natural leaders. Democracy could be made to support an elitist style of politics, and, Federalists hoped, an ordered society as well.

Federalists had little difficulty in presenting the Constitution as continuing the libertarian tradition of republicanism and the embodiment of the people's interests. This was possible because since 1776, political ideals had taken on new meanings, and republican principles had undergone subtle transformations. In their effort to defend the Constitution, Federalists drew together the disparate strands of thought that had emerged throughout the previous decade. Gradually, still not always aware of the consequences, the Federalists created an entirely new conception of politics out of these previously disconnected republican ideas.

At the heart of their emerging persuasion lay the idea of federalism. Here Federalists had to wrestle with the paradoxical idea of simultaneous jurisdiction by two legislative bodies—a clear contradiction of the fixed idea of supreme and indivisible sovereignty. James Wilson, a prominent Pennsylvania jurist, solved this problem at his state's ratification convention. There he claimed that those who argued that competing independent taxing powers—Congress and the state legislatures—could not exist within the same community had entirely misunderstood the nature of sovereignty in America. For Wilson, sovereignty was indeed indivisible, but it did not rest in either the state or the national legislature. Supreme power in America emanated from the people; they were the source of government. The people never surrendered this sovereignty. They merely dispensed portions of it to the various branches and levels of government as they saw fit.

Once sovereignty had been located in the people, the new system of government made perfect intellectual sense, and the Federalists could not restrain their enthusiasm for introducing the power and control of the people into every aspect of the newly created governmental structure. To attack the Constitution now meant to attack the people themselves. "We the People" assumed a transcendent new meaning. Indeed, given the fundamentally different principle upon which the new Constitution rested, it became entirely logical for the Federalists to defend the absence of a bill of rights. Since all power resided in the people, what they did not specifically delegate to Congress they reserved to themselves. Therefore it was not within the national government's power to grant specific rights to the people. For the government to do so would have meant that it comprised the fountain of all power, just as it did in the decadent and despised societies of Europe.

Such contentions revealed the gradually emerging assumptions about government and society that made up the Federalist system. The traditional libertarian division of rulers and people into separate and opposing interests became irrelevant. Instead the old spheres of power and liberty had been fused. The people now held all power; their representatives in the various branches of the government became their servants. Consequently the government itself became the shield of the people's liberties, not a potentially dangerous threat requiring constant scrutiny. Governmental power became, in Federalist literature, indistinguishable from that of the people. Once this view had been established, the Confederation government no longer made any sense. With all power lodged in a single unchecked branch of the government, what was to keep a combination of men from oppressing the very people they were supposed to serve?

The clearest theme that ran through Federalist arguments in the ratification conventions was the need to distribute and separate traditionally mistrusted governmental power. The old conception of a mixed polity no longer made any sense. America, the Federalists argued, was a new, unique republican society of talent and ability with no distinct social orders, only the people. To create a government in which all branches represented the people made perfect sense. All that was necessary was to separate power into distinct executive, judicial, and legislative branches and to balance them against one another. In this way, the entire government, not just the legislature, became a democracy. Thus the Federalists presented the new government as a thoroughly democratic entity based on the needs and desires of the people. The Constitution, in their rhetoric, epitomized traditional republican maxims and represented the culmination of the popular thrust of the Revolution itself.

THE ANTI-FEDERALISTS

Opponents of the Constitution, the Anti-Federalists, did not see it that way. Indeed if any central theme coursed throughout their arguments, it was that the Federalists meant to erect an oppressive aristocracy that would stifle the democratic tendencies fostered by the Revolution. In the New York ratification convention Melancton Smith warned that the new government "will fall into the hands of the few and the great." A Marylander, Timothy Bloodworth, exclaimed that "the great will struggle for power, honor and wealth, the poor become a prey to avarice, insolence, and oppression." A newspaper essay claimed that the Philadelphia convention had created "a monstrous aristocracy" that would "swallow up the democratic rights of the union, and sacrifice the liberties of the people to the power and domination of a few."

Such observations revealed that Anti-Federalists opposed the Constitution for the very reasons that Federalists supported it. They recognized that the new governmental structure would prevent ordinary individuals from gaining election to Congress and would thereby exclude local interests from actual representation in that body. Samuel Chase objected that "the government is not a government of the people" because only the rich and well born would gain election to Congress. Members of the minority in the Pennsylvania ratifying convention recognized that because of the election process, "men of the most elevated rank in life will alone be chosen. The other orders in the society, such as farmers, traders, and mechanics, who all ought to have a competent number of their best informed men in the legislature, shall be totally unrepresented." Melancton Smith in New York remained convinced "that this government is so constituted that the representatives will generally be composed of the first class in the community, which I shall distinguish by the name of the *natural aristocracy* of the country."

These feelings of resentment sprang from a widespread sense of suspicion, hostility, and fear of a hierarchy of outsiders that permeated Anti-Federalism. The Constitution instituted a government of strangers; worse, those strangers were gentlemen who not only had no fellow feeling with simple folk but felt superior to them. Old Amos Singletary during the Massachusetts ratification convention voiced the defiant hostility and deep insecurities of localists: "These lawyers, and men of learning and moneyed men, that talk so finely, and gloss over matters so smoothly, to make us poor illiterate people swallow down the pill, expect to get into Congress themselves; they expect to be managers of this Constitution, and get all the power and all the money into their own hands, and then they will swallow all us little folks like the great *Leviathan*; yes, just as the whale swallowed up Jonah."

These attitudes—antagonism toward aristocracy, commitment to the most intimate participation in government by the widest possible variety of people, devotion to the egalitarian impulses of the Revolution—spawned majoritarian attitudes toward state legislatures but not toward the proposed new Congress.

Although the leadership of the Anti-Federalists included a number of prominent gentlemen—Rawlins Lowndes, George Mason, Richard Henry Lee, George Clinton—these men opposed the Constitution out of a philisophical and intellectual commitment to state government. Anti-Federalism itself emerged from much more visceral emotions. As much a social and a cultural phenomenon as a political movement, it sprang from a reactionary localism that pervaded American society. In the mid-1780s Anti-Federalism was handicapped because its ideas had yet to coalesce into a coherent political ideology. Consequently, in one state convention after another, Anti-Federalists found themselves bullied and embarrassed by their polished, articulate, unified Federalists opponents.

While the Anti-Federalist cause floundered, some individual adherents displayed a keen understanding of the social and political world emerging in America. This was particularly true of William Findley of Pennsylvania, a man who was far more representative of Anti-Federalist thought than gentlemen such as Mason or Clinton. Findley, an Irish immigrant who began life in America as an apprenticed weaver, had risen to become a spokesman for the debtor–paper money interests in the Pennsylvania legislature by the mid-1780s. A self-made man, Findley had never assumed the refinements of gentility—education, affluence, sophistication in speech and dress. Instead he remained an outspoken advocate of middling aspirations, achievements, and resentments. Indeed, he felt a special antagonism toward members of the gentry who looked down upon him and his kind.

Findley never denied serving the interests of his constituents. Indeed, he prided himself upon it and declared that whenever an individual had "a cause of his own to advocate, interest will dictate the propriety of canvassing for a seat" in the legislature. Findley saw nothing wrong with this. To him self-interest was the driving force within American society: "The human soul is affected by wealth, in almost all its faculties. It is effected by its present interests, by its expectations, and by its fears." Findley freely admitted to being self-interested, but he belligerently refused to believe gentlemen were any different. He had no patience with the argument of the genteel that they served in political positions simply to promote the common good. Throughout his terms in the Pennsylvania legislature, Findley had intimate contact with the gentry; the mystique of disinterested aristocratic authority had no power over him. He knew that for all their claims of superiority emanating from knowledge, experience, education, and extensive connections, gentlemen differed from their neighbors only in having more money.

In Findley's mind American society was a heterogeneous mixture composed of "many different classes or orders of people, Merchant, Farmer, Planter Mechanic and Gentry or wealthy Men"; each group with equal claim to the rights and privileges of government. In such a disparate and egalitarian society, no group or class or men could possibly represent the interests of the entire community: "No man when he enters into society, does it from a view to promote the good of others, but he does it for his own good." Consequently the only fair system of representation must be one in which "every order of men in the community . . . can have a share in it." Each local interest must be directly represented in order for the pluralistic society emerging in America to be embodied fully and completely within the government. This belief, combined with their conviction that the Constitution would keep ordinary individuals out of the national government, fed the antagonism Findley and his Anti-Federalist colleagues felt toward the Federalists.

Findley's attacks upon deference and the ability of gentlemen to govern in the interest of a common good was part of an entirely new perception of politics and society. Rather than a harmonious unity that solidified all orders into an organic whole, he saw society divided into disconnected and antagonistic interests. Whether he realized the implications of what he was saying or not, when he and other Anti-Federalists attacked the traditional idea of a natural aristocracy governing in the interest of all, they also indirectly undermined the belief in an organic social order that underlay their own localist brand of republicanism.

Not all of the Anti-Federalists sensed the changes taking place in their society as clearly as Findley, but all expressed an eighteenth-century libertarian distrust of hierarchy that came from a traditional local sense of community. They knew no other language. As they stumbled toward a new understanding of their world, they remained dependent on an anachronistic vocabulary. Bred upon the hostility believed to exist between the spheres of power and liberty, they felt certain that a republican government could exist only in a small geographic region of homogeneous interests and that they must distrust all executive and aristocratical power. Now, however, they watched in horror as the Federalists turned each weapon in their republican arsenal against them. When Anti-Federalists attacked a powerful executive or an independent Senate as potential sources of oppression by rulers set against the people, Federalists scoffed at them and replied that the president anal senators were only agents of the people, not a separate and potentially oppressive interest at all. Whenever Anti-Federalists attacked the Constitution on the grounds that it divided sovereignty, they met the rebuff that sovereignty lay with the people and that to attack the Constitution was to attack the people. When Anti-Federalists demanded a bill of rights—the essence of libertarian republicanism—their opponents made them appear foolish by asking how a government could guarantee rights to the people when the sovereign people themselves limited and restricted the government. Everywhere Anti-Federalists found their own arguments turned back upon them. Republicanism, democracy, the sovereignty of the people—all seemed to have found a home in the Federalist camp.

As long as the powerful localism that permeated American society remained disparate, inchoate, and disconnected from its natural roots within the New World environment, it could not overcome the well articulated ideology of the Federalists. Still, the Anti-Federalist cause enjoyed tremendous popularity. Even without many brilliant debaters, clever parliamentarians, newspaper editors, or men of great individual prestige within their ranks and little, if any, organization, the Anti-Federalists suffered only the narrowest of defeats.

A CHANGING CULTURE

The struggle over the Constitution produced a number of paradoxes and ironic consequences. The Federalists, elitists who wished to create a powerful centralized government controlled by the rich and the well born, constantly spoke in terms of the sovereignty of the people; they presented their case in the most democratic and radical language. Under this guise they managed to create a government that answered their needs—or so they imagined. In 1787 they had little reason to believe that the Constitution might also provide a national framework that could, under changed circumstances, just as easily accommodate the rise of a national democracy. The Anti-Federalists, on the other hand, who wished to create a decentralized government with direct participation by all classes of people, employed an archaic and anachronistic libertarian language of communalism. Yet, in actuality, their behavior belied such an ideal.

An embryonic individualism was tearing at both the hierarchical and localist bases of authority represented by the Federalists and the Anti-Federalists. On the one hand, capitalistic economic practices of the Federalists eroded the social foundation underlying their traditional perception of a natural aristocracy. On the other, the egalitarianism characteristic of localism became increasingly manifested in an individualistic, self-interested behavior that fragmented the communal substructure of localism. As Federalists looked backward to an eighteenth-century ideal of politics and society, Anti-Federalists groped toward a new conception of society and politics more consonant with the transformations taking place within American society. Both groups exhibited thought and behavior characteristic of the newly emerging culture of the American republic.

KEY TERMS

Articles of Confederation: First American national constitution, adopted by the Continental Congress at York, Pennsylvania, November 15, 1777.

Shays' Rebellion: Rural protest movement in central Massachusetts during the winter of 1786–1787, directed against harsh state tax payments that led to repeated farm foreclosures.

James Madison (1751–1836): A member of the Continental Congress (1780–1783) and the Constitutional Convention (1787) who strongly supported ratification of the Constitution and was a contributor to *The Federalist Papers* (1787–1788), which argued the effectiveness of the proposed Constitution; later became the fourth president of the United States (1809–1817).

Alexander Hamilton (1755?–1804): The first U.S. secretary of the treasury (1789–1795), who established the national bank and public credit system and was author of several of *The Federalist Papers.*

John Jay (1745–1829): American diplomat and jurist who served in both Continental Congresses and helped negotiate peace with Great Britain (1782–1783), was the first chief justice of the U.S. Supreme Court (1789–1795) and author of several of *The Federalist Papers.*

DISCUSSION TOPICS

After reading this essay, you should be able to discuss:

1. The differing views of "localists" and "cosmopolitans."

2. The cosmopolitan's fear of democratic excess.

3. The cosmopolitan nature of the Constitution of 1787.

4. The ways in which Madison's ideas combined the localist and cosmopolitan positions.

5. The Federalist and Anti-Federalist views of the Constitution.

Jane Bartram's "Application": Her Struggle for Survival, Stability, and Self-Determination in Revolutionary Pennsylvania

Wayne Bodle

The American Revolution marked a period full of ambiguities for American women. On the one hand, women played a prominent role in securing American independence: producing cloth, managing farms, and supporting boycotts of British goods. Yet, at the same time, women emerged from the revolutionary era disenfranchised and denied an active public role. This seeming paradox has led some historians to argue that American women gained little from the revolutionary experience; gender roles and women's position in society, they claim, remained little changed from colonial days. More recently, however, historians have looked beyond the issue of suffrage and found that the revolutionary experience did indeed alter women's lives, although in small and often subtle ways.

Women played a variety of roles in the revolutionary movement. In the pre-Revolutionary years between 1765 and 1775, women helped to enforce consumer boycotts, acted as protesters in public demonstrations against British policies, manufactured cloth and other domestic goods to replace English imports, and encouraged men to take action against the mother country. During the war years between 1775 and 1783, women supported the military as laundresses and cooks, raised money for Washington's troops, and kept their families together during months and sometimes

"Jane Bartram's 'Application': Her Struggle for Survival, Stability, and Self-Determination in Revolutionary Pennsylvania." *Pennsylvania Magazine of History and Biography*, 115 (1991), pp. 185–220. Reprinted by permission.

years of wartime exile. A few, such as Deborah Sampson Gannett, even served in the Continental Army, disguised as men.

The Revolution thus expanded women's public roles in unexpected and unprecedented ways. Questions of British tyranny and American liberties were not confined to the male realm by any means, as surviving diaries and letters of a wide cross-section of American women make clear. While most revolutionary women probably agreed with the political sentiments of their husbands, fathers, and brothers, many did not, and more than a few formed their own opinions about local and national affairs. As several historians have recently demonstrated, women even redefined the formal political discourse of the Revolutionary era to meet their own experiences and needs.

But whether they advanced their own political opinions or not, American women were forced to take a political stance by the actions of British and American officials. As the Revolutionary War progressed, even the most cautious colonists were forced to choose sides, and Whig and Tory officials alike assumed that a husband's or father's allegiance defined that of his wife or daughter. Thus the wives and daughters of exiled patriots were maltreated by British soldiers and the women of suspected Tory families were hounded by rebel sympathizers, irrespective of the true sentiments of the women involved. Neutrality, the evidence shows, was an impossible luxury during the Revolutionary War, for women as much as for men.

In the end, however, as Wayne Bodle shows in this essay, necessity as much as politics forced the largest number of American women into public roles. As Jane Bartram's testimony before a British compensation commissioner reveals, despite the legal impediment of coverture, which placed a wife's property rights under the sole control of her husband, women were forced to take on the responsibilities of running family farms, artisan shops, and retail stores during the disruptions of the wartime years. Although some were ill-prepared for the undertaking—their husbands having shared with them little about the management of family enterprises—the overwhelming majority took on the added burdens of family direction with determination and successfully steered the family through the travails of wartime disruption. For some women, such as Jane Bartram, the Revolution proved to be an unexpectedly liberating experience.

....

In April 1787 John Anstey, a fact-finder for the Royal Commission on American Loyalists, opened an office in Philadelphia to investigate Pennsylvania compensation claims. Among his first visitors was Jane Bartram, the wife of Alexander Bartram, a Loyalist pottery manufacturer and china dealer who had fled to New York in June 1778 with the British army after its nine-month occupation of Philadelphia. A self-proclaimed patriot, Jane Bartram had remained in Philadelphia when he left. When she sought Anstey's aid in 1787, she had been struggling for nine years to disentangle her fortunes from those of her absent spouse. She appeared in Anstey's office to provide the Commission with a document that represented a critical turning point in that struggle.

We have no account, in her own voice, of Bartram's brief encounter with British officialdom, but something of its awkward resonance lingers in the tone of Anstey's report to his superiors at home. After sketching the facts of the case, he observed that

As this Lady claims a right in opposition to the rights of her Husband, I have thought it advisable to make this report to the Board in London. . . . The object of her Application is, that she may receive the Moiety of what her Husband may or shall receive by way of compensation for losses in consequence of Loyalty, pursuant to the [enclosed] Agreement between her and her husband.

This article explores Jane Bartram's experience in Revolutionary Pennsylvania, focusing on those elements that shaped her response to her abrupt emergence from the privacy of familial and marital circumstances at the start of the Revolution into a widening sphere of personal autonomy and participation in the public culture during the decade after the war.

Whatever else it may have meant to her, the Revolution did not serve Jane Bartram as an initiation in adversity, for her life had [been] intertwined with that circumstance almost from infancy. She was born in the early 1740s as Jane Martin, the daughter of William and Miriam Martin of Whitpain Township in rural Philadelphia County. William Martin, a tailor and part-time farmer, had married Miriam Morgan in 1738 in the Gwynedd Monthly Meeting of Friends. Jane Martin's family life dissolved abruptly with the deaths of both parents in 1747, when she was about five. The Martins left six young children and a small, seriously encumbered estate.

The result of these circumstances for Jane Martin and her siblings was foster care and probably partial or at least temporary separation. In 1750 the administrators obtained a court order to sell the Martin farm and deposit the proceeds with the guardians in trust to cover expenses incurred on the children's behalf. As this legacy was spent, and as the children reached the age of economic utility, they were probably apprenticed or bound out to redeem the cost of their maintenance, and to learn skills or trades that would support them in adulthood.

By 1763, when Jane Martin moved to the city, she probably had come of legal age and acquired, in a foster household or some bound out status, skills that she could employ for her own support. For three years after her arrival in the city, her "conversation" remained as circumspect in Friends' eyes as it had been at Gwynedd. Early in 1767, however, she married Alexander Bartram in Zion Lutheran Church. A committee from the women's meeting met with her and reported that she "chuses to join in Religious Community with the Society of which her Husband is a member, and therefore expects to be disowned." The meeting summarily obliged the newly denominated Jane Bartram. Accusing her of being "so disregardful of the good order established in the Society as to be married by a Priest, to a person not professing with us," it excluded her "from Religious fellowship" until she condemned her misconduct.

Jane Martin's decision to cast her lot with Alexander Bartram proved for her to be—as did the similar choices of many of her contemporaries—the "important crisis" on which much of her subsequent fate would depend. Her eleven years of active marriage with Bartram comprised a monument to the linguistic implications of the term *coverture*. Alexander Bartram's modest visibility in Philadelphia's mercantile community, however, enables us at least to know Jane Bartram's actual whereabouts during these years. Notwithstanding the effective shroud the laws of marriage placed over her separate identity, we can thus discern many of her most important (or at least most determinative) social circumstances. This makes it advisable to know something about Alexander Bartram's life in Revolutionary Philadelphia.

In his 1786 application to the Loyalist Commission for compensation for his losses, Alexander Bartram recalled that he "came to America in 1764 and settled at Philadelphia as a merchant soon after his arrival." Extant records suggest a more gradual progress toward gentility. In 1767 Bartram lived in the city's Middle Ward. A newspaper advertisement that he placed soon after his marriage referred to his "shop in Market-street." He sold imported dry goods and china and domestic pottery to buyers of both wholesale and retail lots of goods, and limited their payment terms to "cash only" transactions.

Bartram's affairs flourished during the decade before the Revolution. In 1771 he advertised a larger array of glass and ceramic goods than he had offered four years earlier, and he announced that he had "got a Pot-house, where he makes all sorts of earthen ware." In 1773, however, he still supplemented his ceramic inventory with "A General Assortment of Spring Goods," and held customers to "Cash or short Credit." The Middle Ward assessors concluded as late as 1773 that Bartram was a "shopkeeper" rather than a "merchant." And while this designation was reversed in 1775, the qualitative evidence remains ambiguous. As late as 1777 a customer in his store could leave with crates of china and glassware, quantities of foodstuffs to serve on those goods, and fine fabrics with which to drape the windows, cover the table, or adorn the host and hostess.

Bartram's aspiration to something more than a humdrum countertop existence is also suggested by his land speculation. In his 1786 Loyalist claim he said that he had lost twelve tracts of unimproved land in Northumberland County and one in Lancaster totaling almost 2,800 acres. He also invested in and near Philadelphia in cleared lands with structural improvements. He never owned his residence or shop in Market Street between Second and Third, but in 1768 he bought a lot in Southwark where he built the "Pot-house" that supplied his shelves. In 1773 he added a small lot nearby and built "five dwelling houses" for rental purposes. In 1776 and 1777 he bought a house and tavern in Woodbury, New Jersey, and a similar complex in Haverford, Chester County, Pennsylvania. Bartram also purchased improved land in Cheltenham Township, Philadelphia County, and in Northampton Township, Bucks County.

From these and other fragmentary records—many of them created by linked Loyalist confiscation and compensation processes that put little premium on objectivity or precise accuracy—we can derive a sketchy picture of Jane Bartram's spouse and of his place in the world. He was clearly more than a precariously situated trader who needed to move a crate of glass at month's end to assure his next rent payment. Just as apparently, however, he was neither a member

of Philadelphia's mercantile establishment nor of its elite. He was gaining ground, perhaps rapidly, at the end of the pre-Revolutionary decade. But his wilderness speculations spoke more of economic aspiration than actuality. Bartram's urban and nearby agricultural investments testify to his mobility and perhaps to his business acumen, but it is difficult to calibrate precisely either his actual wealth or his place on the continuum between the small trader standing behind his countertop and the mercantile grandee sitting in his countinghouse.

In lieu of such precision, we may consider his own quantified estimate of his worth and the more impressionistic appraisals of his witnesses in support of his compensation claim. Bartram swore to the Loyalist commissioners that he had forfeited property in America worth £10,000. His witnesses were more ambiguous in their accounts. Only one would say that the claimant "might be worth £10,000 currency." Others merely observed that he "carried on considerable trade," that he "was considered a man of considerable property in 1775," or that he "was in good circumstances." Joseph Galloway, who as superintendent of the Philadelphia police during the British occupation knew the Loyalist community as well as anyone, summarized Bartram's reputational status by observing that he "was considered a thriving man, and of good credit in Philadelphia, he kept a Shop, he must be worth some money."

Bartram's business records offer glimpses of his personal or family life. He employed various kin as proxies in assembling his modest frontier archipelago. In 1773 and 1774 Helen and Margaret Bartram received warrants for tracts in Northumberland County. In 1773 Jane Bartram was the nominal beneficiary of a survey in the same county. Nearby parcels were carried on the Surveyor General's books for James Alexander Bartram and Ambrose Alexander Bartram. The records produced during Jane's effort in the 1780s to extricate herself from the wreckage of her husband's Revolutionary political choices identify no children other than James Alexander Bartram.

Alexander may thus have brought to their marriage offspring from an earlier union, or Jane Bartram's own family may have been as tragically beset by early mortality as was her parental one three decades before.

Bartram's claim is also comparatively devoid of allusion to his experience with the Revolution itself. Scattered through his papers and the testimony of his witnesses, however, are references that suggest a fuller picture of him than mere accounts of his personal worth. More importantly, they also begin to bring Jane Bartram back, through the mists of coverture, toward the historical light of day. Bartram's economic progress during the 1770s may have disposed him negatively toward the political disorders that intensified during the same period. In 1770 he publicly confessed to having broken the Non-Importation agreements. In his claim he made the almost formulaic statement that he "took no part with the Americans" (i.e., the rebels) in the pre-Revolutionary disturbances. One of his own witnesses, however, testified that Bartram "trained with the Militia early in the Troubles," but added that he still considered him "a good Loyalist." In his narrative Bartram recalled having been imprisoned by outraged Whigs. At one point he said that this occurred in June 1777, and that he had escaped the next night. He later implied that he was still in rebel hands in December of that year, three months after the British came to Philadelphia.

Bartram made the latter statement in support of his claim to a small lot with two houses divided into tenements on Second Street near Christian Street in Southwark. He testified that his wife had purchased the lot on December 19, 1777, while he was a rebel prisoner, and he sought to recover the purchase price of £700. This item was disallowed in 1786, and when Bartram's claim was reheard in 1789, he changed his account to say that Jane had made the purchase "by his advice." One of Bartram's witnesses, however, remembered this lot as "that property his wife bought." This episode may suggest that Jane Bartram was an active participant in family business affairs all along,

or it may show how she, like many wives in the Revolutionary era, found in the absence of a spouse a stimulus to economic initiative.

Whatever the exact chronology of his imprisonment and escape, Bartram returned to occupied Philadelphia in time to establish himself as an unequivocal friend to the King and an outcast from the Revolution. He told the commissioners that he had "assist[ed] in the Barrack department [and] in quartering His Majesty's Troops [and] . . . taking from all suspicious persons Arms and Warlike Stores." By June 1778 Bartram had irrevocably cast his lot with an occupying military force that was ready to abandon Philadelphia. He had been attainted of treason in May 1778 as a member of the first group of suspected collaborators indicted by Pennsylvania's Revolutionary government. A witness later recalled that Bartram had become "very obnoxious to the people in Pennsylvania." When Sir Henry Clinton offered passage to New York in the army's transports to the King's most vulnerable Pennsylvania friends, it was a foregone conclusion that Bartram would take his place on board.

Jane Bartram's situation was different. One of her husband's witnesses testified that she "did not agree in politics," and Alexander acknowledged that when he left the city in 1778 she "staid behind." In 1782, in depicting herself to Pennsylvania authorities as an unjustly displaced patriot, Bartram averred that "ever since the Arrival of the British at Philadelphia [Alexander had] used her grossly ill for her attachment to the cause of American Liberty." Such treatment would have explained her refusal to accompany him into exile. But in a 1785 divorce petition she accused Alexander of having deserted her at the time of the British evacuation. The chaos in Philadelphia in June 1778 would have facilitated the efforts of either party to be rid of the other. The state's records are replete with accounts of women left by their husbands at this time. As for a wife determined not to be dragged away by an abusive (and attainted) spouse, if she were but a few steps beyond his immediate physical control when the ship's lines were cast away—

and fleet enough of foot briefly to maintain that distance—he could have attempted to assert his spousal prerogatives only at grave risk to his own neck. When the British fleet left the city docks on June 18, 1778, Alexander Bartram was aboard and Jane Bartram was not. Although they would remain legally joined until death, and their lives and fates would be painfully and problematically entangled for a decade, their marriage itself was effectively over.

Alone in the Revolutionary capital, Jane Bartram faced many more immediate obstacles to her well-being than opportunities. Even if her political credentials were intact enough and sufficiently well-known to spare her the personal indignity or abuse that an avowed Loyalist such as Grace Galloway endured, many difficulties loomed. In July 1778 Whigs moved quickly and decisively to reassert their ascendancy. Patriot credentials alone did not change the elemental fact of coverture, that a married couple's property was held in the husband's name. The confiscation of property from Loyalist refugees began within days of the departure of the British army. At this time it rapidly became apparent how "obnoxious" Alexander Bartram had been to many of his neighbors.

Records kept by Charles Willson Peale and other agents appointed to administer the confiscation process suggest that Alexander's property *might* have been the first in Philadelphia to be seized and sold. The personal effects left in his house and shop in Market Street were inventoried by July 6. The fact that the couple had rented their residence and store may ironically have benefited Jane Bartram. Even if it was stripped to the walls and floorboards, the space itself would have been exempt from confiscation and available to her as long as she could make rental payments. And confiscation records remind us that she was not really "alone" in Philadelphia. The second entry in Peale's scrawled "summary" of the agents' work recorded the intervention of a "Mr. John Martin"—probably her brother—who claimed most of the "shop goods" found on the site. Peale scoffed at the claim, and Martin might

have been marauding opportunistically on his own behalf. The two siblings also might have been trying to exploit the legal ambiguity of the situation to preserve the retail inventory and thus to give Jane Bartram a better chance to make those rental payments.

By whatever contrivance, Bartram remained in Philadelphia for at least eighteen months after her husband fled to New York. It must have been a scrabbling, bare-boned existence. Late in 1778 she offered a $16 reward for the return of a straying "red and white Cow, very low in flesh, about nine years old," together with its newborn calf. If the space between the wolf and the door could be measured across the bony flanks of an aging bossy, the door in question at least gave entry to a familiar place. The finder was to bring the animals "to the subscriber in Market-street, next door to the Indian King," the site from which Alexander Bartram had long dispensed his mixed inventories of china, glass, fabrics, and provisions. Social security has a spiritual as well as a material dimension. By preserving her long-time home in an environment of constant revolutionary upheaval, Jane Bartram maintained a good deal of that critical amenity.

Her task grew harder in 1779, as inflation accelerated and the grip of the Loyalist confiscation program tightened. Bartram responded by resorting to the inventory diversity that had long served her husband well. In June 1779, as Peale prepared to auction off the Southwark ceramic factory that had supplied the store, she offered to sell "German Steel, and a quantity of Corks." The record is silent as to how she supplied her shop, but she did so at least as late as the fall of 1779, when the town's constables did the field work for the 1780 tax assessments. In his report to the assessors, the Middle Ward constable identified Bartram as a shopkeeper. Although the house rent on the site was £700 per year, Jane was not assessed any tax, which perhaps reflects the precarious monetary circumstances that qualified her for an abatement. It is unclear what these divergent figures reveal about her exact financial situation, her support network(s), and/or her dependency status in the city at this time. If dependent on other parties, she was also responsible for at least one dependent of her own. The constable disclosed that Bartram was living with one child "under age." This was James Alexander Bartram, who Alexander acknowledged in 1786 had remained with his mother.

The Southwark properties were sold in August 1779. The pottery complex alone yielded £7,000 in inflated Continental currency. Charles Willson Peale purchased the lot at Second and Christian Streets that Jane Bartram had acquired two years before. If one citizen's recollection that "the children were considered when [the latter] property was sold" was accurate, any payment that she received may have helped to avert destitution. Political pressures mounted late in 1779 for authorities to deal with the remaining dependents of Loyalist refugees on a collective rather than a case-by-case basis. These pressures grew from internal disputes over Pennsylvania's failing economy. Even if the kin of refugees were not themselves disaffected and thus potential spies or traitors, it was feared they would inevitably become a financial drain on a barely functioning economy. Jane Bartram's allegiance to the Revolution and her demonstrated ability to survive economically availed her little against these pressures. She was probably exiled in the summer of 1780, when authorities summarily ordered the wives of local refugees to leave the state.

Bartram posted bond not to return to Pennsylvania without the Council's permission and left for New York and what must have been an awkward encounter with her estranged spouse. Alexander had by 1780 set up shopkeeping in New York. Jane began laying the groundwork for an early return to Pennsylvania. In seeking permission to come home in 1782, she averred that "while [in New York] as far as [her] influence or assistance . . . extended [she] was as serviceable as in her power in alleviating the distresses of such Americans as had the misfortune of falling into the hands of the British." In May 1782 the Council revoked her bond and allowed Bartram to return to Philadelphia.

The economic crisis of 1779–1780 and the acute fear of a renewed British invasion of Pennsylvania, factors that had provoked the mass expulsion of Loyalist wives, had partially receded by 1782. These circumstances perhaps facilitated the Council's favorable response to Bartram's petition. She also proved to be an astute reader of the political and rhetorical requirements of the situation, for she was a forceful advocate of the possibility of female patriotism. Before recounting the abuse she had suffered at her husband's hands in 1777–1778—her best variation on the "helpless female" theme so admired in "ladies'" petitions by patriarchal political authorities—Bartram launched into the polemical part of her argument. Far from being timorously deferential in tone, her narrative challenged the Council's reasoning in banishing the wives and dependents in the first place. Her punishment, she observed, proceeded "merely from a fault of her Husbands," and she claimed to have always "manifested a friendly and warm desire for the Liberties and rights of the United States of America."

Bartram's protestations of allegiance perhaps satisfied the first of the constraints that had triggered the mass exile of Loyalist spouses, that of political danger to the state's security. Her petition did not even address the second issue, relating to women and dependents as an economic burden on a faltering public economy. The Council may have understood that the endorsers of Bartram's petition would be the guarantors of her material needs. We know almost nothing about the immediate circumstances of her return to Philadelphia, but the hardships of her previous sojourn there would not have lessened in her absence. In 1778 her resourcefulness may have combined with inertia in the aftermath of the British withdrawal to keep an existing enterprise, such as the Bartram shop, in business. On her return in 1782, however, she faced daunting obstacles to resuming operations there, obstacles that went far beyond the obvious start-up costs. Notwithstanding the de facto absence of her husband, she still labored under the legal encumbrances of coverture. Her ability to accumulate property, assume debts, contract or enforce contractual obligations, or do business of almost any kind was constrained by Alexander Bartram's presumptive right to the fruits of her enterprise.

However she supported herself and her child, we know that Bartram attempted to sever her marital ties during this period. Judicial divorces were unavailable in Pennsylvania before 1785, but in some cases the state legislature intervened on petition to resolve intolerable marital problems. In August 1784 Bartram petitioned the Assembly "praying to be divorced from her husband, Alexander Bartram." Perhaps because she did not allege adultery on his part, or because it was considering comprehensive reforms of the state's divorce law, the Assembly tabled her request. She submitted a new petition early in 1785, relating in greater detail Alexander's departure "without leaving a maintenance or support for her or her son," and citing his cruelty to her before deserting. This petition was likewise set aside.

Bartram's objective may have been to reestablish or protect her ability to engage in business as a *feme sole* trader. While Pennsylvania's divorce code before 1785 limited the relief to complaining parties to a divorce *a mensa et thoro* ("from bed and board")—little more than a civilly sanctioned separation agreement—all divorces granted by the legislature in this period were in fact given *a vinculo matrimonii*—or full and complete dissolutions of the marriages in question. The latter relief would remove Jane Bartram's disabilities under coverture. Without such relief her participation in remunerative economic activity on her own behalf would always be performed—if possible at all beyond the subsistence level—at risk that her husband would return to claim the proceeds of those endeavors.

Alexander Bartram did return to Philadelphia in 1785, in the same month that the Pennsylvania legislature passed the new judicial divorce bill. Ironically, it was he and not his wife who

emerged from their encounter with property rights impaired, and the liberalized provision for the dissolution of marriages had nothing to do with Jane Bartram's surprising good fortune in the matter. Bartram had filed an application for compensation with the Loyalist Commission on his arrival in Canada from New York late in 1783. In September 1785 he sailed to Pennsylvania "to procure proofs of [his property's sale under confiscation." Reaching Philadelphia without winter clothing or enough funds to stay long, he apparently expected his quest to proceed smoothly. He quickly discovered, however, the extent of his "obnoxiousness" to his former neighbors. By December he found himself so "reduced in circumstances" that he could not afford the continuing costs of gathering evidence, or even the price of his passage back to Halifax. This predicament brought Bartram face to face with his estranged wife, in a configuration of power relationships undoubtedly different from any they had before experienced.

The consequences of their encounter are engraved in the language of the "Agreement" that John Anstey later perplexedly forwarded to the Loyalist Commission in London. Labeled "Articles of Agreement and Transfer," the document served several ends. Jane Bartram was not even a principal party to the transaction. As a *feme covert*, she was legally barred from contracting with her own spouse. Instead William Johnson and James Stewart of Philadelphia—a bricklayer and a merchant, respectively—stood proxy as her "next friends" in covenant with her husband.

After reciting the sad particulars of the case—the "diverse disputes and unhappy differences" between the Bartrams; the "improp[riety]" of their ever cohabiting again; Jane's "reduc[tion] to penury," and her "intire dependen[ce] on her Friends in Pennsylvania for a support"—the indenture spelled out the terms of the bargain. Johnson and Stewart would "advance" Alexander Bartram £50.5.0 with which to finish collecting his evidence or, failing that, at least to buy a winter coat and book passage back to Nova Scotia to resume prosecuting his claim. For his own part, Bartram agreed to the effective (if not the legal) dissolution both of his marriage and of the prerogatives it gave him over his wife's separate identity and livelihood. He assented to the formalization of the de facto "seperation from Bed and Board which hath long since taken place" between them, and to its continuation "during the term of their joint lives." Moreover, he agreed not "at any time hereafter on any pretense whatsoever [to] molest or disturb the said Jane his wife in her seperate state, nor claim or demand any Estate, Right, Title, Interest or Property in any Lands, Tenements goods, chattels, moneys or effects whatsoever which shall come to her or be acquired by her." Bartram also explicitly acknowledged that such property would be "subject to her Disposition . . . in the same manner as if she were sole and unmarried, nor shall the same nor any part thereof be liable or chargeable with the debts, contracts or incumbrances or to the control of [himself] her said Husband."

Bartram acknowledged that his reasons for coming to terms with his wife included the "natural love and affection he hath and beareth to his son . . . James Alexander Bartram, and for his support, maintenance, education, and advancement in life." The young man had endured a "long fitt of Illness," the costs of which had been "very . . . burthensome to the said Jane Bartram." The indenture allowed Alexander both to discharge the duties of paternal love and to avoid implicitly threatened actions to recover those costs. The trustees were to receive Jane Bartram's share of the compensation award, place it out on loan, and spend the interest for James Bartram's support and education during his minority. When he came of age, they were to pay the principal to Jane and her son "in equal proportions as tenants in common." They had the discretion in the meantime, however, to "lend the whole or any part [of the principal] to Jane Bartram on her own bond, without interest, she supporting, maintaining and educating her said son in lieu of the interest

thereof." If Alexander paid half of his compensation as agreed, the trustees would indemnify him for any financial responsibility for the boy's support, past or future, but if he reneged on the bargain, he would be liable for those costs.

If the agreement comprised a hybrid between a bed and board divorce and a marriage settlement, its latter clauses laid the groundwork for a potential property division far more favorable to Jane Bartram than any she might have received under Pennsylvania's new divorce law. That law provided either for an absolute divorce, in which "all and every the duties, rights and claims accruing to either of the said parties . . . shall cease and determine," or a bed and board separation with discretionary alimony not to exceed "the third part of the annual profits or income of [the husband's] estate, or of his occupation of labor." Alexander Bartram's Pennsylvania property was gone, and he had spent much of his Canadian assets to finance his return to America. His claim against the Crown for £6000 (sterling) thus constituted most of his estate in the world. If their "Agreement" could be enforced, Jane Bartram stood to gain the beneficial use of half of the principal of that sum rather than (at most) one-third of its income.

If the agreement's ultimate implications for Bartram are unclear, its immediate consequences are more readily observable. While its purpose and eventual effect was to assist the Bartrams in disentangling their lives and fortunes, it had the ironic result of increasing their short-term interdependence. With a stake of her own in the outcome of the compensation process, Jane Bartram became an active participant in that process. Alexander returned to Nova Scotia early in 1786 and filed an amended compensation claim there in May. Jane, meanwhile, gathered evidence of his property losses and interceded with Pennsylvania authorities to get that evidence duly certified. She waited on John Nicholson, the state's Comptroller-General, to get certificates for the confiscated lands, only to learn that he "knew nothing of the Property" because the titles had never been officially recorded. Nicholson "directed Mrs. Bartram to cause them to be recorded, in order . . . to enable him to certify that the premises in the deeds mentioned were confiscated as the property of her husband."

When the commissioners in Canada awarded him £797 (sterling), barely more than ten percent of his request, Bartram wrote to his wife in the summer of 1786 and supplied detailed information about the patents in Northumberland County. A year later he asked the London commissioners to "reconsider" the "small[ness]" of the initial grant in light of the "strong proofs" he was then able to present of his "great losses." He attached a sheaf of titles, deeds, and other property records certified by a variety of Pennsylvania and New Jersey public officials. These documents were all dated, copied, or certified between February 1 and September 20, 1786, after Alexander Bartram left Pennsylvania.

Their assembly and transmittal bear marks of Jane Bartram's handiwork. Her efforts had a measurable effect. In 1789 the Commission reheard the case in London and voted to raise Alexander Bartram's award to £1,978, more than double his preliminary compensation.

It is tempting to see something more than the cold hand of coincidence in the juxtaposition between Alexander Bartram's handsomely enlarged compensation award in February 1789 and Jane Bartram's reemergence in the Philadelphia shopkeeping community by the end of that year. By virtue of bottomless reserves of resiliency and resourcefulness—of "application," to construe broadly Anstey's narrow, lawyerly term—supplemented by the help of others and, perhaps, even a belated measure of her husband's goodwill, Bartram had survived the 1780s. Never again in her life would she face such desperate straits.

KEY TERMS

Society of Friends:	The formal name of the religious body commonly known as Quakers.
Encumbered estate:	An estate which includes debts owed to creditors.
Feme sole:	The legal condition of women before marriage in which they had the right to hold and defend property in the courts.
Feme covert:	The legal condition of women after marriage in which all property rights were represented by the husband. This loss of rights was called coverture.
Non-importation agreements:	Agreements of American merchants not to trade with Britain in response to the Townshend Acts of 1767.
Assessors:	Tax assessors.

DISCUSSION TOPICS

After reading this essay, you should be able to discuss:

1. Jane Bartram's legal and social positions as a married women.

2. Alexander Bartram's position in Philadelphia society.

3. Jane Bartram's difficulties in establishing independent political views and property rights.

4. The outline of Jane Bartram's struggle to establish her independence from her husband.

5. The impediments faced by women who sought an independent position in post-Revolutionary society.

11

Absalom Jones: Free Black Leader

Gary B. Nash

The American Revolution wrought profound changes in the lives of the nation's African-American peoples. In the North, the new state governments passed gradual emancipation laws that set slavery on the road to extinction for the thousands of blacks held in bondage above the Mason-Dixon line. In the South, where the continuation of slavery was ensured by the rapid expansion of cotton production after the 1790s, masters found their bondspeople increasingly emboldened by the rhetoric of the Revolution and by the successful desertion of thousands of slaves to the British ranks during the war. While much has been written about post-Revolutionary slavery, until recently historians have paid relatively little attention to the free blacks who resided in the North. Yet scholarship has revealed that the end of slavery in the northern states prompted one of the most dramatic migrations in American history. Fleeing from rural isolation and the legacy of bondage, newly freed blacks flocked to northern cities in search of jobs, communities, and family life.

Of all the northern cities, Philadelphia exerted the greatest magnetic attraction for free blacks. At the center of Philadelphia's free black community stood the religiously oriented Free African Society and the African Church. More than any other institution, independent black churches symbolized and reinforced the African-American quest for racial parity following the Revolution. In this essay, Gary B. Nash tells the story of Absalom Jones, an ex-slave who became one of the leaders of Philadelphia's free black community. By setting Jones's life in the context of the city's developing black religious institutions, Nash reveals the difficulties and prejudice faced by free blacks as well as their steadfast desire to become free and equal citizens of the new republic.

"I, Absalom Jones, was born [a slave] in Sussex [Delaware] on the 6th of November, 1746." So he wrote nearly half a century later when he was a free man, a leader of the free black community in Philadelphia, and the first licensed black minister in the United States. Though hardly noticed in traditional history books, nor even in the recent wave of writing on Afro-American history, the story of Absalom Jones encapsulates much of the experience of the first generation of freed slaves in America. Moreover, his accomplishments, especially his role in establishing the first separate black church in America, entitle him to a place among the "men of mark"—the early black leaders who laid the foundations of modern Afro-American life by fashioning social and religious institutions that carried forward the black quest for freedom and equality after the American Revolution.

His master, Benjamin Wynkoop, took him from the fields, Absalom remembered, when "I was small . . . to wait and attend on him in the house." Removed from the world of field labor, he developed a desire for learning. With pennies given to him from time to time, he recalled, "I soon bought myself a primer and begged to be taught by any body that I found able and willing to give me the least instruction. Soon after this, I was able to purchase a spelling book . . . and a Testament." Literacy could only have increased the distance between him and those of his age who did not live in the big house; and hence Absalom—who had only this slave name—became introspective, or "singular," as he termed it. Then, in 1762, at age 16, his master sold his mother, five brothers, and a sister after deciding to move north to Philadelphia, the Quaker capital of Pennsylvania.

The breaking up of his family, though doubtless traumatic, proved to be a turning point in his life. While bereft of his kin, he was taken to the earliest center of abolitionism in America and to the city where humanitarian reformers had created an atmosphere conducive to education and family formation among slaves.

Thus, while he had to work his master's shop from dawn to dark, Absalom soon prevailed upon Wynkoop to allow him to attend a night school for blacks.

In 1770 Absalom married the slave of his master's neighbor, taking vows in the Anglican church where the Wynkoop family worshipped. Soon after this, encouraged by the abolitionist sentiment that Quakers and others had spread through Philadelphia, he put the tool of literacy to work. Drawing up an appeal for his wife's release, he carried it, with his wife's father at his side, to "some of the principal Friends [Quakers] of this city," asking for their support. "From some we borrowed, and from others we received donations," he recounted. Thereafter, Absalom "made it my business to work until twelve or one o'clock at night, to assist my wife in obtaining a livelihood," and to pay the money that was borrowed to purchase her freedom. It took years to repay the debt. But by 1778, while the American Revolution was occurring, Absalom had apparently discharged his obligations because he was then pleading with his master to allow him to purchase his own freedom. Wynkoop would not consent to this until October 1, 1784—six years after the first of what Absalom remembered as a series of humble requests.

It was probably in 1784, upon gaining his release, that Absalom authenticated his freedom to the world around him by taking the surname Jones. It was a common English name but nonetheless one that *he* had chosen and one that could not be mistaken for the Dutch name of his master whom he had served until the age of 38. But he acted as if he bore his master no grudges. Forbearing and even tempered, he continued to work in Wynkoop's shop. Years later, in an obituary for Jones, it was said that his master "always gave him the character of having been a faithful and exemplary servant, remarkable for many good qualities; especially for his being not only of a peaceable demeanour, but for being possessed of the talent for inducing a disposition to it in others."

Two years after gaining his freedom in Philadelphia, Absalom Jones met another recently freed slave from Delaware named Richard Allen. Allen was much Jones's junior in years but much his senior in his commitment to leading out of physical bondage fellow Africans still enslaved and out of psychological bondage those who had been recently freed. While still a slave, Allen had been converted to Methodism by itinerant preachers during the revolutionary years in Kent County, Delaware. After gaining his freedom in 1780 he spent six years interspersing work as a sawyer and wagon driver with months of riding the Methodist circuits from South Carolina to New York. He learned to preach with great effect to black and white audiences and traveled with some of the leading Methodist sojourners. By the time he arrived in Philadelphia in 1786, full of Methodist zeal and convinced that God had appointed him to special tasks, Allen seems to have completed the crucial psychological middle passage by which those who gained freedom in a legal sense procured as well the emotional autonomy that came only when they overcame servility to whites and dependence upon them.

Invited to preach in the white Methodist church in Philadelphia, Allen soon "raised a Society . . . of forty-two members." Among them was Absalom Jones, who had abandoned Christ Church where his former master worshipped in favor of St. George's Methodist Church. Like taking a surname, this was a step in the forging of a new self-identity, a part of the difficult throwing off of dependency that was indispensable in learning how to live as a fully free person.

Within months of Allen's arrival in Philadelphia Absalom Jones and several other recently freed slaves joined the Methodist preacher to discuss forming an independent black religious society. Religion and education had been the mainsprings of freedom and achievement for all these men. So it was natural that when they looked around them to find the majority of former slaves illiterate and unchurched, they "often communed together

upon this painful and important subject" and determined "to form some kind of religious society." Shortly thereafter, Allen proposed this "to the most respectable people of color in this city," only to be "met with opposition." Leading white Methodists objected even more strenuously, using "very degrading and insulting language to try to prevent us from going on." Nevertheless, out of these deliberations came the Free African Society of Philadelphia, which Jones and Allen founded in April 1787. Though mutual aid was its purported goal, the Society was quasi-religious in character and, beyond that, was an organization for building black strength and pride through collective and independent action. Before we can examine how the Free African Society midwived the birth of the first black churches in North America we must form a mental picture of the world these former bondspersons found themselves in and explore their understanding of the possible strategies that they might adopt in hammering out a post-slavery existence that went beyond mere legal release from thralldom.

Black Philadelphians, like former slaves in other parts of America, had to rethink their relationship to white society in the early days of the Republic. Were they Africans in America who might now return to their homelands? Were they Afro-Americans whose future was bound up in creating a new existence on soil where they had toiled most of their lives but whose cultural heritage was African? Or were they simply Americans with dark skin, who in seeking places as free men and women had to assimilate as quickly as possible to the cultural norms and social institutions of white society?

Outwardly, Philadelphia represented a haven from persecution and an arena of opportunity for manumitted blacks. It was the center of Quaker abolitionism, the location of the national government that had issued ringing phrases about freedom and equality for all, and the capital of the state that in 1780 had passed the first abolition act in America. It was also a bustling maritime center that held out the promise of employment for migrating Afro-

Americans. For all these reasons Philadelphia became a magnet for those released from bondage during the 1780s, and this drawing power also owed something to the considerable sympathy among some of its white inhabitants for freed blacks setting out on the road to freedom. Hence, from a city with about 450 slaves and an equal number of free blacks at the end of the American Revolution Philadelphia grew to contain 2,100 blacks, all but 273 of them free, in 1790, and more than 6,500 blacks, of whom only 55 remained in bondage, in 1800.

In its internal workings, however, Philadelphia was far from ideal for former slaves. The illiterate and often unskilled men and women who trekked there after the Revolution had to compete for jobs with lower-class Irish and German immigrants and did not always find work. Though not disenfranchised by law, free blacks were prohibited by white social pressure from voting. Also, virtually every institution and social mechanism in the city—religious or secular, economic and social—engaged in discriminatory practices which flowed like a natural force from the pervasive belief in black inferiority. The common assumption was that blacks were either innately handicapped or had been irreparably degraded by the experience of slavery.

For black wayfarers who found their way to Philadelphia after the Revolution overcoming patterns of behavior peculiar to slavery became a crucial matter. By its nature, slavery assumed the superiority of the white master class, and even the most benevolent master occupied a power relationship vis-á-vis his slaves that daily reminded blacks of their lowly position and condition. Probably few American slaves believed they were inferior human beings, but slavery required them to act so, and daily behavior became so patterned that dependency and servility developed as a way of life among many of them. Newly freed, they had to face the dominant culture, which was far from ready to treat them as equals and continued to demand deferential comportment from them. We can infer from the fact that almost all the

early black institutions in the North used the adjective "African" in their titles—the Free African Society, the African School, the African Church of Philadelphia—that these ex-slaves identified positively with their ancestral homelands and did not subscribe to the common white characterizations of Africa as a dismal, cultureless environment. Nonetheless, white racism impinged on their lives at every turn and, although not of the virulent form it would assume early in the nineteenth century, it tended to keep cowed the poorest and weakest members of the emerging black communities.

Recognizing the hidebound nature of white attitudes and the psychic scars inflicted by slavery, a few former slaves in the North attempted to solve the problem simply by opting out of American society and returning to Africa. But the small colonization movement of the 1780s that was centered in New England made virtually no impact on black Philadelphians, who overwhelmingly cast their lot with America. Nonetheless, the will to plan rationally, to strive for an independent and dignified existence, and to work for the future of their children depended upon throwing off the incubus of slavery, an institution which had perpetuated itself by exacting a terrible price for black attempts at independent or self-reliant behavior. Some freedmen in Philadelphia believed that in this work of emotional self-reconstruction their future lay not in trying to pry open the doors of white institutions but in building autonomous black organizations where the people emerging from the house of bondage could gather strength, develop their own leaders, and socialize and worship in their own ways.

In the post-Revolutionary era free blacks also had to confront the role that benevolence played in perpetuating feelings of servility and in shaping black–white relations. "There can be no greater disparity of power," writes David Brion Davis, "than that between a man convinced of his own disinterested service and another man who is defined as a helpless object." Thus, white benevolence perpetuated black dependence, often stood in the way of mutual respect, and impeded the growth of positive self-images among freedmen and freedwomen, who could not feel truly free so long as they had to rely on white help in creating a new life for themselves.

Only a few years out of bondage in the 1780s, Philadelphia's free blacks thus lived in a highly fluid situation full of dangers and full of opportunities. Their lowly position and circumscribed means made it imperative to accept the support of benevolent whites who offered education, sometimes jobs, and almost always moral guidance. Likewise, they could hardly hope to obtain the release of their racial brethren still in bondage without white leadership and support. Yet many of them understood that while short-term circumstances required white patronage, the long-term goal must be to stand independent of white largesse.

It is within this ideological context that we can see the Free African Society of Philadelphia as much more than a black mutual aid society. Beginning as an organization in which free blacks were taking the first halting steps toward developing their own leaders and solving their own problems, it became a society which founded churches, assumed a supervisory role over the moral life of the black community, and worked to create a visionary black consciousness out of the disparate human material that had found its way to Philadelphia in this period. But this took time.

While the Free African Society got underway, Richard Allen's preaching and Absalom Jones's quiet aid to those he found in need increased the black congregants at St. George's. Philadelphia's blacks, both slave and free, had married, baptized their children, and attended religious services at most of the city's churches since before the Revolution and had particularly flocked to the Anglican churches, which encouraged them with religious and secular instruction. Now they began transferring their allegiance to the Methodist church, an offshoot of the Anglican church which had declared itself independent only in 1784. This transfer of allegiance is not difficult to understand, for the new Methodist ministers "made no pretensions to literary qual-

ifications," as the first black historian of the African Church of Philadelphia wrote in the 1850s, "and being despised and persecuted as religious enthusiasts, their sympathies naturally turned towards the lowly, who like themselves, were of small estimate in the sight of worldly greatness." Also commending Methodism to former slaves were the well-known antislavery views of founder John Wesley and the Methodist discipline and polity formulated in 1784, which attacked slave trading and slaveholding and barred persons engaged in these practices from holding church offices.

Meanwhile, Jones and Allen enlarged the activities of the Free African Society. In early 1790 the Society attempted to lease the Stranger's Burial ground in order to turn it into a black cemetery under black control. In the next month the Society instituted "a regular mode of procedure with respect to . . . marriages" and began keeping a book of marriage records. Having assumed quasi-ecclesiastical functions, the Society took the final step in September 1790 when a special committee led by Jones recommended the initiation of formal religious services.

All of these enlarged functions bore a decidedly Quakerly stamp, reflecting the strong influence of the Society of Friends on many of the leading members. More particularly, this influence came through the work of Anthony Benezet, the wizened, saintly little Huguenot immigrant who dedicated so much of his life to the Negro's cause. Benezet wrote half a dozen pamphlets against slavery and the slave trade between 1759 and 1784, founded a school for blacks in 1770, and tirelessly devoted himself to it for the rest of his life. In 1780 he personally lobbied with every member of the Pennsylvania legislature to pass a gradual abolition act. When Benezet died in 1784, slaves and free blacks alike turned out en masse to follow his funeral procession to the graveyard and testify to his work on their behalf.

While Quaker support was indispensable to the African Society at first, it also caused difficulties and eventually a deep rift in the black ranks. Quaker humanitarianism was never of the sort that was based on a deep sense of the "likeness among all persons." Quakers held themselves apart from other people, white and black, and in fact the Society of Friends was the only religious group in Philadelphia that refused to accept blacks as members in the 1780s. Theirs was more a policy "of stewardship than a true humanitarianism," and their efforts on behalf of blacks "partook more of condescension than humanitarianism."

The Quakerly leanings of many Free African Society members caused Richard Allen great pain. He made no objections when the African Society adopted Quaker-like visiting committees in early 1788 to call on black families or when they instituted the disownment practices of Quakers in September of that year, to disenroll wayward members. But two months later, when the Society adopted the Friendly practice of beginning meetings with fifteen minutes of silence, Allen led the withdrawal of "a large number" of dissenters whose adherence to Methodism had accustomed them to "an unconstrained outburst of their feelings in religious worship." Allen came no more to meetings of the African Society but privately began convening some of its members in an attempt to stop the drift of the organization toward the practices of the Quakers.

Jones and others made repeated efforts to bring Allen back into the bosom of the group and censured him "for attempting to sow division among us." When their efforts failed, they followed the Quaker procedure of declaring that "he has disunited himself from membership with us." This was in June 1789. Nineteen months later, following four months of deliberations, they began holding formal religious meetings in the Quaker African Schoolhouse.

After Allen's disownment from the Free African Society, the leadership role fell primarily to Absalom Jones. It was the mild-mannered and conciliatory Jones who made the crucial connections in the white community that launched plans for building a black church. The ties with the Society of Friends were wearing thin by the summer of 1791 because many Quakers objected to the Sunday psalm singing by blacks in the Quaker schoolhouse. But Jones had been forging new patronage lines to one of Philadelphia's most influential citizens—the powerful, opinionated doctor, Benjamin Rush. Over the next four years it was Rush who became the Anthony Benezet of the 1790s so far as Philadelphia's free blacks were concerned.

As a young physician before the American Revolution, Rush had written a passionate antislavery pamphlet. But this ardor for the cause had cooled during the war, and he had played no role in the work of the Pennsylvania Abolition Society when it was reestablished in 1784. Then, in a poignant example of trans-Atlantic abolitionist influence, Rush threw himself into the fray in 1787 after reading Thomas Clarkson's recently published *Essay on the Slavery and Commerce of the Human Species*, which in turn had been inspired by Clarkson's reading of Anthony Benezet's *Historical Account of Guinea*, one reading of which convinced him to devote his life to abolitionism. So thoroughly was Rush converted to the free blacks' cause that he immediately joined the Pennsylvania Abolition Society, freed his slave, William Gruber, and shortly thereafter wrote to a friend that "I love even the name of Africa, and never see a Negro slave or freeman without emotions which I seldom feel in the same degree towards my unfortunate fellow creatures of a fairer complexion."

During the summer of 1791 plans went forward for promoting the black church, although white opposition among those who had claimed to be friends of the free blacks surfaced quickly. Working with Absalom Jones, and perhaps with Richard Allen, who had reconciled his differences with members of the African Society, Rush drew up a plan of church government and articles of faith. A white merchant, Robert Ralston, joined Rush in composing subscription papers to be carried about the city to solicit building funds. Aware that many Philadelphians regarded him as impetuous and idiosyncratic, Rush tried to stay in the background, convinced that "the work will prosper the better for my keeping myself out of sight." Rush was hardly capable of self-effacement, however, and word of his role in the plans circulated through the city. Within days of composing the plan of government Rush found himself accosted in the street by William White, rector of Christ Church and recently appointed bishop of the Episcopal Church in Pennsylvania. White "expressed his disapprobation to the proposed African church" because "it originated in pride." Leading Quakers also conveyed their displeasure to Absalom Jones, and the Methodists threatened disownment of any black Methodist who participated in the undertaking. Paternalistic Philadelphians discovered that helping their black brothers gave greater satisfaction than seeing them help themselves.

Such criticism from Anglicans, Quakers, and Methodists, many of whom had been active in the Abolition Society, drove home the lesson that benevolent whites regarded freedmen as deeply inferior and could not abide independent action—pride, Bishop White called it—that challenged that characterization. An early historian of black Methodism, reflecting in 1867 on the final separation of Richard Allen from the white Methodist church, dwelt on precisely this point. "The giant crime committed by the Founders of the African Methodist Episcopal Church," wrote Benjamin Tanner, "was that they dared to organize a Church of men, men to think for themselves, men to talk for themselves, men to act for themselves: A Church of men who support from their own substance, however scanty, the ministration of the Word which they receive; men who spurn to have their churches built for them, and their pastors supported from the coffers of some charitable organization; men who prefer to live by the sweat of their own brow and be free."

No chance yet existed in 1791 for Philadelphia's free blacks to gain the full meaning of freedom through completely independent action. Half of them still lived in the households of whites as domestic servants and hired hands; many had to indenture out their children through the good offices of the Abolition Society; and, as a group, they still were obliged to rely heavily on benevolent white Philadelphians for organizing schools and, in the present case, the African Church. Hence, Absalom Jones and the other black leaders worked closely with Benjamin Rush, Robert Ralston, and other whites in the summer of 1791 to raise subscriptions for their own place of worship. The work went on "swimmingly," Rush reported in August. An "Address of the Representatives of the African Church," an appeal for building funds, was carried to prominent men in the city. This succeeded in garnering some modest contributions, including donations from George Washington and Thomas Jefferson. Attempting to appeal as widely as possible to both blacks and whites, Jones and the other leaders adopted articles of association and a plan of church government "so general as to embrace all, and yet so orthodox in cardinal points as to offend none." But the flow of money soon stopped, perhaps because of the opposition to the church expressed by leading white churchmen. So Jones and Allen decided to broaden their appeal. Believing "that if we put our trust in the Lord, he would stand by us," Allen recounted, they took to the streets in March 1792. "We went out with our subscription paper," recalled Allen, "and met with great success," collecting $360 on the first day.

But thereafter the going got harder and some of the early optimism began to fade. The early subscriptions proved sufficient to buy two adjacent lots on Fifth Street, only a block from the Statehouse, for $450. But most blacks had little to contribute from their meager resources, and most whites seem to have snapped their pocketbooks shut at the thought of a black church. Whereas they had initially responded to the idea of an "African" church as a piece of arrogance on the part of a people so recently released from slavery, they now began calculating the effect on their own churches. "The old and established [religious] societies," wrote Rush, "look shy at them, each having lost some of its members by the new association." Still, Rush did not waver in his conviction that "the poor blacks will succeed in forming themselves into a distinct independent church."

Despite these early difficulties, the resolve of black Philadelphians to form a separate church grew mightily in the fall of 1792 after one of the most dramatic confrontations in early American church history. A number of black leaders were still attending services at St. George's Methodist Church, where the congregation had outgrown the seating capacity. When the white elders decided to expand their house of worship, black Methodists contributed money and labor to the effort. But on the first Sunday after the renovations were completed the elders informed the black worshipers who filed into the church that they must sit in a segregated section of the new gallery rather than along the walls, as had been their custom before. Richard Allen later recounted:

> We expected to take the seats over the ones we formerly occupied below, not knowing any better. We took those seats; meeting had begun, and they were nearly done singing, and just as we got to the seats, the Elder said, "Let us pray." We had not been long upon our knees before I heard considerable scuffling and loud talking. I raised my head up and saw one of the trustees, H——— M———, having hold of the Rev. Absalom Jones, pulling him up off his knees, and saying "You must get up, you must not kneel here." Mr. Jones replied, "Wait until prayer is over, and I will get up, and trouble you no more." With that he beckoned to one of the trustees, Mr. L——— S———, to come to his assistance. He came and went over to William White to pull him up. By this time prayer was over, and we all went out of the church in a body, and they were no more plagued by us in the church.

The St. George's incident confirmed what many blacks had already suspected—that there would be no truly biracial Christian community in the white churches of the city. If they were to worship with dignity, it must be in churches of their own. The first black historian of the black church movement described this striving for dignity in the black exodus from St. George's that followed the discriminatory treatment. It was an "age of general and searching inquiry,"

wrote William Douglass, "into the equity of old and established customs," a time when "a moral earthquake had awakened the slumber of ages" and caused "these humble men, just emerged from the house of bondage . . . to rise above those servile feelings which all their antecedents were calculated to cherish and to assume, as they did, an attitude of becoming men conscious of invaded rights . . ." They were determined, wrote Allen, "to worship God under our own vine and fig tree" and "were filled with fresh vigor to get a house erected to worship God in."

Despite such renewed commitment Jones, Allen, and the other black leaders reluctantly concluded by late 1792 that they could not raise sufficient money to build their African church on the lots they had purchased. To their rescue came the unlikeliest of figures—the Welsh immigrant John Nicholson, who had blazed meteorically onto the Philadelphia scene after the war as state comptroller and high flying speculator in western lands and revolutionary loan certificates. Barely accepted in polite Philadelphia circles, not attached to any church, and uninvolved in the work of the Abolition Society, Nicholson provided what none of the Philadelphia elite would offer—a large loan of $1,000 with which to begin construction. "Humanity, charity, and patriotism never united their claims in a petition with more force than in the present instance," wrote Rush to Nicholson in a letter hand carried by William Gray and Absalom Jones. "You *will* not—you *cannot* refuse their request." Five days later Jones and Gray wrote Nicholson suggesting a 10-year mortgage with "Lawful interest to be paid Quarterly" and pressed their request "for the sake of Religion & Christianity and as this is the first Institution of the kind. . . ."

It took another two months to execute the mortgage and another to draw up building contracts. Finally, in March 1793, as reports of black rebellion in the French West Indies filtered into Philadelphia, the city's free blacks and some of their white benefactors gathered to see earth turned for the church. Richard Allen remembered the day vividly a quarter of a century later. "As I was the first proposer of the African Church, I put the first spade into the ground to dig the cellar for the same. This was the first African Church or meeting house to be erected in the United States of America."

As the workmen completed the African Church in the spring of 1794, Philadelphia's blacks gathered to make a momentous decision about denominational affiliation. Absalom Jones and Allen still favored uniting with the Methodists, even though the white elder stationed in the city remained opposed to a separate black church and "would neither be for us nor have anything to do with us." But the "large majority" favored uniting with the Anglicans (now called Episcopalians), which is understandable in light of the fact that so many of them, both as slaves and free persons, had married, worshiped, and christened their children in the city's three Anglican churches. Steadfast in his conviction that "there was no religious sect or denomination that would suit the capacity of the colored people as well as the Methodist," Allen quietly withdrew again. Nor could he accept the invitation of the majority to be their minister. "I informed them," he wrote later, "that I could not be anything but a Methodist, as I was born and awakened under them, and I could go no further with them, for I was a Methodist, and would leave them in peace and love."

With Allen declining to lead them, the deacons and elders turned to Absalom Jones. He lacked Allen's exhortatory gifts, but his balance, tenacity, education, and dignified leadership all commended him. In July steps were taken to formalize the decision to unite with the Episcopal Church. The black Philadelphians pragmatically agreed to "commit all the ecclesiastical affairs of our church to the government of the Protestant Episcopal Church of North America," while at the same time securing internal control of their church through a constitution that gave them and their successors "the power of choosing our minister and assistant minister," provided that members were to be admitted only

by the minister and churchwardens, and specified that the officers of the church—the vestrymen and deacons—were to be chosen by ballot from among members of at least twelve months standing. Finally, only "men of color, who are Africans, or the descendants of the African race," could elect or be elected into any church office except that of minister and assistant minister. With the help of Benjamin Rush, they had contrived a formula for maintaining black control of the church, while allowing for the absence of trained blacks to fill the ministry.

On July 17, 1794, the African Church of Philadelphia opened its doors for worship. The published account of the dedication ceremony indicates that much of the white ministerial opposition had melted. "The venerable Clergy of almost every denomination, and a number of other very respectable citizens were present," it was noted. Samuel Magaw, rector of St. Paul's Church, gave the sermon from the text "Ethiopia shall soon stretch out her hands unto God." The discourse was from Isaiah: "The people that walked in darkness have seen a great light"—the same epigram that was etched in marble above the church doors.

Magaw's sermon provided a window into the attitudes of Philadelphia's benevolent white leadership at this time. Reconciled to the idea of a black church, they still remained convinced of the free blacks' inferiority and consequently focused on the overriding importance of moral management and social control. Showing his ignorance of the mainsprings of action in the black community, Magaw stressed the need for gratitude and deference on the part of the blacks who crowded the church. They or their fathers, he preached, had come from the heathenish lands of Senegal, Gambia, Benin, Angola, and Congo, and that burden of birth had been increased by the dismal effects of slavery, which "sinks the mind, no less than the body . . . destroys all principle; corrupts the feelings; prevents man from either discerning, or choosing aright in anything." Having been brought from "a land of Pagan darkness, to a land of Gospel light" by white Christian goodness, these former slaves must now maintain their gratitude to those who freed them and donated or loaned money to build the church. They must pray—but not take action—for their brethren still in bondage.

The emphasis in Magaw's sermon was on black passivity and moderation in all things. He warned the black congregation to suppress pride, which he claimed was on the rise among them. Rather they should cultivate "an obliging, friendly, meek conversation." Their church, he counseled them in a perfect display of white paternalism, owed its existence to the benevolent action of whites. That it had been born in strife and had risen only when free blacks defied the passive roles assigned them escaped his notice. But if we set alongside Magaw's dedication sermon the "Causes and Motives" for establishing the African Church, written by Absalom Jones just a month later, we can better comprehend the dialectical struggle that free blacks were engaged in. It is this document, which also announced the decision to name the church St. Thomas's African Episcopal Church of Philadelphia, in honor of the apostle, that indicates the quest for a black ideology and for strategies that would promote strength, security, and meaning in the lives of the first generation of ex-slaves in America. They had been encouraged, Jones wrote, "to arise out of the dust and shake ourselves, and throw off that servile fear, that the habit of oppression and bondage trained us up in." This statement can be taken as almost directly evidence of the influence of Anthony Benezet, under whom Jones and many of the other blacks active in the African Society had been schooled. The Quaker teacher had frontally challenged the deeply rooted doctrine of black inferiority, urged his pupils to regard themselves as "citizens of the world," argued doggedly as early as 1762 that the African environment had produced notable cultures and must not be considered as a place of jungle barbarism, and thus taught his black students that it was the environment of slavery, not innate condition, that turned Africans in America into degraded and defective human beings.

Inspired by Benezet's theories of human brotherhood and the environmentalist argument that it was slavery that had incapacitated Africans in America, Absalom Jones, Richard Allen, and others received further encouragement to strike out on their own from Benjamin Rush and others. An equally important factor in the shedding of the debilitating fear "that the habit of oppression and bondage trained us up in" was the day-to-day accomplishments of Philadelphia's blacks during the decade that followed the Revolution. Through their ability to establish families and residences, by their demonstrated capacity to sustain themselves as free laborers and artisans, and in their success at conducting themselves morally, soberly, and civilly they had proved to themselves the groundless character of the prevalent white view that former slaves were permanently corrupted and unassimilable people.

In drawing up their "Articles of Association" with the Protestant Episcopal Church, Absalom Jones and his cohorts indicated their understanding that, while they had made progress, the road ahead was strewn with barriers that could be surmounted only with the support of white patrons. The Articles announced, in a direct reference to the charges of Bishop White about black "pride," that they wished "to avoid all appearance of evil, by self-conceitedness, or an intent to promote or establish any new human device among us," and hence they had decided to "resign and conform ourselves" to the Episcopal Church of North America. Nonetheless, this was to be a black church, as their constitution spelled out.

In September 1794, one month after the constitution for their church had been accepted by the Convention of the Episcopal Church in Pennsylvania, the trustees and "representatives of the congregation" moved to solidify the racial character of their church by requesting Bishop White to qualify Absalom Jones "to act as our minister." Many years later it was recorded that Jones's "devotion to the sick and dying" during the yellow fever epidemic of 1793 had brought him wide recognition in the black community.

"Administering to the bodily as well as spiritual wants of many poor sufferers, and soothing the last moments of many departing souls among his people, he became greatly endeared to the colored race." The Episcopal Convention took nearly a year before approving Jones as the minister of St. Thomas's, and it did so only after arranging a *quid pro quo* whereby they waived the Greek and Latin requirement for the ministry in exchange for the stipulation that the African church forego the right to send a representative to the yearly convention where denominational policy was set.

Absalom Jones spent nearly a quarter of a century ministering to his flock at St. Thomas's before he died in 1818 at the age of 72. In this role he was far more than a religious leader, for the black church was the center of social, educational, and political life as well. As W. E. B. Du Bois observed, it "is the world in which the Negro moves and acts." Jones's church launched a school for young black children in the late 1790s. It organized several mutual assistance and moral reform societies. Its members stood prominently among petitioners to the state and national legislatures who over the years called for ending the slave trade, abolishing slavery, and repealing discriminatory laws. Both a place of refuge in a hostile white world and a site from which to attack discrimination and exploitation, the church built by the humble slave from Delaware stood at the center of the black struggle for dignity, freedom, and social justice in the new American nation.

KEY TERMS

Methodist circuit: Territory assigned to an itinerant Methodist minister, often in frontier rural areas without settled preachers or established churches.

Christ Church: The principal Episcopal church in Philadelphia.

Quaker abolitionism: Reference to the Quakers, who had been among the earliest and most tenacious proponents of the abolition of slavery.

Huguenot: French Protestants, many of whom sought refuge in America to escape persecution following Louis XIV's revocation of the Edict of Nantes in 1685.

Environmentalist argument: The popular eighteenth-century idea that human personality was primarily shaped and determined by a person's interaction with their surroundings.

DISCUSSION TOPICS

After reading this essay, you should be able to discuss:

1. The means by which a black community formed in Philadelphia.

2. The role of Absalom Jones in the formation of this community.

3. The role of the Quakers in the northern abolition movement.

4. The reasons that free blacks formed separate organizations and congregations.

5. The limits of white benevolence.

12

Tecumseh, the Shawnee Prophet, and American History

R. David Edmunds

The close of the Revolutionary War meant many things to the American people. To some it conferred a guarantee of freedom, to others a return to the peacefulness of everyday life, and to yet others an opportunity to establish a life of independence beyond the Appalachian Mountains. But for Native Americans, the defeat of the British meant the removal of the last defense against expanding American settlements full of farmers hungry for their land. Even before the war ended in 1783, settlers poured onto Indian land in the middle South and the Ohio River valley. There they met tribes that, cut off from a reliable supply of arms and trade goods, had difficulty preventing these incursions on their ancestral land. Moreover, in the eyes of the advancing Americans, who had gained vast military experience during the Revolution, Indians were enemies, having sided with the British during the Revolution in hope of receiving royal protection for their lands.

As tribes were pushed west, small pockets of resistance began to develop. Settler outposts were raided, outlying settlements attacked, farmers and livestock killed. But these remained isolated incidents and offered little prospect for sustained resistance to white incursions. It was against this background that two extraordinary Indian leaders emerged. Tenskwatawa and Tecumseh, Shawnee brothers, learned of the rapacity of American land hunger at an early age and from the dishonor of displacement dreamed of an Indian nation as strong and vigorous as the thirteen colonies that had just won their independence. In different ways they both worked for the revitalization of Native American culture and the securing of an independent nation for all Native Americans. Their quest is the subject of this essay by R. David Edmunds, who offers a different view of the better-known Tecumseh than is generally found in history books.

"Tecumseh, the Shawnee Prophet, and American History: A Reassessment." *Western Historical Quarterly,* 14 (1983), pp. 261–276. Reprinted by permission of *Western Historical Quarterly.*

High upon a granite pedestal overlooking "the Yard" at the United States Naval Academy at Annapolis stands a bronze statue of an Indian warrior. Midshipmen passing in and out of Bancroft Hall traditionally salute the statue before taking examinations in the hope that the renowned warrior's medicine will assist them during their tests. Most midshipmen, if asked whom the statue represents, will reply that it is a replica of Tecumseh, the famous war chief of the Shawnees. In reality, however, the statue was never intended to be Tecumseh. It represents Tamened, a chief among the Delawares.

The midshipmen's incorrect identification of the bronze figure is not surprising, for Americans have long regarded Tecumseh as one of their foremost Indian heroes. He is one of the few militant Indian leaders who was almost universally praised by his white contemporaries. During the War of 1812 both British and American officers spoke highly of the Shawnee, and since his death his image has grown accordingly. Eulogized by historians, Tecumseh has achieved an almost legendary status. His biographers have presented an Indian of superhuman qualities; and Alvin M. Josephy, in his volume *The Patriot Chiefs,* entitles his chapter on the Shawnee as "Tecumseh: The Greatest Indian."

If the white observers and historians have been laudatory in their description of Tecumseh, they have been universal in their condemnation of his brother, Tenskwatawa, the Shawneee Prophet. Both British and American leaders denounced the holy man as a "pretender" and a "coward," and historians have enlarged upon such qualities to present an image of a charlatan who manipulated the tribesmen for his own purposes. While Tecumseh's political and military movement is pictured as logical and praiseworthy, the Prophet represents the darker side of Indian life. A religious fanatic, Tenskwatawa is presented as riding his brother's coattails to a position of minor prominence.

Unquestionably, the Shawnee brothers emerged to positions of leadership during a period of great stress for Native Americans. Although the Treaty of Greenville supposedly had drawn a line between Indian and American lands in Ohio, the treaty was ignored. Frontier settlement continued to advance north from the Ohio Valley, threatening the remaining Indian land base in the region. Meanwhile, white hunters repeatedly trespassed onto Indian lands to hunt game needed by the tribesmen, and by the first decade of the nineteenth century game was becoming scarce. The fur trade declined in a similar manner, and after 1800 many warriors were hard pressed to provide for their families. Not suprisingly, the Indians retaliated by stealing settlers' livestock, and the resulting clashes produced casualties on both sides. Obviously, both Indians and whites suffered, but losses were much larger among the natives. Governor William Henry Harrison of Indiana admitted that "a great many of the Inhabitants of the Fronteers [*sic*] consider the murdering of the Indians in the highest degree meritorious," while Governor Arthur St. Clair of the Northwest Territory reported that "the number of those unhappy people [the Indians] who have been killed since the peace at Greenville . . . is great enough to give serious alarm for the consequences."

Much of the Indian–white conflict was triggered by alcohol. Frustrated over their declining political and economic status, beleaguered tribesmen drowned their sorrows in frontier whiskey. Although illegal, alcohol was in plentiful supply, and brawls resulting from the Bacchanalia spread social chaos throughout the Indian villages. Once-proud warriors quarreled among themselves or abused their kinsmen, while others retreated into drunken stupors. Some Shawnees, weakened by their dissipation, fell victims to influenza, smallpox, and other diseases. Others sat passively in their lodges, bewildered by the changes swirling around them. Meanwhile, the clans—traditional kinship systems designed to regulate and provide cohesiveness among the separate Shawnee villages— were unable to cope with the multitude of problems besetting the tribe.

Overwhelmed by the chaos within their villages, the Shawnees pondered the causes. Although many tribesmen realized that the majority of their problems emanated from outside sources such as loss of lands, economic deterioration, injustice, and alcohol, others suspected darker elements and probed inward, examining the fabric of tribal society. Predictably, traditional Shawnees concluded that much of their trouble resulted from witchcraft, for the fear of witches and their evil power permeated Shawnee culture, and neighboring tribes believed the Shawnees to have a particular affinity for sorcery and the supernatural.

The basis for such fear lay deep in tribal tradition. The Shawnees believed that in the dim past, when they first crossed the Great Water in search of their homeland, they had been opposed by a huge water serpent who represented the evil powers in the universe. Although their warriors had killed the serpent, witches had saved part of its body, which still held a potent and malevolent power. Contained in medicine bundles, this evil had been passed down through the ages and was used by witches to spread disorder throughout the tribe.

The balance between order and chaos formed a focal point for Shawnee cosmology. The Shawnees believed they were a people chosen by the great power in the universe—"the Master of Life"—to occupy the center of the earth and bring harmony to the world. For their assistance, the Master of Life provided the Shawnees with a sacred bundle possessing powerful medicine that could be used for good. He also gave the tribe a series of laws regulating their personal conduct. If the Shawnees cherished the bundle, and used its medicine properly, and if they followed the sacred laws, they would prosper and their world would be orderly. But if witches gained the ascendancy, or if the Shawnees relinquished the ways of their fathers, their lives would be full of turmoil. In the years following the Treaty of Greenville, many traditional Shawnees believed that the witches had gained the upper hand.

Not surprisingly, many associated the Americans with these forces of evil. The Shawnees believed that the sea was the home of the Great Serpent—the embodiment of disorder. Their forefathers had always warned that pale-skinned invaders might emerge from the water to disrupt the harmony of the Shawnee homeland. Since the Americans had first appeared on the eastern seashore, many tribesmen were certain the invaders were the children of the Serpent, intent upon the Indians' downfall. In 1803 Shawnees at Fort Wayne informed Indian agents that their ancestors had stood on the eastern seashore, watching as a strange ship came over the horizon.

> At first they took it to be a great bird, but they soon found it to be a monstrous canoe filled with the very people who had got the knowledge which belonged to the Shawnees. After these white people had landed, they were not content with having the knowledge which belonged to the Shawnees, but they usurped their lands also.—But these things will soon end. The Master of Life is about to restore to the Shawnees their knowledge and their rights and he will trample the Long Knives under his feet.

And even Black Hoof, a government chief committed to the American cause, admitted, "The white people has spoiled us. They have been our ruin."

Yet the same chaos that threatened the tribesmen also produced a man who promised them deliverance. Known as a Lalawethika ("The Noisemaker" or "Loud Mouth"), the man had been born in 1775 on the Mad River in eastern Ohio. Prior to Lalawethika's birth, his father had been killed by the Americans and his mother had abandoned him when he was only four years old. Raised by a sister, his childhood had been overshadowed by two older brothers, Chiksika and Tecumseh. Lalawethika never excelled as a hunter or a warrior, and during his adolescence he became an alcoholic. Following the Treaty of Greenville he lived in a small village headed by Tecumseh, where he unsuccessfully aspired to the status of shaman. But in April 1805 this alcoholic ne'er-do-well experienced a vision that changed his life and propelled him to the forefront of Indian leadership.

While lighting his pipe from the fire in his lodge, Lalawethika collapsed, falling into a coma so deep his wife and neighbors believed him to be dead. As his wife began her mourning song he astonished his family by first stirring, then regaining consciousness. Visibly shaken, he informed the gathered onlookers that indeed he had died and had visited heaven, where the Master of Life had shown him both an Indian paradise and a hell where eternal fires lay in wait for sinful tribesmen. Alcoholics like himself suffered the most, for molten lead was poured down their throats until flames shot out their nostrils. Amidst much trembling, Lalawethika vowed to renounce his former ways and never again drink the white man's whiskey. No longer would he be known as Lalawethika. Henceforward he would be called Tenskwatawa—"The Open Door"—a name symbolizing his new role as a holy man destined to lead his people down the narrow road to paradise.

In the following months Tenskwatawa experienced other visions and enlarged upon his doctrine of Indian deliverance. Much of his teachings addressed the decline of traditional moral values among the Shawnees and other tribes. Tenskwatawa claimed he "was particularly appointed to that office by the Great Spirit" and that his "sole object was to reclaim the Indians from bad habits and to cause them to live in peace with all mankind." While he continued to denounce whiskey as "poison and accursed," he also condemned the violence that permeated tribal society. He urged warriors to treat each other as brothers, to stop their quarreling, and to refrain from striking their wives and children. Husbands and wives should remain faithful to each other, and marriages should be monogamous. Shawnee warriors currently married to more than one woman "might keep them," but such marriages displeased the Master of Life.

Convinced that his forefathers had enjoyed a happier existence, the new Shawnee Prophet attempted to revitalize some facets of traditional tribal culture. Indeed, much of Tenskwatawa's teaching was nativistic in both tone and content.

He asked his followers to return to the communal life of the past and to renounce all desire to accumulate property as individuals. Those tribesmen who hoarded their possessions were doomed, but others who shared with their kinsmen, "when they die are happy; and when they arrive in the land of the dead, will find their wigwams furnished with everything they had on earth." He also instructed them to use only the food, implements, and dress of their fathers. Pork, beef, and mutton were unclean, and the tribesmen were instructed to eat only the game they killed in the forests. Neither were the Indians to eat bread, but only corn, beans, and other crops raised by their ancestors. Stone or wood implements should replace metal tools, and although guns could be used for self-defense, the warriors were to hunt with bows and arrows. With the exception of weapons, all items of American manufacture were to be discarded. In a similar manner, the Indians were to dress in skin or leather clothing and were ordered to shave their heads, leaving only the scalp lock of their forefathers. False gods should be forgotten, but the tribesmen should pray to the Master of Life, asking that he return fish to the streams and game to the forest. To assist his disciples, Tenskwatawa provided them with sacred "prayer sticks." The sticks were inscribed with pictographs illustrating certain spirits who would help the tribesmen in their supplications. If the Shawnees were faithful and their hearts pure, the Master of Life would restore order, the earth would be fruitful, and they would prosper.

While Tenskwatawa attempted to revitalize some part of the Shawnee culture, he condemned others. He warned that many of the traditional dances and ceremonies no longer had any meaning and offered new ones in their place. He also instructed his followers to throw away their personal medicine bundles, which he claimed had been powerful in the past, but no longer possessed the potency needed to protect the Shawnees from the new dangers that threatened them. Tenskwatawa alone spoke for the Master of Life, and only those tribesmen who subscribed to the new faith would ever know happiness. But his disciples would be rewarded above all men, for they alone would eventually "find your children or your friends that have long been dead restored to life."

If the Prophet condemned some of the old religious practices, he was particularly suspicious of those tribesmen who held religious beliefs differing from his own. At best those shamans or medicine men who opposed his doctrine were misguided fools. At worst they were witches, in league with the Great Serpent to spread disorder among the tribes. And the Prophet did not limit his accusations to religious leaders. For the holy man, religion and politics were the same. He had been chosen by the Master of Life to end the chaos in the Shawnee world. All those who opposed him also opposed the Master of Life. Therefore, he was particularly suspicious of tribesmen who were becoming acculturated or who had been converted to Christianity. Such men also were suspect of witchcraft. Unless they repented, they too should be destroyed.

Tenskwatawa's distrust of those Indians who adhered to American values reflected his general condemnation of the Long Knives. He informed his followers that the Master of Life had made the British, French, and Spanish, but the Americans were the children of the Great Serpent. In his visions Tenskwatawa had seen the Americans take the form of a great crab that crawled from the sea, and the Master of Life had told him, "They grew from the scum of the great water when it was troubled by the Evil Spirit. And the froth was driven into the woods by a strong east wind. They are numerous, but I hate them. They are unjust. They have taken away your lands, which were not made for them." Only if the Indians rejected the Americans would order ever be restored to the Shawnee world. The Prophet instructed his people to cease all contact with the Long Knives. If they met an American in the forest, they might speak to him from a distance, but they should avoid touching him or shaking his hand. They were also forbidden to trade Indian foods to their white neighbors, for these provisions were the special gifts of the Master of Life, to be used by his children, not the spawn of the Serpent. Tenskwatawa instructed his disciples to cut their ties with frontier merchants, and "because they [the Americans] have cheated you," the Indians were to pay "no more than half their credits." Moreover, Indian women married to American men should return to their tribes, and the children of such unions were to be left with their fathers.

The new faith soon spread to other tribes, who like the Shawnees were unable to adjust to the great changes sweeping around them. By the autumn of 1805 warriors from the Delawares and Wyandots were traveling to Greenville, Ohio, where the Prophet had established a new village. There Tenskwatawa converted the visitors, then sent them back to proselytize their home villages. The Delawares proved particularly susceptible to the new religion, and during the late winter of 1806 they accused about one dozen of their tribesmen of witchcraft. In March 1806 the Prophet journeyed to the Delaware villages, where he examined the captives, exonerating some, but condemning others. The Delawares eventually burned four of their kinsmen before the witch-hunt terminated. Predictably, all those burned were converted Christians whose acculturation made them more suspicious.

The witch-hunt among the Delawares frightened Moravian missionaries associated with the tribe and brought a storm of protest from government officials. During the spring of 1806 Harrison wrote to the Delawares denouncing the Prophet and asking, "If he is really a prophet, ask him to cause the sun to stand still—the moon to alter its course—the rivers to cease to flow—or the dead to rise from their graves. If he does these things, you may believe that he has been sent from God."

Ironically, Harrison's challenge played into Tenskwatawa's hands. In the spring of 1806 several astronomers had traveled through Indiana and Illinois locating observation stations to study an eclipse of the sun scheduled to occur on June 16. Although Harrison either ignored or forgot about the event, the Prophet remembered. Among the Shawnees such an eclipse was known as a "Black Sun," an event surrounded with dread and portending future warfare. Accepting Harrison's challenge, in early June Tenskwatawa surprised even his closest followers by promising to darken the sun. On June 16, while his disciples and skeptics both assembled in his village, the Prophet remained secluded in his lodge throughout most of the morning, but as the noon sun faded into an eerie twilight he stepped forth exclaiming, "Did I not speak the truth? See the sun is dark!" He then assured his audience that he would restore the sun's former radiance, and as the eclipse ended even those tribesmen who still remembered him as Lalawethika, the drunken loudmouth, now were convinced of his medicine.

Following the eclipse, the Prophet's influence spread rapidly. During the summer of 1806 Kickapoos from the Wabash visited his village, were converted, and by the following summer their towns in eastern and central Illinois had become seedbeds for the new religion. Early in 1807 large numbers of Potawatomis and Ottawas from the Lake Michigan region traveled to Greenville and then carried the new faith back to the western Great Lakes. One of the Ottawas, Le Magouis, or "the Trout," became a special envoy for Tenskwatawa and journeyed into upper Michigan where he taught the Prophet's doctrines to the Chippewas. The results were phenomenal. At Chequamegon Bay hundreds of Chippewas gathered opposite Madeline Island to "dance the dances and sing the songs" of the new deliverance. Subscribing to the Prophet's instructions, they threw their medicine bags into Lake Superior and made plans to visit the holy man in Ohio. In the following months so many tribesmen were en route to the Prophet's village that white traders found most of the Chippewa towns along the southern shores of Lake Michigan deserted. The Menominees, Sacs, and Winnebagos also were swept up in the religious frenzy, and during the summer of 1807 they trekked to Greenville in large numbers.

Unable to comprehend the religious nature of the movement, American officials at first believed that Tenskwatawa was only a figure-head controlled by more traditional chiefs among the Shawnees. During 1807 several groups of American agents arrived at the Prophet's village to investigate the character of the new movement. After meeting with Tenskwatawa, most of the envoys agreed that the holy man was the dominant Indian leader in the village. Moreover, the Prophet was able to persuade them that his religion posed no threat to the government. But Harrison and other officials refused to admit that the movement was an indigenous uprising, resulting from desperate conditions among the Indians. Instead, they charged that the Prophet was actually a British agent, intent upon raising the tribes against the United States.

Yet the British were as mystified about Tenskwatawa as were the Americans. During the summer of 1807 British agents were active among the Indians of Michigan and Wisconsin, but they remained suspicious of the Prophet. Although they invited the Shawnee to visit them in Canada, he refused. In response, William Clause, Deputy Superintendent of Indian Affairs for Upper Canada, warned other Indians to avoid him, speculating that the holy man might be working for the French.

The large numbers of Indians who journeyed to Tenskwatawa's village enhanced his prestige, but they also alarmed white settlers in Ohio. Moreover, the influx of tribesmen exhausted Tenskwatawa's food supply, and he was hard pressed to feed his followers. In November 1807 the Potawatomis suggested that he withdraw from Greenville and establish a new village on the Tippecanoe River in Indiana. The new site would be much less exposed to white influence and was located in a region where game was more plentiful. Therefore, in April 1808 the Prophet and his followers abandoned Ohio and moved to Prophetstown.

The withdrawal to Indiana temporarily removed Tenskwatawa from white scrutiny, but his logistical problems continued. Since Prophetstown was located further west, it was more accessible to potential converts, and during 1808 and 1809 Indians flocked to the new village in numbers surpassing those who had visited him at Greenville. Although the villagers planted fields of corn and scoured the surrounding countryside for game, they could not feed the multitude. To obtain additional food, the Prophet brazenly turned to the Americans. In June 1808 he sent a delegation of warriors to Harrison assuring the governor of his peaceful intentions and asking for provisions. The Indians were so persuasive that Harrison sent food to Prophetstown and invited Tenskwatawa to meet with him in Vincennes. Two months later, in August 1808, the Prophet and his retinue arrived at Vincennes and spent two weeks conferring with Harrison. The governor was astonished at "the considerable talent of art and address" with which Tenskwatawa mesmerized his followers. Moreover, the holy man's pleas of friendship toward the United States were so convincing that Harrison provided him with additional stores of food and gunpowder and reported to his superiors that his earlier assessments of the Shawnee were in error, for "the influence which the Prophet has acquired will prove advantageous rather than otherwise to the United States."

Tenskwatawa was also able to hoodwink John Johnston, the Indian agent at Fort Wayne. In May 1809 he met with Johnston, and although the agent previously had expressed misgivings about the Prophet's motives, Tenskwatawa assured him of his friendship. The Shawnee spent four days, denying "in the most solemn manner, having any view inimical to [the Americans'] peace and welfare." Indeed, when the conference ended, Johnston, like Harrison, exonerated the holy man from all charges and reported, "I have taken much pains and have not been able to find that there existed any grounds for the alarm."

But the facade of friendship was too fragile to last. Although the Prophet feigned goodwill toward the government, he could not control his followers, many of whom were no less devious in their relations with the United States. As Indian depredations spread along the Wabash

Valley, Harrison became convinced of the Shawnee's duplicity. During the summer of 1809 Tenskwatawa again visited with the governor in Vincennes, but this time Harrison was less hospitable. Tenskwatawa's protestations of friendship had little impact, and Harrison informed the War Department that his suspicions of the Prophet "have been strengthened rather than diminished in every interview I have had with him since his arrival." Moreover, by the summer of 1809 Harrison was making preparations for the Treaty of Fort Wayne, and he assumed that such a transaction would terminate any pretense of amity between the government and the holy man.

Harrison was correct. The Treaty of Fort Wayne, signed in September 1809, ceded over three million acres in Indiana and Illinois to the United States. Negotiated by friendly chiefs among the Miamis, Delawares, and Potawatomis, the treaty was adamantly opposed by Tenskwatawa. In response, he redoubled his efforts to win new disciples. Messengers were sent to the Ottawas and Potawatomis, and many Wyandots who earlier had shunned the new faith now were converted to the Prophet's teachings. Once again Harrison received reports that the Indians were burning witches, and friendly chiefs among the Miamis and Piankashaws complained that warriors long faithful to the government now were flocking to Prophetstown.

Concerned over the new upsurge in the Prophet's influence, Harrison sent informers to the Tippecanoe and invited Tenskwatawa to again meet with him in Vincennes, but the holy man refused. He also ignored an invitation by the governor to travel to Washington and meet with the president. Instead, he informed Harrison that the recent treaty was illegal and threatened to kill all those chiefs who had signed it. He also vowed that the lands would never be settled by white men and warned Harrison to keep American settlement south of the mouth of the Vermillion River.

The Treaty of Fort Wayne ended any pretense of cooperation between Tenskwatawa and the government. By 1810 the lines were drawn.

Tenskwatawa and his movement were unequivocally opposed to American expansion, and in the years following the treaty the anti-American sentiment was both transformed and intensified.

Tecumseh's role in the formation of this movement was entirely a secondary one. He subscribed to the new faith and lived with the Prophet at Greenville, where he assisted his brother in meeting the delegations of both Indian and white visitors. Tecumseh sometimes spoke in council upon such occasions, but no more so than Blue Jacket, Roundhead, or other Indians prominent in the village. In 1807 he accompanied a group of tribesmen who met with Governor Thomas Kirker of Ohio, but in this instance he spoke in defense of his brother, convincing the governor that the Prophet and his movement were no threat to peace. Although primary materials from this period are full of references to the Prophet, almost none mention Tecumseh. Most accounts of Tecumseh's activities during these years are from the "reminiscences" of American observers recorded decades later.

Indeed, Tecumseh did not challenge the Prophet's position of leadership until 1810, two years after the move to Prophetstown and five years after the religious movement's beginnings. During 1808 Indians continued to flock to Prophetstown to see the holy man, not his brother; and in that year it was the Prophet, not Tecumseh, who met with Harrison at Vincennes. In the summer of 1808 Tecumseh did visit Malden seeking supplies for the Indians at Prophetstown, but he made no claims to leadership; and British accounts of the visit, which are quite specific in listing other Indians' names, refer to him only as "the Prophet's brother," not as Tecumseh, a chief among the Shawnees.

The springboard to Tecumseh's emergence was the Treaty of Fort Wayne. From Tecumseh's perspective it was obvious that the religious emphasis of his brother could no longer protect the remaining Indian land base. During the summer of 1809 he visited a few Indian villages in Illinois, but after the treaty Tecumseh took a new initiative and began to travel widely, emphasizing a political and military solution to the Indians' problems. The tribesmen should still adhere to the new religion, but they should abandon their old chiefs who remained friendly to the Americans. Instead, all warriors should politically unite under Tecumseh, for in his own words, "I am the head of them all. . . . I am alone the acknowledged chief of all the Indians."

Therefore, for two years—in 1810 and 1811—Tecumseh traveled extensively among the Indians of the West. During these years he met twice with Harrison, who reported to his superiors that Tecumseh now had emerged as "really the efficient man—the Moses of the family." In this period Tecumseh slowly eclipsed the Prophet's position of leadership, but ironically as the character of the Indian movement changed, its appeal to the tribesmen declined. In 1810 and 1811 parties of warriors recruited by Tecumseh temporarily joined the village at Prophetstown, but their numbers never approached the multitude of Indians who earlier had flocked to the Prophet. And although the Prophet no longer dominated the movement, he continued to exercise considerable influence. For example, his ability to convince his followers that they could easily obtain a victory over the Americans contributed to their ill-fated attack upon Harrison's forces at the Battle of Tippecanoe in 1811. Obviously, after the battle the Prophet's influence was broken, and Tecumseh remained the dominant leader of the battered movement. But Tecumseh's preeminence was of short duration, for he was killed less than two years later, on October 5, 1813, at the Battle of the Thames.

It is evident, therefore, that the Prophet, not Tecumseh, was the most important figure in the emergence of the Indian movement prior to the War of 1812. Tecumseh used the widespread religious base earlier established by his brother as the foundation for his unsuccessful attempt to unite the tribes politically and militarily. Although the Prophet has been pictured as either a charlatan or a religious fanatic whose teachings seem quite bizarre, such an appraisal reflects an ethnocentric bias. He certainly seemed logical to the Indians, and for several years he exercised a widespread influence throughout the Old Northwest. In retrospect, such a phenomenon is not surprising. In times of oppression native American peoples have often turned to a religious deliverance. The Shawnee Prophet fits into a historical pattern exemplified by the Delaware Prophet, Handsome Lake, Wovoka and the Ghost Dance, and many others. Indeed, Tecumseh's emphasis upon political and military unification was much less typical than the Prophet's messianic nativism.

This reassessment does not mean that Tecumseh was not a remarkable man. Indeed, he was a brave and farsighted leader who sacrificed his life for his people. But the real Tecumseh stands on his own merits. He does not need the romantic embellishments of ethnocentric historians. Tragically, the Tecumseh who has emerged from the pages of history is, in many respects, a "white man's Indian."

KEY TERMS

Treaty of Greenville: 1795 treaty between the United States and the Indians of the Ohio River valley following the Indian defeat at the Battle of Fallen Timbers in 1794 which ceded much of Ohio to the United States.

Bacchanalia: Originally a Roman festival honoring Bacchus, the god of wine; in general, drunken revelry.

Moravian missionaries: Members of the Unitas Fratrum, an evangelical Christian communion, who in 1740 founded a religious colony at Bethlehem, Pennsylvania, and directed much of their energies toward converting backcountry Indians to Christianity.

Treaty of Fort Wayne: 1809 treaty between the United States and the Indians of the Ohio River valley ceding three million acres of Indiana Territory Indian land on the Wabash River to the United States.

DISCUSSION TOPICS

After reading this essay, you should be able to discuss:

1. The strategic position held by Indians in the trans-Appalachian West.

2. Tenskwatawa's role in creating a pan-Indian resistance movement.

3. Tecumseh's role in the movement.

4. The main points of revitalization movements.

5. The reasons why the two brothers' movement failed.

PART THREE

An Expanding People

In the forty years leading to the Civil War, the United States grew in many dramatic ways. The population more than doubled between 1820 and 1860 and, equally important, the mixture of peoples who made up the country's population became more diverse. Mexicans and new groups of Native Americans were annexed by the expanding nation, while Germans, Irish, and Chinese immigrants flocked to its coastal cities and inland farms. The nation grew physically as well. Of the twenty-three states that made up the union in 1820, only Louisiana lay west of the Mississippi River; by the beginning of the Civil War, the nation counted eleven new states, all but three of them in the trans-Mississippi West. In 1860 the United States stretched from the Atlantic to the Pacific.

Not only did the nation's economy grow during the antebellum years, but the Northeast developed into an early industrial center. In the northern states, what had been a region of independent farmers, artisans, and shopkeepers became increasingly a region of employers and their dependent employees. In the southern states, the international demand for cotton rejuvenated the system of plantation slavery that led the two regions along increasingly divergent courses.

The forces of agrarian change that drove tens of thousands of eastern farmers to seek better fortunes in the West are the subject of Robert A. Gross's essay "Culture and Cultivation." The growing penetration of national and international markets into rural Concord, Massachusetts, transformed the lives of its residents, Gross argues, forcing them to balance their family- and community-oriented lives against the impersonal forces of the marketplace. In Concord, as in the rest of the United States, the American Revolution set in motion social, economic, and political forces that would transform everyday life in the early nineteenth century.

The human side of northern economic transformation is analyzed in essays by Ronald Schultz and Christine Stansell. Looking at the dynamic religious culture of Philadelphia artisans at a time when their craft system was under unrelenting assault by sweatshops and by competition from cheaper and less-skilled immigrant labor, Schultz shows that religion played a central role in craftsmen's response to their economic predicament. In New York City, on the other hand, the concerns of poor women—especially those who were heads of households—involved more than maintaining their families. By the middle of the nineteenth century, these women also had to deal with middle- and upper-class reformers who used charity as a form of social engineering, granting aid to those whom they judged "respectable" and denying it to those who clung to the culture of the streets. As Stansell argues, the conflict over the "uses of the streets" was as much a struggle over the proper role of women in the new industrial order as a confrontation between women of different social classes.

As the northern states industrialized and pioneers settled the western states, the South experienced an economic renaissance based not on industry but on a new staple crop: cotton. In "Gouge and Bite, Pull Hair and Scratch," Elliott J. Gorn analyzes the culture of ordinary white male southerners. Violence was endemic in a society that relied on physical coercion to maintain discipline among its slave labor force, and, as abolitionists often claimed, the ubiquitousness of violence distorted white society as well as black.

The Civil War has long occupied a privileged place in American history. The spectacle of American fighting American, of family pitted against family, has fired the imagination of generations of Americans, beginning as soon as the war ended. Historians, too, have felt the urgency of conflict and the importance of the issues involved, but their professional concerns turn more to explaining the causes and impact of the war. In "Advocate of the Dream," Stephen B. Oates takes us inside the mind of the sixteenth president as he grappled with the weightiest issues of our nation's history. Oates concludes that Lincoln was, in every respect, a man of abiding principle. Although often cloaked in romance, the actual battles of the Civil War were anything but romantic. In "Heroes and Cowards," Bell I. Wiley recounts the frightening experience of combat as seen through the eyes of ordinary Confederate soldiers. There was little romance in the everyday struggles of Civil War soldiers to remain healthy, warm, fed, and alive.

PAST TRACES

The early textile factories that began to dot the landscape of the rural northeast in the late eighteenth and early nineteenth centuries brought forth a divided response from Americans at large as well as the women who worked there. While some saw the mills in a positive light, as ways of adding to the number of scarce jobs in the countryside or as a means to make the United States a self-sufficient manufacturing nation, others saw in the mills a reflection of contemporary England where similar mills had ushered in a regime of poverty, ill health, and low morals. In this document, Lucy Larcom, an early worker in the Lowell, Massachusetts, cotton mills and a fledgling poet, recounts her experiences at the power loom with a degree of ambivalence that was characteristic of early women mill operatives. What did it mean that mill workers were viewed as mere "hands" rather than as individuals? And what effect did the monotonous routine of factory work have on women's minds? Larcom offers no solutions here, but instead points to a set of problems that occupied the minds of many Americans in early industrial America.

An Idyl of Work

But this was waste,—this woman-
    faculty
Tied to machinery, part of the machine.
That wove cloth when it might be
    clothing hearts
And minds with queenly raiment. She
    foresaw
The time must come when mind itself
    would yield
To the machine, or leave the work to
    hands
Which were hands only.
. . . These [women] counted but as
    "hands!" named such! . . .
It must not be at all, or else their toil
Must be made easier, larger its
    reward! . . .
Here was a problem, then,
For the political theorist: how to save
Mind from machinery's clutches.

The rumbling wheels and rattling bands
All in succession roll,
The regulator swiftly moves;
And regulates the whole . . .

The bales of cotton soon are brought,
And from the Picker flows
Swift through the cards and breakers
    come,
And to the Speeder goes.

With rapid flight the Speeder flies
T'is pleasing to behold,
The roping round the bobins wind,
One half can near be told.

The next we know the spinners call
For roping to be brought,
It's carried from the carding room,
And on their spindles caught.

Come, listen friends, and you, I tell
What spinners they can do,
The roping they will quick convert,
To warp and filling to.

Another sight I now behold,
It is a pleasing scene,
The warp is taken soon as spun,
And wound around the beam.

Then soon it's carried out of sight,
Into the dressing room,
It's warped and dressed all complete,
And fitted for the loom.

The slaie and harness is prepared,
Each thread for to convene,
The looms are placed in rows
   throughout,
The weavers stand between.

The shuttle now is swiftly thrown,
It flies from end to end
And they stand ready all the while,
Each broken thread to mend. . . .

13

Culture and Cultivation: Agriculture and Society in Thoreau's Concord

Robert A. Gross

For the first three hundred years of its existence, the United States was predominantly a land of farmers. As late as 1800, more than nine out of ten people lived in agrarian towns and villages, where most of them were members of small, independent farming families. Regulated by the yearly cycle of the seasons and the daily rhythms of the field and barnyard, life on these farms changed little between the seventeenth and early nineteenth centuries. Life in these pastoral communities centered on land and family, and even such apparently economic transactions as the purchase of land and the borrowing of money were family affairs undertaken in the spirit of neighborliness. But as regional and international commerce expanded after the American Revolution and new markets in the trans-Appalachian South and West fostered the beginnings of industrialization, farmers found themselves dealing with a rapidly changing world in which contracts and money were valued more than neighborliness and community.

In this essay, Robert A. Gross explores the transformation of northern agriculture between the Revolution and the Civil War by focusing on the well-known town of Concord, Massachusetts. As markets expanded in post-Revolutionary America, they placed an ever-increasing number of new products within the reach of farmers and rural artisans, who had previously produced by themselves most of the goods their families needed. It was this intense contact with a growing market in manufactured goods and agricultural products, a market in which local merchants played a defining role, that transformed social and economic relationships in rural Massachusetts, increasing farmers' independence of their neighbors while at the same time undermining the social and economic basis of traditional community life. But, as Gross reminds us, this rural transformation was a slow and uneven process that took generations—not years—

to complete. Despite the growing importance of market relationships, many of the family and community values of 1800 continued to direct everyday life there as late as the Civil War.

Gross's account of rural Massachusetts entering a new age reminds us of one of the historian's greatest concerns: tracing both change and continuity. New England farms changed—sometimes dramatically—in the early nineteenth century, but as Gross also shows, much in rural life remained untouched by the new system of agrarian capitalism as late as the Civil War.

....

The town of Concord, Massachusetts, is usually thought of as the home of minutemen and transcendentalists—the place where "the embattled farmers" launched America's war for political independence on April 19, 1775, and where Ralph Waldo Emerson and Henry David Thoreau, more than a half-century later, waged their own struggles for intellectual independence, both for themselves as writers and for American culture as a whole. But in the late nineteenth century, Concord acquired a distinction it never possessed in the years when it was a seedbed of revolutionary scholars and soldiers. It became a leading center of agricultural improvement. Thanks to the coming of the railroad in 1844, Concord farmers played milkmen to the metropolis and branched out into market gardening and fruit raising as well. Concord was nursery to a popular new variety of grape, developed by a retired mechanic-turned-horticulturist named Ephraim Bull. And to crown its reputation, the town called the cultural capital of antebellum America by Stanley Elkins became the asparagus capital of the Gilded Age. Concord was, in short, a full participant in yet another revolution: the agricultural revolution that transformed the countryside of New England in the middle decades of the nineteenth century.

The progress of that agricultural revolution forms my central theme. The minutemen of 1775 inhabited a radically different world from that of their grandchildren and great-grandchildren on the eve of the Civil War. We know the general outlines of how things changed—that farmers gradually abandoned producing their own food, clothing, and tools and turned to supplying specialized, urban markets for a living. In the process, they rationalized their methods and altered the ways they thought about their work. Theirs was a new world in which modern science was wedded to agricultural capitalism. But the process by which that world came into being is little known. Historians have given their attention chiefly to more dramatic events—to the rise of cities and factories, to the story of Boston and Lowell. No less important was the revolution in the countryside. Without it, the creation of an urban-industrial society would have been impossible.

Together, the city and the country underwent a great transformation. The years from around 1800 to 1860 comprise what Emerson called an "age of Revolution"—a time "when the old and the new stand side by side and admit of being compared; when the energies of all men are searched by fear and by hope; when the historic glories of the old can be compensated by the rich possibilities of the new era." What could be a better time to be alive, Emerson asked. That is essentially the inquiry I am undertaking—an inquiry into what it was like to make and to experience the great transition to modern agricultural capitalism in Concord.

The agricultural revolution did not come suddenly in an irresistible wave of change. The process was a slow and uneven one, proceeding by fits and starts and sometimes encountering setbacks along the way. Some things never really changed at all, and not until the end of the period, with the coming of the railroad, had a new world truly been born.

All of this, of course, can be said only with the historian's benefit of hindsight. To the participants in the process, who did not know the outcomes, the transition must have been at times a deeply unsettling experience. It challenged old habits and practices, demanded new responses while promising only uncertain rewards, and swept up those who wanted only to be left alone, comfortably carrying on their fathers' ways. Even those farmers and entrepreneurs who successfully rode the tide must have had their doubts. Those who resisted or just plain failed said little about their fate, succumbing to what Thoreau saw as lives of "quiet desperation." In the effort to reconstruct the experience of the transition, Thoreau's observations bear close reading. Thoreau was the most powerful and articulate critic of agricultural capitalism that America produced in the decades before the Civil War.

Had a visitor come to Concord around 1800 and lived through the 1850s, he would certainly have been unprepared for the ways things changed. At the opening of a new century, the agricultural economy was very much tied to the past. In the size of their farms, in the crops and livestock they raised, in the ways they used the land, farmers still carried on as their fathers had.

For one thing, the number of farms was the same in 1800 as it had been in 1750 and 1771: about 200. And the average size of a farm was no bigger in 1800 than it had been before: around sixty acres. These were unchanging facts of life in eighteenth-century Concord; nothing— not even revolution, war, and depression— would alter them in the slightest.

This fundamental stability in the number and size of farms was no accident, no haphazard outcome of social evolution. It was a deliberate creation, a rational adaptation to the conditions of farming and family life in the preindustrial, household economy. This arrangement of farms on the landscape arose in response to a basic dilemma Concord began to encounter as early as the 1720s: there were too many young people in town and not enough land for them all—not enough, at least, for them to support families in

the usual way. Markets did not exist to sustain comfortable livings on very small farms. Nor would the farming methods of the day have enabled the yeomen of Concord to produce substantial surpluses had the demand for them suddenly appeared. As a result, so long as families continued to be fruitful and multiply as successfully as they did and so long as death continued to stalk New Englanders less relentlessly than it did people in the Old World, the people of Concord would have to face up to the inevitable outcome. There was a fundamental imbalance between numbers and resources. Something would have to give.

As it turned out, what gave was the aspiration of colonial patriarchs to settle all their sons close by on family lands. As early as the 1720s, it was becoming clear that some estates in Concord could not be split up "without Spoiling the Whole." Instead, increasingly, one son—often, but not invariably, the eldest— would inherit the homestead intact. The other children would have to go into trade, take portions and dowries in cash, or, in what was commonly the case, move away and settle on frontier lands. In effect, a continuing exodus of young people to new lands underwrote the stability of Concord's farms. Emigration was the key to the future, to insuring that old patterns would go on unchanged. That mechanism worked so successfully that the colonial framework of farming in Concord—some 200 farms of about sixty acres on the average—survived intact not just until 1800 but until the eve of the Civil War. No matter how much things changed, young people growing up on farms in nineteenth-century Concord had in common with their eighteenth-century forebears the expectation that most would move away and make new lives in another town.

For those who stayed behind on the homesteads around 1800, farming went on in traditional ways. In the household economy of Concord the needs of the family and the labor it supplied largely determined what was produced and in what amounts. This does not mean that farms were self-sufficient. Farmers normally strove to obtain a surplus of goods to exchange with neighbors and to enter into the stream of trade. Given the limited markets and the constraints on production in the eighteenth century, surpluses were necessarily small. Most farmers lacked the incentive or the capacity to participate extensively in trade.

Indeed, most farmers even lacked the ability to be fully self-sufficient. Historians have been led astray by the image of the independent yeoman, wholly dependent on his own resources, that eighteenth-century writers like J. Hector St. John Crèvecoeur have handed down to us. What we would think of as the basic necessities of colonial husbandry—plows, oxen, pastures, sheep—were absent on a great many farms. A third of Concord's farmers did not own oxen, and if they were like the farmers in the towns of Groton, Marlborough, and Dedham, whose inventories have been examined by Winifred Rothenberg at Brandeis University, half of them did not possess a plow and three-quarters (72 percent) had no harrow (this was the case down to 1840). Nor were farmers in Concord any more self-sufficient in the production of textiles. Almost half had no sheep in 1771, and in 1750 some 56 percent raised no flax at all.

What did people do, then, for basic necessities? They borrowed from neighbors or kin, exchanged goods or labor with others, or resorted to the store. Perhaps most often, they made do with what they had. This was a world of scarcity in which expectations were modest and always circumscribed. People had to accept the fact that labor and capital were required to supply all one's necessities "from within." It was the rich—the large landholders and the men who combined farming with a profitable trade—who could aspire to independence. It was they who produced most of the flax in Concord in 1750, planting about one-fourth to one-half an acre on the average, which is what the books say the ordinary farmer usually had. And it was they who could provide a wise variety of their own foods. The wealthy were able to take care of these needs precisely because

they were engaged in trade, thereby acquiring the resources to hire labor and diversify livestock and crops. Market participation and self-sufficiency were not at opposite ends of a spectrum. Rather, market dependence without facilitated independence within. So when we read about the self-sufficient farmer, we should be skeptical: he was the exceptional man, uniquely favored by fortune. The editor of *Old Farmer's Almanack*, Robert Bailey Thomas, spoke for a good many readers when he remarked that "there is a great satisfaction derived from living as much as possible upon the produce of one's own farm." But it was a satisfaction that only a few farmers ever enjoyed. Although independence was the general ambition, interdependence was the inescapable fact of life.

The world of trade, then, offered a way out of the pervasive dependency of farmers on one another—out of the constant borrowing back and forth, the necessity of exchanging work, the endless keeping of accounts to ascertain one's standing in the community-wide network of credits and debts. And trade in agricultural surpluses played an important role in colonial Concord, shaping the principal uses to which people put their lands. Throughout the second half of the eighteenth century, farmers in Concord and elsewhere in eastern Massachusetts kept most of their improved land in grass. In Ipswich, over 90 percent of the improved land in 1771 was in meadows and pasture; in Concord that year, 80 percent. In a sense, farmers were doing what came naturally; the soil was well suited to raising grass. But it was the pull of urban markets that prompted farmers to emphasize their mowing and grazing lands. Concord was beef country in the late colonial era. The agricultural economy was based on cereals—mainly rye and corn—for home consumption and beef for market.

This was an extensive agricultural regime, where farmers saved on labor by exploiting land. The trouble was that by the eve of the Revolution, the land was losing its capacity to support livestock. Between 1749 and 1771, cattle holdings increased by a fifth, but to feed them farmers had to expand their pasturage by 84 percent, even though sheep raising was declining sharply. Concord was starting to experience a serious agricultural decline. Indeed, so poor was the town's farming reputation that it blighted the marriage prospects of a young cabinet maker and farmer named Joseph Hosmer. It is said that when he asked for the hand of a wealthy farmer's daughter in Marlborough, Massachusetts, in 1759, he was rejected out of hand. "Concord plains are sandy," complained the father. "Concord soil is poor; you have miserable farms there, and no fruit. There is little hope that you will ever do better than your father, for you have both farm and shop to attend to, *and two trades spoil one.* Lucy shall marry her cousin John; he owns the best farm in Marlboro', and you must marry a Concord girl, who cannot tell good land from poor." Joseph Hosmer ultimately won the girl, but he had to pasture his cattle outside of Concord—in Rutland and Princeton, Massachusetts.

By 1801, though still very much bound to the past, Concord was beginning to feel the stirrings of agricultural change. Markets were opening up everywhere for farmers, thanks to the extraordinary prosperity the United States enjoyed during the era of the Napoleonic wars. The port cities—merchants to the world in the 1790s and early 1800s—boomed, and so, in turn, did their hinterland. Concord farmers began to raise substantial surpluses of rye, wood, and hay for the market. They met the needs not only of Boston and Charlestown but also of the rapidly growing non-farming population at home. Between 1771 and 1801, the share of Concord's population engaged in crafts and trade doubled, from 15 percent to 33 percent.

The agricultural economy remained essentially what it had been: an economy based on cereals, grasses, and cattle. It would stay that way up through 1840. That year 86 percent of the improved land lay in meadows and pasture. But within that framework, farmers steadily devoted more and more of their energies to producing for market. They raised three principal

commodities for sale: oats, hay, and wood. The production of oats was clearly geared to city markets; it far outstripped the growth in the numbers of horses in Concord, and it clearly paralleled the periods of most rapid increase for Boston and Lowell. Expanded hay production came as a result of the increasing conversion of pastures and unimproved land to what were called "English and upland meadows," land plowed and seeded with clover, timothy, and herd's-grass. Adoption of English hay was the major agricultural improvement of the era, and Concord farmers took it up with zeal. They cultivated meadowlands for cash, while relying on the natural river meadows of the Concord and Assabet rivers to feed their own livestock. As a result, the average farmer doubled his production of English hay from 4 to 8 tons between 1801 and 1840, while his output of fresh meadow hay barely increased from about 8 to 8.5 tons. For the most part, the land converted to English hay was made available by the clearing of vast woodlands for market.

At the same time as farmers were concentrating on these staples, they also sought out new crops. They experimented with teasels, broomcorn, and silk, none of which worked. They added potatoes for both family use and sale. A few wealthy farmers engaged in commercial wool growing on a large scale, raising flocks of one thousand or so sheep before the entire business collapsed in the 1830s from cheap western competition. Far more typical were the small-scale efforts of men like "Uncle Ben" Hosmer—Joseph's younger brother—to assemble surpluses for sale.

By 1840 wagons and roads had so improved that a good deal of butter was being made and sold in Concord. But it was not until the coming of the railroad that large-scale production of milk, eggs, fruits, and garden vegetables became truly profitable in Concord. Before then, small farmers like Ben Hosmer had to concentrate on bulky goods—oats, hay, and wood—supplemented by whatever other surpluses they could get. And note that it was Dinah Hosmer, not Ben, who put up the butter and eggs.

In these circumstances, it is not surprising that farmers continued the effort to supply their own necessities, even as they sought new products for market. To be sure, they were quick to abandon raising their own cloth when cheap textiles started streaming out of the new mills. But a great many farmers never had been able to furnish their own linen or wool. When it came to foodstuffs, they still did as much as they could for themselves. Rye steadily declined in relative importance from 1800 to 1840, but even in 1840 three-quarters of the farmers in town still raised enough for their bread. The same holds true for fodder crops. English hay went to market; the fresh meadows fed livestock at home.

This combination of production for both markets and home use meant, in practice, that farmers were adding greatly to the burdens of their work. One crop was not substituted for another. Farmers simply exploited themselves more intensively than ever. Once they had spread their labor over the land, plowing shallowly, manuring thinly, and cultivating infrequently, with the result that yields were low. That was acceptable when farmers chiefly raised grain crops for family use and the profits came from grazing livestock. But now farmers depended for a living on far more intensive work: chopping wood, reclaiming land for English hay, digging potatoes, making butter, and occasionally even nursing mulberry bushes.

Farmers not only labored more intensively than ever. They did so in a radically new setting. By the mid-1820s, the evidence strongly suggests that hired labor had come to supplant family labor on the farm. Between 1801 and 1826 the ranks of landless men in Concord expanded from around 150 to 250, even as opportunities in crafts and trade stagnated and the number of farms remained unchanged. Those laborers must have been doing something for a living. Since farmers' sons were continuing the exodus out of Concord—but at an earlier age and to lands farther and farther from home—it is likely the laborers were taking their place. The hired hand had become a commonplace figure on the farm

as early as 1815. Thomas's "Farmer's Calendar" for May of that year assumed that farmers had already "hired a man for a few months, to help along with your work," and it offered this advice: "If you have a good faithful one, then set store by him and treat him well, and, mind me now, don't you fret.—*Steady, boys, steady*, is the song for a farmer—If you get yourself into a habit of continually fretting, as some do, then it is ten to one if you can get good men to work for you. But some prefer a dull, lazy lubber, because he is cheap! but these *cheap* fellows I never want on my farm."

Thomas's comments suggest that a calculating, even suspicious spirit dominated the relations between farmers and their help. Where once farm boys had labored for their fathers out of duty, love, and an expectation that they would inherit land of their own someday, now it was money—and money alone—that kept help working on the farm. The social relations of production were imbued with the ethos of agricultural capitalism.

The same rationalizing, economizing impulse transformed the work customs of the community. As late as 1840, many farmers still lacked basic resources to do their work, even as they added to the demands on themselves. Nonetheless, they gave up cooperative practices like the huskings and apple bees of old. These were now condemned as uneconomical and wasteful "frolics," given over to heavy drinking and coarse entertainment. When one writer in the *Concord Gazette* of 1825 wistfully lamented the disappearance of bundling, country dances, and "the joyous huskings" of the past, he was roundly denounced by another for peddling immorality in the press. Neighborly sharing and cooperation probably diminished in another way as well. Agricultural reformers urged farmers to be as sparing as possible in "changing works." Again the *Old Farmer's Almanack* tells the changing sentiment. "There are some," Thomas complained in 1821, "who cannot bear to work alone. If they have a yard of cabbages to hoe, they must call in a neighbour to change work. Now this is very pleasant, but it tends to lounging and idleness and neglect of business; for we cannot always have our neighbours at work with us." Concord farmers likely took such advice; in *Walden*, Thoreau assumes that the farmer characteristically works alone and is starved for company by the time he comes back from the fields. An era had come to an end: farmers now relied on the claims of cash rather than the chain of community to do their work.

Edward Jarvis, a prominent nineteenth-century medical reformer who grew up in Concord, celebrated this development as a positive force in social life. "The people of Concord are none the less kind, sympathetic and generous than their fathers, but they are stronger in body and in beast. They are more self-sustaining, and it is better that each should do his own work, with his own hands or by such aid as he can compensate in the ordinary way. . . . The world's work is now as well and completely done as ever and people both individually and socially are as happy and more prosperous, and are loving, generous and ready to aid in distress, poverty, and sickness, wherever these shall present themselves, in any family or neighborhood."

Jarvis wrote in 1878, at the end of the long transition, and he summarized as progress what small farmers at the time may have experienced as a very mixed blessing. Huskings may have wasted corn; changing works may have been a bother; and the exchange of goods and labor among farmers could sometimes end up in hard feelings and lawsuits on both sides. Still, the farmer who lacked money to hire all the help he needed had no alternative but to depend on his neighbors or exploit himself to the hilt.

Even before the railroad era, then, Concord farmers had entered the world of modern capitalism, with its characteristic institutions of money and markets. Producing for market had

not, however, wholly displaced traditional activities on the farm; men still tried to furnish their food from within. This attempt to combine new demands with old ones added significantly to the burden of farm work; it amounted to a speed-up: more output in less time.

The intensification of farm work accelerated even more sharply after the railroad linked Concord more tightly and speedily to Boston market. The goods that the city demanded were those that required long hours of unremitting toil. Dairying was probably to become the most important. Between 1800 and 1840, as farmers turned to making butter for sale, the average herd of cows on a farm rose slightly from $4\frac{1}{2}$ to 5. The next decade saw that figure increase again to 6. More dramatically, the proportion of men owning ten cows or more doubled from 11 to 22 percent. It was in the 1840s, too, that farmers began on a large scale to reclaim the many acres of boggy meadow in town for English hay. This was immensely costly and labor-intensive work. Those who could afford it hired Irish laborers to do the job; increasingly, cheap foreign labor displaced native help. Finally, the demand for wood boomed in these years; so vigorously did farmers respond to the market that by 1850 they had reduced the forests of Concord to a mere tenth of the town. Some people were already alarmed at the prospect of timber running out. In short, the steady chopping of the ax; the bustle of men spading up meadows, hauling gravel, and raking hay; the clanging of milk pails—these were the dominant sounds on Concord's farms in the 1840s. These sounds reverberate through *Walden*, and all of them finally were orchestrated to the movements of that locomotive whose piercing whistle as it swept into town announced the triumph of a new order of things.

KEY TERMS

Ralph Waldo Emerson (1803–1882): One of America's most renowned writers and a central figure of American transcendentalism, whose poems, orations, and especially his essays are regarded as landmarks in the development of American thought and literary expression.

Henry David Thoreau (1817–1862): A seminal figure in the history of American thought who spent much of his life in Concord, Massachusetts, where he became associated with the New England transcendentalists; best-known for his "Civil Disobedience" (1849) and *Walden* (1854).

Napoleonic Wars: European wars fought between Britain and France, 1799–1815. The need for provisions caused by the wars provided American farmers with exceptionally lucrative markets for their produce.

DISCUSSION TOPICS

After reading this essay, you should be able to discuss:

1. The aims of small farmers in rural America after the Revolution.

2. The nature of the economic and social changes that overtook family farmers in the early nineteenth century.

3. The ways in which farmers responded to these changes.

4. The extent to which their aims changed during the post-Revolutionary years.

14

God and Workingmen: Popular Religion and the Formation of Philadelphia's Working Class, 1790–1830

Ronald Schultz

The growth of factories in the first half of the nineteenth century was the most visible aspect of American industrialization. The creation of large three- and four-story buildings housing hundreds of operatives who worked to the rhythm of steam- or water-driven machinery presented a striking contrast to the predominantly rural scale and pace of American life.

But while the factory system has long been the hallmark of America's transformation from an agrarian to an industrial nation, the most important industrial changes took place not in the factory but in the small artisan shops that dominated the American economy before the Civil War. In these shops, skilled craftsmen, who had learned their trades through long years of apprenticeship and journeyman training, controlled their daily output, the quality of their products, and the rhythm of work itself following long-established craft rules and customs.

Beginning in the early nineteenth century, however, growing numbers of merchants and master craftsmen began to view the slow pace of craft production as a hindrance in their quest to supply large quantities of cheap manufactured goods to rapidly expanding western and southern markets. Breaking craft skills into simple, easily learned tasks and hiring semiskilled and unskilled workers to perform them, these early

"God and Workingmen: Popular Religion and the Formation of Philadelphia's Working Class, 1790–1830," reprinted from *Religion in a Revolutionary Age*, eds. Ronald Hoffman and Peter J. Albert. (Charlottesville, VA: University Press of Virginia), pp. 125–155. Reprinted with the permission of the University Press of Virginia.

manufacturers undercut the craft system and placed all aspects of production under their control. The demise of the craft system meant more than changes in work regimes, however; it announced the end of an ancient culture and way of life as well.

Artisans responded to the demise of their way of life in numerous ways. Some accepted their fate with resignation while others attempted to escape the downward slide into dependency by joining the ranks of manufacturing employers. But for many artisans, the answer to their plight lay in the organization of craft unions. Beginning in the 1820s, skilled artisans in New York City, Philadelphia, and other American production centers formed themselves into craft unions that attempted to restore the artisan voice to the workplace and to stem their declining social and economic fortunes. In this study of Philadelphia artisans at the cusp of industrialization, Ronald Schultz explores the role that religion played in the organization of the nation's first workingmen's movement. Organized religion proved to be a double-edged sword for Philadelphia craftsmen, Schultz tells us, for it could demand personal rejection of worldly concerns and lead to the acceptance of new industrial conditions as easily as it could reinforce artisan values and serve as an ally in the struggle to restore the artisans' independent position in American society. This tension between worldly and otherworldly religious concerns would never be fully reconciled and would continue to mark the relationship between religion and the American labor movement well into the twentieth century.

....

In ways we are only beginning to understand, the age of the American Revolution was also the formative age of America's working class. Between the mobilization for Independence of the mid-1770s and the final political resolution of the Revolution in the 1820s, laboring-class Americans experienced a profound transformation in their personal and working lives.

As the nation's economy turned from colonial dependence to embrace industrial independence, the give-and-take of the small shop and the uneven rhythms of craft production gave way to the increasing regularity and limited autonomy of manufactories and the putting-out system. In the process of confronting the rise of manufacturing and the declining fortunes of their unique way of life, American artisans and less skilled workingmen forged a working-class movement from the raw material of craft traditions, popular politics, and rational religion.

Post-Revolutionary Philadelphia was a religious battleground. Responding to what the Rev. Robert Adair described as "a moral wilderness" of unchurched apprentices, journeymen, and poor working people, representatives of small sects and major denominations combed the city for laboring-class converts. In meeting halls, on street corners, from storefront churches—even in an occasional tavern—urban itinerants preached, cajoled, and exhorted "plain and unlettered" Philadelphians to join the ranks of the pious. City ministers embarked on this search for new souls because they were concerned and anxious. As they walked the back streets and alleys of laboring-class neighborhoods, they drew back from what they described as the "ignorance and vice" and the "moral degradation" of laboring-class parents and their "poor and ignorant children prowling the streets" without the "wholesome restraints" of religion. For the new breed of itinerants, laboring-class Philadelphia was both a test of their moral courage and an unparalleled opportunity for redemption on a massive scale.

Philadelphia's urban itinerants shared with many of their clerical contemporaries a middle-class disdain for the unruliness of laboring-class life. Yet the rough-hewn lifestyles they witnessed on their daily rounds were stubbornly real and thriving, for post-Revolutionary Philadelphia was a city in the midst of enormous social change. To begin with, there were simply more people. On the eve of the Revolution the city was already the largest in America with a population of more than 25,000. Postwar prosperity and the growth of cloth and iron manufacturing in the early nineteenth century brought thousands of new immigrants from Britain to join a flood of migrants from rural Pennsylvania and other seaboard states. By 1800 Philadelphia contained 81,000 inhabitants, nearly half living in the rapidly growing laboring-class suburbs of the Northern Liberties and Southwark. The 1810 federal census enumerated more than 111,000 residents, and when the workingmen's movement peaked in 1830, the city held nearly 189,000 people.

This influx of people changed the scale of social relations in Philadelphia. No longer did craftsmen, merchants, and shopkeepers live side by side along the same street or lane as they had in the colonial city. Instead, by the turn of the nineteenth century, affluent and laboring-class Philadelphians lived in separate neighborhoods with their own distinctive ways of life. As a result, after 1800 the "better" and "poorer" sort saw and knew each other less well than at any previous time in the city's history. Increasingly isolated in their own neighborhoods, middle- and upper-class men and women gradually came to view their working-class counterparts with suspicion—as an alien and potentially dangerous people.

This growing distance between the everyday experiences and the diverse cultures of the city's upper, middling, and lower ranks ultimately became one of the engines of nineteenth-century urban evangelicalism and helped thrust Philadelphia into the forefront of post-Revolutionary benevolence. But if the growing rift in the city's class structure troubled urban itinerants, it was the changing nature of the city's work force that worried them more. Throughout the colonial era Philadelphia's reputation as a manufacturing center rested on the output of hundreds of small shops housing a working master, one or two journeymen, and a

like number of apprentices, indentured servants, or slaves. Only comparatively large enterprises like shipyards and ropewalks required a greater number of craftsmen and laborers, and the city never supported more than a handful of these highly capitalized establishments.

By 1820, however, Philadelphia was no longer a craftsman's city. Now manufactories and putting-out concerns began to appear among the small shops that continued to dot the urban landscape. Employing young, half-trained apprentices and career-stalled journeymen, these early industrial enterprises divided tasks, increased hours, and, in the process, drove production up and prices down in ruinous competition with Philadelphia's small masters. The eclipse of the traditional craft system was evident as early as 1820 when more than a third of the city's workers labored in medium- and large-scale manufactories and uncounted others earned their livelihoods as dependent outworkers.

Even in the remaining smaller shops work relations were vastly different from those of colonial times. By the end of the Revolution, lifelong journeymen and apprentices working on wage contracts had already begun to replace traditionally independent craftsmen. This trend accelerated after the turn of the century, as mushrooming southern and western markets along with growing competition from larger and better capitalized manufacturers drove independent masters to cut costs the only way they could—by cheapening the price of labor. By hiring boys as laborers rather than apprentices, and by working them alongside journeymen increasingly trapped in a downward cycle of wage labor and dependence, small masters cut their costs and weakened craft traditions as well. By 1820 apprentice and journeyman had become nostalgic atavisms for what were, in fact, simply younger and older wage workers.

Immigration added a final note of change to the city's burgeoning manufacturing economy. Soon after the postwar economy stabilized in the mid-1790s, low-paid Irish laborers, artisans, and handloom weavers flocked to Philadelphia, swelling the already substantial ranks of the city's laboring poor. Coming at a time when even British- and American-born mariners, laborers, and tailors could support their families only by periodic resort to private and public poor relief, the arrival of the Irish only lowered already minimal wages and placed greater strain on a rudimentary relief system.

Viewing the human costs of this rapidly disintegrating craft economy at close range, urban proselytizers set about the task of social reconstruction, armed with a mixture of religious zeal, personal determination, and a deep sense of moral righteousness. The Methodists were the first onto the field, attempting as early as the 1760s to revive the laboring-class enthusiasm that had lain dormant in Philadelphia since George Whitefield's enormously successful revivals of the 1740s and 1750s. Directing their urban efforts from a sail loft along the Delaware riverfront, Thomas Webb, a British soldier turned itinerant, Edward Evans, a ladies' shoemaker, and James Emerson, a seller of orange-lemon shrubs, created Philadelphia Methodism with a distinctively plebeian cast. The church retained this laboring-class identification during the uncertain years of the Revolution and into the 1780s and 1790s. By 1794 slightly more than half the city's white male Methodists were workingmen, and by 1801 that proportion had grown to 68 percent.

The rapid growth of American Methodism in the post-Revolutionary era owed much to the denomination's characteristic expectation that proselytes would confirm their conversion by becoming active bearers of their newfound faith. The Methodist discipline encouraged the creation of a lay ministry, and while only a handful might advance from class leader to full-fledged itinerant, many more took on missionary efforts closer to home. In 1803, to cite but one example, a group of Philadelphia craftsmen, most of them cordwainers, created the Hospitable Society as a vehicle for missionary work among the city's laboring poor. Traveling door to door, the visiting committee braved the "frequent insults and abuse" that greeted them at many laboring-class homes to bring a message of "relief" and personal salvation "to their fellow creatures." Although apparently much more successful in converting wives than workingmen, the intensive campaign of the Hospitable Society did reap its share of male converts, some of whom spread the word among their mates. In this way, Methodism expanded its laboring-class membership until, between 1830 and 1840, independent churches existed in each of Philadelphia's working-class suburbs and four of every five male members worked for his living.

The success of the Methodists in attracting working-class members elicited two sorts of reactions from the city's other denominations. The Quakers, Anglicans, and Lutherans were for the most part comfortable with the social composition of their existing congregations. Although Anglicans and Quakers were prominent among the city's many benevolent organizations, some of which touched the lives of the laboring poor, their churches made no direct attempts to recruit among working people. Other denominations were less complacent and organized themselves to follow the Methodist example. The Presbyterians, especially, trod close to the heels of the Methodists. Heirs, with the Methodists, of the Great Awakening, New Side Presbyterianism claimed a humble following through the Revolution and into the post-Revolutionary decades. In 1804, well before Methodist itinerants moved from the city into the laboring-class suburbs, the Presbyterians built a church in the Northern Liberties to accommodate the sailors and maritime craftsmen who were coming to dominate the district. If they met with only modest success in the early years—the 1804 subscription listed nearly as many merchants as workingmen—within a decade almost half the membership of the Northern Liberties church came from the district's working class.

The Rev. James Patterson was elected pastor of the Northern Liberties church in September 1813. Finding that "the number that regularly attended upon religious instruction . . . was not very encouraging," Patterson borrowed a technique from local Methodists and began visiting door-to-door in the narrow streets and back alleys of the Liberties. Unlike the reception accorded the members of the Methodist Hospitable Society a decade earlier, Patterson found the district more cordial, and before long his church was too small for his expanding congregation. Part of his success stemmed from his open distaste for deference and moralistic priggishness, attitudes he shared with many workingmen. As his successor in the Northern Liberties pulpit noted, Patterson possessed a "perfect disrelish of everything that savoured of affected dignity," and he frankly pitied any man who "had nothing but his clerical robes to entitle him to the confidence and respect of men."

Patterson was clearly the right man for his "plain and unlettered" congregation of workingmen and their families. His popularity was confirmed when, in January 1816, he inaugurated a seven-month-long revival. Preaching to overflow crowds, initially for seventy-six consecutive nights and then, after a brief respite, for another ninety, Patterson beat on the themes of Presbyterian doctrine: the total depravity of the heart, salvation through the sacrifice of the Son of God, and the dreadful doom awaiting those who rejected the gospel. By the end of his spiritual marathon, Patterson lay ill and exhausted, but his Northern Liberties church counted 180 new communicants and many more were said to have joined neighboring congregations because of his preaching.

The powerful effect of Patterson's preaching on his predominantly young working-class audience is preserved in a journal entry he made late in the revival. In it Patterson recounts the story of a young journeyman who experienced conversion the day after attending the revival. "While sitting on his work-bench," the entry begins, "he was powerfully convicted by reading the well known hymn, 'Alas, and did my Saviour bleed.' He fell upon his knees beside his workbench, and cried aloud for mercy. This was the means of awakening four of his shop-mates to see and feel their danger as sinners, and to plead

for salvation. They continued in supplication til mid-night, when they began to rejoice in hope, and to praise God for redeeming love."

In James Patterson the Presbyterians had their best hope for victory in the competition for laboring-class souls. Yet neither Patterson's determined oratory nor the Methodists' self-expanding system of converts managed to capture more than a minority of Philadelphia workingmen for the militias of Christ. Even as he enjoyed the satisfaction of a successful revival, Patterson endured the street corner taunts of young journeymen and apprentices who called after him mockingly, "brimstone, fire and brimstone." Nor could Patterson or the Methodists stop the growing number of masters and employers who worked their apprentices and journeymen on Sunday. And what could anyone do with the master baker who forbade his fourteen-year-old apprentice to read the New Testament, warning him that "it will fill your head with foolish freaks"?

Working-class religiosity ran in many veins, and active proselytizing and enthusiastic revivals could not hope to tap them all. Again, it was the Rev. James Patterson who, unknowingly, demonstrated this. In an 1819 journal entry, Patterson considered his failure to convert a mariner whose wife was about to join the Presbyterian Church. Forcing his wife to accompany him on a country excursion the very Sunday she was to join Patterson's church, the mariner, apparently ill with tuberculosis, suffered a pulmonary lesion and was carried back to the city nearly dead. It was a weak and ashen-faced man whom Patterson confronted when he visited the couple's home shortly afterward. Realizing the gravity of the man's illness, the parson asked him whether he had made peace with God and was prepared to die. With that, the mariner flew into a rage and bellowed at Patterson, "I want no popish stuff, and no pope about me when I am going to die." Calming somewhat, he continued, "I am very weak, I don't wish you to talk to me." Undaunted, Patterson declined to leave and instead asked the mariner whether he believed the scriptures to be the word of God. By now incredulous, the sailor sprang from his sofa and turned to Patterson exclaiming, "I am astonished that you would ask any one such a question in an enlightened land." He then looked about the room for his pistols and threatened to shoot Patterson if he did not leave. Patterson departed unharmed and the mariner died a few months later, but not before calling a Universalist minister to his side.

This small glimpse of working-class life reveals another aspect of popular religion in the post-Revolutionary era. Like the beleaguered mariner, many workingmen viewed the missionary impulses of the Methodists and Presbyterians as an invasion of their world and an imposition on their way of life. This explains both the rough reception accorded the Hospitable Society's visiting committee in 1803 and the taunts that James Patterson endured fifteen years later. If they wanted religion, many laboring-class Philadelphians seemed to be saying, they would find it for themselves.

And so many did, finding a religion that fit with their views, often in surprising places. The dying mariner of Patterson's memoir found his religion with a Universalist minister. Likewise, Joe Holden, a New York blacksmith, thought that Universalism "may not be so bad after all" and undertook his own study of the matter. Large numbers of Philadelphia craftsmen followed suit. As early as 1796, Benjamin Rush, an early convert to Universalism, noted the laboring-class appeal of Elhanan Winchester's Sunday evening lectures on universal salvation. Rush's observation is confirmed by the 1793 subscription list of Winchester's First Universalist Church, in which nearly two-thirds of the identifiable signers were workingmen. If we add the 8 percent who were shopkeepers, grocers, and innkeepers—men with close ties to the city's craftsmen—fully 71 percent of the church's subscribers were members of Philadelphia's still amorphous working class.

If Universalism was primarily a region that attracted craftsmen, small shopkeepers, and a handful of liberal intellectuals in the late eigh-

teenth century, it was even more so during the first three decades of the following century. A tally of the surviving pew books for the years 1814–25 reveals a membership dominated by the city's *menu peuple*. In this crucial period of working-class formation, 91 percent of the identifiable members fell within this plebeian group, while fully 78 percent listed working-class occupations. Here, then, was a religion that spoke to the needs and desires of city workingmen. While the numerical strength of Universalism's plebeian appeal is remarkable in itself, it is made even more so by the fact that the Universalists, unlike the Methodists and Presbyterians, did not proselytize or mount revivals but attracted their following by simple lectures delivered in a moderate-sized church situated in Lombard Street, some distance from the city's largest working-class neighborhoods. That Philadelphia craftsmen and small shopkeepers were willing to tramp across the city on Sunday evenings to attend lectures and services speaks eloquently for the powerful attraction that drew the city's working classes to Universalism.

There were thus many paths that Philadelphia workingmen might walk in search of salvation. Some followed lay preachers into the Methodist connection and took their religion from the intimacy and fellowship of weekly class meetings. Others ran with open hearts to the message of emotional revelation that sputtered from fiery Presbyterians. Still others marked out their own path and moved with measured gait to embrace the democratic salvation offered by Universalism. But knowing the paths taken is not yet to understand the place of religion in the formation of Philadelphia's working class. What did Methodism, Presbyterianism, or Universalism offer workingmen? Was it hope for a better future, respite from the swift flow of social change, or strength to forge new collective identities in a rising manufacturing economy? An answer to these questions can only be found by placing the appeal of these plebeian denominations against the backdrop of Philadelphia's emerging working-class movement and the popular moral tradition that informed it.

Philadelphia's working-class movement developed over the course of a century, beginning with the political mobilization of city craftsmen during the 1720s and ending with the creation of distinctive working-class organizations at the close of the 1820s. In the course of this long and complex history, only the outlines of which can be sketched here, a unique set of popular intellectual traditions powerfully shaped the making of the city's working class.

More a group of closely connected attitudes about work, community, and social justice than a fully articulated ideology, the small-producer tradition was the moral code by which artisans lived out their productive lives. At its core was a simple statement of the labor theory of value, or as it was more commonly rendered before the nineteenth century, the social value of labor. Beginning with the rise of urban guilds to political prominence in the twelfth century, English and European craftsmen asserted the linked claims that their labor alone was responsible for the transformation of nature into socially useful goods and that this social usefulness entitled them to respect and well-being within their communities. By the time of the English Civil War, this simple idea had developed into what would become the typical artisan claim of the eighteenth and nineteenth centuries: that labor represented the basis of community life and the foundation of all collective wealth.

From the artisan's claim that civil society rested on the foundation of his labor, it was a short distance to the corollary notion that the craftsmen's collective contribution to the commonwealth placed them on an equal footing with other members of the community. Thus, it was no accident that artisans and small farmers were notorious advocates of democratic political reforms from at least the time of the English Civil War. Claiming the rights of "freeborn Englishmen," small producers defended their rights to jury trial by their peers, to due process of law, and, if not the right to vote, then at least their right to be heard on the hustings. In the American context, artisan struggles during and after the Revolution would expand these rights to include manhood suffrage and the right of ordinary citizens to hold elective office. Whether encountered in England or America, however, artisan notions of free-born rights ran at odds with the prevailing notions of political rights and privileges propounded by large property holders and their political supporters. Against the claim that only the possession of substantial property provided a man with a true interest in society, artisans countered that the attainment of a skill and the social indispensability of productive labor combined to give all workingmen at least as great a stake in society as that claimed by the wealthy landowner or merchant.

In the end, however, artisans derived their notion of equality from practice rather than high political theory. Since the Middle Ages, membership in a trade conferred upon craftsmen the right to voice their opinions, to vote, and to hold formal office or informal positions of authority within their trade organizations. In short, it gave them the right to determine the affairs of their trade in conjunction with their fellow craftsmen. Thus, in drawing together popular notions of free-born rights with the rough democracy of the shop and informal trade society, artisans came to view themselves as equals, not only with other workingmen, but also with the wealthiest and most powerful members of society.

The third pillar of the small-producer tradition was competency. Few terms were as ubiquitous among artisans and other small producers as this. In its most basic form, competency was the lifelong ability of an artisan to provide a comfortable existence for his family through his own labor. A competency was the promise of moderate well-being and financial independence purchased through the early acquisition of a skill and the lifelong practice of a trade. For Anglo-American craftsmen, entry into a trade meant entering into a covenant with the community, a covenant in which the artisan offered a life of productive labor to the community in return for the respect of his peers and an independent life free from protracted want.

A sense of community-mindedness completed the small-producer tradition. Artisanal notions of community derived from the internal structure of the trades as well as from the local nature of craft production itself. Petty production in early America was typically production for a local market where producers and customers not only knew each other but were bound by intimate ties of custom and clientage. Under these conditions, in which artisans depended upon personal goodwill for their livelihood, the maintenance of community bonds was crucial to the smooth operation of the craft system.

But beyond the nature of small production itself, artisanal ideas about community developed from the communal organization of the craft workshop. Almost all artisans worked in small establishments with a handful of other craftsmen and apprentices. Even in larger enterprises like shipyards and metal works, craftsmen worked in gangs or crews that were seldom composed of more than a dozen men. Human relationships in these small-scale conditions were intimate and characterized by a norm of mutuality and cooperation. The shop was a little community where work rules, the pace of production, and personal relationships were governed to a considerable degree by the workers themselves. When artisans turned their attention to the larger community around them, they naturally referred to the daily operations of their shops as a guide. Much as earlier craft guilds looked to the operations of the workshop when they sought to create regulations for the conduct of their trades, artisans relied upon the world of the shop when they sought a model for the proper functioning of the community in which they lived.

Artisans, then, viewed community, like their craft, as an association of individuals who labored together for the benefit of all. A well-run society, like a well-regulated trade, required the subordination of individual self-interest and acquisitiveness to the collective well-being of its members. Just as artisans arranged shop tasks and the pace of production to ensure that there was work enough for all, so craftsmen saw a proper community as one in which labor and its rewards were shared with fairness and equality

and in which no productive member lacked in essentials while others had a more than ample supply. What craftsmen could not abide was a society where a few men lived on the fruits of the workingmen's labor and deprived producers of their just recompense.

These qualities—the value of labor, equality, competency, and community—made up the small-producer tradition. Together they represented the intellectual and moral standard against which Philadelphia artisans measured the religious appeals of Methodist class leaders, Presbyterian evangelists, and Universalist ministers. As events were to prove, those appeals led city workingmen along two, very different, paths.

> Blessed are the poor in spirit for they,
> Towards heav'ns kingdom are far on the way.
>
> In lowly rev'rence let me come,
> And bow in heart before thy awful throne.

The words are those of John Cox, a humble Philadelphia shoemaker, amateur poet, and ardent spokesman for working-class piety. His seven hundred-odd lines of uneven verse represent one of the few direct statements of laboring-class religiosity that have come down to us and reveal the unmistakable accents of the evangelical appeal among the working classes.

In England, as E. P. Thompson noted long ago, Methodism and other evangelical confessions offered solace and spiritual recompense to the victims of industrial change, albeit at the price of a lifelong obedience and servility that extended well beyond the spiritual kingdom into the texture of everyday life. In Philadelphia the evangelical message was more complex and equivocal, and the conditions of its auditors were altogether different. Unlike England, where the crushing weight of state repression joined with severe industrial dislocation to make of Methodism a "chiliasm of despair," laboring-class Philadelphians faced a more gradual industrial transformation with the power of manhood suffrage securely in their hands. Accordingly, evangelical religion offered craftsmen a more positive, if ultimately limiting, message. In their simple theology as well as in their spontaneous and democratic style, urban itinerants appealed to a working class that had successfully thrown off the bonds of colonial deference and had begun to demand a politics as plain and direct as their small-producer ethos. In this sense, evangelicalism was part of the larger cultural emergence of artisans and lesser workingmen into the public life of the post-Revolutionary era.

But in the wider view, the evangelical appeal touched something deeper than the Revolutionary political experiences of ordinary men and women. In the postwar years, Methodist and Presbyterian evangelists opened the doors of Christian brotherhood to Philadelphia's working people. In its early stages, post-Revolutionary evangelicalism held forth the prospect of a religion that could encompass both searing emotionality and traditional notions of artisanal respectability. Under the cover of institutional legitimacy provided by their class meetings and shoestring congregations, workingmen and their families found the freedom to express the mutual release of emotion that was an essential part of working-class culture, a culture that the city's more established churches eschewed and condemned. Unlike the city's more staid clerics, urban itinerants exhorted their congregations to *feel* the power of God's grace and their own shared religiosity. At the same time they provided their parishioners with institutional channels—churches, class meetings, and love feasts—that cloaked their expressive emotionality with a measure of public respectability.

What ordinary Philadelphians sought in evangelical religion was collective commitment and shared experience, the mutual validation of belief and community that comes from rituals of collective catharsis and experiential piety. A nineteenth-century mariner described this evangelical appeal with great poignancy: "What I likes along o'preachin'," he told a traveling evangelist, is "when a man is a-preachin' at me I want him to take somert hot out of his heart and shove it into mine,—that's what I calls preachin'." It was by taking "somert hot" from their hearts and sharing it with their congregations that urban evangelists created the electric waves of piety that washed over their rough-hewn flocks. From the end of the Revolution until well into the next century, these plebeian proselytizers provided a respectable venue for those who thought, as did an anonymous Boston sailor, that "faith is suth'n like Tinder: shut it up and it will go out, but give it vent and it will burn." Urban evangelicalism blew across a smoldering working-class piety that had long been ignored by more conventional churches and ignited flames of enthusiasm that would shape the lives of large numbers of working people for generations to come.

The shared experiences of conversion, prayer, and public testimony built powerful and lasting bonds between preachers, class leaders, and rank-and-file believers At the same time, the evangelical emphasis on the individual's responsibility for salvation, nurtured and confirmed within the circle of collective fellowship, conveyed a sense of self-worth and community esteem that paralleled traditional craft feelings and norms. For many craftsmen and deskilled workingmen, the competency and self-respect that was lost in the decline of the craft system might be redeemed in the class meeting and evangelical congregation. In the end, it was this combined search for secular redemption, personal recognition, and spiritual salvation that brought floods of working-class converts into Philadelphia's Methodist and Presbyterian churches in the years following the Revolution.

But for all its positive attributes—its democratic inclusiveness, its fostering of personal and collective worth, its promise of spiritual redemption—evangelicalism carried with it the heavy baggage of its Calvinist heritage. Despite its evident humanism and the genuine concern of street preachers and class leaders to bring religion to the poor, urban evangelicalism was haunted by the notion of the depravity of man. In the final analysis, urban itinerants brought religion to the working-class as a way of tempering the sin and meanness that they saw as inherent in human nature, especially as it was manifested among the nation's lower orders. In the evangelists' eyes, mankind was by nature evil, and righteous living was, for all men and women, the labor of Sisyphus. Once unremitting depravity was accepted as the essence of human nature, asceticism and fear became the only pathways to salvation. Herein lay the central tension in the evangelical message to the working class: accept God's love and you may regain your competency and self-respect, but involve yourself too much with worldly concerns and you face eternal damnation from a wrathful, punishing God.

John Cox's *Rewards and Punishments* captures this tension exactly, in its title as well as its verse. Cox begins by offering the promise of restored competency and general prosperity that would be God's reward to a regenerate Philadelphia:

Filled with God's grace, our city will shine bright,
And over the world will cast resplendent light;
Our enemies shall never do us harm,
For he will help us with outstretched arm.

All that is required to achieve this urban millennium is for the men and women of the city to bridle their passions and learn the lesson of humility:

Let us arise and shake ourselves from dust,
And he will help us overcome our lust;
His goodness he will extend to every soul,
If they will subject be to his control.

This is the message of a loving God, a God ever ready to "help us with outstretched arm." But, let human pridefullness and arrogance triumph, and the project fails. Here Cox's God takes on a more ominous countenance:

With base ingratitude ye did despise
My statutes, and from me did turn your eyes,
And for this thing I on you will send terror,
As long as you will still persist in error.

The path is clearly marked: this way, reward; that way, punishment. Like Christian, John Bunyan's archetypal seeker, Philadelphians are offered choices and a moral road map. One path leads to the postmillennial Celestial City, all others lead to urban poverty and degrading dependency. Aware of the uncertainty of the human heart, Cox closes his promise with a characteristic evangelical warning wrapped within a threat: "If that we his blessed task forsake, / He'll on our heads his dreadful anger shake."

For John Cox and workingmen who thought like him, the evangelical message of repressive deliverance promised the resurrection of a world of small producers, a world in which their labor would lead not only to competency but to simple respect. Most artisans in post-Revolutionary Philadelphia shared these aspirations and many spent their lives searching for a way to redeem what they saw as the lost promise of the American Revolution. Some, like Cox, found that way in an evangelical religion that traded laboring-class solidarity for the fellowship of the class meeting and, perhaps, a small measure of worldly success.

By rejecting the solidarity of the emerging labor movement for the consolation of faith, submission, not struggle became the center of Cox's religion:

Let us with pleasure bear each dispensation,
In ev'ry rank of life and ev'ry station;
Let us become as clay in [a] potter's hand
To mould in any form at his command.

In the end, it was submission rather than organization that would finally yield both temporal and spiritual rewards:

Let us in all things to his will submit,
With patience undergo all he thinks fit:
And if unto the end we him adore,
We will receive of him a heav'nly store.

This was one side of working-class religion; restraint, repression, and self-denial operating through submission and fear to produce a life of satisfaction and self-esteem. All that was required was to reject the tavern, the Sunday excursion, the camaraderie of games and gambling, and, along with it, the journeymen's society and mutuality, the integument of working-class culture. What would be left in the end was not a working class but "respectable" workingmen indistinguishable in sentiment from their middle-class employers.

There was, of course, another side to working-class religion and it was, in many ways, the more important of the two. It was the side that empowered rather than diminished working-class life. Unlike Methodism and evangelical Presbyterianism, both of which still bore the marks of Puritanical Calvinism in their message of denial and submission, this alternative to overweening piety offered democratic salvation as well as an open acceptance of the working-class way of life. In Philadelphia, this brighter side of working-class religion found its most forceful expression in the doctrines and organizations of the Universalist Church.

Part of a widespread reaction to predestinarian doctrines in the years following the Revolution, Universalism embraced the notion of salvation for everyone. Against John Cox's paradoxical image of a benevolent yet ultimately vengeful God, Universalists counterposed the God of pure love—a God who, in the end, understood human frailties and forgave human transgressions. The message of the Universalists was thus a simple but powerful one: all will be saved.

Translated from doctrine into practice, Universalism took on a distinctively laboring-class voice as early as the 1790s in the form of didactic hymns. Written to instruct as well as entertain, hymnody became the vehicle for Universalism's popular appeal. Something of this plebeian appeal can be sensed in Abner Kneeland's "Invitation to the Gospel," with its imagery of plenty and social leveling:

> Hear ye that starve for food,
> By feeding on the wind,
> Or vainly strive with earthly good,
> To fill an empty mind.

> The Lord of Love has made,
> A soul reviving feast,
> And lets the world, of every grade,
> To rich provision taste.

Universalist hymnody also contained more direct appeals, as in Elhanan Winchester's paean to "America's Future Glory and Happiness," which focused on the central theme of the craftsman's creed, a life of competency:

> No more the labour'r pines, and grieves,
> For want of plenty round;
> His eyes behold the fruitful sheaves,
> Which makes his joys abound.

Such working-class themes ran through many Universalist hymns, but their appeal to city workingmen ran deeper still. In their hymns and preaching, Universalists often spoke of a community of love in ways that echoed the solidarity of tight-knit journeymen's societies and the mutuality of the larger working-class community:

> How sweet is the union of souls,
> In harmony, friendship and love;
> Lord help us, this union to keep,
> In *union* God grant we may meet.

This was written in 1808, a time when masters and journeymen were being relentlessly driven apart by the new manufacturing economy, a time during which the Democratic-Republican party was dividing itself into opposing manufacturing and working-class wings. Reading these lines against the evidence of an emerging working-class movement, it would have been difficult for many Philadelphia workingmen to separate the union of Christian fellowship from early craft unions.

In the end, this was the most remarkable aspect of the Universalist–working-class connection. While the Universalist credo mirrored traditional artisan values better than the doctrines of any other denomination, it was not beliefs that ultimately mattered. It was organization. From its inception, the Universalist Church was a meeting ground for the leaders (and at least some of the rank-and-file) of Philadelphia's working-class movement.

We can date the beginnings of the post–Revolutionary workers' movement from the formation of the Democratic Society of Pennsylvania in 1793. Organized by old

Antifederalists and a new generation of opposition politicians, the Democratic Society brought Philadelphia craftsmen into organized politics for the first time since the 1770s. The political connection of Philadelphia Universalism was evident the same year, when 39 percent of the church's subscribers were also listed as members of the Democratic Society.

As the Democratic Society broadened into the Democratic-Republican party and, early in the nineteenth century, the party began to organize workingmen into neighborhood political clubs, the Universalist Church continued to play an informal organizing role. Not only did the church count such Democratic-Republican luminaries as Alexander James Dallas and Matthew Clarkson among its members, but, more importantly, it also included two of the city's most prominent working-class leaders on its rolls. Anthony Cuthbert, a mastmaker and member of one of Philadelphia's most prominent artisan families, and Israel Israel, an innkeeper and political champion of the early nineteenth-century workingmen's movement, were both active Universalists from the 1790s through the 1820s. Israel, who first earned his reputation among craftsmen for his selfless efforts in laboring-class neighborhoods during the yellow fever epidemic of 1794, became one of the most important popular leaders of the early nineteenth century.

The paucity of church records for the first two decades of the nineteenth century limits our understanding of the church's organizing role in those years, but the continued presence of popular leaders such as Cuthbert and, especially, Israel, coupled with the increasing working-class presence in the church itself, strongly suggests the church's importance to the emerging working-class movement. This importance was underlined when the workers' movement took on an institutional structure during the late 1820s. The creation of the Mechanics' Union of Trade Associations in 1827 and the Workingmen's party the following year marked the formation of America's first working class. Led by William Heighton, a local shoemaker of English birth, the Mechanics' Union and the Workingmen's party forged artisan intellectual traditions and popular politics into a powerful working-class presence in Philadelphia. Universalism played more than a minor role in this process, for not only was Heighton a follower of Universalist doctrines, he also organized the Mechanics' Union through a series of meetings held in the city's Universalist churches.

Religion played an important part in Heighton's ambitious and multifaceted plan to restore the producing classes—farmers, mechanics, and laborers—to their rightful place in American society. In an address delivered at the newly gathered Second Universalist Church, located near the working-class suburb of the Northern Liberties, Heighton outlined his plan. The cause of the continuing economic and social decline of Philadelphia's working classes, he declared, was the growing dominance of the "avaricious accumulators and ungenerous employers" of the city. This class of "aristocratic accumulators," Heighton told his working-class audience, consisted of social and economic parasites who obtained their livelihoods solely from the fruits of other men's labor. The degraded condition of Philadelphia workingmen, he explained, came not from human moral failings or the wrath of a displeased God, but from the unrestrained greed of men who lived by exploiting the city's working classes.

In time, Heighton hoped to set the united working classes of the city against this growing class of accumulators. In the meantime, he maintained that it was the duty of Philadelphia's "legislative, judicial, and theological classes" to exercise "their influence to remedy [the workers'] degraded condition." Yet, as Heighton painstakingly pointed out, none of these classes had thus far brought any degree of social justice to the workingman's door, and the clergy had failed most egregiously of all.

In the course of his public indictment of Philadelphia's reforming clergy, Heighton outlined the proper role of religion in a future republic of labor. As he saw it, the social and moral obligation of the clergy was not simply to "teach evangelical truths" but "to teach the absolute necessity of undeviating justice between man and man." While he thought that true Christian ministers ought to be living "imitators of those primitive Christians who had 'all things in common,'" Heighton found instead that most Philadelphia clerics remained blind to the "legalized extortion" practiced on the city's working classes. "Why do they not point out the enormous injustice of one class of men possessing legal authority to take advantage of the necessities of another?" he asked. And why had the denominational clergy not directed "the power of their reasoning, and the thunders of their eloquence against the unjust and vice-creating system of conflicting interest—a system so directly opposed to that adopted by . . . the Prince of Peace?"

If the established clergy were shameless in their failure to speak out against this pernicious evil, the evangelists were, for Heighton, the most culpable of all. Taking aim at the city's Methodist and evangelical Presbyterian ministers, he pointed to the futility of their quest for working-class redemption in a world structured by industrial capitalism. With barely disguised contempt Heighton warned his listeners that "not all the fervent intercessions of prayer, not all the influence of pathetic exhortation, nor all the declarations of divine denunciation, can ever arrest the progress of sin while the system of individual interest and competition is supported." For Heighton, the only hope for redemption lay not in working-class piety within the present system but in a united effort by clergy and workingmen alike to overturn that system in the name of social justice.

Religion, then, was closely bound up with Heighton's vision of a republic of independent producers; the competition and individual interest of the wage-labor market was a moral injustice, to be sure, but it was also a sin. The interest of the clergy and the interest of workingmen were consequently the same: the creation of a moral society founded in social justice. "If the clergy would arrest the fatal march of vice," Heighton advised, "let them direct their attacks on its fountain head." "The grand nursery of sin must be destroyed," he added, "before they can cherish any reasonable hopes of a general and permanent reformation in our country." Thus the republic of labor would be more than a society of loosely associated producers; it would be God's true community.

In the broadest sense, then, religion occupied a prominent place in Philadelphia's working-class movement because that movement went well beyond a simple strengthening of workers' market capacities. Heighton's aim, whether in the Mechanics' Union or the Workingmen's party, was to reform American society, to make America into the moral community that both clergy and workingmen saw as the nation's brightest promise. As husbandmen of public and private morality, the American clergy could do much to bring about this reformation, if only they would direct "their talents, their learning, and their influence . . . against the mainspring of all evil, and source of every crime." If all of America's clerics would follow the example of their Universalist brethren and unite with the nation's working people in the project of labor reform, "religion [would] extend, and flourish in all its sublime and harmonious beauties" throughout the entire nation.

Popular religion thus played an important role in the formation of Philadelphia's working class. While some workingmen retreated into the quiescence of evangelical piety and finally turned their backs on the working-class movement, many others turned to religion as a moral force that underwrote their own traditions and pointed toward a more hopeful future. While much, much more remains to be done before we can fully understand the place of religion in early working-class life, the case of the Universalists and Philadelphia's workingmen's movement suggests that religion could be a powerful ally in the workingmen's quest for economic and social justice.

KEY TERMS

Benevolence: A middle-class movement that originated in the nation's churches which sought to dispense aid and religious ideas to the poor.

Evangelicalism: A form of religious exhortation that emphasizes direct emotional experience on the part of both minister and congregation.

Plebeian: Nonelite men and women.

George Whitefield (1714–1770): Follower of John Wesley in England who preached widely in the American colonies and was a central figure in the Great Awakening of the mid-eighteenth century, instrumental in establishing Methodism in America.

Benjamin Rush (1745–1813): American physician, politician, and educator; a signer of the Declaration of Independence, involved in nearly every reform movement in the early United States, and especially known for promoting the abolition of slavery and the humane treatment of the mentally handicapped.

John Bunyan (1628–1688): English Baptist preacher and author of *Pilgrim's Progress*, the most popular religious tract after the Bible in America. *Pilgrim's Progress* is an allegorical tale of Christian's journey from the City of Destruction to the Celestial City.

DISCUSSION TOPICS

After reading this essay, you should be able to discuss:

1. The major social and economic changes experienced by working people in post-Revolutionary Philadelphia.

2. The origin and growth of evangelical religion in the city.

3. The differing appeals of evangelical and rational religion to Philadelphia artisans.

4. The reasons why these two very different forms of religious expression both found adherents among laboring-class Philadelphians.

5. The impact these two religious forms had on early unionizing efforts.

15

Women, Children, and the Uses of the Streets: Class and Gender Conflict in New York City, 1850–1860

Christine Stansell

The years between 1820 and 1860 witnessed the development of an intensive campaign to redefine the proper place of women in American society. Coming at a time of intense social and cultural change, the impulse to create a distinctively American conception of womanhood and definition of female virtue spread rapidly throughout America. Depicting the home as a domestic haven in an increasingly competitive and commercial world, the "Cult of True Womanhood" attributed to women a vital function in maintaining republican virtue during a threatening period of industrialization and urbanization. This "Cult of True Womanhood" prescribed a series of characteristics for women, as guardians of national virtue, to cultivate. Of these, the most important were religious piety, moral purity, submissiveness to men, and the maintenance of the home as place of comfort and moral education.

While many women embraced the virtues of "true womanhood," a life of domesticity was never a real possibility for poor and working-class women. Forced to work in order to maintain their families and lacking the resources and leisure necessary to maintain a middle-class household, these working women carved out lives regulated by their own distinctive social and cultural values. But, as Christine Stansell reveals in this essay, this working-class women's culture came into increasing conflict with the domestic ideal of middle- and upper-class women reformers in the course of the nineteenth

"Women, Children, and the Uses of the Streets: Class and Gender Conflict in New York City, 1850–1860." *Feminist Studies*, 8:2, (1982) pp. 309–335. Reprinted by permission of the publisher, Feminist Studies, Inc., c/o Women's Studies Program, University of Maryland, College Park, MD 20742.

century. Offering moral advice and economic aid to working-class women through a growing network of benevolent organizations, Bible societies, and temperance associations, these middle-class women sought to force working-class women from the public world of the streets and tenements into the private world of domesticity. By granting assistance only to those women who would adopt their notions of respectable living, these reforming women attempted to make the domestic ideal a universal reality in antebellum America.

On a winter day in 1856, an agent for the Children's Aid Society (CAS) of New York encountered two children out on the street with market baskets. Like hundreds he might have seen, they were desperately poor—thinly dressed and barefoot in the cold—but their cheerful countenances struck the gentleman, and he stopped to inquire into their circumstances. They explained that they were out gathering bits of wood and coal their mother could burn for fuel and agreed to take him home to meet her. In a bare tenement room, bereft of heat, furniture, or any other comforts, he met a "stout, hearty woman" who, even more than her children, testified to the power of hardihood and motherly love in the most miserable circumstances. A widow, she supported her family as best she could by street peddling; their room was bare because she had been forced to sell her clothes, furniture, and bedding to supplement her earnings. As she spoke, she sat on a pallet on the floor and rubbed the hands of the two younger siblings of the pair from the street. "They were tidy, sweet children," noted the agent, "And it was very sad to see their chilled faces and tearful eyes." Here was a scene that would have touched the heart of Dickens, and seemingly many a chillier mid-Victorian soul. Yet in concluding his report, the agent's perceptions took a curiously harsh turn.

Though for her pure young children too much could hardly be done, in such a woman there is little confidence to be put . . . it is probably, some cursed vice has thus reduced her, and that, if her children be not separated from her, she will drag them down, too.

Such expeditions of charity agents and reformers into the households of the poor were common in New York between 1850 and 1860. So were such harsh and unsupported judgments of working-class mothers, judgments which either implicitly or explicitly converged in the new category of the "dangerous classes." In this decade, philanthropists, municipal authorities, and a second generation of Christian evangelicals, male and female, came to see the presence of poor children in New York's streets as a central element of the problem of urban poverty. They initiated an ambitious campaign to clear the streets, to change the character of the laboring poor by altering their family lives, and, in the process, to eradicate poverty itself. They focused their efforts on transforming two elements of laboring-class family life, the place of children and the role of women.

There was, in fact, nothing new about the presence of poor children in the streets, nor was it new that women of the urban poor should countenance that presence. For centuries, poor people in Europe had freely used urban public areas—streets, squares, courts, and marketplaces—for their leisure and work. For the working poor, street life was bound up not only with economic exigency, but also with childrearing, family morality, sociability, and neighborhood ties. In the nineteenth century, the crowded conditions of the tenements and the poverty of great numbers of metropolitan laboring people made the streets as crucial an arena as ever for their social and economic lives. As one New York social investigator observed, "In the poorer portions of the city, people live much and sell mostly out of doors."

How, then, do we account for this sudden flurry of concern? For reformers like the agent from CAS, street life was antagonistic to ardently held beliefs about childhood, womanhood, and, ultimately, the nature of civilized urban society. The middle class of which the reformers were a part was only emerging, an economically illdefined group, neither rich nor poor, just beginning in the antebellum years to assert a distinct cultural identity. Central to its self-conception was the ideology of domesticity, a set of sharp ideas and pronounced opinions about the nature of a moral family life. The sources of this ideology were historically complex and involved several decades of struggles by women of this group for social recognition, esteem, and power in the family. Nonetheless, by midcentury, ideas initially developed and promoted by women and their clerical allies had found general acceptance, and an ideology of gender had become firmly embedded in an ideology of class. Both women and men valued the home, an institution which they perceived as sacred, presided over by women, inhabited by children, frequented by men. The home preserved those social virtues endangered by the public world of trade, industry, and politics; a public world which they saw as even more corrupting and dangerous in a great city like New York.

Enclosed, protected, and privatized, the home and the patterns of family life on which it was based thus represented to middle-class women and men a crucial institution of civilization. From this perspective, a particular geography of social life—the engagement of the poor in street life rather than in the enclave of the home— became in itself evidence of parental neglect, family disintegration, and a pervasive urban social pathology. Thus in his condemnation of the impoverished widow, the CAS agent distilled an entire analysis of poverty and a critique of poor families: the presence of her children on the streets was synonymous with a corrupt family life, no matter how disguised it might be. In the crusade of such mid-Victorian reformers to save poor children from their parents and their class lie the roots of a long history of middle-class intervention in working-class fami-

lies, a history which played a central part in the making of the female American working class.

Many historians have shown the importance of antebellum urban reform to the changing texture of class relations in America, its role in the cultural transformations of urbanization and industrialization. Confronted with overcrowding, unemployment, and poverty on a scale theretofore unknown in America, evangelical reformers forged programs to control and mitigate these pressing urban problems, programs which would shape municipal policies for years to come. Yet their responses were not simply practical solutions, the most intelligent possible reactions to difficult circumstances; as the most sensitive historians of reform have argued, they were shaped by the world view, cultural affinities, conceptions of gender, class prejudices, and imperatives of the reformers themselves. Urban reform was an interaction in which, over time, both philanthropists and their beneficiaries changed. In their experience with the reformers, the laboring poor learned—and were forced—to accommodate themselves to an alien conception of family and city life. Through their work with the poor, the reformers discovered many of the elements from which they would forge their own class and sexual identity, still ill-defined and diffuse in 1850; women, particularly, strengthened their role as dictators of domestic and familial standards for all classes of Americans. The reformers' eventual triumph in New York brought no solutions to the problem of poverty, but it did bring about the evisceration of a way of urban life and the legitimation of their own cultural power as a class.

The conflict over the streets resonated on many levels. Ostensibly the reformers aimed to rescue children from the corruptions and dangers of the city streets; indeed the conscious motives of many, if not all, of these well-meaning altruists went no further. There were many unquestioned assumptions, however, on which their benevolent motives rested, and it is in examining these assumptions that we begin to see the challenge which these middle-class people unwittingly posed to common practices of the poor. In their cultural offensive, reformers sought to impose on the poor conceptions of childhood and motherhood drawn from their own ideas of domesticity. In effect, reformers tried to implement their domestic beliefs through reorganizing social space, through creating a new geography of the city. Women were especially active; while male reformers experimented, through a rural foster home program, with more dramatic means of clearing the streets, middle-class ladies worked to found new working-class homes, modeled on their own, which would establish a viable alternative to the thoroughly nondomesticated streets. Insofar as the women reformers succeeded, their victory contributed to both the dominance of a class and of a specific conception of gender. It was, moreover, a victory which had enduring and contradictory consequences for urban women of all classes. In our contemporary city streets, vacated, for the most part, of domestic life yet dangerous for women and children, we see something of the legacy of their labors.

CHILDREN'S USES OF THE STREETS

Unlike today, the teeming milieu of the New York streets in the mid-nineteenth century was in large part a children's world. A complex web of economic imperatives and social mores accounted for their presence there, a presence which reformers so ardently decried. Public life, with its panoply of choices, its rich and varied texture, its motley society, played as central a role in the upbringing of poor children as did private, domestic life in that of their more affluent peers. While middle-class mothers spent a great deal of time with their children (albeit with the help of servants), women of the laboring classes condoned for their offspring an early independence—within bounds—on the streets. Through peddling, scavenging, and the shadier arts of theft and prostitution, the streets offered children a way to earn their keep, crucial to making ends meet in their households. Street life also provided a home for children without families—the orphaned and abandoned—and an alternative to living at home for the espe-

cially independent and those in strained family circumstances.

Such uses of the streets were dictated by exigency, but they were also intertwined with patterns of motherhood, parenthood, and childhood. In contrast to their middle- and upper-class contemporaries, the working poor did not think of childhood as a separate stage of life in which girls and boys were free from adult burdens, nor did poor women consider mothering to be a full-time task of supervision. They expected their children to work from an early age, to "earn their keep" or to "get a living," a view much closer to the early modern conceptions which Philippe Ariès describes in *Centuries of Childhood*. Children were little adults, unable as yet to take up all the duties of their elders, but nonetheless bound to do as much as they could. To put it another way, the lives of children, like those of adults, were circumscribed by economic and familial obligations. In this context, the poor expressed their care for children differently than did the propertied classes. Raising one's children properly did not mean protecting them from the world of work; on the contrary, it involved teaching them to shoulder those heavy burdens of labor which were the common lot of their class, to be hardworking and dutiful to kin and neighbors. By the same token, laboring children gained an early autonomy from their parents, an autonomy alien to the experience of more privileged children. But there were certainly generational tensions embedded in these practices: although children learned independence within the bounds of family obligation, their self-sufficiency also led them in directions that parents could not always control. When parents sent children out to the streets, they could only partially set the terms of what the young ones learned there.

Streetselling, or huckstering, was one of the most common ways for children to turn the streets to good use. Through the nineteenth century, this ancient form of trade still flourished in New York alongside such new institutions of mass marketing as A.T. Stewart's department store. Hucksters, both adults and children, sold all manner of necessities and delicacies. In the downtown business and shopping district, passers-by could buy treats at every corner: hot sweet potatoes, bake-pears, teacakes, fruit, candy, and hot corn. In residential neighborhoods, hucksters sold household supplies door to door: fruits and vegetables in season, matchsticks, scrub brushes, sponges, strings, and pins. Children assisted adult hucksters, went peddling on their own, and worked in several low-paying trades which were their special province: crossing-sweeping for girls; errandrunning, bootblacking, horseholding, and newspaperselling for boys. There were also the odd trades in which children were particularly adept, those unfamiliar and seemingly gratuitous forms of economic activity which abounded in nineteenth-century metropolises; one small boy whom a social investigator found in 1859 made his living in warm weather by catching butterflies and peddling them to canary owners.

Younger children, too, could earn part of their keep on the streets. Scavenging, the art of gathering useful and salable trash, was the customary chore for those too small to go out streetselling. Not all scavengers were children; there were also adults who engaged in scavenging full-time, ragpickers who made their entire livelihoods from "all the odds and ends of a great city." More generally, however, scavenging was children's work. Six- or seven-year-olds were not too young to set out with friends and siblings to gather fuel for their mothers. Small platoons of these children scoured neighborhood streets, ship and lumber yards, building lots, demolished houses, and the precincts of artisan shops and factories for chips, ashes, wood, and coal to take home or peddle to neighbors. "I saw some girls gathering cinders," noted Virginia Penny, New York's self-styled Mayhew. "They burn them at home, after washing them."

The economy of rubbish was intricate. As children grew more skilled, they learned how to turn up other serviceable cast-offs. "These gatherers of things lost on earth," a journal had called them in 1831. "These makers of something out of nothing." Besides taking trash home

or selling it to neighbors, children could peddle it to junk dealers, who in turn vended it to manufacturers and artisans for use in industrial processes. Rags, old rope, metal, nails, bottles, paper, kitchen grease, bones, spoiled vegetables, and bad meat all had their place in this commercial network. The waterfront was especially fruitful territory: there, children foraged for loot which had washed up on the banks, snagged in piers, or spilled out on the docks. Loose cotton shredded off bales on the wharves where the southern packet ships docked, bits of canvas and rags ended up with paper- and shoddy-manufacturers (shoddy, the cheapest of textiles, made its way back to the poor in "shoddy" ready-made clothing). Old rope was shredded and sold as oakum, a fiber used to caulk ships. Whole pieces of hardware—nails, cogs, and screws—could be resold: broken bits went to iron- and brass-founders and coppersmiths to be melted down; bottles and bits of broken glass, to glassmakers. The medium for these exchanges were the second-hand shops strung along the harbor which carried on a bustling trade with children despite a city ordinance prohibiting their buying from minors. "On going down South Street I met a gang of small Dock Thieves . . . had a bag full of short pieces of old rope and iron," William Bell, police inspector of second-hand shops, reported on a typical day on the beat in 1850. The malefactors were headed for a shop like the one into which he slipped incognito, to witness the mundane but illegal transaction between the proprietor and a six-year-old boy, who sold him a glass bottle for a penny. The waterfront also yielded trash which could be used at home rather than vended: tea, coffee, sugar, and flour spilled from sacks and barrels, and from the wagons which carried cargo to nearby warehouses.

The growth of the street trades meant that increasing numbers of children worked on their own, away from adult supervision. This situation magnified the opportunities for illicit gain, the centuries-old pilfering and finagling of apprentices and serving-girls. When respectable parents sent their children out to scavenge and peddle, the consequences were not always what they intended: these trades were an avenue to theft and prostitution as well as to an honest living. Child peddlers habituated household entryways, with their hats and umbrellas and odd knickknacks, and roamed by shops where goods were often still, in the old fashion, displayed outside on the sidewalks. And scavenging was only one step removed from petty theft. The distinction between gathering spilled flour and spilling flour oneself was one which small scavengers did not always observe. Indeed, children skilled in detecting value in random objects strewn about the streets, the seemingly inconsequential, could as easily spot value in other people's property. As the superintendent of the juvenile asylum wrote of one malefactor, "He has very little sense of moral rectitude, and thinks it but little harm to take small articles." A visitor to the city in 1857 was struck by the swarms of children milling around the docks, "scuffling about, wherever there were bags of coffee and hogshead of sugar." Armed with sticks, "they 'hooked' what they could." The targets of pilfering were analogous to those of scavenging: odd objects, unattached to persons. The prey of children convicted of theft and sent to the juvenile house of correction in the 1850s included, for instance, a bar of soap, a copy of the *New York Herald*, lead and wood from demolished houses, and a board "valued at 3¢." Police Chief George Matsell reported that pipes, tin roofing, and brass doorknobs were similarly endangered. Thefts against persons, pickpocketing and mugging, belonged to another province, that of the professional child criminal.

Not all parents were concerned about their children's breaches of the law. Reformers were not always wrong when they charged that by sending children to the streets, laboring-class parents implicitly encouraged them to a life of crime. The unrespectable poor did not care to discriminate between stolen and scavenged goods, and the destitute could not afford to. One small boy picked up by the CAS told his benefactors that his parents had sent him out chip picking with the instructions "you can take it wherever you can find it"—although like many

children brought before the charities, this one was embroidering his own innocence and his parents' guilt. But children also took their own chances, without their parents' knowledge. By midcentury, New York was the capital of American crime, and there was a place for children, small and adept as they were, on its margins. Its full-blown economy of contraband, with the junk shops at the center, allowed children to exchange pilfered and stolen goods quickly and easily: anything, from scavenged bottles to nicked top hats could be sold immediately.

As scavenging shaded into theft, so it also edged into another street trade, prostitution. The same art of creating commodities underlay both. In the intricate economy of the streets, old rope, stray coal, rags, and sex all held the promise of cash, a promise apparent to children who from an early age learned to be "makers of something out of nothing." For girls who knew how to turn things with no value into things with exchange value, the prostitute's act of bartering sex into money would have perhaps seemed daunting, but nonetheless comprehensible. These were not professional child prostitutes; rather, they turned to the lively trade in casual prostitution on occasion or at intervals to supplement other earnings. One encounter with a gentleman, easy to come by in the hotel and business district, could bring the equivalent of a month's wages in domestic service, a week's wages seamstressing, or several weeks' earnings huckstering. Such windfalls went to pay a girl's way at home or, more typically, to purchase covertly some luxury—pastries, a bonnet, cheap jewelry, a fancy gown—otherwise out of her reach.

Prostitution was quite public in antebellum New York. It was not yet a statutory offense, and although the police harassed streetwalkers and arrested them for vagrancy, they had little effect on the trade. Consequently, offers from men and inducements from other girls were common on the streets, and often came a girl's way when she was out working. This is the reason a German father tried to prevent his fourteen-year-old daughter from going out scavenging when she lost her place in domestic service. "He said, 'I don't want you to be a rag-picker. You are not a child now—people will look at you—you will come to harm,'" as the girl recounted the tale. The "harm" he feared was the course taken by a teenage habitue of the waterfront in whom Inspector Bell took a special interest in 1851. After she rejected his offer of a place in service, he learned from a junk shop proprietor that, along with scavenging around the docks, she was "in the habit of going aboard the Coal Boats in that vicinity and prostituting herself." Charles Loring Brace, founder of the CAS, claimed that "the life of a swill-gatherer, or coal-picker, or chiffonier [rag-picker] in the streets soon wears off a girl's modesty and prepares her for worse occupation," while Police Chief Matsell accused huckster-girls of soliciting the clerks and employees they met on their rounds of counting houses.

While not all girls in the street trades were as open to advances as Brace and Matsell implied, their habituation to male advances must have contributed to the brazenness with which some of them could engage in sexual bartering. Groups of girls roamed about the city, sometimes on chores and errands, sometimes only with an eye for flirtations, or being "impudent and saucy to men," as the parents of one offender put it. In the early 1830s, John R. McDowall, leader of the militant Magdalene Society, had observed on fashionable Broadway "females of thirteen and fourteen walking the streets without a protector, until some pretended gentleman gives them a nod, and takes their arm and escorts them to houses of assignation." McDowall was sure to exaggerate, but later witnesses lent credence to his description. In 1854, a journalist saw nearly fifty girls soliciting one evening as he walked a mile up Broadway, while diarist George Templeton Strong referred to juvenile prostitution as a permanent feature of the promenade in the early 1850s: "no one can walk the length of Broadway without meeting some hideous troop of ragged girls." But despite the entrepreneurial attitude with which young girls ventured into prostitution, theirs was a grim choice, with hazards which, young as they were, they could not always foresee. Nowhere can we see more clearly the complexities of poor children's lives in the public city. The life of the streets taught them self-reliance and the arts of survival, but this education could also be a bitter one.

The autonomy and independence which the streets fostered through petty crime also extended to living arrangements. Abandoned children, orphans, runaways, and particularly independent boys made the streets their home: sleeping out with companions in household areas, wagons, marketplace stalls, and saloons. In the summer of 1850, the *Tribune* noted that the police regularly scared up thirty or forty boys sleeping along Nassau and Ann streets; they included boys with homes as well as genuine vagabonds. Police Chief Matsell reported that in warm weather, crowds of roving boys, many of them sons of respectable parents, absented themselves from their families for weeks. Such was Thomas W., who came to the attention of the CAS; "sleeps in stable," the case record notes. "Goes home for clean clothes; and sometimes for his meals." Thomas's parents evidently tolerated the arrangement, but this was not always the case. Rebellious children, especially boys, evaded parental demands and discipline by living on the streets full-time. Thus John Lynch left home because of some difficulty with his father: he was sent on his parents' complaint to the juvenile house of correction on a vagrancy charge.

Reformers like Matsell and the members of the CAS tended to see such children as either orphaned or abandoned, symbols of the misery and depravity of the poor. Their perception, incarnated by writers like Horatio Alger in the fictional waifs of sentimental novels, gained wide credibility in nineteenth-century social theory and popular thought. Street children were essentially "friendless and homeless," declared Brace. "No one cares for them, and they care for no one." His judgment, if characteristically harsh, was not without truth. If children without parents had no kin or friendly neighbors to whom to turn, they were left to fend for themselves. Such was the story of the two small children of a deceased stonecutter, himself a widower. After he died, "they wandered around, begging cold victuals, and picking up, in any way they were able, their poor living." William S., fifteen years old, had been orphaned when very young. After a stay on a farm as an indentured boy, he ran away to the city, where he slept on the piers and supported himself by carrying luggage off passenger boats: "William thinks he has seen hard times," the record notes. But the testimony garnered by reformers about the "friendless and homeless" young should also be taken with a grain of salt. The CAS, a major source of these tales, was most sympathetic to children who appeared before the agents as victims of orphanage, desertion, or familial cruelty; accordingly, young applicants for aid sometimes presented themselves in ways which would gain them the most favor from philanthropists. The society acknowledged the problem, although it claimed to have solved it: "runaways frequently come to the office with fictitious stories . . . Sometimes a truant has only one parent, generally the mother, and she is dissipated, or unable to control him. He comes to the office . . . and tells a fictitious story of orphanage and distress." Yet in reality, there were few children so entirely exploited and "friendless" as the CAS believed.

Not surprisingly, orphanage among the poor was a far more complex matter than reformers perceived. As Carol Groneman has shown, poor families did not disintegrate under the most severe difficulties of immigration and urbanization. In the worst New York slums, families managed to keep together and to take in those kin and friends who lacked households of their own. Orphaned children as well as those who were temporarily parentless—whose parents, for instance, had found employment elsewhere—typically found homes with older siblings, grandparents, and aunts. The solidarity of the laboring-class family, however, was not as idyllic as it might seem in retrospect. Interdependence also bred tensions which weighed heavily on children, and in response, the young sometimes chose—or were forced—to strike out on their own. Step-relations, so

common in this period, were a particular source of bad feelings. Two brothers whom a charity visitor found sleeping in the streets explained that they had left their mother when she moved in with another man after their father deserted her. If natural parents died, step-parents might be particularly forceful about sending children "on their own hook." "We haven't got no father nor mother," testified a twelve-year-old wanderer of himself and his younger brother. Their father, a shoemaker, had remarried when their mother died; when he died, their stepmother moved away and left them, "and they could not find out anything more about her."

Moreover, the difficulties for all, children and adults, of finding work in these years of endemic underemployment created a kind of half-way orphanage. Parents emigrating from New York could place their boys in apprenticeships which subsequently collapsed and cast the children on their own for a living. The parents of one boy, for example, left him at work in a printing office when they moved to Toronto. Soon after they left, he was thrown out of work; to support himself he lived on the streets and worked as an errand boy, news boy, and bootblack. Similarly, adolescents whose parents had left them in unpleasant or intolerable situations simply struck out on their own. A widow boarded her son with her sister when she went into service; the boy ran away when his aunt "licked him." Thus a variety of circumstances could be concealed in the category of the street "orphan."

All these customs of childhood and work among the laboring poor were reasons for the presence of children, girls and boys, in the public life of the city, a presence which reformers passionately denounced. Children and parents alike had their uses for the streets. For adults, the streets allowed their dependents to contribute to their keep, crucial to making ends meet in the household economy. For girls and boys, street life provided a way to meet deeply ingrained family obligations. This is not to romanticize their lives. If the streets provided a way to meet responsibilities, it was a hard and bitter, even a cruel one. Still, children of the laboring classes lived and labored in a complex geography, which reformers of the poor perceived only as a stark tableau of pathology and vice.

To what degree did their judgments of children redound on women? Although reformers included both sexes in their indictments, women were by implication more involved. First, poverty was especially likely to afflict women. To be the widow, deserted wife, or orphaned daughter of a laboring man, even a prosperous artisan, was to be poor; female self-support was synonymous with indigence. The number of self-supporting women, including those with children, was high in midcentury New York: in the 1855 census report for two neighborhoods, nearly 60 percent of six hundred working women sampled had no adult male in the household. New York's largest charity reported in 1858 that it aided 27 percent more women than men. For women in such straits, children's contributions to the family income were mandatory. As a New York magistrate had written in 1830: "of the children brought before me for pilfering, nine out of ten are those whose fathers are dead, and who live with their mothers." Second, women were more responsible than men for children, both from the perspective of reformers and within the reality of the laboring family. Mothering, as the middle class saw it, was an expression of female identity, rather than a construction derived from present and past social conditions. Thus the supposedly neglectful ways of laboring mothers reflected badly not only on their character as parents, but also on their very identity as women. When not depicted as timid or victimized, poor women appeared as unsavory characters in the annals of reformers: drunken, abusive, or, in one of the most memorable descriptions, "sickly-looking, deformed by over work . . . weak and sad-faced." Like prostitutes, mothers of street children became a kind of half-sex in the eyes of reformers, outside the bounds of humanity by virtue of their inability or unwillingness to replicate the innate abilities of true womanhood.

REFORMERS AND FAMILY LIFE

In the 1850s, the street activities of the poor, especially those of children, became the focus of a distinct reform politics in New York. The campaign against the streets, one element in a general cultural offensive against the laboring classes which evangelical groups had carried on since the 1830s, was opened in 1849 by Police Chief Matsell's report to the public on juvenile delinquency. In the most hyperbolic rhetoric, he described a "deplorable and growing evil" spreading through the streets. "I allude to the constantly increasing number of vagrants, idle and vicious children of both sexes, who infest our public thoroughfares." Besides alerting New York's already existing charities to the presence of the dangerous classes, Matsell's expose affected a young Yale seminarian, Charles Loring Brace, just returned from a European tour and immersed in his new vocation of city missionary. Matsell's alarmed observations coalesced with what Brace had learned from his own experiences working with boys in the city mission. Moved to act, Brace in 1853 founded the CAS, a charity which concerned itself with all poor children, but especially with street "orphans." Throughout the 1850s, the CAS carried on the work Matsell had begun, documenting and publicizing the plight of street children. In large measure because of its efforts, the "evil" of the streets became a central element in the reform analysis of poverty and a focus of broad concern in New York.

Matsell, Brace, and the New York philanthropists with whom they associated formed—like their peers in other northeastern cities—closely connected network of secular and moral reformers. Unlike philanthropists in the early nineteenth century, who partook of an older attitude of tolerance to the poor and of the providential inevitability of poverty, mid-Victorians were optimistic that poverty could be abolished by altering the character of their almoners as workers, citizens, and family members. The reformers of the streets were directly concerned with the latter. In their efforts to teach the working poor the virtues of the middle-class home as a means of self-help, they laid the ideological and programmatic groundwork for a sustained intervention in working-class family life.

There were, then, greater numbers of children in the New York streets after 1845, and their activities were publicized as never before. Faced with an unprecedented crisis of poverty in the city, reformers fastened on their presence as a cause rather than a symptom of impoverishment. The reformers' idea that the curse of poor children lay in the childrearing methods of their parents moved toward the center of their analysis of the etiology of poverty, replacing older notions of divine will. In the web of images of blight and disease which not only reflected but also shaped the midcentury understanding of poverty, the tenement house was the "parent of constant disorders, and the nursery of increasing vices," but real parents were the actual agents of crime. In opposition to the ever more articulate and pressing claims of New York's organized working men, this first generation of "experts" on urban poverty averred that familial relations rather than industrial capitalism were responsible for the misery which any clear-headed New Yorker could see was no transient state of affairs. One of the principal pieces of evidence of "the ungoverned appetites, bad habits, and vices" of laboring-class parents was the fact that they sent their offspring out to the streets to earn their keep.

The importance of domesticity to the reformers' own class identity fostered this shift of attention from individual moral shortcomings to the family structure of a class. For these middle-class city dwellers, the home was not simply a place of residence; it was a focus of social life and a central element of class-consciousness, based on specific conceptions of femininity and childrearing. There, secluded from the stress of public life, women could devote themselves to directing the moral and ethical development of their families. There, protected from the evils of the outside world, the young could live out their childhoods in innocence, freed from the necessity of labor, cultivating their moral and intellectual faculties.

From this vantage point, the laboring classes appeared gravely deficient. When charity visitors, often ladies themselves, entered the households of working people, they saw a domestic sparseness which contradicted their deepest beliefs about what constituted a morally sustaining family life. "[Their] ideas of domestic comfort and standard of morals, are far below our own," wrote the Association for Improving the Condition of the Poor (AICP). The urban poor had intricately interwoven family lives, but they had no *homes*. Middle-class people valued family privacy and intimacy: among the poor, they saw a promiscuous sociability, an "almost fabulous gregariousness." They believed that the moral training of children depended on protecting them within the home; in poor neighborhoods, they saw children encouraged to labor in the streets. The harshness and intolerance with which midcentury reformers viewed the laboring classes can be partly explained by the disparity between these two ways of family life. "Homes—in the better sense—they never know," declared one investigating committee; the children "graduate in every kind of vice known in that curious school which trains them—the public street." The AICP scoffed at even using the word: "Homes . . . if it is not a mockery to give that hallowed name to the dark, filthy hovels where many of them dwell." To these middle-class women and men, the absence of home life was not simply due to the uncongenial physical circumstances of the tenements, nor did it indicate the poor depended upon another way of organizing their family lives. Rather, the homelessness of this "multitude of half-naked, dirty, and leering children" signified an absence of parental love, a neglect of proper childrearing which was entwined in the habits and values of the laboring classes.

MIDDLE-CLASS WOMEN AND THE CHILDREN'S AID SOCIETY

Rather than encouraging girls to break away from their families, the ladies sought the opposite: to create among the urban laboring classes a domestic life of their own. They aimed to mold future wives and mothers of a reformed working class: women who would be imbued with a belief in the importance of domesticity and capable of patterning their homes and family lives on middle-class standards.

It was this strategy of change which would eventually dominate attempts to reform working-class children. The ladies envisioned homes which would reorganize the promiscuously sociable lives of the poor under the aegis of a new, "womanly" working-class woman. In the CAS industrial schools and Lodging-House, girls recruited off the streets learned the arts of plain sewing, cooking, and housecleaning, guided by the precept celebrated by champions of women's domestic mission that "nothing was so honorable as industrious *house-work*." These were skills which both prepared them for waged employment in seamstressing and domestic service and outfitted them for homes of their own: as the ladies proudly attested after several years of work, their students entered respectable married life as well as honest employment. "Living in homes reformed through their influence," the married women carried on their female mission reformers by proxy.

Similarly, the women reformers instituted meetings to convert the mothers of their students to a new relationship to household and children. Classes taught the importance of sobriety, neat appearance, and sanitary housekeeping: the material basis for virtuous motherhood and a proper home. Most important, the ladies stressed the importance of keeping children off the streets and sending them to school. Here, they found their pupils particularly recalcitrant. Mothers persisted in keeping children home to work and cited economic reasons when their benefactresses

upbraided them. The CAS women, however, considered the economic rationale a pretense for the exploitation of children and the neglect of their moral character. "The larger ones were needed to 'mind' the baby," lady volunteers sardonically reported, "or go out begging for clothes . . . and the little ones, scarcely bigger than the baskets on their arms, must be sent out for food, or chips, or cinders." The Mother's Meetings tried, however unsuccessfully, to wean away laboring women from such customary practices to what the ladies believed to be a more nurturant and moral mode of family life: men at work, women at home, children inside.

In contrast to the male reformers [of the CAS], the women of the society tried to create an intensified private life within New York itself, to enclose children within tenements and schools rather than to send them away or incarcerate them in asylums. There is a new, optimistic vision of city life implied in their work. With the establishment of the home across class lines, a renewed city could emerge, its streets free for trade and respectable promenades, and emancipated from the inconveniences of pickpockets and thieves, the affronts of prostitutes and hucksters, the myriad offenses of working-class mores and poverty. The "respectable" would control and dominate public space as they had never before. The city would itself become an asylum on a grand scale, an environment which embodied the eighteenth-century virtues of reason and progress, the nineteenth-century virtues of industry and domesticity. And as would befit a city for the middle class, boundaries between public and private life would be clear: the public space of the metropolis would be the precinct of men, the private space of the home, that of women and children.

KEY TERMS

Magdalene Society: A middle-class reform society which sought to reform prostitutes, provide them with alternative occupations, and thus end prostitution in the early United States.

Charles Dickens (1812–1870): English novelist noteworthy for his portrayal of the lives of the poor.

DISCUSSION TOPICS

After reading this essay, you should be able to discuss:

1. The ways in which children contributed to the working-class family economy.

2. The viewpoints of middle-class reformers concerning working-class children.

3. The contrasting views of their own children held by working-class women.

4. The clash of cultures revealed by these differing viewpoints concerning children in the streets.

"Gouge and Bite, Pull Hair and Scratch": The Social Significance of Fighting in the Southern Backcountry

Elliott J. Gorn

Violence was an integral part of everyday life in antebellum America. In the nation's cities, members of competing fire companies routinely fought one another for the right to put out fires, local sporting matches often turned into general brawls, and bearbaiting and cockfighting continued to be favorite popular pastimes. On the western frontier, white encroachment and Indian resistance regularly led to the shedding of blood, and in every community court dockets recorded an alarming number of assaults, batteries, and other forms of criminal violence. As antebellum reformers never tired of pointing out, unrestrained violence seemed to be an essential component of the American character.

But while violence was endemic to antebellum society, nowhere did it play such a crucial social role as in the American South. Since the colonial era, southern men were notorious for the frequency and ferocity with which they fought one another, often for seemingly insignificant reasons. To call someone a "Scotsman" or a "rogue" was enough to provoke a fray that might cost a combatant his eye, his ear, or even his life. In this essay, Elliott J. Gorn surveys the ubiquitous violence of the American South and attempts to explain this peculiar regional trait by pointing to three interrelated characteristics. According to Gorn, the undeveloped state of the market economy emphasized fierce loyalties to kin and locality while the hard life of the backcountry promoted drinking, joking, and fighting as forms of personal release. Status and reputation in this rough-and-tumble world accrued to those who took personal risks lightly and were willing to inflict pain and permanent injury without flinching. In the southern backcountry, Gorn suggests, violence was truly the measure of a man.

"'Gouge and Bite, Pull Hair and Scratch': The Social Significance of Fighting in the Southern Backcountry." *American Historical Review*, 90, pp. 18–43. Copyright © 1985 by Elliott J. Gorn. Reprinted by permission of the author.

"I would advise you when You do fight Not to act like Tygers and Bears as these Virginians do—Biting one anothers Lips and Noses off, and *gowging* one another—that is, thrusting out one anothers Eyes, and kicking one another on the Cods, to the Great damage of many a Poor Woman." Thus, Charles Woodmason, an itinerant Anglican minister born of English gentry stock, described the brutal form of combat he found in the Virginia backcountry shortly before the American Revolution. Although historians are more likely to study people thinking, governing, worshiping, or working, how men fight—who participates, who observes, which rules are followed, what is at stake, what tactics are allowed—reveals much about past cultures and societies.

The evolution of southern backwoods brawling from the late eighteenth century through the antebellum era can be reconstructed from oral traditions and travelers' accounts. As in most cultural history, broad patterns and uneven trends rather than specific dates mark the way. The sources are often problematic and must be used with care; some speculation is required. But the lives of common people cannot be ignored merely because they leave few records. "To feel for a feller's eyestrings and make him tell the news" was not just mayhem but an act freighted with significance for both social and cultural history.

As early as 1735, boxing was "much in fashion" in parts of Chesapeake Bay, and forty years later a visitor from the North declared that, along with dancing, fiddling, small swords, and card playing, it was an essential skill for all young Virginia gentlemen. The term "boxing," however, did not necessarily refer to the comparatively tame style of bare-knuckle fighting familiar to eighteenth-century Englishmen. In 1746, four deaths prompted the governor of North Carolina to ask for legislation against "the barbarous and inhuman manner of boxing which so much prevails among the lower sort of people." The colonial assembly responded by making it a felony "to cut out the Tongue or pull out the eyes of the King's Liege People."

Five years later the assembly added slitting, biting, and cutting off noses to the list of offenses. Virginia passed similar legislation in 1748 and revised these statutes in 1772 explicitly to discourage men from "gouging, plucking, or putting out an eye, biting or kicking or stomping upon" quiet peaceable citizens. By 1786 South Carolina had made premeditated mayhem a capital offense, defining the crime as severing another's bodily parts.

Laws notwithstanding, the carnage continued. Philip Vickers Fithian, a New Jerseyite serving as tutor for an aristocratic Virginia family, confided to his journal on September 3, 1774:

> By appointment is to be fought this Day near Mr. *Lanes* two fist Battles between four young Fellows. The Cause of the battles I have not yet known; I suppose either that they are lovers, and one has in Jest or reality some way supplanted the other; or has in a merry hour called him a *Lubber* or a *thick-Skull*, or a *Buckskin*, or a *Scotsman*, or perhaps one has mislaid the other's hat, or knocked a peach out of his Hand, or offered him a dram without wiping the mouth of the Bottle; all these, and ten thousand more quite as trifling and ridiculous are thought and accepted as just Causes of immediate Quarrels, in which every diabolical Strategem for Mastery is allowed and practiced.

The "trifling and ridiculous" reasons for these fights had an unreal quality for the matter-of-fact Yankee. Not assaults on persons or property but slights, insults, and thoughtless gestures set young southerners against each other. To call a man a "buckskin," for example, was to accuse him of the poverty associated with leather clothing, while the epithet "Scotsman" tied him to the low-caste Scots-Irish who settled the southern highlands. Fithian could not understand how such trivial offenses caused the bloody battles. But his incomprehension turned to rage when he realized that spectators attended these "odious and filthy amusements" and that the fighters allayed their spontaneous passions in order to fix convenient dates and places, which allowed time for rumors to spread and crowds to gather. The Yankee concluded that only devils, prostitutes, or monkeys could sire creatures so unfit for human society.

Descriptions of these "fist battles," as Fithian called them, indicate that they generally began like English prize fights. Two men, surrounded by onlookers, parried blows until one was knocked or thrown down. But there the similarity ceased. Where as "Broughton's Rules" of the English ring specified that a round ended when either antagonist fell, southern bruisers only began fighting at this point. Enclosed not inside a formal ring—the "magic circle" defining a special place with its own norms of conduct—but within whatever space the spectators left vacant, fighters battled each other until one called enough or was unable to continue. Combatants boasted, howled, and cursed. As words gave way to action, they tripped and threw, gouged and butted, scratched and choked each other. "But what is worse than all," Isaac Weld observed, "these wretches in their combat endeavor to their utmost to tear out each other's testicles."

Around the beginning of the nineteenth century, men sought original labels for their brutal style of fighting. "Rough-and-tumble" or simply "gouging" gradually replaced "boxing" as the name for these contests. Before two bruisers attacked each other, spectators might demand whether they proposed to fight fair—according to Broughton's Rules—or rough-and-tumble. Honor dictated that all techniques be permitted. Except for a ban on weapons, most men chose to fight "no holts barred," doing what they wished to each other without interference, until one gave up or was incapacitated.

The emphasis on maximum disfigurement, on severing bodily parts, made this fighting style unique. Amid the general mayhem, however, gouging out an opponent's eye became the sine qua non of rough-and-tumble fighting, much like the knockout punch in modern boxing. The best gougers, of course, were adept at other fighting skills. Some allegedly filed their teeth to bite off an enemy's appendages more efficiently. Still, liberating an eyeball quickly became a fighter's surest route to victory and his most prestigious accomplishment. To this

end, celebrated heroes fired their fingernails hard, honed them sharp, and oiled them slick. "You have come off badly this time, I doubt?" declared an alarmed passerby on seeing the piteous condition of a renowned fighter. "'Have I,' says he triumphantly, shewing from his pocket at the same time an eye, which he had extracted during the combat, and preserved for a trophy."

As the new style of fighting evolved, its geographical distribution changed. Leadership quickly passed from the southern seaboard to upcountry counties and the western frontier. Although examples could be found throughout the South, rough-and-tumbling was best suited to the backwoods, where hunting, herding, and semisubsistence agriculture predominated over market-oriented, staple crop production. Thus, the settlers of western Carolina, Kentucky, and Tennessee, as well as upland Mississippi, Alabama, and Georgia, became especially known for their pugnacity.

The social base of rough-and-tumbling also shifted with the passage of time. Although brawling was always considered a vice of the "lower sort," eighteenth-century Tidewater gentlemen sometimes found themselves in brutal fights. These combats grew out of challenges to men's honor—to their status in patriarchal, kin-based, small-scale communities—and were woven into the very fabric of daily life. Rhys Isaac has observed that the Virginia gentry set the tone for a fiercely competitive style of living. Although they valued hierarchy, individual status was never permanently fixed, so men frantically sought to assert their prowess—by grand boasts over tavern gaming tables laden with money, by whipping and tripping each other's horses in violent quarter-races, by wagering one-half year's earnings on the flash of a fighting cock's gaff. Great planters and small shared an ethos that extolled courage bordering on foolhardiness and cherished magnificent, if irrational, displays of largess.

Piety, hard work, and steady habits had their adherents, but in this society aggressive self-assertion and manly pride were the real marks of status. Even the gentry's vaunted hospitality demonstrated a family's community standing, so conviviality itself became a vehicle for rivalry and emulation. Rich and poor might revel together during "public times," but gentry patronage of sports and festivities kept the focus of power clear. Above all, brutal recreations toughened men for a violent social life in which the exploitation of labor, the specter of poverty, and a fierce struggle for status were daily realities.

During the final decades of the eighteenth century, however, individuals like Fithian's young gentlemen became less inclined to engage in rough-and-tumbling. Many in the planter class now wanted to distinguish themselves from social inferiors more by genteel manners, gracious living, and paternal prestige than by patriarchal prowess. They sought alternatives to brawling and found them by imitating the English aristocracy. A few gentlemen took boxing lessons from professors of pugilism or attended sparring exhibitions given by touring exponents of the manly art. More important, dueling gradually replaced hand-to-hand combat. The code of honor offered a genteel, though deadly, way to settle personal disputes while demonstrating one's elevated status. Ceremony distinguished antiseptic duels from lower-class brawls. Cool restraint and customary decorum proved a man's ability to shed blood while remaining emotionally detached, to act as mercilessly as the poor whites but to do so with chilling gentility.

Slowly, then, rough-and-tumble fighting found specific locus in both human and geographical landscapes. We can watch men grapple with the transition. When an attempt at a formal duel aborted, Savannah politician Robert Watkins and United States Senator James Jackson resorted to gouging. Jackson bit Watson's finger to save his eye. Similarly, when "a low fellow who pretends to gentility" insulted a distinguished doctor, the gentleman responded with a proper challenge. "He had scarcely uttered these words, before the other flew at him, and in an instant turned his eye out of the socket, and while it hung upon his cheek, the fellow was barbarous enough to endeavor to pluck it entirely out." By the new century, such ambiguity had lessened, as rough-and-tumble fighting was relegated to individuals in backwoods settlements. For the next several decades, eye-gouging matches were focal events in the culture of lower-class males who still relished the wild ways of old.

"The indolence and dissipation of the middling and lower classes of Virginia are such as to give pain to every reflecting mind," one anonymous visitor declared. "Horse-racing, cockfighting, and boxing-matches are standing amusements, for which they neglect all business; and in the latter of which they conduct themselves with a barbarity worthy of their savage neighbors." Thomas Anburey agreed. He believed that the Revolution's leveling of class distinctions left the "lower people" dangerously independent. Although Anburey found poor whites usually hospitable and generous, he was disturbed by their sudden outbursts of impudence, their aversion to labor and love of drink, their vengefulness and savagery. They shared with their betters a taste for gaming, horse racing, and cockfighting, but "boxing matches, in which they display such barbarity, as fully marks their innate ferocious disposition," were all their own. Anburey concluded that an English prize fight was humanity itself compared to Virginia combat.

Another visitor, Charles William Janson, decried the loss of social subordination, which caused the rabble to reinterpret liberty and equality as licentiousness. Paternal authority—the font of social and political order—had broken down in America, as parents gratified their children's whims, including youthful tastes for alcohol and tobacco. A national mistrust of authority had brought civilization to its nadir among the poor whites of the South. "The lower classes are the most abject that, perhaps, ever peopled a Christian land. They live in the woods and deserts and many of them cultivate no more land than will raise them corn and cabbages, which, with fish, and occasionally a piece of pickled pork or bacon, are their constant food. . . . Their habitations are more wretched than can be conceived; the huts of the poor of Ireland, or even the meanest Indian wig-wam, displaying more ingenuity and greater industry." Despite their degradation—perhaps because of it—Janson found the poor whites extremely jealous of their republican rights and liberties. They considered themselves the equals of their best-educated neighbors and intruded on whomever they chose. The gouging match this fastidious Englishman witnessed in Georgia was the epitome of lower-class depravity:

> We found the combatants . . . fast clinched by the hair, and their thumbs endeavoring to force a passage into each other's eyes; while several of the bystanders were betting upon the first eye to be turned out of its socket. For some time the combatants avoided the *thumb stroke* with dexterity. At length they fell to the ground, and in an instant the uppermost sprung up with his antagonist's eye in his hand!!! The savage crowd applauded, while, sick with horror, we galloped away from the infernal scene. The name of the sufferrer was John Butler, a Carolinian, who, it seems, had been dared to the combat by a Georgian; and the first eye was for the honor of the state to which they respectively belonged.

Janson concluded that even Indian "savages" and London's rabble would be outraged by the beastly Americans.

While Janson toured the lower South, his countryman Thomas Ashe explored the territory around Wheeling, Virginia. A passage, dated April 1806, from his *Travels in America* gives us a detailed picture of gouging's social context. Ashe expounded on Wheeling's potential to become a center of trade for the Ohio and upper Mississippi valleys, noting that geography made the town a natural rival of Pittsburgh. Yet Wheeling lagged in "worthy commercial pursuits, and industrious and moral dealings." Ashe attributed this backwardness to the town's frontier ways, which attracted men who specialized in drinking, plundering Indian property, racing horses, and watching cock-fights. A Wheeling Quaker assured Ashe that mores were changing, that the underworld ele-

ment was about to be driven out. Soon, the godly would gain control of the local government, enforce strict observance of the Sabbath, and outlaw vice. Ashe was sympathetic but doubtful. In Wheeling, only heightened violence and debauchery distinguished Sunday from the rest of the week. The citizens' willingness to close up shop and neglect business on the slightest pretext made it a questionable residence for any respectable group of men, let alone a society of Quakers.

To convey the rough texture of Wheeling life, Ashe described a gouging match. Two men drinking at a public house argued over the merits of their respective horses. Wagers made, they galloped off to the race course. "Two thirds of the population followed:—blacksmiths, shipwrights, all left work: the town appeared a desert. The stores were shut. I asked a proprietor, why the warehouses did not remain open? He told me all good was done for the day: that the people would remain on the ground till night, and many stay till the following morning." Determined to witness an event deemed so important that the entire town went on holiday, Ashe headed for the track. He missed the initial heat but arrived in time to watch the crowd raise the stakes to induce a rematch. Six horses competed, and spectators bet a small fortune, but the results were inconclusive. Umpires' opinions were given and rejected. Heated words, then fists flew. Soon, the melee narrowed to two individuals, a Virginian and a Kentuckian. Because fights were common in such situations, everyone knew the proper procedures, and the combatants quickly decided to "tear and rend" one another—to rough-and-tumble—rather than "fight fair." Ashe elaborated: "You startle at the words tear and rend, and again do not understand me. You have heard these terms, I allow, applied to beasts of prey and to carnivorous animals; and your humanity cannot conceive them applicable to man: It nevertheless is so, and the fact will not permit me the use of any less expressive term."

The battle began—size and power on the Kentuckian's side, science and craft on the Virginian's. They exchanged cautious throws and blows, when suddenly the Virginian lunged at his opponent with a panther's ferocity. The crowd roared its approval as the fight reached its violent denouement:

> The shock received by the Kentuckyan, and the want of breath, brought him instantly to the ground. The Virginian never lost his hold; like those bats of the South who never quit the subject on which they fasten till they taste blood, he kept his knees in his enemy's body; fixing his claws in his hair, and his thumbs on his eyes, gave them an instantaneous start from their sockets. The sufferer roared aloud, but uttered no complaint. The citizens again shouted with joy. Doubts were no longer entertained and bets of three to one were offered on the Virginian.

But the fight continued. The Kentuckian grabbed his smaller opponent and held him in a tight bear hug, forcing the Virginian to relinquish his facial grip. Over and over the two rolled, until, getting the Virginian under him, the big man "snapt off his nose so close to his face that no manner of projection remained." The Virginian quickly recovered, seized the Kentuckian's lower lip in his teeth, and ripped it down over his enemy's chin. This was enough: "The Kentuckyan at length *gave out*, on which the people carried off the victor, and he preferring triumph to a doctor, who came to cicatrize his face, suffered himself to be chaired round the ground as the champion of the times, and the first *rougher-and-tumbler*. The poor wretch, whose eyes were started from their spheres, and whose lip refused its office, returned to the town to hide his impotence, and get his countenance repaired." The citizens refreshed themselves with whiskey and biscuits, and then resumed their races.

Ashe's Quaker friend reported that such spontaneous races occurred two or three times a week and that the annual fall and spring meets lasted fourteen uninterrupted days, "aided by the licentious and profligate of all the neighboring states." As for rough-and-tumbles, the Quaker saw no hope of suppressing them. Few nights passed without such fights; few mornings failed to reveal a new citizen with mutilated features. It was a regional taste, unrestrained by law or authority, an inevitable part of life on the left bank of the Ohio.

What can we conclude about the culture and society that nourished rough-and-tumble fighting? The best place to begin is with the material base of life and the nature of daily work. Gamblers, hunters, herders, roustabouts, rivermen, and yeomen farmers were the sorts of persons usually associated with gouging. Such hallmarks of modernity as large-scale production, complex division of labor, and regular work rhythms were alien to their lives. Recent studies have stressed the premodern character of the southern uplands through most of the antebellum period. Even while cotton production boomed and trade expanded, a relatively small number of planters owned the best lands and most slaves, so huge parts of the South remained outside the flow of international markets or staple crop agriculture. Thus, backcountry whites commonly found themselves locked into a semi-subsistent pattern of living. Growing crops for home consumption, supplementing food supplies with abundant game, allowing small herds to fatten in the woods, spending scarce money for essential staples, and bartering goods for the services of part-time or itinerant trades people, the upland folk lived in an intensely local, kin-based society. Rural hamlets, impassable roads, and provincial isolation—not growing towns, internal improvements, or international commerce—characterized the backcountry.

Even men whose livelihoods depended on expanding markets often continued their rough, premodern ways. Characteristic of life on a Mississippi barge, for example, were long periods of idleness shattered by intense anxiety, as deadly snags, shoals, and storms approached. Running aground on a sandbar meant backbreaking labor to maneuver a thirty-ton vessel out of trouble. Boredom weighed as heavily as danger, so tale telling, singing, drinking, and gambling filled the empty hours. Once goods were taken on in New Orleans, the men began the thousand-mile return journey against the current. Before steam power replaced muscle, bad food and whiskey fueled the gangs who day after day, exposed to wind and water, poled the river bottoms or strained at the cordelling ropes until their vessel reached the tributaries of the Missouri or the Ohio. Hunters, trappers, herdsmen, subsistence farmers, and other backwoodsmen faced different but equally taxing hardships, and those who endured prided themselves on their strength and daring, their stamina, cunning, and ferocity.

Such men played as lustily as they worked, counterpointing bouts of intense labor with strenuous leisure. What travelers mistook for laziness was a refusal to work and save with compulsive regularity. "I have seen nothing in human form so profligate as they are," James Flint wrote of the boatmen he met around 1820. "Accomplished in depravity, their habits and education seem to comprehend every vice. They make few pretensions to moral character; and their swearing is excessive and perfectly disgusting. Although earning good wages, they are in the most abject poverty; many of them being without anything like clean or comfortable clothing." A generation later, Mark Twain vividly remembered those who manned the great timber and coal rafts gliding past his boyhood home in Hannibal, Missouri: "Rude, uneducated, brave, suffering terrific hardships with sailorlike stoicism; heavy drinkers, course frolickers in moral sties like the Natchez-under-the-hill of that day, heavy fighters, reckless fellows, every one, elephantinely jolly, foul witted, profane; prodigal of their money, bankrupt at the end of the trip, fond of barbaric finery, prodigious braggarts; yet, in the main, honest, trustworthy, faithful to promises and duty, and often picaresquely magnanimous." Details might change, but penury, loose morality, and lack of steady habits endured.

Boatmen, hunters, and herdsmen were often separated from wives and children for long periods. More important, backcountry couples lacked the emotionally intense experience of the bourgeois family. They spent much of their time apart and found companionship with members of their own sex. The frontier town or crossroads tavern brought males together in surrogate brotherhoods, where rough men paid little deference to the civilizing role of women and the moral uplift of the domestic family. On the margins of a booming, modernizing society, they shared an intensely communal yet fiercely competitive way of life. Thus, where work was least rationalized and specialized, domesticity weakest, legal institutions primitive, and the market economy feeble, rough-and-tumble fighting found fertile soil.

Just as the economy of the southern backcountry remained locally oriented, the rough-and-tumblers were local heroes, renowned in their communities. There was no professionalization here. Men fought for informal village and county titles; the red feather in the champion's cap was pay enough because it marked him as first among his peers. Paralleling the primitive division of labor in backwoods society, boundaries between entertainment and daily life, between spectators and participants, were not sharply drawn. "Bully of the Hill" Ab Gaines from the Big Hatchie Country, Neil Brown of Totty's Bend, Vernon's William Holt, and Smithfield's Jim Willis—all of them were renowned Tennessee fighters, local heroes in their day. Legendary champions were real individuals, tested gang leaders who attained their status by being the meanest, toughest, and most ruthless fighters, who faced disfigurement and never backed down. Challenges were ever present; yesterday's spectator was today's champion, today's champion tomorrow's invalid.

Given the lives these men led, a world view that embraced fearlessness made sense. Hunters, trappers, Indian fighters, and herdsmen who knew the smell of warm blood on their hands refused to sentimentalize an environment filled with threatening forces. It was not that backwoodsmen lived in constant danger but that violence was unpredictable. Recreations like cockfighting deadened men to cruelty, and the gratuitous savagery of gouging matches reinforced the daily truth that life was brutal, guided only by the logic of superior nerve, power, and cunning. With families emotionally or physically distant and civil institutions weak, a man's role in the all-male society was defined less by his ability as a breadwinner than by his ferocity. The touchstone of masculinity was unflinching toughness, not chivalry, duty, or piety. Violent sports, heavy drinking, and impulsive pleasure seeking were appropriate for men whose lives were hard, whose futures were unpredictable, and whose opportunities were limited. Gouging champions were group leaders because they embodied the basic values of their peers. The successful rough-and-tumbler proved his manhood by asserting his dominance and rendering his opponent "impotent," as Thomas Ashe put it. And the loser, though literally or symbolically castrated, demonstrated his mettle and maintained his honor.

Here we begin to understand the travelers' refrain about plain folk degradation. Setting out from northern ports, whose inhabitants were increasingly possessed by visions of godly perfection and material progress, they found southern upcountry people slothful and backward. Ashe's Quaker friend in Wheeling, Virginia, made the point. For Quakers and northern evangelicals, labor was a means of moral self-testing, and earthly success was a sign of God's grace, so hard work and steady habits became acts of piety. But not only Yankees endorsed sober restraint. A growing number of southern evangelicals also embraced a life of decorous self-control, rejecting the hedonistic and self-assertive values of old. During the late eighteenth century, as Rhys Isaac has observed, many plain folk disavowed the hegemonic gentry culture of conspicuous display and found individual worth, group pride, and transcendent meaning in religious revivals. By the antebellum era, new evangelical waves washed over class lines as rich and poor alike forswore such sins as drinking, gambling, cursing, fornication, horse racing, and dancing. But conversion was far from universal, and, for many in backcountry settlements like Wheeling, the evangelical idiom remained a foreign tongue. Men worked hard to feed themselves and their kin, to acquire goods and status, but they lacked the calling to

prove their godliness through rigid morality. Salvation and self-denial were culturally less compelling values, and the barriers against leisure and self-gratification were lower here than among the converted.

Moreover, primitive markets and the semi-subsistence basis of upcountry life limited men's dependence on goods produced by others and allowed them to maintain the irregular work rhythms of a precapitalist economy. The material base of backwoods life was ill suited to social transformation, and the cultural traditions of the past offered alternatives to rigid new ideals. Closing up shop in mid-week for a fight or horse race had always been perfectly acceptable, because men labored so that they might indulge the joys of the flesh. Neither a compulsive need to save time and money nor an obsession with progress haunted people's imaginations. The backcountry folk who lacked a bourgeois or Protestant sense of duty were little disturbed by exhibitions of human passions and were resigned to violence as part of daily life. Thus, the relative dearth of capitalistic values (such as delayed gratification and accumulation), the absence of a strict work ethic, and a cultural tradition that winked at lapses in moral rigor limited society's demands for sober self-control.

Not just unconverted poor whites but also large numbers of the slave-holding gentry still lent their prestige to a regional style that favored conspicuous displays of leisure. As C. Vann Woodward has pointed out, early observers, such as Robert Beverley and William Byrd, as well as modern-day commentators, have described a distinctly "southern ethic" in American history. Whether judged positively as leisure or negatively as laziness, the southern sensibility valued free time and rejected work as the consuming goal of life. Slavery reinforced this tendency, for how could labor be an unmitigated virtue if so much of it was performed by despised black bondsmen? When southerners did esteem commerce and enterprise, it was less because piling up wealth contained religious or moral value than because productivity facilitated the leisure ethos. Southerners could therefore work hard without placing labor at the center of their ethical universe. In important ways, then, the upland folk culture reflected a larger regional style.

Thus, the values, ideas, and institutions that rapidly transformed the North into a modern capitalist society came late to the South. Indeed, conspicuous display, heavy drinking, moral casualness, and love of games and sports had deep roots in much of Western culture. As Woodward has cautioned, we must take care not to interpret the southern ethic as unique or aberrant. The compulsions to subordinate leisure to productivity, to divide work and play into separate compartmentalized realms, and to improve each bright and shining hour were the novel ideas. The southern ethic anticipated human evil, tolerated ethical lapses, and accepted the finitude of man in contrast to the new style that demanded unprecedented moral rectitude and internalized self-restraint.

The American South also shared with large parts of the Old World a taste for violence and personal vengeance. Long after the settling of the southern colonies, powerful patriarchal clans in Celtic and Mediterranean lands still avenged affronts to family honor with deadly feuds. Norbert Elias has pointed out that postmedieval Europeans routinely spilled blood to settle their private quarrels. Across classes, the story was the same:

> Two associates fall out over business; they quarrel, the conflict grows violent; one day they meet in a public place and one of them strikes the other dead. An innkeeper accuses another of stealing his clients; they become mortal enemies. Someone says a few malicious words about another; a family war develops. . . . Not only among the nobility were there family vengeance, private feuds, vendettas. . . . The little people too—the hatters, the tailors, the shepherds—were all quick to draw their knives.

Emotions were freely expressed: jollity and laughter suddenly gave way to belligerence; guilt and penitence coexisted with hate; cruelty always lurked nearby. The modern middle-class individual, with his subdued, rational, calculating ways, finds it hard to understand the joy sixteenth-century Frenchmen took in ceremonially burning alive one or two dozen cats every Midsummer Day or the pleasure eighteenth-century Englishmen found in watching trained dogs slaughter each other.

Despite enormous cultural differences, inhabitants of the southern uplands exhibited characteristics of their forebears in the Old World. The Scots-Irish brought their reputation for ferocity to the backcountry, but English migrants, too, had a thirst for violence. Central authority was weak, and men reserved the right to settle differences for themselves. Vengeance was part of daily life. Drunken hilarity, good fellowship, and high spirits, especially at crossroads taverns, suddenly turned to violence. Traveler after traveler remarked on how forthright and friendly but quick to anger the backcountry people were. Like their European ancestors, they had not yet internalized the modern world's demand for tight emotional self-control.

Above all, the ancient concept of honor helps explain this shared proclivity for violence. According to the sociologist Peter Berger, modern men have difficulty taking seriously the idea of honor. American jurisprudence, for example, offers legal recourse for slander and libel because they involve material damages. But insult—publicly smearing a man's good name and besmirching his honor—implies no palpable injury and so does not exist in the eyes of the law. Honor is an intensely social concept, resting on reputation, community standing, and the esteem of kin and compatriots. To possess honor requires acknowledgment from others; it cannot exist in solitary conscience. Modern man, Berger has argued, is more responsive to dignity—the belief that personal worth inheres equally in each individual, regardless of his status in society. Dignity frees the evangelical to confront God alone, the capitalist to make contracts without customary encumbrances, and the reformer to uplift the lowly. Naked and alone man has dignity; extolled by peers and covered with ribbons, he has honor.

Anthropologists have also discovered the centrality of honor in several cultures. According to J. G. Peristiany, honor and shame often preoccupy individuals in small-scale settings, where face-to-face relationships predominate over anonymous or bureaucratic ones. Social standing in such communities is never completely secure, because it must be validated by public opinion, whose fickleness compels men constantly to assert and prove their worth. Julian Pitt-Rivers has added that, if society rejects a man's evaluation of himself and treats his claim to honor with ridicule or contempt, his very identity suffers because it is based on the judgment of peers. Shaming refers to that process by which an insult or any public humiliation impugns an individual's honor and thereby threatens his sense of self. By risking injury in a violent encounter, an affronted man—whether victorious or not—restores his sense of status and thus validates anew his claim to honor. Only valorous action, not words, can redeem his place in the ranks of his peer group.

Bertram Wyatt-Brown has argued that this Old World ideal is the key to understanding southern history. Across boundaries of time, geography, and social class, the South was knit together by a primal concept of male valor, part of the ancient heritage of Indo-European folk cultures. Honor demanded clan loyalty, hospitality, protection of women, and defense of patriarchal prerogatives. Honorable men guarded their reputations, bristled at insults, and, where necessary, sought personal vindication through bloodshed. The culture of honor thrived in hierarchical rural communities like the American South and grew out of a fatalistic world view, which assumed that pain and suffering were man's fate. It accounts for the pervasive violence that marked relationships between southerners and explains their insistence on vengeance and their rejection of legal redress in settling quarrels. Honor tied personal identity to public fulfillment of social roles. Neither bourgeois self-control nor internalized conscience determined status; judgment by one's fellows was the wellspring of community standing.

In this light, the seemingly trivial causes for brawls enumerated as early as Fithian's time—name calling, subtle ridicule, breaches of decorum, displays of poor manners—make sense. If a man's good name was his most important possession, then any slight cut him deeply. "Having words" precipitated fights because words brought shame and undermined a man's sense of self. Symbolic acts, such as buying a round of drinks, conferred honor on all, while refusing to share a bottle implied some inequality in social status. Honor inhered not only in individuals but also in kin and peers; when members of two cliques had words, their tested leaders or several men from each side fought to uphold group prestige. Inheritors of primal honor, the southern plain folk were quick to take offense, and any perceived affront forced a man either to devalue himself or strike back violently and avenge the wrong.

The concept of male honor takes us a long way toward understanding the meaning of eye-gouging matches. But backwoods people did not simply acquire some primordial notion without modifying it. Definitions of honorable behavior have always varied enormously across cultures. The southern upcountry fostered a particular style of honor, which grew out of the contradiction between equality and hierarchy. Honorific societies tend to be sharply stratified. Honor is apportioned according to rank, and men fight to maintain personal standing within their social categories. Because black chattel slavery was the basis for the southern hierarchy, slave owners had the most wealth and honor, while other whites scrambled for a bit of each, and bondsmen were permanently impoverished and dishonored. Here was a source of tension for the plain folk. Men of honor shared freedom and equality; those denied honor were implicitly less than equal—perilously close to a slave-like condition. But in the eyes of the gentry, poor whites as well as blacks were outside the circle of honor, so both groups were subordinate. Thus a herdsman's insult failed to shame a planter since the two men were not on the same social level. Without a threat to the gentleman's honor, there was no need for a duel; horsewhipping the insolent fellow sufficed.

Southern plain folk, then, were caught in a social contradiction. Society taught all white men to consider themselves equals, encouraged them to compete for power and status, yet threatened them from below with the specter of servitude and from above with insistence on obedience to rank and authority. Cut off from upper-class tests of honor, backcountry people adopted their own. A rough-and-tumble was more than a poor man's duel, a botched version of genteel combat. Plain folk chose not to ape the dispassionate, antiseptic, gentry style but to invert it. While the gentleman's code of honor insisted on cool restraint, eye gougers gloried in unvarnished brutality. In contrast to duelists' aloof silence, backwoods fighters screamed defiance to the world. As their own unique rites of honor, rough-and-tumble matches allowed backcountry men to shout their equality at each other. And eye-gouging fights also dispelled any stigma of servility. Ritual boasts, soaring oaths, outrageous ferocity, unflinching bloodiness—all proved a man's freedom. Where the slave acted obsequiously, the backwoodsman resisted the slightest affront; where human chattels accepted blows and never raised a hand, plain folk celebrated violence; where blacks could not jeopardize their value as property, poor whites proved their autonomy by risking bodily parts. Symbolically reaffirming their claims to honor, gouging matches helped resolve painful uncertainties arising out of the ambiguous place of plain folk in the southern social structure.

Backwoods fighting reminds us of man's capacity for cruelty and is an excellent corrective to romanticizing premodern life. But a close look also keeps us from drawing facile conclusions about innate human aggressiveness. Eye gouging represented neither the "real" human animal emerging on the frontier, nor nature acting through man in a Darwinian struggle for survival, nor anarchic disorder and communal breakdown. Rather, rough-and-tumble fighting was ritualized behavior—a product of specific cultural assumptions. Men drink together, tongues loosen, a simmering of old rivalry begins to boil; insult is given, offense taken, ritual boasts commence; the fight begins, mettle is tested, blood redeems honor, and equilibrium is restored. Eye gouging was the poor and middling whites' own version of a historical southern tendency to consider personal violence socially useful—indeed, ethically essential.

Rough-and-tumble fighting emerged from the confluence of economic conditions, social relationships, and culture in the southern backcountry. Primitive markets and the semisubsistence basis of life threw men back on close ties to kin and community. Violence and poverty were part of daily existence, so endurance, even callousness, became functional values. Loyal to their localities, their occupations, and each other, men came together and found release from life's hardships in strong drink, tall talk, rude practical jokes, and cruel sports. They craved one another's recognition but rejected genteel, pious, or bourgeois values, awarding esteem on the basis of their own traditional standards. The glue that held men together was an intensely competitive status system in which the most prodigious drinker or strongest arm wrestler, the best tale teller, fiddle player, or log roller, the most daring gambler, original liar, skilled hunter, outrageous swearer, or accurate marksman was accorded respect by the others. Reputation was everything, and scars were badges of honor. Rough-and-tumble fighting demonstrated unflinching willingness to inflict pain while risking mutilation—all to defend one's standing among peers—and became a central expression of the all-male subculture.

Eye gouging continued long after the antebellum period. As the market economy absorbed new parts of the backcountry, however, the way of life that supported rough-and-tumbling waned. Certainly by mid-century the number of incidents declined, precisely when expanding international demand brought ever more upcountry acres into staple production. Towns, schools, churches, revivals, and families gradually overtook the backwoods. In a slow and uneven process, keelboats gave way to steamers, then railroads; squatters, to cash crop farmers; hunters and trappers, to preachers. The plain folk code of honor was far from dead, but emergent social institutions engendered a moral ethos that warred against the old ways. For many individuals, the justifications for personal violence grew stricter, and mayhem became unacceptable.

Ironically, progress also had a darker side. New technologies and modes of production could enhance men's fighting abilities. "Birmingham and Pittsburgh are obliged to complete . . . the equipment of the 'chivalric Kentuckian,'" Charles Agustus Murray observed in the 1840s, as bowie knives ended more and more rough-and-tumbles. Equally important, in 1835 the first modern revolver appeared, and manufacturers marketed cheap, accurate editions in the coming decade. Dueling weapons had been costly, and Kentucky rifles or horse pistols took a full minute to load and prime. The revolver, however, which fitted neatly into a man's pocket, settled more and more personal disputes. Raw and brutal as rough-and-tumbling was, it could not survive the use of arms. Yet precisely because eye gouging was so violent—because combatants cherished maimings, blindings, even castrations—it unleashed death wishes that invited new technologies of destruction.

With improved weaponry, dueling entered its golden age during the antebellum era. Armed combat remained both an expression of gentry sensibility and a mark of social rank. But in a society where status was always shifting and unclear, dueling did not stay confined to the upper class. The habitual carrying of weapons once considered a sign of unmanly fear, now lost some of its stigma. As the backcountry changed, tests of honor continued, but gunplay rather than fighting tooth-and-nail appealed to new men with social aspirations. Thus, progress and technology slowly circumscribed rough-and-tumble fighting, only to substitute a deadlier option. Violence grew neater and more lethal as men checked their savagery to murder each other.

KEY TERMS

Scots-Irish: The people of Scotland who settled in northern Ireland and their descendents, especially those who migrated to America.

Cordelling ropes: Ropes attached to a canal barge allowing the barge to be towed through a canal.

Celtic: Reference to ancient inhabitants of Ireland.

Darwinian: A theory of biological evolution developed by Charles Darwin and others, stating that all species of organisms arise and develop through the natural selection of small, inherited variations that increase the individual's ability to compete, survive, and reproduce.

DISCUSSION TOPICS

After reading this essay, you should be able to discuss:

1. The importance of honor in defining southern masculinity.

2. The differing forms of honor found among elite and common southern men.

3. The ways in which risking one's life and limb in a "rough-and-tumble" established one's reputation.

4. The role of violence in southern life.

17

Advocate of the Dream

Stephen B. Oates

No American president has been as mythologized as Abraham Lincoln. Whether revered as the savior of the Union or condemned as the cause of the Civil War and the subsequent decline of the South, the sixteenth president has appeared larger than life since he took the oath of office in 1861. In this reconsideration of the man behind the myth, Stephen B. Oates examines Lincoln's commitment to a moral vision of national prosperity and political equality open to all Americans. Oates suggests that the "American dream" of material reward for individual effort was Lincoln's guiding philosophy from his early days as a young politician in Illinois through his final days as leader of the victorious Union.

The greatest challenge to this dream of moderate mobility was the continued existence of slavery in the southern states, and it haunted Lincoln throughout his public life. From his unsuccessful senatorial campaign of 1858, during which he declared that the nation could not exist "half slave and half free," through his wartime emancipation of southern slaves, Lincoln dealt with the complex moral, economic, and political issues raised by slavery with a mixture of principle and pragmatism. Ultimately, Oates argues, it was Lincoln's creative struggle with the conundrum of slavery and individual liberty that ensured his greatness as a leader.

From *Abraham Lincoln: The Man Behind the Myths* by Stephen B. Oates (New York: Harper & Row, 1984) pp. 57–88. Copyright © 1984 by Stephen B. Oates. Reprinted by permission of HarperCollins Publishers.

1. THE BEACON LIGHT OF LIBERTY

In presidential polls taken by *Life* magazine in 1948, the *New York Times Magazine* in 1962, and the *Chicago Tribune Magazine* in 1982, historians and political scholars ranked Lincoln as the best chief executive in American history. They were not trying to mythologize the man, for they realized that errors, vacillations, and human flaws marred his record. Their rankings indicate, however, that the icon of mythology did rise out of a powerful historical figure, a man who learned from his mistakes and made a difference. Indeed, Lincoln led the lists because he had a moral vision of where his country must go to preserve and enlarge the rights of all her people. He led the lists because he had an acute sense of history—an ability to identify himself with a historical turning point in his time and to articulate the promise that held for the liberation of oppressed humanity the world over. He led the lists because he perceived the truth of his age and embodied it in his words and deeds. He led the lists because, in his interaction with the spirit and events of his day, he made momentous *moral* decisions that affected the course of humankind.

It cannot be stressed enough how much Lincoln responded to the spirit of his age. From the 1820s to the 1840s, while Lincoln was growing to manhood and learning the art and technique of politics, the Western world seethed with revolutionary ferment. In the 1820s, revolutions broke out not only in Poland, Turkey, Greece, Italy, Spain, and France, but blazed across Spain's ramshackle South American empire as well, resulting in new republics whose capitals rang with the rhetoric of freedom and independence. The Republic of Mexico even produced laws and promulgations that abolished slavery throughout the nation, including Mexico's subprovince of Texas. In that same decade, insurrection panics rocked the Deep South, especially the South Carolina tidewater, as America's disinherited Africans reflected the revolutionary turbulence sweeping the New World. In 1831, in an effort to liberate his people, a visionary slave preacher named Nat Turner incited the most violent slave rebellion in American history, a revolt that shook the South to its foundations and cleared the way for the Great Southern Reaction against the human-rights upheavals of the time. In the 1830s, a vociferous abolitionist movement sprang up in the free states; Great Britain eradicated slavery in the Empire; and impassioned English emancipators came to crusade in America as well. In distant Russia, Czar Nicholas I established an autonomous communal structure for Russia's millions of serfs—the first step in their eventual emancipation two decades later. In the 1840s, while Lincoln practiced law and ran for Congress, reformist impulses again swept Europe. Every major country there had liberal parties that clamored for representative government, self-rule, civil liberties, and social and economic reform. In 1848, the year Congressman Lincoln denounced "Mr. Polk's War" against Mexico, defended the right of revolution, and voted against slavery expansion, revolutions again blazed across Europe, flaring up first in France against the July Monarchy, then raging through Italy and central Europe. These were revolutions against monarchy, despotism, exploitation by the few, revolutions that tried to liberate individuals, classes, and nationalities alike from the shackles of the past. In sum, it was an age of revolution, a turbulent time when people throughout the Western world were searching for definitions of liberty, fighting and dying for liberty, against reactionary forces out to preserve the status quo.

Out in Illinois, Lincoln identified himself with the liberating forces of his day. In fact, he became the foremost political spokesman for those impulses in the United States, a man with a world view of the meaning and mission of his young country in that historic time.

From earliest manhood, Lincoln was a fervent nationalist in an age when a great many Americans, especially in Dixie, were aggressive localists. His broad outlook began when he was an Indiana farm boy tilling his father's mundane wheatfield. During lunch breaks, when he was not studying grammar and rhetoric, Lincoln would peruse Parson Weems's eulogistic biography of George Washington, and he would daydream about the Revolution and the origins of the Republic, daydream about Washington, Jefferson, and Madison as great national statesmen who shaped the course of history. By the time he became a politician in the 1830s, Lincoln idolized the Founding Fathers as apostles of liberty (never mind for now that many of those apostles were also southern slaveowners). Young Lincoln extolled the Fathers for beginning a noble experiment in popular government on these shores, to demonstrate to the world that a free people could govern themselves without hereditary monarchs and aristocracies. And the foundation of the American experiment was the Declaration of Independence, which in Lincoln's view proclaimed the highest political truths in history: that all men were created equal and entitled to liberty and the pursuit of happiness. This meant that men like Lincoln were not chained to the conditions of their births, that they could better their station in life and realize the rewards of their own talent and toil.

A good example, Lincoln believed, was his political idol, Whig national leader Henry Clay of Kentucky. Born into a poor farm family, Clay lifted himself all the way to the United States Senate and national and international fame. For Lincoln, this taught a "profitable lesson"—"it teaches that in this country, one can scarcely be so poor, but that, if he *will*, he *can* acquire sufficient education to get through the world respectably." Thanks to the Declaration, which guaranteed Americans "the right to rise," Lincoln himself had acquired enough education to "get through the world respectably." Thus he had a deep, personal reverence for the Declaration and insisted that all his political sentiments flowed from that document.

All his economic beliefs derived from that document, too. Indeed, Lincoln's economics were as nationalistic and deeply principled as his politics. Schooled in the Whig doctrine of order and national unity, Lincoln advocated a strong federal government to maintain a pros-

perous, stable economy for the benefit of all Americans—"the old and the young, the rich and the poor, the grave and the gay, of all sexes and tongues, and colors and conditions," as he would say. Thus he championed a national bank, internal improvements financed by the federal government, federal subsidies to help the states build their own canals, turnpikes, and railroads, and state banks whose task was to ensure financial growth and stability. "The legitimate object of government," Lincoln asserted later, "is to do for the people what needs to be done, but which they can not, by individual effort, do at all, or do so well, for themselves."

Lincoln's national economic program was part of his large vision of the American experiment in popular government. By promoting national prosperity, stability, and unity, his economics would help guarantee his "American dream"— the right of all Americans to rise, to harvest the full fruits of their labors, and so to better themselves as their own talent and industry allowed. Thus the American experiment ensured two things essential to liberty: the right of self-government and the right of self-improvement.

Nor was the promise of America limited to the native-born. Her frontier, Lincoln said, should function as an outlet for people the world over who wanted to find new homes, a place to "better their conditions in life." For Lincoln, the American experiment was the way of the future for nations across the globe. A child of the Enlightenment, the American system stood as a beacon of hope for "the liberty party throughout the world."

Yet this beacon of hope harbored a monstrous thing, a relic of despotism in the form of Negro slavery. In Lincoln's view, bondage was the one retrograde institution that disfigured the American experiment, and he maintained that he had always hated it, as much as any abolitionist. His family had opposed slavery, and he had grown up and entered politics thinking it wrong. In 1837, his first public statement on slavery, Lincoln contended that it was "founded both on injustice and bad policy," and he never changed his mind. But before 1854 (and the significance of this date will become clear), Lincoln generally kept his own counsel about slavery and abolition. After all, slavery was the most inflammable issue of his generation, and Lincoln observed early on what violent passions Negro bondage—and the question of race that underlay it—could arouse in white Americans. In his day, slavery was a tried and tested means of race control in a South dedicated to white supremacy. Moreover, the North was also a white supremacist region, where the vast majority of whites opposed emancipation lest it result in a flood of southern "Africans" into the free states. And Illinois was no exception, as most whites there were anti-Negro and anti-abolition to the core. Lincoln, who had elected to work within the American system, was not going to ruin his career by trumpeting an unpopular cause. To be branded as an abolitionist in central Illinois—his constituency as a legislator and a U.S. congressman—would have been certain political suicide.

Still, slavery distressed him. He realized that it should never have existed in a self-proclaimed free and enlightened Republic. He who cherished the Declaration of Independence understood only too well how bondage mocked and contradicted that noble document. Yes, he detested slavery. It was a blight on the American experiment in popular government, the one institution that robbed the Republic of its just example in the world, robbed the United States of the hope it should hold out to oppressed people everywhere.

He opposed slavery, too, because he had witnessed some of its evils firsthand. In 1841, on a steamboat journey down the Ohio River, he saw a group of manacled slaves on their way to the cruel cotton plantations of the Deep South. Lincoln was appalled at the sight of those chained Negroes. Fourteen years later he wrote that the spectacle "was a continual torment to me" and that he saw something like it every time he touched a slave border. Slavery, he said, "had the power of making me miserable."

Again, while serving in Congress from 1847 to 1849, he passed slave auction blocks in Washington, D.C. In fact, from the windows of the Capitol, he could observe the infamous "Georgia pen"—"a sort of Negro livery stable," as he described it, "where droves of negroes were collected, temporarily kept, and finally taken to southern markets, precisely like droves of horses." The spectacle offended him. He agreed with a Whig colleague that the buying and selling of human beings in the United States was a national disgrace. Accordingly Lincoln drafted a gradual abolition bill for the District of Columbia. But powerful southern politicians howled in protest, and his own Whig support fell away. At that, Lincoln dropped the bill and sat in gloomy silence as Congress rocked with debates—with drunken fights and rumbles of disunion—over the status of slavery in the territories. Shocked at the behavior of his colleagues, Lincoln confessed that slavery was the one issue that threatened the stability of the Union.

Yet Attorney Lincoln had to concede that bondage was a thoroughly entrenched institution in the southern states, one protected by the U.S. Constitution and a web of national and state laws. This in turn created a painful dilemma for Lincoln: a system he deeply loved had institutionalized a thing he abominated. What could be done? Lincoln admitted that the federal government had no legal authority in peacetime to harm a state institution like slavery. And yet it should not remain in what he considered "the noblest political system the world ever saw."

Caught in an impossible predicament, Lincoln persuaded himself that if slavery were confined to the South and left alone there, time would somehow solve the problem and slavery would ultimately die out. Once it was no longer workable, he believed, southern whites would gradually liberate the blacks on their own. They would do so voluntarily.

And he told himself that the Founding Fathers—that Washington, Jefferson, and Madison—had felt the same way, that they too had expected slavery to perish some day. In Lincoln's interpretation, the Fathers had tolerated slavery as a necessary evil, one that could not be removed where it already existed without causing wide-scale chaos and destruction. But, Lincoln contended, they had taken steps to restrict the growth of bondage (had prohibited it in the old Northwest Territories, had outlawed the international slave trade) and thus to place the institution on the road to extinction. And he decided that this was why the Fathers had not included the words *slave* or *slavery* in the Constitution. When bondage did disappear, "there should be nothing on the face of the great charter of liberty suggesting that such a thing as negro slavery had ever existed among us."

So went Lincoln's argument before 1854. Thanks to the Founding Fathers, slavery was on its way to its ultimate doom. And he believed that southerners and northerners alike accepted this as axiomatic. The task of his generation, Lincoln thought, was to keep the Republic firmly on the course charted by the Fathers, guiding America toward that ultimate day when slavery would finally be removed, the nation righted at last with her own ideals, and popular government preserved for all humankind. It was this vision—this sense of America's historic mission in the progress of human liberty—that shaped Lincoln's beliefs and actions throughout his mature years.

Still, despite his passionate convictions about popular government and human liberty, Lincoln before the Civil War did not envision black people as permanent participants in the great American experiment. On the contrary, he feared that white Americans were too prejudiced to let Negroes live among them as equals. If it was impossible for blacks to be completely free in America, then he preferred that they be free somewhere else. Once slavery died out in Dixie, he insisted that the federal government should colonize all blacks in Africa, an idea he got from Henry Clay.

Of course, emancipation and colonization would depend entirely on the willingness of southerners to cooperate. Lincoln hoped and assumed that they would. Before the Civil War, he always sympathized with the mass of southern whites and thought of them inherently humane and patriotic. After all, Lincoln him-self was a native Kentuckian, and *he* loved the American experiment and tried to be a fair-minded man. He said of southern whites and slavery, "They are just what we would be in their situation. When it is said that the institution exists, and that it is very difficult to get rid of . . . I can understand and appreciate the saying." Yet he thought the great majority of southern whites "have human sympathies, of which they can no more divest themselves then they can of their sensibility to physical pain." Because of their human sympathies, he assumed that they would abolish slavery when it became necessary to do so.

Assumptions aside, though, Lincoln had no evidence that southerners would ever voluntarily surrender their slaves, voluntarily give up their status symbols and transform their cherished way of life founded on the peculiar institution. In 1832, the year Lincoln entered politics, Virginia had actually considered emancipation and colonization (in the aftermath of Nat Turner's insurrection), but had rejected colonization as too costly and complicated to carry out. And neither they nor their fellow southerners were about to emancipate their blacks and leave them as free people in a white man's country. As a consequence, they became adamantly determined that slavery should remain on a permanent basis, not just as a labor device, but as a means of race control in a region brimming with Negroes.

Yet Lincoln clung to the notion that slavery would eventually perish in Dixie, that southerners were rational men who would gradually liberate their blacks when the time came. And he clung to the belief that somehow, when the time did come, the Republic would pay out all the millions of dollars necessary to compensate slave-owners for their losses and ship more than three million blacks out of the country. And he assumed, too, that southerners would consent to the deportation of their entire labor force.

2. THIS VAST MORAL EVIL

Then came 1854 and the momentous Kansas-Nebraska Act, brainchild of Senator Stephen A.

Douglas of Illinois. Douglas's measure overturned the old Missouri Compromise line, which excluded slavery from the vast northern area of the old Louisiana Purchase territory. The act then established a new formula for dealing with slavery in the national lands: now Congress would stay out of the matter, and the people of each territory would decide whether to retain or outlaw the institution. Until such time as the citizens of a territory voted on the issue, southerners were free to take slavery into most western territories, including the new ones of Kansas and Nebraska. These were carved out of the northern section of the old Louisiana Purchase territory. Thanks to the Kansas-Nebraska Act, a northern domain once preserved for freedom now seemed open to a proslavery invasion.

At once a storm of free-soil protest broke across the north, and scores of political leaders branded the Kansas-Nebraska Act as part of a sinister southern plot to extend slave territory and augment southern political power in the national capital. Had not the pro-southern Pierce administration and powerful southern politicians like Senator David R. Atchison of Missouri helped Douglas ram the measure through Congress? Had not every southern senator but two voted in favor of it? Were not Missouri border captains vowing to make Kansas a gateway for proslavery expansion to the Pacific?

There followed a series of political upheavals. The old Whig party disintegrated, and in its place emerged the all-northern Republican party, dedicated to blocking slavery extension, saving the cherished frontier for free white labor, and dismantling southern power in Washington. At the same time, a civil war blazed up in Kansas, as proslavery and free-soil pioneers came into bloody collisions on the prairie there—proof that slavery was far too volatile ever to be solved as a purely local matter.

No one was more upset about Kansas-Nebraska than Lincoln. In his view, the southern-controlled Democratic party—the party that dominated the presidency, the Senate, and the Supreme Court—had launched a revolt against the Founding Fathers and the entire course of the Republic as far as slavery was concerned. Now bondage was not going to die out in the South. It was going to grow and expand and continue indefinitely, as slaveholders dragged manacled black people across the West, adapting slave labor to mines and farms and whatever conditions they found there. Now southern leaders would create new slave states on the frontier and make bondage powerful and permanent in America. Now the Republic would never remove the cancer that afflicted its political system—would never remove a "cruel wrong" that marred her global image and made a mockery of the Declaration.

Lincoln plunged into the antiextension fight. He campaigned for the national Senate. He joined the Republicans and became head of the new party in Illinois. He inveighed against the "Slave Power" and its insidious "new designs" to place bondage on the road to expansion and perpetuity. He spoke with an urgent sense of mission that gave his speeches a searching eloquence—a mission to save the American experiment, turn back the tide of slavery expansion, restrict the peculiar institution once again to the South, and place it back on the road to extinction, as Lincoln believed the Founding Fathers had so placed it.

Still, he could not believe that the southern people were involved in the new slave policy. No, they were beguiled by scheming Democratic politicians—by Douglas and southern leaders in Washington and back in Dixie, who were out to enlarge slave territory under the guise of popular sovreignty, under the pretext that it was all "a sacred right of self-government." On the stump in Illinois, Lincoln engaged in a rhetorical dialogue with the southern people, speaking as though they were in his audiences. He did not fault them for the origin of slavery; he bore them no ill-will of any kind. He still believed in their intrinsic decency and sense of justice, still believed that they too regarded slavery as wrong—that they too felt there was humanity in the Negro. Do you deny this? he asked them at

Peoria in 1854. Then why thirty-four years ago did you join the North in branding the African slave trade as an act of piracy punishable death? "Again," Lincoln went on, "you have amongst you, a sneaking individual, of the class of native tyrants, known as the 'SLAVEDEALER.' He watches your necessities, and crawls up to buy your slave, at a speculating price. If you cannot help it, you sell to him; but if you can help it, you drive him from your door. You despise him utterly. You do not recognize him as a friend, or even as an honest man. Your children must not play with his; they must rollick freely with the little negroes, but not with the 'slave-dealers' children. If you are obliged to deal with him, you try to get through the job without so much as touching him. It is common with you to join hands with the men you meet; but with the slave dealer you avoid the ceremony—instinctively shrinking from the snaky contact."

Now why is this? Lincoln asked southern whites. Is it not because your human sympathy tells you "that the poor negro has some natural right to himself—that those who deny it, and make mere merchandise of him, deserve kickings, contempt and death?" He beseeched southerners not to deny their true feelings about slavery. He beseeched them to regard bondage strictly as a necessity, as the Fathers had so regarded it, and to contain its spread as those "old-time men" had done.

"Fellow countrymen—Americans south, as well as north," Lincoln cried, let us prevent the spirit of Kansas-Nebraska from displacing the spirit of the Revolution. "Let us turn slavery from its claims of 'moral right,' back upon its existing legal rights . . . and there let it rest in peace. Let us re-adopt the Declaration of Independence, and with it, the practices, and policy, which harmonize with it. Let north and south—let all Americans—let all lovers of liberty everywhere—join the great and good work. If we do this, we shall not only have saved the Union; but we shall have so saved it, as to make, and to keep it, forever worthy of the saving."

But Lincoln's entreaties fell on deaf ears in Dixie. Across the region, in an age of revolutionary agitation, proslavery apologists disparaged the Declaration of Independence and the idea of human equality as "a self-evident lie." They trumpeted Negro bondage as a great and glorious good, sanctioned by the Bible and ordained by God throughout eternity. They contended that Negroes were subhuman and belonged in chains as naturally as cattle in pens. Cranky George Fitzhugh even exhorted southerners to destroy free society (or capitalism), revive the halcyon days of feudalism, and enslave all workers—white as well as black. And he ranted at abolitionists for allying themselves with the "uncouth, dirty, naked little cannibals of Africa." Because "free society" was "unnatural, immoral, unchristian," the proslavery argument went, "it must fall and give way to a slave society—a system as old as the world." For "two opposite and conflicting forms of society cannot, among civilized men, co-exist and endure. The one must give way and cease to exist—the other become universal." "Free society!" shrieked one Alabama paper. "We sicken of the name! What is it but a conglomeration of greasy mechanics, filthy operatives, small-fisted farmers, and moonstruck theorists?"

Such pronouncements made Lincoln grimace. They convinced him that a contemptible breed of men had taken over in the South and "debauched" the public mind there about the moral right of slavery. "The slave-breeders and slave-traders are a small, odious and detested class, among you," he wrote a southern friend; "and yet in politics, they dictate the course of all of you, and are as completely your masters, as you are the masters of your own negroes." But to Lincoln's despair, proslavery, anti-northern declarations continued to roar out of Dixie. Worse still, in 1857 the pro-southern Supreme Court handed down the infamous Dred Scott decision, which sent Republicans reeling. In it, the court decreed that Negroes were inferior beings who were not and never had been United States citizens and that the Constitution and Declaration were whites-only charters that did not apply to them. What was more, the court ruled that neither Congress nor a territorial government could outlaw slavery in the national lands, because that would violate southern property rights as guaranteed by the Fifth Amendment. As Lincoln and other Republicans observed, the net effect of the decision was to legalize slavery in all federal territories from Canada to Mexico.

The ominous train of events from Kansas-Nebraska to Dred Scott shook Lincoln to his foundations. By 1858, he and a lot of other Republicans began to see a treacherous conspiracy at work in the United States—a plot on the part of the southern leaders and their northern Democratic allies to reverse the whole course of modern history, to halt the progress of human liberty as other reactionary forces in the world were attempting to do. As Lincoln and his colleagues saw it, the first stage of the conspiracy was to betray the Fathers and expand bondage across the West, ringing the free North with satellite slave states. At the same time, proslavery theorists were out to discredit the Declaration and replace the idea of the equality of men with the principles of inequality and human servitude. The next step, Lincoln feared, would be to nationalize slavery. The Supreme Court would hand down another decision, one declaring that states could not exclude slavery either because that too violated the Fifth Amendment. Then the institution would sweep into Illinois, sweep into Indiana and Ohio, sweep into Pennsylvania and New York, sweep into Massachusetts and New England, sweep all over the northern states, until at last slavery would be nationalized and America would end up a slave house. At that, as Fitzhugh advocated, the conspirators would enslave all American workers regardless of color. The northern free-labor system would be expunged, the Declaration of Independence overthrown, self-government abolished, and the conspirators would restore despotism with class rule, an entrenched aristocracy, and serfdom. All the work since the Revolution of 1776 would be annihilated. The world's best hope—America's experiment in popular government—would be destroyed, and humankind would spin backward into feudalism.

For Lincoln, the Union had reached a monumental crisis in its history. If the future of a free America was to be saved, it was imperative that Lincoln and his party block the conspiracy in its initial stage—the expansion of slavery onto the frontier. To do that, they demanded that slavery be excluded from the territories by federal law and once again placed on the road to its ultimate doom. In 1858 Lincoln set out after Douglas's Senate seat, inveighing against the Little Giant for his part in the proslavery plot and warning Illinois—and all northerners beyond—that only the Republicans could save their free-labor system and their free government.

Now Lincoln openly and fiercely declaimed his antislavery sentiments. He hated the institution. Slavery was "a vast moral evil" he could not but hate. He hated it because it degraded blacks and whites alike. He hated it because it violated America's *"central idea"*—the idea of equality and the right to rise. He hated it because it was cruelly unjust to the Negro, prevented him from eating "the bread that his own hands have earned," reduced him to "stripes, and unrewarded toils." He hated slavery because it imperiled white Americans, too. For if one man could be enslaved because of the color of his skin, Lincoln realized, then any man could be enslaved because of skin color. Yet, while branding slavery an evil and doing all they could to contain it in Dixie, Lincoln and his Republican colleagues would not, legally could not, molest the institution in those states where it already existed.

Douglas, fighting for his political life in free-soil Illinois, lashed back at Lincoln with unadulterated race baiting. Throughout the Great Debates of 1858, Douglas smeared Lincoln and his party as Black Republicans, as a gang of radical abolitionists out to liberate southern slaves and bring them stampeding into Illinois and the rest of the North, where they would take away white jobs and copulate with white daughters. Douglas had made such accusations before, but never to the extent that he did in 1858. Again and again, he accused Lincoln of desiring intermarriage and racial mongrelization.

Lincoln did not want to discuss such matters. He complained bitterly that race was not the issue between him and Douglas. The issue was whether slavery would ultimately triumph or ultimately perish in the United States. But Douglas understood the depth of anti-Negro feeling in Illinois, and he hoped to whip Lincoln by playing on white racial fears. And so he kept warning white crowds: Do you want Negroes to flood into Illinois, cover the prairies with black settlements, and eat, sleep, and marry with white people? If you do, then vote for Lincoln and the "Black Republicans." But *I* am against Negro citizenship, Douglas cried. I want citizenship for whites only. I believe that this government "was made by the white man, for the benefit of the white man, to be administered by white men." "I do not question Mr. Lincoln's conscientious belief that the negro was made his equal, and hence his brother"—great laughter at that—"but for my own part, I do not regard the negro as my equal, and positively deny that he is my brother or any kin to me whatever."

Such allegations forced Lincoln to take a stand. It was either that or risk political ruin in white-supremacist Illinois. What he said carefully endorsed the kind of racial discrimination then enforced by Illinois law. Had he not done so, as one scholar had reminded us, "the Lincoln of history simply would not exist." At Charleston, Illinois, Lincoln conceded that he was not and never had been in favor "of making voters or jurors of Negroes, nor of qualifying them to hold office, nor to intermarry with white people." There was, he said at Ottawa, "a physical difference" between the black and white races that would "probably" always prevent them from living together in perfect equality. And Lincoln wanted the white race to have the superior position so long as there must be a difference. Therefore any attempt to twist his views into a call for perfect political and social equality was "but a specious and fantastic arrangement of words by which a man can prove a horse chestnut to be a chestnut horse."

We shall probably never know whether Lincoln was voicing his own personal convictions in speeches like these, given the heat of political debate before all-white audiences. To be sure, this is one of the most hotly disputed areas of Lincoln scholarship, with several white historians siding with Bennett and Harding and labeling Lincoln a white supremacist. Certainly in the 1850s he had ambivalent feelings about what specific social and political rights black people ought to enjoy. But so did a good many principled and dedicated white abolitionists. When compared to the white-supremacist, anti-Negro attitudes of Douglas and most other whites of that time, Lincoln was an enlightened man in the matter of race relations. In those same 1858 debates, he consistently argued that if Negroes were not the equal of Lincoln and Douglas in moral or intellectual endowment, they *were* equal to Lincoln, Douglas, and "every living man" in their right to liberty, equality of opportunity, and the fruits of their own labor. (Later he insisted that it was bondage that had "clouded" the slaves' intellects and that Negroes were capable of thinking like whites.) Moreover, Lincoln rejected "the counterfeit argument" that just because he did not want a black woman for a slave, he therefore wanted her for a wife. He could just let her alone. He could let her alone so that she could also enjoy her freedom and "her natural right to eat the bread she earns with her own hands."

While Douglas (like the Supreme Court) empathically denied that the Declaration of Independence applied to Negroes, Lincoln's position held that it did. The Negro was a man; Lincoln's "ancient faith" taught him that all men were created equal; therefore there could be no "moral right" in one man's enslaving another. As historian Richard N. Current has said, Lincoln left unstated the conclusion of his logic: that there was no moral right in one man's making a political and social inferior of another on grounds of race.

In the debate at Alton, Lincoln took his reasoning even further as far as the Declaration was concerned. "I think the authors of that notable document intended to include *all* men," Lincoln said, "but they did not intend to declare all men equal in *all respects*. They did not mean to say all were equal in color, size, intellect, moral development, or social capacity." What they meant was that all men, black as well as white, were equal in their inalienable rights to life, liberty, and the pursuit of happiness. When they drafted the Declaration, they realized that blacks did not then have full equality with whites, and that whites did not at that time have full equality with one another. The Founding Fathers did not pretend to describe America as it was in 1776. "They meant to set up a standard maxim for free society," Lincoln said, "which should be familiar to all, and revered by all; constantly labored for, and even though never perfectly attained, constantly spreading and deepening its influence, and augmenting the happiness and value of life to all people of all colors everywhere."

By stressing "to all people of all colors everywhere," Lincoln reminded his countrymen that the American experiment remained an inspiration for the entire world. But he reminded them, too, as historian Current has noted, that "it could be an effective inspiration for others only to the extent that Americans lived up to it themselves." No wonder Lincoln said he hated Douglas's indifference toward slavery expansion. "I hate it because of the monstrous injustice of slavery itself," Lincoln explained at Ottawa. "I hate it because it . . . enables the enemies of free institutions, with plausibility, to taunt us as hypocrites."

Exasperated with Douglas and white Negrophobia in general, Lincoln begged American whites "to discard all this quibbling about this man and the other man—this race and that race and the other race as being inferior," begged them to unite as one people and defend the ideal of the Declaration of Independence and its promise of liberty and equality for all humankind.

Lincoln's remarks, however, aggravated a lot of common people in Illinois; they voted for Douglas candidates in 1858 and helped return Lincoln's rival to the Senate.* The historical Lincoln even lost Springfield and Sangamon County, because of his controversial views on slavery and the Negro, as one historian has argued, were too advanced for his neighbors. If we are to understand Lincoln's attitudes on slavery and race, it is imperative that we weigh them in proper historical context. We can learn nothing, nothing at all, if his words are lifted from their historical setting and judged only by the standards of another time.

3. MY DISSATISFIED FELLOW COUNTRYMEN

We return to why Lincoln still ranks as the best President Americans have had. In large measure, it was because of his sense of history and his ability to act on that. It was because he saw the slavery problem and the future of his country in a world dimension. He saw that what menaced Americans of his day affected the destinies of people everywhere. On the stump in Illinois, Ohio, and New York, he continued to warn free men of the heinous efforts to make bondage permanent in the United States. He would not let up on his countrymen about the *moral* issue of slavery. "*If slavery is not wrong,*" he warned them, "*nothing is wrong.*" He would not let up on "the miners and sappers" of returning despotism, as he called proslavery spokesmen and their northern allies, and on the historical crisis threatening his generation, a crisis that would determine whether slavery or freedom—despotism or popular government, the past or the future—would triumph in his impassioned time.

Yet in the late 1850s Lincoln's goal was not the presidency. One of the more popular misconceptions about him was that he had his eye on the White House even in the Great Debates. Yet there is not a scintilla of reliable evidence to support this. What Lincoln wanted, and wanted fervently, was a seat in the national Senate, because in the antebellum years it was the

---

*In those days, state legislatures chose U.S. Senators. Lincoln hoped to win by persuading Illinois voters to elect Republican rather than Democratic candidates to the legislature.

Senate that featured the great orators of the day—men like Daniel Webster, John C. Calhoun, and especially Lincoln's idol, Henry Clay. The presidency, by contrast, was a mundane administrative job that offered little to a man of Lincoln's oratorical abilities. No, he preferred the national Senate, because in that august body he could defend the containment of slavery, defend free labor, defend popular government and the American experiment, in speeches that would be widely read and preserved for posterity in the *Congressional Globe*. As a loyal Republican, he would take any respectable national office that would simultaneously "advance our cause" and give him personal fulfillment. But throughout 1859 and early 1860, he kept his eye on Douglas's Senate seat in 1864.

So it was that Lincoln kept assailing Douglas for his role in the proslavery plot Lincoln saw at work in his country. And he reminded northerners of the republican vision of a future America—a better America than now existed—an America of thriving farms and bustling villages and towns, an America of self-made agrarians, merchants, and shopkeepers who set examples and provided jobs for self-improving free workers—an America, however, that would never come about if slavery, class rule, and despotism triumphed in Lincoln's time.

Meanwhile, he kept trying to reach the southern people, to reason with them about slavery and the future of the Union, to woo them away from their reactionary leaders. He observed how ironic it was that the Democrats had abandoned their Jeffersonian heritage and that the Republicans—supposedly the descendants of the old Federalists—now defended Jeffersonian ideals. He warned southerners that "This is a world of compensations; and he who would *be* no slave, must consent to *have* no slave. Those who deny freedom to others, deserve it not for themselves."

"I think Slavery is wrong, morally, and politically," he told southern whites at Cincinnati in 1859, still speaking to them as though they were his audience. "I desire that it should gradually

terminate in the whole Union." But "I understand you differ radically with me upon this proposition." You believe that "Slavery is a good thing; that Slavery is right; that it ought to be extended and perpetuated in this Union." But we Republicans not only disagree with you; we are going to "stand by our guns" and beat you in a fair election. Yet we will not hurt you. We will treat you as Washington, Jefferson, and Madison treated you, and will leave slavery alone where it already exists among you. "We mean to remember that you are as good as we are; that there is no difference between us other than the difference of circumstances. We mean to recognize and bear in mind always that you have as good hearts in your bosoms as other people, or as we claim to have, and treat you accordingly. We mean to marry your girls when we have a chance—the white ones I mean— [laughter] and I have the honor to inform you that I once did have a chance that way."

But he cautioned southerners about their threats to disrupt the Union should the Republicans win the government in 1860. How will disunion help you? Lincoln demanded. If you secede, you will no longer enjoy the protection of the Constitution, and we will no longer be forced to return your fugitive slaves. What will you do—build a wall between us? Make war on us? You are brave and gallant, "but man for man, you are not better than we are, and there are not so many of you as there are of us." Because you are inferior in numbers, "you will make nothing by attempting to master us."

Despite Lincoln's reassurances, southern spokesmen derided the Republicans as warmongering abolitionists out to destroy the southern way of life based on slavery. In October, 1859, they got all the evidence they needed that this was so. Old John Brown and a handful of revolutionaries—most of them young, five of them black—invaded Harpers Ferry in an attempt to incite a full-scale slave rebellion. Though the raid failed and Brown was captured and hanged, the South convulsed in hysteria, as rumors of slave uprisings and abolitionist invasions pummeled the region. For their part, southern politicians pronounced the raid a Republican conspiracy, a mad and monstrous scheme to drown the South in rivers of blood. During a tour in the embattled Kansas Territory, Lincoln denied such accusations and argued that hanging Brown was just. But he warned southerners that "if constitutionally we elect a President, and therefore you undertake to destroy the Union, it will be our duty to deal with you as old John Brown has been dealt with."

At Cooper Union the following year, Lincoln responded to continued southern imputations about the Republicans and John Brown. "You charge that we stir up insurrections among your slaves," Lincoln said. "We deny it; and what is your proof? Harpers Ferry! John Brown!! John Brown was no Republican; and you have failed to implicate a single Republican in his Harpers Ferry enterprise." But he saved his most eloquent remarks for his fellow Republicans. Since they intended southerners no harm and promised over and over to leave their slaves alone, what then was the dispute about? "The precise fact upon which depends the whole controversy" was that southerners thought slavery right and Republicans thought it wrong. "Thinking it right, as they do, they are not to blame for desiring its full recognition, as being right; but, thinking it wrong, as we do, can we yield to them? Can we cast our votes with their view, and against our own? In view of our moral, social, and political responsibilities, can we do this?" No, the Republicans' sense of duty would not let them yield to southern demands about slavery. Nor would Republicans be frightened from their duty by threats of disunion and destruction to the government. "LET US HAVE FAITH THAT RIGHT MAKES MIGHT, AND IN THAT FAITH, LET US, TO THE END, DARE TO DO OUR DUTY AS WE UNDERSTAND IT."

Impressed by his impassioned oratory and firm commitment to party principles, and impressed too by his availability, the Republicans chose Lincoln to be their standard bearer in 1860, to run for President on their free-soil, free-labor platform.

Lincoln, for his part, accepted the nomination because he was as ambitious as he was deeply principled. While he preferred to serve the Republican cause on Capitol Hill, he would work for it wherever the party wanted to put him so long as it was a meaningful national office. And in 1860 that was the White House. In Lincoln, as it turned out, the Republicans chose a candidate more unbending in his commitment to Republican principles than anybody else they might have selected. As the Republican standard bearer, Lincoln was inflexible in his determination to prohibit slavery in the territories by national law and to save the Republic (as he put it) from returning "class," "caste," and "despotism." He exhorted his fellow Republicans to stand firm in their duty: to brand slavery as an evil, contain it in the South, look to the future for slavery to die a gradual death, and promise colonization to solve the question of race. Someday, somehow, the American house must be free of slavery. That was the Republican vision, the distant horizon Lincoln saw.

Yet, for the benefit of southerners, he repeated that he and his party would not interfere with slavery in Dixie. The federal government had no constitutional authority in peacetime to tamper with a state institution like slavery.

But southerners in 1860 were in no mood to believe anything Lincoln said. In their eyes, he was a "horrid looking wretch," another John Brown, "a black-hearted abolitionist fanatic" who lusted for Negro equality. There were, of course, a number of loyal Unionists in the South who pleaded for reason and restraint, who beseeched their fellow southerners to wait for an overt Republican act against them before they did anything rash. For most, though, Brown's Harpers Ferry invasion was all the overt action they intended to tolerate. For all classes in Dixie, from poor whites in South Carolina to rich cotton planters in Mississippi, Lincoln personified the feared and hated *Yankee*—the rapacious entrepreneur, the greasy mechanic, the mongrel immigrant, the frothing abolitionist, the entire "free-love, free-nigger" element, all of whom in southern eyes had combined in Lincoln's party. In him, southerners saw a monster who would send a Republican army into Dixie to free the slaves by gunpoint and whip up a racial storm that would consume their farms and plantations, their investments, their wives and daughters. Even if the South had to drench the Union in blood, exclaimed an Alabama paper, "the South, the loyal South, the Constitutional South, would never submit to such humiliation and degradation as the inauguration of Abraham Lincoln."

For Lincoln, the slavedealers had indeed assumed leadership in Dixie, and he would never compromise with them over a single plank in the Republican platform. Anyway, he still refused to believe that the South's blustery spokesmen truly reflected popular sentiment there. "The people of the South," he remarked during the obstreperous 1860 campaign, "have too much good sense, and good temper, to attempt the ruin of the government." He agreed with his advisers that southern Unionism was too powerful for secession to triumph. Surely, he reasoned, the southern people shared his own sentiments about the future of the American experiment. Surely, like the powerful southerners who helped found the country, like Washington, Jefferson, and Madison, the southern people of his day believed in the Declaration of Independence, which was their charter of liberty as much as his own and that of the Republicans. Surely the southern people would reject the forces of reaction in the world and come around to Lincoln's view, to stand with those who sought the liberation and uplift of the human spirit.

On election day, November 6, telegraph dispatches across the country carried the crucial news: Lincoln had defeated his three leading opponents—John Breckinridge of the southern Democrats, Douglas of the northern Democrats, and John Bell of the Constitutional Union ticket—and was to be the sixteenth president. Lincoln had won, not because his foes were split, but because he carried California and Oregon and every northern state except New Jersey, which divided its electoral votes between him and Douglas. In the electoral college, where Lincoln gained his triumph, his total vote exceeded that of his combined opponents by a margin of 187 to 123. In popular votes, though, Lincoln was a minority President, with 1,866,452 ballots compared to 2,815,617 for his combined foes. Many factors were involved in this confusing and raucous contest, but the fact remains that the majority of Americans in 1860 regarded Lincoln as too radical and dangerous to occupy the White House. Of course, you don't learn about this in the story of Lincoln as Man of the People.

In the Deep South, newspapers screamed with headlines about Lincoln, and people thronged the streets of southern cities with talk of secession everywhere. "Now that the black radical Republicans have the power," asserted a South Carolinian, "I suppose they will [John] Brown us all." Of course, Lincoln and his party did not have the power. They had only won the presidency. The Democrats, though divided, still controlled the Supreme Court and both houses of Congress, and would have demolished any abolition bill the Republicans might have introduced there. But for southerners that stormy winter, the nation had reached a profound turning point: an all-northern party avowedly hostile to slavery had gained control of the executive branch of the government. In the Deep South, a white man reading his newspaper could rehearse what was bound to follow. With the North's supremacy in population and drift toward abolition and revolutionary violence, that party was certain to win the rest of the government one day and then attack slavery in Dixie. Better, then, to strike for southern independence now than to await the Republican blow. Thus, even before Lincoln could be inaugurated, the seven states of the Deep South—with their heavy slave concentrations—left the Union and established the slave-based Confederacy. As a South Carolina resident explained to President Buchanan: "Slavery with us is no abstraction—but a *great* and *vital fact*. Without it our every comfort would be taken from us. Our wives, our children, made un-happy—education, the light of knowledge—all lost and our *people ruined for ever. Nothing short of separation from the Union can save us.*" The editor of the Montgomery *Mail* agreed. "To remain in the Union is to lose all that white men hold dear in government. We vote to get out."

In Springfield, President-elect Lincoln admitted that there were "some loud threats and much muttering in the cotton states," but insisted that the best way to avoid disaster was through calmness and forbearance. What reason did southerners have to be so incensed? What had the Republicans done to them? What southern rights had they violated? Did not southerners still have the fugitive slave law? Did they not have the same Constitution they had lived under for seventy-odd years? "Why all this excitement?" asked Lincoln. "Why all these complaints?"

With the border states also threatening to secede, Lincoln seemed confused, incredulous, at what was happening to his country. He seemed not to understand how he appeared in southern eyes. He kept telling himself that his advisers were right, that southern Unionism would somehow bring the errant states back. He could not accept the possibility that *his* election to the presidency might cause the collapse of the very system which had enabled him to get there. The irony of that was too distressing to contemplate.

In his Inaugural Address of March 4, 1861, Lincoln pleaded for southern whites to understand the Republican position on slavery. He assured them once again that he would not molest slavery in Dixie, that he had no legal right to molest it there. He even approved the original Thirteenth Amendment, just passed by Congress, that would have explicitly guaranteed slavery in the southern states. Lincoln endorsed the amendment because he deemed it consistent with Republican ideology. And in his conclusion he spoke personally to the southern people, as he had done so often since 1854: "In *your* hands, my dissatisfied fellow countrymen, and not in *mine*, is the momentous issue of civil war.

The government will not assail *you*. You can have no conflict, without being yourselves the aggressors. *You* have no oath registered in Heaven to destroy the government, while *I* shall have the most solemn one to 'preserve, protect and defend' it.

"I am loth to close. We are not enemies, but friends. We must not be enemies. Though passion may have strained, it must not break our bonds of affection. The mystic chords of memory, stretching from every battlefield, and patriot grave, to every living heart and hearthstone, all over this broad land, will yet swell the chorus of the Union, when again touched, as surely they will be, by the better angels of our nature."

In Dixie, excitement was so great that men read in Lincoln's words, not conciliation, but provocation. The feverish Charleston *Mercury* even blasted it as a declaration of war. At that very moment, in fact, war threatened to break out in Charleston harbor, where hostile rebel cannon ringed Fort Sumter and its lonely Union flag. The Confederates had already seized every U.S. fort in Dixie except for Sumter and one other in the Florida Gulf. Now Sumter became a symbol for both sides, as the rebels demanded that Lincoln surrender it and angry Union men exhorted him to hold.

In the ensuing crisis, Lincoln clung to the belief that the southern people would overthrow the secessionists and restore the southern states to the Union. But he had little time to wait, for the Sumter garrison was rapidly running out of provisions. Should he send a relief expedition? But what if that betrayed southern Unionists and detonated a civil war? In "great anxiety" about what to do, Lincoln consulted repeatedly with his Cabinet and with high-ranking officers of the army and navy, but they gave him conflicting advice. Far from being an aggressive tyrant who forced the innocent South to start the war, the historical Lincoln vacillated over Sumter, postponed a decision, suffered terribly. He told an old Illinois friend that "all the troubles and anxieties" of his life could not equal those that beset him during the Sumter nightmare. They were so great, Lincoln said, that he did not think it possible to survive them.

Then a report from an emissary he had sent to Charleston smashed his hope that the crisis could be peacefully resolved. The emissary reported that South Carolinians had "no attachment to the Union," and that some wanted a clash with Washington to unite the Confederacy. Moreover, Unionism was equally dead everywhere else in Dixie, and the seceded states were "irrevocably gone." There was no conceivable way that Lincoln could avoid an armed collision with southern rebels: if he did not hold Sumter, he would have to stand somewhere else or see the government collapse.

It was a rude awakening for Lincoln, who had placed great faith in the potency of southern Unionism, who had always thought that southern white people loved the country as much as he and shared his faith in the American promise. Well, he had been wrong. Out of that sobering realization, out of everything he held dear about the Union, out of all his suffering, came a decision to stand firm. After all, he had won the presidency in a fair and legal contest. He would not compromise his election mandate. He would preserve the Union and the principle of self-government on which the Union was based: the right of a free people to choose their leaders and expect the losers to acquiesce in that decision. If southerners disliked him, they could try to vote him out of office in 1864. But he was not going to let them separate from the Union, because that would set a catastrophic precedent that any unhappy state could leave the Union at any time. For Lincoln, the philosophy of secession was "an ingenious sophism" southerners had contrived to vindicate their rebellion. This sophism held that each state possessed "some omnipotent, and sacred supremacy," and that any state could lawfully and peacefully leave the Union without its consent. "With rebellion thus sugar coated," Lincoln complained, southern leaders "have been drugging the public mind of their section for more than thirty years." Yet it was a preposterous argument. The Constitution specifically stated that the Constitution and the national laws made under it were the supreme law of the land. Therefore the states could not be supreme as the secessionists claimed; the Union was paramount and permanent, and could not be legally wrecked by a disaffected minority. The principle of secession was disintegration, Lincoln said. And no government based on that principle could possibly endure.

Yes, he would hold Fort Sumter. In that imperiled little garrison in Charleston Harbor, surrounded by rebel batteries and a hostile population, Lincoln saw the fate of popular government hanging in the balance. He would send a relief expedition to Sumter, and if the Confederates opened fire, the momentous issue of civil war was indeed in their hands.

And so the fateful events raced by: the firing on the fort, Lincoln's call for 75,000 troops, the secession of four border states, and the beginning of war. Deeply embittered, Lincoln grumbled about all the "professed Union men" in Dixie who had gone over to the rebellion. And he looked on in distress as one supposedly loyal southerner after another resigned from the United States Army and headed south to enlist in the rebel forces. It depressed him immeasurably. He referred to Robert E. Lee, Joseph E. Johnston, John Bankhead Magruder, and all like them as traitors. And in his public utterances he never again addressed the southern people as though they were in his audiences. Instead he spoke of them in the third person, calling them rebels and insurrectionaries—a domestic enemy engaged in treason against his government.

And so the Civil War had come—a war that no reasonable man in North or South had wanted. What began as a ninety-day skirmish on both sides swelled instead into a vast inferno of destruction with consequences beyond calculation for those swept up in its flames. For Lincoln, the country was out of control, threatening to annihilate everyone and everything, all promise and all hope, and he did not think he could bear the pain he felt. His election had provoked this madness, and he took it personally. Falling into a depression that would plague him throughout his embattled presidency, he remarked that the war was the supreme irony of his life: that he who sickened at the sight of blood, who abhorred stridency and physical violence, who dreamed that "mind, all conquer-ing *mind*," would rule the world someday, was caught in a national holocaust, a tornado of blood and wreckage with Lincoln himself whirling in its center.

KEY TERMS

Whig: A member of the Whig party; with the Democratic party, one of the two dominant political parties of the second quarter of nineteenth-century America.

Deep South: The states of Alabama, Georgia, Louisiana, Mississippi, and South Carolina.

Northwest Territories: The north-central region of the United States extending from the Ohio and Mississippi rivers to the Great Lakes.

Harper's Ferry: The national arsenal at Harper's Ferry, Virginia.

Cooper Union: An educational institution in New York City which carried on extensive programs of adult education.

DISCUSSION TOPICS

After reading this essay, you should be able to discuss:

1. Lincoln's views about slavery.

2. Lincoln's notions of the importance of opportunity in America.

3. The ways in which the Kansas-Nebraska Act and the Dred Scott decision were turning points in Lincoln's thinking about the South and the Union.

4. The reasons growing numbers of southerners came to view Lincoln as a radical intent upon abolishing slavery.

18

Heroes and Cowards

Bell I. Wiley

The drama and sacrifice of war have occupied an important place in the American popular imagination for more than a century. Ironically, this fascination with the travails of warfare exists despite the fact that Americans have seldom experienced warfare directly. The security offered by the Atlantic and Pacific oceans as well as the relative military weakness of this country's northern and southern neighbors have largely allowed Americans to escape the debilitating effects of wars fought on their own territory. Only in the Revolutionary War, the War of 1812, and the Civil War did Americans find their farms, towns, and cities turned into battlefields and the civilian population menaced by contending armies.

The greatest of these internal wars was the Civil War of 1861–1865. Not only did the war claim over 600,000 American lives, destroy millions of dollars in property, and end a whole way of life, but it was also the only war in which American fought American. In this essay, Bell I. Wiley takes us beyond the exploits of military leaders and the movements of whole armies to the gritty experiences of the ordinary Confederate soldier. Wars are a collection of battles, and it was the danger and anarchy of conflict that tested the resolve of the ordinary soldier. Some, as Wiley poignantly reveals, became heroes and others cowards in the process, but none escaped the experience of combat unchanged.

From *The Life of Johnny Reb: The Common Soldier of the Confederacy* by Bell Irvin Wiley (Baton Rouge, LA: Louisiana State University Press, 1970), pp. 68–89. Copyright © 1970, 1971, 1978 by Bell I. Wiley. Reprinted by permission of Louisiana State University Press.

While it may be granted that there were significant changes in the reactions of soldiers as they became accustomed to combat, the fact remains that the experiences and behavior of those taking part in Confederate battles followed the same general pattern. These more or less common characteristics must be described in some detail.

When an encounter with the Yankees was expected certain preliminaries were necessary. One of these was the issue of extra provisions, accompanied by the order to "cook up" from three to five days' rations, so that time would not have to be taken for the preparation of food during the anticipated action. This judicious measure generally fell short of its object because of Johnny Reb's own characteristics: he was always hungry, he had a definite prejudice against baggage, and he was the soul of improvidence. Sometimes the whole of the extra ration would be consumed as it was cooked, and rarely did any part of it last for the full period intended. About the same time that food was dispensed the general in command would address his men for the purpose of firing their spirit and inspiring them to deeds of valor. Soldiers en route to Shiloh, for example, were thus charged by Albert Sidney Johnston:

I have put you in motion to offer battle to the invaders of your country. With the resolution and disciplined valor becoming men fighting, as you are, for all worth living or dying for, you can but march to a decisive victory over the agrarian mercenaries sent to subjugate and despoil you of your liberties, property, and honor. Remember the precious stake involved; remember the dependence of your mothers, your wives, your sisters, and your children on the result; remember the fair, broad, abounding land, the happy homes, and the ties that would be desolated by your defeat.

The eyes and the hopes of eight millions of people rest upon you. You are expected to show yourselves worthy of your race and lineage; worthy of the women of the South, whose noble devotion in this war has never been exceeded in any time. With such incentives to brave deeds and with the trust that God is with us, your general will lead you confidently to the combat, assured of success.

Presently each man would be given a supply of ammunition. This was delayed as long as possible, so that the powder would not become damped through carelessness of the men. If Confederates held the initiative, the issue of ammunition would take place the night before the attack; but if the Rebs were on the defensive, without any definite knowledge of the time of assault, the issue of cartridges had to take place at an earlier stage. The customary allotment to each fighter was from forty to sixty rounds, a round being a ball and enough powder for a single shot.

Prior to their issue lead and powder for each load had, for convenience, been wrapped in a piece of paper with the bullet at one end, the powder behind it, and the other end closed with a twist or a plug to hold the powder in place. This improvised cartridge was cylindrical in shape, somewhat resembling a section of crayon. When Johnny Reb loaded his gun—usually a muzzle loader—he bit off the twisted end so that the powder would be exploded by the spark when the trigger was pulled, dropped the cartridge in the muzzle, rammed in a piece of wadding and waited for the opportunity to draw bead on a Yankee. Surplus rounds were kept in a cartridge box—a leather or metal container that hung from the belt—or in a haversack, or in trouser pockets.

Knapsacks and other baggage not actually needed on the field were supposed to be left in the rear with the quartermaster, but officers always had trouble preventing their men from throwing aside their equipment at random. After Bull Run and Shiloh most soldiers did not have to be cautioned about their canteens, as the acute suffering from thirst experienced in those engagements was a sufficient reminder to carry well-filled water tins into subsequent fights.

The day of battle finally comes. The men are roused from sleep at a very early hour, perhaps two or three o'clock. The well-known call to arms is an extended beat of the snare drum known as the "long roll." After the lines are drawn up officers inspect equipment, giving particular attention to ammunition, to see that all is in readiness.

Then a few words of advice and instruction: Do not shoot until you are within effective musket range of the enemy; fire deliberately, taking care to aim low, and thus avoid the over-shooting to which you have been so markedly susceptible in previous battles. If you merely wound a man so much the better, as injured men have to be taken from the field by sound ones; single out a particular adversary for your fire, after the example of your sharpshooting forefathers at Bunker Hill and New Orleans. When possible pick off the enemy's officers, particularly the mounted ones, and his artillery horses. Under all conditions hold your ranks; avoid the natural but costly inclination to huddle together under heavy fire. When ordered to charge, do so at once and move forward rapidly; you are much less apt to be killed while going steadily forward than if you hesitate or retreat; but in case you have to fall back, do so gradually and in order; more men are killed during disorganized retreat than at any other time; if your objective is a battery, do not be terrorized—artillery is never as deadly as it seems; a rapid forward movement reduces the battery's effectiveness and hastens the end of its power to destroy. Do not pause or turn aside to plunder the dead or to pick up spoils; battles have been lost by indulgence in this temptation. Do not heed the calls for assistance of wounded comrades or stop to take them to the rear; details have been made to care for casualties, and the best way of protecting your wounded friends is to drive the enemy from the field. Straggling under any guise will be severely punished. Cowards will be shot. Do your duty in a manner that becomes the heroic example your regiment has already set on earlier fields of combat.

Orders to march are now given, and to the waving of colors and the stirring rhythm of fife and drum the regiments proceed to their appointed place in the line of battle. As the dawn mist clears away, a scene of intense activity is revealed on all sides. Surgeons are preparing their kits; litter bearers and ambulances are ominously waiting. Arrived at their place in line, the men wait for what seem interminable hours while other units are brought into position. There is some talk while they wait, though less than earlier in the war. Comrades quietly renew mutual pledges to seek out those who are missing at the battle's end—for help if they are wounded and for protection of belongings and notification of homefolk if they are dead. A few men read their testaments, some mutter soft prayers—a devout captain is observed standing with the Bible in hand reading aloud to his Mississippians, but this scene is unusual. Here and there a soldier bites off a chew of tobacco and joins a host of comrades whose jaws are already working. Very rarely an officer or a private sneaks a swig of "How Come You So" to bolster his spirit for the ordeal ahead. Everywhere suspense bears down with crushing force, but is indicated largely by silence.

Presently the rattle of musketry is heard in front. Skirmishers must have made contact with enemy pickets. All are alert. A signal gun is fired and the artillery joins in with accumulating fury. At last the command—"Forward!"—and an overpowering urge to make contact with the enemy. Soon lines of blue are discernible. Comrades begin to fall in increasing numbers. Now the shout, lost perhaps in the din of battle—"Charge!"— accompanied by a forward wave of officer's saber and the line leaps forward with the famous "Rebel yell."

This yell itself is an interesting thing. It was heard at First Manassas and was repeated in hundreds of charges throughout the war. It came to be as much a part of a Rebel's fighting equipment as his musket. Once, indeed, more so. Toward the end of an engagement near Richmond in May 1864, General Early rode up to a group of soldiers and said, "Well, men, we must change them once more and then we'll be through." The response came back, "General, we are all out of ammunition." Early's ready retort was, "Damn it, holler them across." And, according to the narrator, the order was literally executed.

The Confederate yell is hard to describe. An attempt to reproduce it was made a few years ago when Confederate veterans re-enacted battle scenes in Virginia. But this, by the very nature of things, was an inadequate representation. Old voices were too weak and incentive too feeble to create again the true battle cry. As it flourished on the field of combat, the Rebel yell was an unpremeditated, unrestrained and utterly informal "hollering." It had in it a mixture of fright, pent-up nervousness, exultation, hatred and a pinch of pure deviltry. Yelling in attack was not peculiar to Confederates, for Yanks went at Rebels more than once with "furious" shouts on their lips. But the battle cry of Southerners was admittedly different. General "Jube" Early, who well understood the spirit of his soldiers, made a comparison of Federal and Confederate shouting as a sort of aside to his official report of the battle of Fredericksburg. "Lawton's Brigade, without hesitating, at once dashed upon the enemy," he said, "with the cheering peculiar to the Confederate soldier, and which is never mistaken for the studied hurrahs of the Yankees, and drove the column opposed to it down the hill." Though obviously invidious, the general's observation is not wholly inaccurate.

The primary function of the rousing yell was the relief of the shouter. As one Reb observed after a fight in 1864, "I always said if I ever went into a charge, I wouldn't holler! But the very first time I fired off my gun I hollered as loud as I could, and I hollered every breath till we stopped." At first there was no intention of inspiring terror in the enemy, but the practice soon attained such a reputation as a demoralizing agent that men were encouraged by their officers to shout as they assaulted Yankee positions. In the battle of Lovejoy's Station, for instance, Colonel Clark cried out to his Mississippians, "Fire and charge with a yell." Yankees may not have been scared by this Rebel throatsplitting, but they were enough impressed to set down in their official reports that the enemy advanced "yelling like fiends," or other words to the same effect.

But those Rebs who are now charging at the Yankees know that yelling is only a small part of their business. Yankee lines loom larger as the boys in gray surge forward. Now there is a pause for aiming, and the roar of countless muskets, but the individual soldier is hardly conscious of the noise or the kick of his weapon. Rarely does he have time to consider the effectiveness of his shot. He knows that scores of Yankees are falling, and his comrades as well, but he cannot attend to details of slaughter on either side. He drops to his knee, fumblingly bites off and inserts a cartridge, rams it home with a quick thrust of the rod, then rises and dashes forward with his fellows. On they go, these charging Rebs, feeling now that exaltation which comes after the fight gets under way. "There is something grand about it—it is magnificent," said Robert Gill of his experience under fire near Atlanta. "I feel elated as borne along with the tide of battle."

Presently there is an obvious slowing down of the advance, as resistance increases and attacking ranks become thin. Artillery fire comes in such force as to shatter good-sized trees, and men are actually killed by falling limbs. The lines of gray seem literally to bend beneath the weight of canister and grape, and yelling soldiers lean forward while walking as if pushing against the force of a wind. Slaughter becomes so terrible that ditches run with blood. The deafening noise is likened by one Reb to "a large cane brake on fire and a thunder storm with repeated loud thunder claps." The flight of shells (called "lamp posts" and "wash kettles" according to their size and shape) reminds Robert Gill of "frying on a large scale only a little more so"; and Maurice Simons thinks of a partridge flying by, "only we would suppose that the little bird had grown to the size of an Eagle." Some of the men, unable to confront this holocaust, seek the protection of rocks, trees, and gullies. Others of stronger nerve close the gaps and push onward.

The overwhelming urge to get quickly to the source of danger brings an end to loading and shooting. With one last spurt the charging troops throw themselves among their adversaries, gouging with bayonets, swinging with clubbed muskets, or even striking with rocks, fence rails and sticks. Presently one side or the other gives way, and the charge is over.

But not the battle. Before the day's fighting is completed there will be several charges, each followed by lulls for reorganization. And perhaps the conflict, as at Gettysburg, will extend to a second and third day, each characterized by repetitions of attack over various portions of the field; or perhaps the main action, as at Fredericksburg, will be defensive, staving off repeated Federal assaults.

Moving to the charge, though by far the most dramatic part of fighting, actually made up only a small portion of a soldier's experience in battle. There were hours of lying on the ground or of standing in line, perhaps under the heat of a boiling sun, while troops on other parts of the field carried out the tasks assigned them. Then there was endless shifting, to bolster a weak spot here, to cut off an enemy salient there, or to replenish ammunition. These and many other activities, coupled with repeated advances on enemy positions, took a heavy toll of the soldier's strength.

As the day wore on he was increasingly conscious of exhaustion. Though accustomed before the war to long hours of labor on the farm or extended jaunts in pursuit of game, he found fighting the hardest work he had ever done. Fatigue was sharpened by the fact that rest and food had been scarce during the days before the battle. By midafternoon his strength was often so depleted that he could hardly load and fire his gun, if indeed he was able to stand at all. Those who fought at Shiloh may have joined in the postwar criticism of Beauregard for not pushing the battle as Sunday's sun sank in the west, but officers' reports made soon after the fight show that most of the men were so exhausted that further aggression was impossible.

Increasing with the combatant's fatigue came intolerable thirst. Sweating in the grime and dust, he had emptied his canteen early in the day, hoping to refill it from some stream. But rarely was there any such chance. If he were lucky enough to reach a pond he was apt to find it so choked with the dead and wounded as to be unfit for use. But even so, that soldier considered himself lucky who could sweep aside the gory scum and quench his thirst by greedy draughts of the muddy water underneath.

If the battle happened to be in winter, as at Murfreesboro, Fredericksburg, or Nashville, the suffering from thirst was not so intense. But the exposure to cold was hardly less severe. Discomfort was increased by damp weather, scarcity of clothing, and the inability to make fires. At Murfreesboro, for instance, soldiers lay in line of battle for nearly a week under a cold rain without fire.

When the combat extended over several days, as was frequently the case, hunger was added to other discomforts. At Gettysburg Washington Artillerymen became so famished that a captain sent a detail to gather food from the haverstacks of Federal dead. Many other hungry soldiers were not so fortunate as to have this opportunity.

The coming of night usually brought a rest from fighting, but not from suffering. The disorganization which characterized Confederate battles often separated the soldier from his regiment. The command of duty, plus a desire to know the lot of his friends, would cause him, tired to the point of prostration though he was, to set out on a tedious search for his fellows. When he found the scattered remnants of his company he would probably discover that some messmate, committed to his care by mutual pledge before the battle, was missing. Then he must make a round of the battlefield and the emergency hospitals, inquiring patiently, calling out the name of his friend, and scanning by candlelight the ghastly faces of dead and wounded. The quest might end in happy discovery, but more likely it would prove futile. At last the weary soldier would fall down on the ground. And in spite of the piteous cries of the wounded he would sink at once into heavy slumber.

The morrow of a battle, whether its duration was for one or several days, was in some respects more trying than the conflict itself. Scenes encountered in the burial of the dead were strange and appalling: there a dead Yankee lying on his back "with a biscuit in his hand and with one mouthful bitten off and that mouthful still between his teeth"; here "the top of a man's Skull Hanging by the Hair to a Limb some 8 or 9 feet from the ground"; yonder another "man Siting behind a large oak tree his head . . . shot off"; to the right a small, whining dog curled up in the arms of a dead Yankee, refusing to be coaxed from its erstwhile master; to the left a lifeless Reb sprawled across the body of a well-dressed Federal, the gray-clad's hand in the Northerner's pocket—a gruesome warning to those who are tempted to plunder during battle; farther on, the field is strewn with nude figures blackened and mutilated by a fire that swept across the dry foliage in the wake of the fight. One of the burying party working in Federal-traversed territory is shocked to find that before his arrival "the hogs got a holt of some of the Yankey dead." In any direction one chances to gaze lie heaps of disfigured bodies; to a rural-bred Georgian the scene following Fredericksburg suggested "an immense hog pen and then all killed."

After a prolonged summer encounter the task was unusually repulsive. Wrote a soldier who helped in the burial of the Gettysburg dead:

> The sights and smells that assailed us were simply indescribable—corpses swollen to twice their original size, some of them actually burst asunder with the pressure of foul gases and vapors. . . . The odors were nauseating and so deadly that in a short time we all sickened and were lying with our mouths close to the ground, most of us vomiting profusely.

While some were burying the dead, others were walking about picking up spoils. Trinkets of all sorts, such as Yankee letters, diaries, photographs and pocket knives were much in demand as souvenirs to be sent home to relatives. "I am going to send you a trophie that come off the battlefield at Gettysburg," wrote a Reb to his sister. "I got three pictures out of a dead Yankees knapsack and I am going to send you one. . . . The pictures are wrapped up in a letter from the person whose image they are. . . . She signed her name A. D. Spears and she lived in Main somewhere, but I could not make out

where she lived." Occasionally Rebs laughed over the sentimental contents of such letters. Some soldiers profited financially from their plundering of battlefields. Following the Franklin engagement of December 1864 George Athey wrote:

> I got agood knapsack fuol of tricks whitch I sold $4.5 dolars worth out of it and cepe as mutch as I wanted.

Articles essential to personal comfort were eagerly gathered up. After the Seven Days' Battles a Reb wrote exultantly:

> We have had a glorious victory with its rich Booty A many one of our boys now have a pair of Briches a nice Rubber cloth & a pair of Blankets also a pair or more of Small Tent Cloths.

The avidity with which an impoverished Confederate might pounce upon the riches left in the wake of Federal defeat, as well as the unhappy consequence of overenthusiasm, is evidenced by an entry in a Tennessean's diary following the battle of Seven Pines:

> I awoke quite early yesterday morning, and everything seemed very quiet, I went over the field seeing what I could see. Here were Sutlers' tents, filled with luxuries, oranges, lemons, oysters, pineapples, sardines, in fact, almost everything that I could think of. My first business was to eat just as much as I possibly could, and that was no small amount, for I had been living on hard tack for several days. I then picked out a lot of stationary, paper, envelopes, ink, pens and enough to fill one haversack, then I found a lot of puff bosomed linen shirts, and laid in a half dozen together with some white gloves and other little extras enough to fill another haversack. Then I filled another with nuts and candies and still another with cheese. With this load, I wandered around picking up some canteens to carry back to the boys. Then adding to my load such articles as a sword, an overcoat, etc. . . . I quickened my pace and before I had gone twenty steps, the Yankees opened fire . . . and the balls whistled around me in a perfect shower. I had about two hundred yards to go before reaching my regiment and by the time I reached it, I had thrown away all my plunder.

If the battle ended in defeat, falling back might be so hurried as to leave the dead and wounded in Federal hands. This, added to the increased hardships of retreat and the disappointment of being whipped, caused the soldier's cup to overflow with bitterness.

But whether victorious or not, Johnny Reb began within a remarkably short time to recall and to enjoy the interesting and humorous detail of the combat. Campfire groups must have delighted in teasing Private Joseph Adams about losing his pants when a shell exploded near him at Murfreesboro; and there was doubtless plenty of laughter when M. D. Martin told how a shell cut off his two well-stocked haversacks and scattered hardtack so promiscuously that "several of the boys were struck by the biscuits, and more than one thought he was wounded."

James Mabley could always get a good laugh with his story of the Reb at Chancellorsville who while in the act of drawing a bead on a Yank was distracted by a wild turkey lighting in a tree before him; the Federal was immediately forgotten, and in an instant the crack of this Reb's gun brought the turkey to the ground.

The men of Gilmor's Battalion never tired of asking their colonel after a valley engagement of 1864 "if spades are trumps"; for during this fight a ball went all the way through an unopened deck of cards that he was carrying in his inside coat pocket, stopping only at the last card, the ace of spades.

Almost everyone could tell of a "close shave" when a bullet hit a knapsack, perforated a hat, or spent itself by passing through a bush immediately in front, to fall harmlessly to the ground in plain view. One soldier marveled at hearing through the din of battle the cry of John Childress as he fell: "I am killed, tell Ma and Pa goodbye for me."

Then someone may have mentioned the tragic case of Jud and Cary Smith, Yale-educated brothers from Mississippi. While in the act of lying down under fire, the younger, Cary, putting his hand under his coat, found his inner garments covered with blood; and with only the exclamation "What does this mean?" he died. Jud was so overwhelmed with grief that he spent the entire night muttering affectionate words over his brother's corpse. He passed the next day and night in unconsolable solitude. The third day was that of Malvern Hill, and when the first charge took place Jud kept on going after his comrades fell back under the murderous fire, and he was never seen or heard of again. After the father learned of the fate of his two sons he joined Price's army as a private soldier; when his regiment charged at Iuka, he followed the example set by Jud at Malvern Hill, and he likewise was never heard of again.

But there was not much lingering on tragic notes. It was more pleasant to talk of how Jeb Stuart at Second Manassas beguiled the Yankees into exaggerated ideas of Rebel strength by having his men drag brush along the roads to stir up huge clouds of dust; or of how the Yankee General Banks was duped into abandoning several strong positions during his Red River campaign by such Confederate ruses as sending drummers out to beat calls, lighting superfluous campfires, blowing bugles, and "rolling empty wagons over fence rails"; or of how George Cagle, while lying on a ridge at Chickamauga, kept at work four or five muskets gathered from incapacitated comrades, and as Yankee bullets whistled overhead he simulated the activity of an artillery unit, giving such commands as "attention Cagle's Battery, make ready, load, take aim, fire"; of how Sergeant Nabors scared nervous Yankee prisoners who asked him at Atlanta if he were going to kill them by replying, "That's our calculation; we came out for that purpose."

By no means was all of the fighting in the open field. Warring in trenches—Johnny Reb usually called them "ditches"—made its appearance in the spring of 1862 on the Virginia peninsula where Magruder's army was entrenched for a month. At Vicksburg, where Pemberton's troops were under siege for forty-seven days, soldiers spent most of the time in earthworks along the line, or in caves to the rear. During the Atlanta campaign Rebs of the

Army of Tennessee saw considerable trench warfare. But by far the longest stretch of this sort of campaigning was done by Lee's troops, who spent the greater part of the war's last year in ditches around Petersburg.

Occasionally the routine of trench fighting was broken by an assault of one army or the other, but the time was mostly spent in desultory exchanges of artillery and musket fire. The Federals, being the besiegers and having vastly superior resources, did the larger part of the firing. So unlimited, indeed, were their supplies of ammunition that they could make the countryside reverberate with repeated discharges of their heavy cannon.

The defenders of Vicksburg were subjected to heavier fire than any other trench fighters in the war. Back of them lay the Mississippi, dotted with gunboats, and before them were the troops of Grant and Sherman well equipped with artillery. The besieged were deficient in both guns and ammunition. Hemmed in thus by superior forces and equipment, conscious of their inability to give effective retaliation, living on ever dwindling rations, suffering from a shortage of drinking water and cut off largely from their friends, they were subjected day after day and night after night to a cannonading that was so severe at times as to make heads ache from the concussion. One of the defenders wrote in his diary at the midpoint of siege:

The fighting is now carried on quite systematically . . . in the morning there seems to be time allowed for breakfast, when all at once the work of destruction is renewed. There is about an hour at noon & about the same at sunset, taking these three intervals out the work goes on just as regularly as . . . on a well regulated farm & the noise is not unlike the clearing up of new ground when much heavy timber is cut down! Add to that the nailing on of shingles by several men & one has a pretty good idea of the noise. It might be supposed that a score of villages had sprung up all round him & that the inhabitants were vieing with each other to see who could be the most industrious.

The caves dug in the hillside were poor protection against the heavy shells that came screeching through the air with varying notes of terror. If one lifted his head ever so little above the earthworks, the crack of a sharpshooter's rifle, followed instantly by a dull thud, would announce the doom of another Reb. A man who was slightly wounded in the trenches stood in considerable danger of being more seriously injured, if not killed outright, as he traversed the open space between battle line and hospital. Life under such conditions became a torturing ordeal, and the situation was not helped by jesting speculation as to the prospective comforts of Johnson's Island, Camp Chase and Camp Douglas.

In the trenches before Atlanta and Petersburg existence was not so perilous nor so gloomy as at Vicksburg. Common to all, however, was the intolerable heat of the summer sun. Some men sought alleviation by building little brush arbors along the trenches. The sultriness of the ditches became so unbearable at night that some of the men resorted to sleeping on the edge—and when the Federal batteries opened they would simply roll over to safety. But immunity from danger in the Atlanta and Petersburg trenches was only comparative. The killing and wounding of men by Federal sharpshooting and artillery fire were of such common occurrence as hardly to elicit notice save by the company to which the casualty belonged.

The number of killed and wounded would have been much greater but for the skill of the men in side-stepping arched shots. "The mortars are thrown up a great height," wrote an Alabamian from Petersburg, "and fall down in the trenches like throwing a ball over a house—we have become very perfect in dodging them and unless they are thrown too thick I think I can always escape them at least at night." He added that the dugouts which they contrived at intervals along the trenches and which they were wont to call bombproofs were not impervious at all to mortar shells, and that "we always prefer to be out in the ditches—where by using strategy and skill we get out of their way." So confident did the troops become of their ability to escape these lobbed shots of the Yankees that they would keep up a derisive yelling throughout a bombardment.

During periods of truce ladies from Petersburg made several visits to the lines, walking down the ditches in their cumbersome hoop skirts to see how bombproofs were made, climbing upon the parapets to get a look at the Yankees, giggling and oh-ing at the strange sights confronting them. Both Federals and Rebs enjoyed these interludes in crinoline but some of the latter could not refrain from mischievously expressing the wish that the Yanks would throw a few shells over to see if the fair visitors would shake with terror or raise the Rebel yell.

But these tantalizing glimpses of Petersburg belles afforded only brief respite from the terrible filth, the smothering heat of summer and the cold of winter, the rain and mud of all seasons, the restricted movement and the countless other deprivations that made trench warfare the most unpleasant aspect of Confederate soldierhood. Open fighting with all its dangers was immeasurably preferable to such existence as this.

But what of valor and of cowardice on the field of battle? There were numerous manifestations of both, though many more of the former than of the latter. Deeds of Rebel bravery, individual and collective, were of such common occurrence as to be quite beyond all estimation. A few definite instances will serve as examples of the glory that lighted up the fields of Manassas, of Shiloh, of Antietam, of Gettysburg, of Spottsylvania—and of countless others.

At Shiloh Private Samuel Evans refused to go to the rear when a ball passed through both cheeks, "but remained and fought for a considerable length of time, cheering on the men and loading and shooting as fast as he could." An officer who saw his men reduced from twenty-eight to twelve as he led them into the ravaging fire at Seven Pines cried out as he fell pierced through the heart, "Boys, I am killed, but you press on." Private Ike Stone was severely wounded at the beginning of the Murfreesboro fight, but he paused only to bind up his injuries, and when his captain was incapacitated Stone

took charge of the company and led it valorously through the battle, this despite a second wound. In the thick of this same fight Sergeant Joe Thompson was overwhelmed with the impulse to take a prisoner; leaping ahead of his comrades he overtook the retreating Federal column, seized a Yank and started to the rear with him; but this man having been shot down in his grasp, Thompson ran back to the still-retreating lines, seized a second Federal and brought him away safely. When Private Mattix's left arm was so seriously injured that he could no longer fire his musket, he went to his commanding officer and said, "Colonel, I am too badly wounded to use my gun but can carry the flag; may I?" Before this three standard-bearers had been shot down in succession, but when the requested permission was given him, Mattix seized the staff, stepped boldly in front of the regiment, and carried the colors throughout the remainder of the contest.

In his official report of Second Manassas Major J. D. Waddell, commanding Toombs' Georgians, said that he "carried into the fight over 100 men who were barefoot, many of whom left bloody foot-prints among the thorns and briars through which they rushed, with Spartan courage and really jubilant impetuosity, upon the serried ranks of the foe." Colonel E. C. Cook of the Thirty-second Tennessee Infantry reported after Chickamauga that one of his men, J. W. Ellis, who had marched for six weeks without shoes, "went thus into battle and kept up his company at all times till wounded."

At Chickamauga Private Mayfield was wounded in the thigh by a Minié ball and at the same time dazed by a shell. Litter bearers picked him up and were carrying him to the rear when he recovered from the shock and sprang to the ground with the remark, "This will not do for me," and rushed back to continue the fight. In this same engagement Private McCann fought gallantly until his ammunition was exhausted; then he picked up cartridge boxes of the dead and wounded and coolly distributed ammunition among his comrades. When the colonel commended his heroic conduct McCann asked that his bravery be cited in the official report of the battle. Shortly afterward he received a mortal wound and as he was borne dying to the rear, he turned smiling to his colonel and reminded him of the promise of honorable mention.

Of all the brave those who were entrusted with the colors had the most consistent record. Almost every official report of regimental commanders mentions the courageous action of standard-bearers. To keep the flag flying was a matter of inestimable pride, and its loss to the enemy was an incalculable disgrace. Consequently men vied with each other for the honor of holding the cherished emblem aloft in the thickest of the fight. The Federals, knowing the close association of morale and colors, and being easily able to single out standard-bearers because of their conspicuousness, were wont to concentrate an unusually heavy fire upon them. Literally thousands of those who aspired to the honor of carrying and guarding the flags paid for the privilege with their lives.

"In my two color companies," reported Colonel Jenkins of the Palmetto Sharpshooters after Seven Pines, "out of 80 men who entered 40 were killed and wounded, and out of 11 in the color guard, 10 were shot down, and my colors pierced by nine balls passed through four hands without touching the ground." At Antietam the First Texas Infantry lost eight standard-bearers in succession, and at Gettysburg, the Twenty-sixth North Carolina lost fourteen. At Antietam also, the flag of the Tenth Georgia—which regiment lost fifty-seven per cent of its men and officers in this one engagement—received forty-six shots. The standard of Lyle's Regiment was torn to tatters at Corinth, and color-bearer Sloan when last seen by his comrades was "going over the breast works waving a piece over his head and shouting for the Southern Confederacy."

Color Sergeant Rice of the Twenty-eighth Tennessee Infantry, downed by a bullet at Murfreesboro, still clung to the flag, holding it aloft as he crawled on his knees until a second shot brought death and delivered him of his trust. On another part of this bloody field Color Sergeant Cameron advanced too far ahead of his comrades and was captured. He tore the flag from its staff, concealed it on his person, carried it to prison with him, escaped and brought it back to be unfurled anew above its proud followers.

Murfreesboro likewise afforded the setting for perhaps the most extraordinary of all color-bearer feats. While this contest raged at its greatest fury the opposing lines came very near each other in that portion of the field occupied by the Nineteenth Texas Cavalry (dismounted). A Yankee standard carrier stood immediately to the front of the Texas Color Sergeant, A. Sims, waving his flag and urging the blue column forward. Sergeant Sims, construing this as something of a personal insult, rushed forward, planted his own flag staff firmly on the ground with one hand and made a lunge for that of his exhorting adversary with the other. At the moment of contact, both color-bearers, Yankee and Rebel, "fell in the agonies of death waving their banners above their heads until their last expiring moments." The Texas standard was rescued, but not until one who rushed forward to retrieve it had also been shot down.

Confederate authorities sought to stimulate the men by offering medals and badges to those who were cited by officers. Unable to supply these emblems, Congress passed an act in October 1862 providing for the publication of a Roll of Honor after each battle which should include the names of those who had best displayed their courage and devotion. Such lists were read at dress parades, published in newspapers and filed in the adjutant general's office. As a further inducement commissions were offered to those who should distinguish themselves, and special inscriptions were placed on flags of those regiments that captured artillery or gave other proof of unusual achievement. But the most effective incentive was probably that of personal and family pride. This was strikingly evidenced by the remark of a Georgian to his brother after Franklin: "I am proud to say that there was no one between me and the Yankees when I was wounded."

Cowardice under fire, being a less gratifying subject than heroism, has not received much attention from those who have written or talked of the Confederate Army. Of the various sources of information on this obscure point the most fertile are the official reports of battles by commanders of units ranging from regiments to armies. But the most numerous of these reports—those submitted by regimental commanders—are characterized by a reluctance to admit wholesale cowardice because of possible reflections on the conduct of the commanders themselves. This reluctance sometimes resulted in misrepresentation of the rankest sort, as in the following case: After the attack on Battery Wagner, Morris Island, South Carolina, July 18, 1863, Colonel Charles W. Knight, commanding the Thirty-first North Carolina Regiment, said in closing his report, "It is useless to mention any officer or man, when all were acting coolly and bravely." In the body of his report he mentioned being repulsed, but there is absolutely no suggestion of bad conduct on the part of the regiment. But when Knight's superior, General William B. Taliaferro, reported the battle, he said: "The Thirty-first North Carolina could not be induced to occupy their position, and ingloriously deserted the ramparts. . . . I feel it my duty to mention . . . [their] disgraceful conduct."

In the reports of higher ranking officers, who could admit bad conduct of portions of their commands with more impunity than colonels, and in the wartime letters and diaries of the common soldiers, much testimony on the subject may be found. This evidence shows clearly that Confederate soldiers were by no means immune to panic and cowardice.

At First Manassas a few Rebs fled into the woods when shells began to fly. There was disgraceful conduct at the beginning of McClellan's peninsula campaign, when General D. H. Hill wrote that "several thousand soldiers . . . have fled to Richmond under pretext of sickness. They have even thrown away their arms that their flight might not be impeded." At Seven Pines there were a few regiments that "disgracefully left the battle field with their colors."

General W. H. C. Whiting in reporting the battle of Gaines's Mill said: "Men were leaving the field in every direction and in great disorder . . . men were skulking from the front in a shameful manner; the woods on our left and rear were full of troops in safe cover from which they never stirred." At Malvern Hill, General Jubal Early encountered "a large number of men retreating from the battle-field," saw "a very deep ditch filled with skulkers," and found a "wood filled with a large number of men retreating in confusion."

Men ran, skulked and straggled by the hundreds at Shiloh. A Tennessee regiment took fright during an advance, ran back on supporting lines crying, "Retreat! Retreat!" and caused great confusion; but they were rallied and set in motion toward the Federal position; again they were overcome with fear, and this time they rushed back so precipitately that they ran over and trampled in the mud the color-bearer of the regiment behind them. A Texas regiment behaved in the same manner; placed in line of battle it began firing, but before the guns had all been discharged, "it broke and fled disgracefully from the field." An officer who attempted to bring back the fugitives and threatened to report them as "a pack of cowards" was told that "they did not care a damn" what they were called, they would not follow him. When General W. J. Hardee tried to rally another demoralized regiment he was fired on by its members. Some of the straggling for which Shiloh was notorious was due to circumstances that exonerate those involved, but there can be no doubt that a large part of those who found various pretexts for leaving the firing line were playing the coward. Said Colonel O. F. Strahl in his official report: "On Monday morning we . . . had a great number of stragglers attached to us. The stragglers demonstrated very clearly this morning that they had strayed from their own regiments because they did not want to fight. My men fought gallantly until the stragglers ran and left them and began firing from the rear over their heads. They were then compelled to fall to the rear. I rallied them several times and . . .

finally left out the stragglers." General Beauregard clinched this evidence in his official report: "Some officers, non-commissioned officers, and men abandoned their colors early in the first day to pillage the captured encampments; others retired shamefully from the field on both days while the thunder of cannon and the roar and rattle of musketry told them that their brothers were being slaughtered by the fresh legions of the enemy."

General Bushrod Johnson reported that at Murfreesboro troops on his right became demoralized and "men of different regiments, brigades, divisions, were scattered all over the fields," and that he was almost run over, so precipitate was their fight. Captain Felix Robertson said that he had never seen troops so completely broken as those demoralized at Murfreesboro. "They seemed actuated only by a desire for safety," he added. "I saw the colors of many regiments pass, and though repeated calls were made for men of the different regiments, no attention was paid to them."

At Chancellorsville and Gettysburg the conduct of the soldiers seems to have been exceptionally good. This may have been due in some part to vigorous efforts of General Lee and of the War Department early in 1863 to tighten up the discipline of the Army of Northern Virginia. The fighting before Vicksburg was marred by shameful conduct in the action of May 16, 1863, of which General Pemberton said: "We lost a large amount of artillery. The army was much demoralized; many regiments behaved badly," and Colonel Edward Goodwin reported of a small number of troops immediately in front of him:

> At this time our friends gave way and came rushing to the rear panicstricken. . . . I brought my regiment to the charge bayonets, but even this could not check them in their flight. The colors of three regiments passed through. . . . We collared them, begged them, and abused them in vain.

The wholesale panic which seized Confederate troops at Missionary Ridge was as notorious as it was mystifying. A soldier who took part in the battle wrote in his diary, "In a few minutes the whole left gave way and a regular run commenced." After a retreat of several hundred yards, this Reb's battalion rallied momentarily, "but it was in such a confused mass that we made but a feeble resistance, when all broke again in a perfect stampede." His conviction was that the troops acted disgracefully, that they "did not half fight."

General Bragg in his official report of the fight said that "a panic which I had never witnessed seemed to have seized upon officers and men, and each seemed to be struggling for his personal safety, regardless of his duty or character." He added that "no satisfactory excuse can possibly be given for the shameful conduct of the troops on our left in allowing their line to be penetrated. The position was one which ought to have been held by a line of skirmishers against any assaulting column, and wherever resistance was made the enemy fled in disorder after suffering heavy loss. Those who reached the ridge did so in a condition of exhaustion from the great physical exertion in climbing, which rendered them powerless, and the slightest effort would have destroyed them." What stronger indictment could there be of any soldiery by its general-in-command!

But the woeful tale is not ended. In connection with Early's campaign of 1864 in the Shenandoah Valley occurred some of the most disgraceful running of Confederate history. After an engagement near Winchester on July 23, General Stephen Ramseur wrote his wife:

> My men behaved shamefully—They ran from the enemy. . . . The entire command stampeded. I tried in vain to rally them & even after the Yankees were checked by a few men I posted behind a stone wall, they continued to run all the way to the breastworks at Winchester—& many of them threw away their guns & ran on to Newton 6 miles beyond. They acted cowardly and I told them so.

On September 19, 1864, during another hard fight near Winchester, a panic of unprecedented proportions struck the ranks of Early's army. Regiment after regiment broke and fled back toward the town. General Bryan Grimes appalled by the demoralization and fearful that his brigade would succumb to it, threatened "to blow the brains out of the first man who left ranks," and then moved over to confront the fugitives, waving his sword and giving many a Reb the full weight of its flashing blade. But fleeing regiments, increasing now in number, could not be stopped. They poured into the town, out of the valley pike, and some continued their disordered course for miles beyond. "The Ladies of Winchester came into the streets and beged them crying bitterly to make a stand, for their sakes if not for their own honor," wrote a captain who witnessed the rout; but "the cowards did not have the shame to make a pretense of halting."

A month later at Cedar Creek, plunder combined with cowardice to inflict upon Early's veterans one of the most shameful defeats of the war. In the morning, by brilliant action, the Confederates pounced upon the Federals and drove them from their camps. As the Southern lines advanced large numbers of soldiers and officers turned aside, against positive orders, and began to ransack the rich stores abandoned by the foe. While the victors were absorbed in pillage, the Federals rallied, and in the afternoon they counterattacked. The disorganized Confederates broke first on the left, and then all along the line. Efforts of division commanders and of others who attempted to stay the tide of panic was to no avail, and the field was utterly abandoned.

"It was the hardest day's work I ever engaged in," Grimes said, "trying to rally the men. Took over flags at different times, begging, commanding, entreating the men to rally—would ride up and down the lines, beseeching them by all they held sacred and dear, to stop and fight, but without any success. I don't mean my Brigade only, but all."

Price's Missouri expedition of 1864 was marked by an instance of large-scale panic. When the Federals attacked the Confederate rear on October 25, near Carthage, Missouri, demoralization set in. As Price rode rapidly to the point of danger he "met the divisions of Major-Generals Fagan and Marmaduke retreating in utter and indescribable confusion, many of them having thrown away their arms. They were deaf to all entreaties or commands, and in vain were all efforts to rally them."

While the Atlanta campaign seems to have been remarkably free of demoralization under fire, there were at least two instances involving a considerable number of men. In a skirmish on June 9, 1864, a Texas cavalry unit that had a distinguished record in battle broke upon slight contact with the Federal cavalry, and fled in a manner described as disorderly and shameful by General Ross. Later, in the Battle of Jonesboro, August 31, 1864, an advancing brigade of Confederates halted without orders when it came to the Federal picket line, the men seeking shelter behind piles of rails. They seemed "possessed of some great horror of charging breastworks," reported Colonel Bushrod Jones, "which no power of persuasion or example could dispel."

The last instance of large-scale panic during the war was at Nashville, December 16, 1864. On this occasion the division of General Bate, when assaulted about four o'clock in the afternoon by the Federals, began to fall back in great confusion and disorder. In a few moments the entire Confederate line was broken, and masses of troops fled down the pike toward Franklin. All efforts to rally the troops proved fruitless. General Bate in his official report leaves the impression that the rout, due to extenuating circumstances, cast little if any reproach upon his men. But General Hood, in chief command, was evidently of contrary opinion, as he says that Confederate loss in killed and wounded was small, implying that withdrawal took place without much resistance. He says further that the break came so suddenly that artillery guns could not be brought away. Captain Thomas J. Key says in his diary that "General Bate's division . . . shamefully broke and fled before the Yankees were within 200 yards of them," and that there "then ensued one of the most disgraceful routs" that it had ever been his misfortune to witness.

There were innumerable cases of individual cowardice under fire. When men are assembled in such large numbers, especially when many of them are forced into service, a certain proportion are inevitably worthless as fighters. Some of those who fled wanted earnestly to act bravely, but they had not the power to endure fire unflinchingly. This type is well exemplified by the Reb who covered his face with his hat during the battle of Fredericksburg, and who later, when told that his turn at the rifle pits was imminent, "made a proposition that he would go out from camp and strip" and let his comrades "get switches and whip him as much as they wanted" if they would obtain his release from the impending proximity to Federal fire. A similar case was encountered by Colonel C. Irvine Walker. A man had been reported for cowardly behavior on the field. Walker called him to task and told him that he would be watched closely during the next engagement. When the time came the colonel went over to check his performance as the regiment advanced. "I found him in his place," reported Walker, "his rifle on his shoulder, and holding up in front of him a frying pan." The man was so scared that he sought this meager protection, yet he moved forward with his company and was killed.

Another case of infamy converted to valor was cited by Colonel William Stiles, of the Sixtieth Georgia Infantry. During a charge this officer saw a robust Reb drop out of line and crouch behind a tree; the colonel slipped up and gave him a resounding whack across the back with the flat of his sword, and shouted, "Up there, you coward!"

The skulker, thinking evidently that he was the mortal victim of a Yankee shot, "clasped his hands, and keeled over backwards, devoutly ejaculating, 'Lord, receive my spirit!'"

After momentary bafflement, Stiles kicked the prostrate soldier violently in the ribs, exclaiming simultaneously, "Get up, sir! The Lord wouldn't receive the spirit of such an infernal coward."

The man sprang up with the joyful exclamation, "Ain't I killed? The Lord be praised," grabbed his musket, rejoined his comrades, and henceforth conducted himself with courage.

Other officers had less success. Men who had no shoes were often excused from fighting, and a good many soldiers took advantage of this rule by throwing away their shoes on the eve of conflict. Others left the field under pretext of helping the wounded to the rear, and this in spite of strict orders against removal of casualties by anyone except those specifically detailed for the purpose. Still others feigned sickness or injury. A favorite ruse was to leave one's own regiment during the confusion of battle, and then to evade duty by a pretense of endless and futile searching for the outfit intentionally abandoned.

Infuriated officers would curse these shirkers, beat them with swords and even threaten them with shooting, and on occasion carry out their threats on the spot. Commanders would place file-closers in the rear with instruction to arrest, and in some instances to shoot down, those who refused to do their duty. Courts-martial sentenced great numbers to hard and disgraceful punishments. Private soldiers covered spineless comrades with scorn and ridicule. But these measures were only partially effective.

There can be no doubt that the trying conditions under which Confederate soldiers fought contributed to the bad performance of some on the field of battle. Men often went into combat hungry and remained long under fire with little or nothing to eat. Sometimes, as at Antietam and Gettysburg, they fought after exhausting marches. Many of those who participated in the routs at Chattanooga and at Nashville were without shoes. Often the Confederate artillery protection was inadequate. The superior number of the Federals made Rebel flanks unduly vulnerable, and flank sensitiveness was the cause of more than one panic. Casualties among line officers were unusually heavy, and replacement with capable men was increasingly difficult after 1863.

When all of these factors are considered, it is rather remarkable that defection under fire was not more frequent than it actually was. Those soldiers who played the coward, even granting that the offenders totaled well up in the thousands, were a very small proportion of the Confederate Army. Taken on the whole of his record under fire, the Confederate private was a soldier of such mettle as to claim a high place among the world's fighting men. It may be doubted that anyone else deserves to outrank him.

KEY TERMS

Skirmishers: Lightly armed, highly mobile troops who fought outside major battle lines.

Pickets: Lightly entrenched defensive positions.

DISCUSSION TOPICS

After reading this essay, you should be able to discuss:

1. The daily experiences of war.

2. The ways in which southern soldiers exhibited courage.

3. The ways in which southern soldiers also exhibited cowardice.

4. The ways in which the Confederate army stimulated courage and discountenanced cowardice.